Contemporary Systems Analysis

■ ■ ■

5th Edition

Contemporary
Systems Analysis

■ ■ ■

Marvin Gore
Mt. San Antonio College

John Stubbe
Mt. San Antonio College

B&E TECH **Business and
Educational Technologies**
A Division of Wm. C. Brown Communications, Inc.

 **Business and Educational Technologies**

Book Team

Publisher *Sue Simon*
Acquisitions Editor *Paul Ducham*
Managing Developmental Editor *Linda M. Meehan*
Production Editor *Kay Driscoll*
Designer *Kristyn A. Kalnes*
Art Editor/Art Processor *Rachel Imsland*
Photo Editor *Carrie Burger*

 Wm. C. Brown Communications, Inc.

President and Chief Executive Officer *G. Franklin Lewis*
Corporate Senior Vice President, President of WCB Manufacturing *Roger Meyer*
Corporate Senior Vice President and Chief Financial Officer *Robert Chesterman*
Corporate Vice President and General Manager, Brown & Benchmark *Tom Doran*
Corporate Vice President and General Manager, Wm. C. Brown Publishers *Beverly Kolz*

Cover © Gabe Palmer/The Stock Market

Copyedited by Nikki Herbst

The credits section for this book begins on page 513 and is considered an extension of the copyright page.

A Times Mirror Company

Library of Congress Catalog Card Number: 92–73562

ISBN 0–697–07697–0

Printed in the United States of America by Wm. C. Brown Communications, Inc., 2460 Kerper Boulevard, Dubuque, IA 52001

10 9 8 7 6 5 4 3 2 1

Brief Contents

Preface   xvii

■ **Unit 1 Contemporary Systems Analysis and Design 2**

    1   Contemporary Information Systems Analysis and Design   4

    2   A Business as an Information System   32

■ **Unit 2 Managing the Computer Information Systems Project 62**

    3   Communication and Documentation   64

    4   Project Management   88

■ **Unit 3 Information Systems Engineering 114**

    5   Data Flow Diagrams and the Data Dictionary   116

    6   Computer-Assisted Systems Engineering (CASE)   152

■ **Unit 4 The Study Phase 172**

    7   Initial Investigation   176

    8   System Performance Definition   206

    9   Candidate System Evaluation   240

    10   Study Phase Report and Review   266

    Exhibit 1 The Study Phase Report—OARS Case Study   274

■ **Unit 5 The Design Phase 288**

    11   Detailed System Design   292

    12   Data Modeling   310

    13   Output Design   332

    14   Input Design   350

    15   Design Phase Report and Review   364

    Exhibit 2 The Design Phase Report—OARS Case Study   372

■ Unit 6   The Development and Operation Phases 394

    16   Preparing for Implementation 402
    17   Computer Program Development 422
    18   Development Phase Report and Review 440
    Exhibit 3 The Development Phase Report—OARS Case Study 446
    19   System Operation and Change Management 466

Glossary 495
Credits 513
Index 515

Table of Contents

Preface   xvi

unit 1

Contemporary Systems Analysis and Design   2

Chapter One

Contemporary Information Systems Analysis and Design   4

Preview   4
Objectives   5
Key Terms   5
Computer Information Systems   6
   Information System Concepts   6
   Business Information Systems   10
The Systems Development Life Cycle   11
   The Life-Cycle Phases   11
   The Life-Cycle Flowchart   12
     The Life-Cycle Activities   12
     Life-Cycle Management and
     Documentation   12

Systems Analysis and the Systems
   Analyst   14
   Systems Analysis   14
   The Systems Analyst   14
   Careers in Systems Analysis   14
     Performing Systems Analysis   14
     Opportunities and
     Compensation   15
     Personal Qualifications   15
   The User and the SDLC   17
     Information Resource
     Management   17
     Distributed Data Processing   17
     The Concept of Usability   19
Evolution of Information Systems
   Engineering   19
   Classical Life-Cycle Methodology   19
   Structured Analysis and Design
    Methods   21
   Prototyping   22
     Definition of Prototyping   22
     Prototyping Version of the SDLC
     22
Automating the Systems Development
   Life Cycle   24
   The Forces of Change   24
   Automated Systems Development
    Life-Cycle Tools   25
     Task-Oriented Tools   25
     Computer-Assisted Systems
     Engineering (CASE)   26

Summary 27
For Review 29
For Discussion 29
For Exercise: Quality Management and
    Computer Information Systems
    30

2

Chapter Two

A Business as an Information System
32

Preview 32
Objectives 33
Key Terms 3
Business System Characteristics 34
    Business Goals and Objectives 34
    A Business: A System of Systems 34
Describing the Business Organization
    38
    The Organization Chart 38
    The Organization Function List 44
Information Structure of a Business 44
    Product Flow and Information Flow
    44
    Information Generators 48
Management Uses of Information 48
    Information System Levels 48
    Feedback and Control 51
Quality Management 53
    Total Quality Management (TQM)
    53
    TQM and Information Systems: The
    Agile Enterprise 58
Summary 58
For Review 59
For Discussion 59
For Exercise: Organization Chart for
    NEWDREAM Corporation 60

2

unit

Managing the Computer
Information Systems Project 62

3

Chapter Three

Communication and Documentation 64

Preview 64
Objectives 65
Key Terms 65
The Elements of Communication 66
    The Communication Process 66
    Toward More Effective
    Communication 66
Interviewing Techniques 69
Technical Writing 70
    Technical Writing Defined 70
    Types of Technical Writing 70
        Policies and Procedures 70
        Narratives 71
        Specifications 72
        Manuals 72
        Reports 72
Presentations 73
    Preparing for the Presentation 73
    Scheduling the Presentation 73
    The Presentation Outcome 74
Generating the Documentation 76
    Word Processing 77
    Presentation Graphics 77
        Types of Basic Charts 77
        Development of Effective Charts
        81
        Graphics Software 81

Desktop Publishing   84
   Word Publishing   84
   Text/Graphics Formatting   84
Summary   86
For Review   86
For Discussion   87
For Exercise: Communicating with
   Charts   87

unit

3

Information Systems Engineering
114

Chapter Four

Project Management   88

Preview   88
Objectives   89
Key Terms   89
The Systems Team   90
   The Team Members   90
   The Principal User   91
   Roles and Responsibilities
    Throughout the SDLC   91
   Joint Application Design (JAD)   92
   Usability Engineering   92
Project Planning and Reporting   93
   Progress Planning and Status
    Reporting   93
   Cost Planning and Status Reporting
    96
   Performance Indices and Charts   97
Critical Path Networks   100
   Critical Path Method (CPM)   102
   Program Evaluation and Review
    Technique (PERT)   104
Project Reviews   110
   Purposes of Project Reviews   110
   The Project Review Package   111
Summary   111
For Review   112
For Discussion   112
For Exercise: Critical Path Network for
   the Janis Corporation   113

Chapter Five

Data Flow Diagrams and the Data
Dictionary   116

Preview   116
Objectives   117
Key Terms   117
Structured Analysis and Design   118
   Separating the What From the How
    118
   Documentation Needs   118
Data Flow Diagrams   119
   Definition of a Data Flow Diagram
    119
   Data Flow Diagram Transformations
    and Decomposition   120
   Guidelines for Drawing Data Flow
    Diagrams   127
The Data Dictionary   127
   Data Elements and Data Structures
    127
   Data Dictionary Definition and
    Entries   131
   Entities and Attributes   135
   Entity-Relationship Diagrams   135
Identification Codes   136
   The Code Plan   136
Common Types of Codes   137
   Sequence Codes   137
    Simple Sequence Code   137
    Block Sequence Code   138

Group Classification Code   139
Significant Digit Code   140
Alphanumeric Codes   140
   Mnemonic Codes   141
   Alphabetic Derivation Codes
   142
Process Specification   143
Decision Tables   143
Decision Trees   145
Structured English   146
Summary   147
For Review   148
For Discussion   149
For Exercise 1: Data Flow Diagram
   Representation of the Systems
   Development Life Cycle   149
For Exercise 2: Understanding Codes
   150

Chapter Six

Computer-Assisted Systems Engineering (CASE)   152

Preview   152
Objectives   153
Key Terms   153
Pathways to Case   154
   Search for Productivity and Quality
   154
   Hardware and Software
   Developments   154
      Microcomputers   154
      Micro to Mainframe Link   155
User Involvement in the SDLC   157
Nonprocedural Languages   158
   Applications Generators   158
   Query Languages and Report
   Generators   158
   Fourth Generation Languages (4GLs)
   159
Structured Methodologies   159
   Evolution of Structured
   Methodologies   159

Classification of Structured
   Methodologies   160
      Process-Oriented Model   160
      Data-Oriented Model   160
      Object-Oriented Model   161
CASE Products   162
   Tools and Workbenches   162
   Categories of CASE Products   163
   Components of CASE Products   165
      Basic CASE Tools   165
      Advanced CASE Tools   166
   CASE and the SDLC   167
Summary   168
For Review   169
For Discussion   170
For Exercise: Potential for CASE   170

unit 4

The Study Phase   172

Chapter Seven

Initial Investigation   176

Preview   176
Objectives   177
Key Terms   177
Problem Identification   178
   Need Identification   178
   The Information Service Request
   178
The Initial Investigation   181
   Project Initiation   181
   Background Analysis   184
   Fact-Finding Techniques   184
      Data Collection   185
      Correspondence and
        Questionnaires   185
      Personal Interviews   186
      Observation   188
      Research   189

Fact-Analysis Techniques   189
   Data Element Analysis   190
   Input-Output Analysis   191
   Recurring Data Analysis   195
   Report Use Analysis   195
   Results of Analysis   195
User Review   198
  Modified Information Service
   Request   198
  Project Directive   200
Summary   202
For Review   202
For Discussion   203
For Exercise: The Hollerith Card
   Company   203

Chapter Eight

System Performance Definition   206

Preview   206
Objectives   207
Key Terms   207
Transition from the Logical to the
   Physical Model   208
Example System—ABCO Corporation:
   On-line Accounts Receivable
   System (OARS)   208
  ABCO History   208
  OARS Initial Investigation   210
  Project Directive   213
Logical Model of the New System   218
General Constraints   222
  Statement of General Constraints
   222
  Example System: General Constraints
   223
Specific Objectives   224
  Identification and Ranking of
   Specific Objectives   224
  Example System: Specific Objectives
   225

Output Description   225
  Output Identification and
   Description   225
  Example System: Output Description
   228
Summary   238
For Review   238
For Discussion   238
For Exercise: OARS Hierarchy Chart
   239

Chapter Nine

Candidate System Evaluation   240

Preview   240
Objectives   241
Key Terms   241
Purposes of a Candidate System
   Evaluation   242
Steps in a Candidate System Evaluation
   242
  Step 1: Develop the System
   Candidates   243
  Step 2: Perform Preliminary
   Evaluation of System Candidates
   246
  Step 3: Prepare Detailed
   Descriptions of Candidates   247
  Step 4: Identify Meaningful System
   Characteristics   252
  Step 5: Determine Performance and
   Cost for Each Candidate   252
  Step 6: Weight the System
   Performance and Cost
   Characteristics   260
  Step 7: Select the "Best" System
   261
The General System Design   262
Summary   264
For Review   264
For Discussion   265
For Exercise: Candidate Evaluation
   Matrix   265

Chapter Ten

Study Phase Report and Review 266

Preview 266
Objectives 267
Key Terms 267
Performance Specification 268
Study Phase Report 268
  Structure and Content 268
  Example Study Phase Report 271
Study Phase Review 271
Summary 272
For Review 272
For Discussion 273

Exhibit 1 The Study Phase Report—OARS Case Study 274

5 unit

The Design Phase 288

Chapter Eleven

Detailed System Design 292

Preview 292
Objectives 293
Key Terms 293
Detailed Design Specifications 294
  General System Design 294
  Identifying Processing Requirements 294
  Identifying Control Requirements 302
  Identifying Reference Manual Requirements 303

Test Requirements 303
  Identification of Test Requirements 303
  Structured Walk-throughs 304
Hardware Acquisition 304
Summary 307
For Review 308
For Discussion 308
For Exercise: Vendor Evaluation Matrix 308

Chapter Twelve

Data Modeling 310

Preview 310
Objectives 311
Key Terms 311
Objectives of Data Modeling 312
Understanding the Data and Data Flows 312
  Data Flow Diagrams 312
  The Data Dictionary 312
Understanding the Relationships between Entities 312
  Entity-Relationship Diagrams (ERDs) 314
  Drawing Entity-Relationship Diagrams 315
Normalization of Files 317
  Purpose of Normalization 317
  Normal Forms 317
Data Base Management Systems 320
  DBMS Components 322
  DBMS Functions 323
  DBMS Architectures 324
  Data Base Management Systems and the Personal Computer 326
  The Data Base Administrator (DBA) 326
The Prototyping Engine 327
  Attributes of the Prototyping Engine 327
  The Prototyping Cycle 328

Summary   330
For Review   331
For Discussion   331
For Exercise: File Normalization   331

Chapter Thirteen

Output Design   332

Preview   332
Objectives   333
Key Terms   333
General Principles of Output Design   334
Printer Output   334
  Designing Effective Printer Layouts   334
  Printer Layout Forms   334
  Prototyping Printer Outputs   340
  Graphics and Desktop Publishing   340
Visual Display Terminal Screen Output   344
  Designing Effective Screen Layouts   344
  Screen Layout Forms   344
Summary   347
For Review   348
For Discussion   348
For Exercise: Output Display Design   348

Chapter Fourteen

Input Design   350

Preview   350
Objectives   351
Key Terms   351
Source Document Design   352
  Source Document Design Responsibility   352

Principles of Source Document Design   352
  Ease of Data Recording   352
  Ease of Use   353
  Required Data   353
  Cost Considerations   354
  Automated Source Document Design   355
  Source Document Control   355
VDT Input Screen Design   357
  Designing Effective Input Screen Layouts   357
  Screen Layout Forms   358
  Prototyping VDT Screens   359
Input Scanners   360
Summary   362
For Review   363
For Discussion   363
For Exercise: Input Form Design   363

Chapter Fifteen

Design Phase Report and Review   364

Preview   364
Objectives   365
Key Terms   365
Design Specification   366
Design Phase Report   366
  Structure and Content   366
  Example Design Phase Report   368
Design Phase Review   368
Summary   369
For Review   369
For Discussion   370

Exhibit 2 The Design Phase Report—OARS Case Study   372

unit 6

The Development and Operation Phases 394

Development Phase Activities 394
Operation Phase Activities 398

Chapter Sixteen

Preparing for Implementation 402

Preview 402
Objectives 403
Key Terms 403
Implementation Planning 404
  The Implementation Process 404
  The Implementation Plan 404
Test Plans 404
  Bottom-Up Computer Program
    Development 405
  Top-Down Computer Program
    Development 407
  Formal Test Planning 409
Training 411
  Training: An Overview 411
  Programmer Training 411
  Operator Training 412
  User Training 413
  Management Orientation 415
Equipment Installation 415
Conversion 416
  Conversion: An Overview 416
  Conversion Activities (Development
    Phase) 416
    Procedures Conversion 416
    Program Conversion 416
    File Conversion 416
  Changeover Plan (Operation Phase)
    417
Implementation Management 419
Summary 420
For Review 421
For Discussion 421
For Exercise: Development Phase PERT
    Network 421

Chapter Seventeen

Computer Program Development 422

Preview 422
Objectives 423
Key Terms 423
Creating a Computer Program 424
  Defining the Problem 424
  Planning the Problem Solution 424
  Writing the Program 424
  Testing the Program 425
  Completing the Program
    Documentation 425
Procedural Programming Languages
    425
  Structured Programming Concepts
    426
  Program Coding and Debugging
    Example 426
  Structured Walk-Throughs 429
Nonprocedural Progamming Languages
    429
  Structured Query Language (SQL)
    432
  Natural Languages 435
  Object-Oriented Languages 435
  Code Generators 436
Summary 436
For Review 437
For Discussion 437
For Exercise: Computer Program
    Development Report 438

Chapter Eighteen

Development Phase Report and Review
440

Preview 440
Objectives 441
Key Terms 441
System Specification 442
Development Phase Report 442
    Structure and Content 442
    Example Development Phase Report
    444
Development Phase Review 444
Summary 445
For Review 445
For Discussion 445

*Exhibit 3 The Development
Phase Report—OARS Case
Study 446*

Chapter Nineteen

System Operation and Change
Management 466

Preview 466
Objectives 467
Key Terms 467
Changeover 468
    The Changeover Crisis 468
    Changeover Activities 469
    User Turnover 471

Routine Operation 471
    Organizing for Data Processing 471
    Data Processing Standards 474
        The Standards Manual 474
        Customer Relations 475
        Security 475
Performance Review and Evaluation
    477
    Performance Review Board 477
    Post-Installation Review 478
    Periodic Review 480
Change Management 481
    Guidelines for System Modification
    481
    Change Control 484
    Redevelopment Engineering 487
        Reverse Engineering 488
        Reengineering 489
Summary 490
For Review 492
For Discussion 492
For Exercise: Coping with Change in
    the "Real World" 493

Glossary 495
Credits 513
Index 515

Preface

"Today's supercomputer is tomorrow's hundred-MIPS personal computer."
Allen Kay, Apple Computer

"The "3G" workstation will become available in the 1990s. It will execute one giga-instruction per second, have a gigabyte of memory and include a gigabyte bus; it will cost less than $10,000."
Raj Reddy, Carnegie Mellon University

The Agile Enterprise

In the 1970s and 1980s we learned that information was a critical commodity upon which the productivity of our economy depended. This established the importance of the design and development of effective computer-related business systems and led to the recognition of systems analysis as an important and growing career field for information system professionals. The information systems designers of the 1990s face even greater challenges than did those of preceding decades. We have entered a period of accelerated change in the social, economic, political, legal, and technological environments in which our businesses and industries must excel in order to compete for local and global markets. In all areas change is occurring so rapidly that we have been propelled into the era of the *agile enterprise,* where "agile" means the ability to anticipate and to quickly react to an external environment that is event- and customer-driven.

Competition has made it clear that two necessary enterprisewide attributes for survival and success in the 1990s are flexible, very fast-response computer information systems and an unrelenting focus on quality as measured by customer satisfaction. The term *computer integrated enterprise (CIE)* is aptly applied to industries that possess the first attribute, and the term *total quality management (TQM)* describes the processes adopted by industries committed to an unrelenting focus on quality improvement and on goods or services that not only meet, but exceed customer expectations.

Because of these contemporary events we feel that it is appropriate to name this revision of *Elements of Systems Analysis,* our widely adopted textbook, *Contemporary Systems Analysis.* Computer information systems and the systems development life cycle (SDLC) process for developing these systems remain at the core of *Contemporary Systems Analysis.* Within the context of the SDLC, we emphasize tools and techniques, such as *prototyping,* that is, developing and refining a model of an information system, that make possible the rapid development and modification of the information systems that enable an enterprise to respond to changes in the business environment.

Although the ultimate customer affected by computer-related business information systems is an external user of goods or services, our focus is on the internal customers for whose use these systems are developed. All of the principles of TQM apply toward ensuring that these users receive a quality system that meets or exceeds their expectations. Thus CIE and TQM are recurring topics in *Contemporary Systems Analysis,* where a principal theme is "agile systems for agile enterprises."

The continuing impact of change among the information technologies is manifest in the following key forecasts for the 1990s that appeared in a publication of the Computer Society of the Institute of Electrical and Electronic Engineers for which the theme was "The Promise of the Next Decade."[1] The forecasts are for

1. A rapid rate of performance growth in computer technology and architectures for all computers, from mainframe to microcomputer, with order of magnitude increases in reliability and extensive workload sharing among many processors operating in parallel.
2. Very large increases in storage capacities for directly addressable internal memory and for external storage devices, including memory hierarchies, CD-ROM, and digital optical disks.
3. An accelerated trend toward the distribution of information and computing power to users through high-performance local and wide area networks, leading to extensive client/server linkages from microcomputers to mainframes.
4. Dramatic advances in user-centered computer interfaces, providing multimedia, i.e., combination of text, graphics, image, and speech, and exhibiting some artificial intelligence capabilities.
5. Continuation of the breakdown of the traditional division between home and work, with increasing use of small, portable computers and high-definition, multifunction displays ranging in size from pocket to wall.

Collectively, these technological trends support the quick response required by competitive enterprises. For example, successful retailers have acquired the agility needed to be profitable in a rapidly changing, consumer-sensitive marketplace. These retailers know that a multimonth planning cycle is not adequate. They depend upon the Universal Product Code (UPC) and Electronic Data Interchange (EDI) to capture sales data for internal use, such as inventory management, and for direct transmission to the computer information systems of their manufacturers so that production schedules can continuously anticipate demand. These and other computer information systems of increasing complexity make the task of the systems analyst, who is the principal developer of applications software for computer information systems, a daunting one.

---

[1]"The Promise of the Next Decade," *Computer,* Vol. 24, No. 9, Sept. 1991, Los Alamitos, CA.

Fortunately, powerful computer-based information systems engineering tools and techniques are also emerging. Systems analysts are now able to automate many of the structured analysis and design techniques used in lieu of, or in conjunction with, traditional methods. Time-consuming paper and pencil tasks are being accomplished quickly and efficiently by computer-assisted systems engineering (CASE) workbenches. Rapid applications development (RAD) tools such as prototyping can speed up the life-cycle process and produce higher-quality systems for less cost. The new methodologies are changing the teaching and practice of systems analysis, and they are the motivators that led to *Contemporary Systems Analysis.*

Goal and Scope of This Book

The goal of *Contemporary Systems Analysis* is to provide students with a comprehensive introduction to the information engineering skills that they, as future users or systems analysts, will need to work in a competitive, computer-integrated business environment. In this highly interactive work situation, the need and opportunities for cooperation between systems analysts and information systems users throughout the entire SDLC will be greatly amplified.

Contemporary Systems Analysis provides a balanced treatment of the four phases of the SDLC: study, design, development, and operation. Although current in its coverage, the text does not overly stress a specific tool or technique. Rather, it is designed to provide the student with the perspective needed to identify and select the combination of tools and techniques most appropriate to solving a particular business problem.

A three-tiered approach is taken toward contemporary practices in systems analysis and design. The tiers are as follows:

1. *The systems development life cycle (SDLC)* as a methodology for managing complex software projects.
2. *Structured systems analysis and design techniques* for analyzing existing systems and developing top-down performance specifications for new or improved systems.
3. *Concurrent prototyping* as a means of speeding up the life-cycle process and providing continuous validation of system performance, including the presentation of computer-assisted systems engineering (CASE) as a powerful analysis, design, and development tool.

Throughout the text a user-oriented, TQM emphasis is maintained. This emphasis has three salient attributes consistent with the feedback nature of the SDLC: continuous improvement, user involvement, and focus on the *usability* of the information system, which is the worth or quality of the system as perceived by its users. This perception is the ultimate measure of the success or failure of a computer information system.

New Features of the Text

The features that distinguish *Contemporary Systems Analysis* from the predecessor text by Gore and Stubbe are the following:

1. Inclusion of TQM as an important topic, and one that reinforces the concept that customer-perceived "usability" is the measure of the value of the system.
2. Updating of all topics consistent with observed and projected changes in hardware and software development technologies.
3. Consolidation of related materials, such as technology and project management.
4. Expanded treatment of rapid applications development, including data-driven, event-driven, and prototyping techniques.
5. Emphasis on microcomputer/workstation (vs. mainframe) solutions in a networked, distributed data processing environment.
6. Inclusion of end-of-chapter "For Exercise" mini-exercises designed to illustrate and amplify important topics.
7. An in-text SDLC case study that reflects the growing importance of client/server relationships among mainframes, midrange computer systems, and user workstations.
8. Two new student workbooks, each developed to illustrate a current and industry-relevant case study.

Other Special Features of the Text

Special features of the text that are consistent with its goals and scope are as follows:

1. **Support for an accompanying "hands-on" laboratory.** The text and student workbook are designed so that assignments may be completed in a microcomputer equipped laboratory using popular spreadsheet, data base, and graphics software packages designed for use with IBM PC and compatible or Macintosh microcomputers. Midrange and microcomputer CASE products can be used with many assignments. One of the most popular CASE methodologies is Excelerator, which will be given to adopters of this text.[2]
2. **A presentation and learning reinforcement sequence consistent with the SDLC sequence of activities.** Major concepts, tools, and techniques that are applicable throughout the SDLC are introduced in the first three units of the text. These include: information and business system concepts, communications and documentation, project management, data flow diagrams, and CASE tools. The next four units follow the SDLC sequence of activities and provide opportunities to apply these tools to activities characteristic of the study, design, development, and operation phases.

---

[2] *Excelerator,* a well-known CASE methodology, is a product of Intersolve, Inc., and adopters of *Contemporary Systems Analysis* will receive a free copy that can be used on two computers. Additional copies are available for a small fee.

3. **Use of in-text learning aids:**
   Each major unit begins with an overview that introduces the chapters in that unit and explains the relationships among them.

   Each chapter begins with a preview and statement of measurable student learning objectives, followed by a list of key terms and their definitions. Key terms appear in boldface type in the text, and other significant terms are italicized.

   Each chapter includes a summary that synopsizes the main points and ''For Discussion'' questions that expand upon major concepts and related issues.

   ''For Exercise'' mini-assignments are included in all chapters in which important tools or techniques are presented.

   A glossary that includes all key (boldfaced) and significant (italicized) terms serves as a study aid and ready reference.

4. **An Integrated Learning Package.** *Contemporary Systems Analysis* is an integrated learning package that is comprised of:
   The text itself with the features described above.

   A student workbook accompanied by an instructors' solutions manual. The workbook, which is new to this edition, is entitled *Champion, an Agile Industry,* and it reflects the major themes of the text. It contains assignments that parallel significant chapter topics. These assignments are more comprehensive than the ''For Exercise'' mini-assignments that appear in the text, and they are designed to require a higher level of critical thinking.

   A second workbook, under development, will be available to new or continuing adopters of the text. This will provide an opportunity to give alternate assignments. Both workbooks will be updated to maintain currency.

   High-quality transparency masters for all significant figures and an extensive test bank.

5. **A comprehensive instructor's manual.** The manual:
   Describes unit and chapter goals.

   Identifies measurable student performance objectives.

   Lists key points indexed to page and figure number.

   Provides answers to ''For Discussion'' questions and ''For Exercise'' mini-assignments at the end of each chapter.

   Contains chapter quizzes and unit examinations, with answers.

6. **A continuous, integrated, in-text case study.** The case study is a unified presentation of all the major activities that occur throughout the SDLC phases. It can serve as a practical reference for subsequent seminar or actual systems projects.

Contemporary Systems Analysis is designed to serve both as a text for an introductory course in systems analysis and as a guidebook for students in an advanced, project-oriented course. It is designed to meet not only the needs of information systems majors, but also those of all business students because they, too, will interact with computer information systems throughout their professional careers.

Acknowledgments

Contemporary Systems Analysis owes its existence, first, to the students who were responsible for the real-time testing of the manuscript and who have, often unknowingly, contributed to the many revisions of the materials that resulted in the creation of this text.

Also, we wish to express our appreciation for the frank assessments, recommendations, and comments provided by reviewers of the manuscript in its various stages of development. The positive evaluations encouraged us, and the critical critiques stimulated us to analyze and improve our efforts. Those to whom we are particularly indebted for a value-added product are: M. Gordon Hunter, Nanyang Technological University, Singapore; Arline Sacks, Northern Virginia Community College; Bob Miller, College of New Caledonia/Prince George, B.C.; Charles P. Bilbrey, James Madison University; Susan Helms, St. Mary's College of Minnesota; Don Mann, Oakland Community College; Gary L. Sharp, Laramie County Community College; Carol Clark, Middle Tennessee State University; Dale D. Gust, Central Michigan University; Carl W. Penziul, Corning Community College; Raymond Yu, Douglas College; Kinder Deo, Douglas College; John Blackwell, Douglas College; Joan Smulders, Douglas College; Gail Corbitt, California State University–Chico.

Finally, we owe a great debt of thanks to the editorial teams at Wm. C. Brown Publishers who had the patience to "stick with us" through an extended writing and production schedule. With your support, we believe that, in the end, we have produced a textbook and teaching tools that are, indeed, contemporary. Thank you Linda Meehan, and Paul Ducham.

Marvin Gore
John Stubbe
Walnut, California

Contemporary Systems Analysis and Design

A major goal of *Contemporary Systems Analysis* is to introduce you to the methods, tools, and techniques you will need to participate effectively in the design, development, and use of modern computer information systems. Accordingly, the purpose of the two chapters in Unit One is to provide a framework of essential concepts that will reoccur and be reinforced throughout the text.

Chapter 1, "Contemporary Information Systems Analysis and Design," is designed to assist you to develop a working vocabulary and a background of concepts essential to the field of systems analysis. You will become familiar with information system terms, such as system, systems analysis, systems analyst, computer information system, and business information system. The chapter describes the jobs performed by and the promising career opportunities for systems analysts. It introduces the concept of the systems development life cycle (SDLC) as an organized process, called a methodology, for the design and development of effective computer-based business information systems. The chapter traces the evolution of information systems engineering from classical to structured methods and introduces prototyping, an increasingly important technique for reducing SDLC time and cost. Also, it introduces computer-assisted systems engineering (CASE) as a powerful analysis, design, and development tool in an era marked by increasing information systems complexity and the emergence of the computer-integrated enterprise.

Chapter 2, "A Business as an Information System," further examines the systems characteristics of businesses and describes how businesses are organized to accomplish their goals and objectives. The chapter describes and explains the structure and use of organization charts and organization function lists. It emphasizes the information structure of a business by distinguishing between product flow and information flow and by linking business information needs to external and internal information generators. Also, the four information levels in an enterprise are identified, and the principal characteristics of each are discussed as they relate to management uses of information.

The principles of total quality management (TQM) are introduced and related to the systems development life cycle (SDLC) and to business organization and management—with a focus on developing quick-response information systems for agile enterprises.

Chapter

1

■ ■ ■

Contemporary Information Systems Analysis and Design

Preview

Because the computer-based information systems upon which the productivity of our economy depends are becoming increasingly complex, an organized approach to their design and development is essential. Systems analysis, which is a structured process, or methodology, for identifying and solving problems, provides this approach. Using tools and techniques based on the concept of a life cycle through which all business information systems must pass, systems analysts are able to manage information resources and to create systems that increase the productivity of their users.

Many of these tools and techniques are, themselves, automated. Their application to the systems development life cycle is called computer-assisted systems engineering. As they continue to evolve, the systems engineering methodologies increasingly will contribute to the ability of competitive companies to access and use the information needed to respond to rapidly changing conditions. The emergence and growth of companies, called computer-integrated enterprises, that have successfully consolidated and focused corporatewide information systems will continue, and these companies will dominate the global marketplace as we enter the next century.

Objectives

1. You will be able to describe fundamental information system concepts using a basic computer information systems vocabulary.
2. You will be able to recognize the systems development life cycle (SDLC) flowchart for a business information system and to describe the principal characteristics of each of the four life-cycle phases.
3. You will be able to explain the importance of systems analysis as a method for designing and developing effective computer information systems.
4. You will be able to demonstrate awareness of the jobs performed by systems analysts, the career opportunities in systems analysis, and the qualifications needed for success in the field of systems analysis.
5. You will be able to explain how the life-cycle methodologies for systems analysis and design have evolved and will be able to distinguish among the principal features of the classical, structured, and prototyping approaches.
6. You will be able to define prototyping and to describe the prototyping model of the systems development life cycle.
7. You will recognize the importance of automating the SDLC and will be able to discuss the use of CASE tools and their relationship to the computer-integrated enterprise.

Key Terms

systems analysis   a structured process for designing and developing effective computer information systems.

computer information system (CIS)   in this text, a computer-based business information system.

system   a combination of resources working together to convert inputs into outputs.

business information system   a system that uses resources to convert data into the information needed to accomplish the purposes of the business.

life cycle   the period of the creation and existence of a business information system.

systems development life cycle (SDLC) a sequence of related activities through which all business information systems must pass. The four life-cycle phases are: study, design, development, and operation.

baseline specification   any one of the three essential systems development life-cycle reference documents: performance specification, design specification, or system specification.

systems analyst   a person who performs systems analysis during any, or all, of the life-cycle phases.

usability   the worth, or quality, of a system as perceived in the value system of its principal users.

prototyping   a technique for speeding up the development of a computer information system by working with a model of that system that evolves into a final design specification.

computer-assisted systems engineering (CASE)   an engineering approach toward automating all phases of the systems development life-cycle methodology.

computer-integrated enterprise (CIE) an enterprise in which all elements, from business plan to delivery of a product or service, are linked by an organized and shared collection of information.

Computer Information Systems

Information System Concepts

Computers and computer-based information systems continue to revolutionize the manner in which our economy functions. Because they make possible the accurate decision-making needed to respond to shorter product life cycles and rapidly changing business situations, computer information systems have become indispensable power tools upon which the productivity and global markct-share of business and industry depend. In the United States at present approximately three-quarters of all workers are involved either in the creation, manipulation, or use of information or in the development, manufacturing, or marketing of information processing products and services. We are witnessing the emergence of the **computer-integrated enterprise,** or **CIE,** which is an enterprise in which all elements, from business plan to delivery of a product or service, are linked by an organized and shared collection of information.

Prominent among competitive CIEs are manufacturing industries in which business functions and manufacturing operations are integrated across the entire enterprise. This type of CIE is referred to as *computer-integrated manufacturing, or CIM.* For example, the IBM Corporation, which is the world's largest manufacturer of computer hardware and software, not only is developing and marketing CIM products but also has made a corporatewide commitment to apply CIM internally. The "circular" factory in figure 1.1 is a CIM enterprise model that shows the six functional areas characteristic of manufacturing industries. Figure 1.2 adds to this model a picture of the integrated information systems needed to effectively manage the data needed in a CIM environment. Also, consider the office, which is a universal business support area. As shown in figure 1.3, office tasks have been converted from "typing and filing" to the use of networks of electronic systems for word processing, information storage and retrieval, and local and remote communications.

As the foregoing examples illustrate, it has become clear that in the future our economic well-being will depend upon increasingly complex communications and computer-centered information systems. Therefore, the study of **systems analysis** as a structured process for designing and developing effective computer-related business information systems is important. The ability to define and apply basic systems concepts is essential to the study of computer-related business information systems, commonly referred to as **computer information systems,** or **CIS.**

In a very general sense, we can view a system as a group of related parts that work together as a unit. The definition of a system that we will use in this book is based upon that concept; however, our working definition is less general and more specific to the study of business information systems. We define a **system** to be a combination of resources working together to convert inputs into outputs, and we will further refine this definition as we proceed. The conversion process is depicted in figure 1.4. As this figure shows, the resources used by a system include personnel, facilities, materials, and equipment. Usually, we consider the inputs to the system to be *data,* which are recordable facts. The outputs of a system are interpreted, or processed, data, which are called *information.* Thus data are a form of raw information.

■ Figure 1.1   The enterprise model. The enterprise model for a factory shows the six major functional areas that make up a manufacturing enterprise. Computer-integrated manufacturing, CIM, uses information technology to achieve competitive advantages by integrating these functions in order to speed up new product design and development; reduce production planning time; improve plant floor operations; improve product quality, reliability, and serviceability; optimize inventory management; and reduce delivery times.

(Reference: IBM, The Computer Integrated Manufacturing (CIM) Enterprise, U.S. Marketing and Services, Dept. ZW1, White Plains, NY 10604)

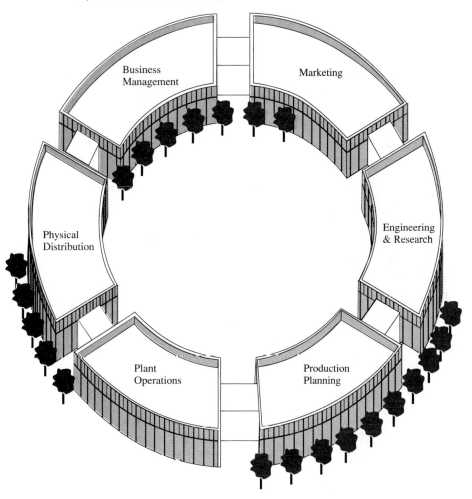

Managing data in the CIM environment. A CIM architecture must provide for the access and presentation of information in ways that meet the needs of individual users. This is accomplished by setting up and managing a hierarchy of storage functions. These include local data files, designed to meet the needs within a functional area; a data store which provides a base for enterprisewide data integration, standardization, and control; and a repository which provides users with access to information formatted to best meet their needs.

(Reference: IBM, The Computer Integrated Manufacturing (CIM) Enterprise, U.S. Marketing and Services, Dept. ZW1, White Plains, NY 10604)

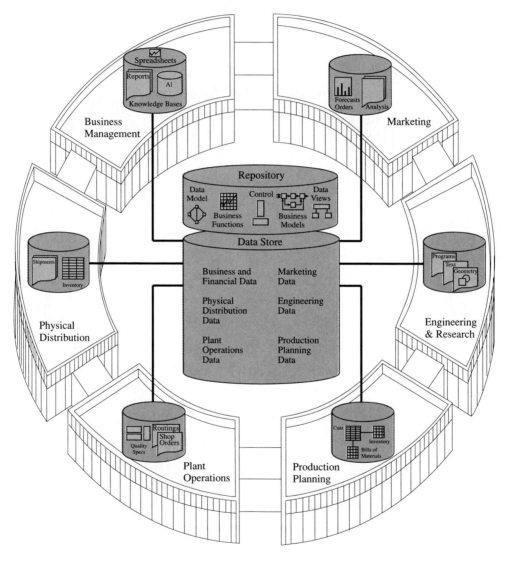

■ Figure 1.3   An automated office. The office of the 1990s will be fully automated. Corporate headquarters will include executive workstations, word processing and data entry stations, data storage (micrographic) facilities, and data reproduction services (intelligent copiers) links. The "hub" of the office will be the corporate communications system, which will support teleconferencing, electronic mail, and connectivity with remote users.

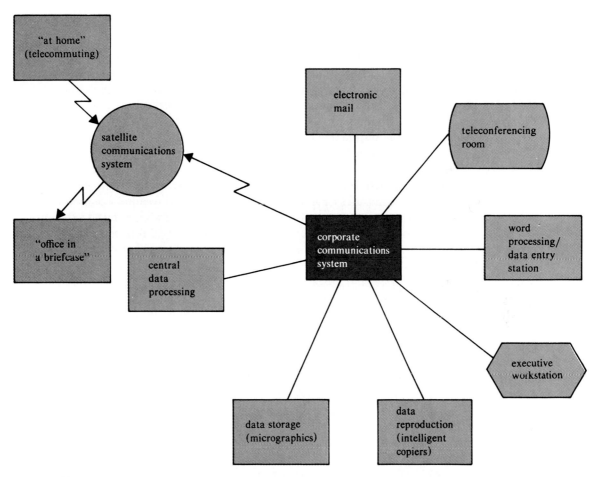

■ Figure 1.4   A system definition. A system is a combination of resources working together to convert inputs into outputs. In a business system, which converts data into information, the principal resources are personnel, facilities, materials, and equipment.

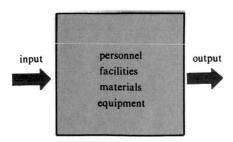

It is important to note that information that is the output of one system may become the input data to another system because it must be further refined for other uses. An example is a computer information system that summarizes data at a regional level and also provides the regional summary information to a national marketing manager as an input to a strategic planning and decision-making process.

Business Information Systems

A business information system is a particular type of system. It uses resources to convert data into the information needed to accomplish the purposes of the business. Generally, these purposes are to provide goods or services. An example of a business information system that supports the purposes of a business is a retail store system that converts sales transaction data into information needed to prepare customer billings, manage inventory, schedule product delivery, and calculate profit and loss. Another example is a financial system that enables customers of a bank to enter personal identification data into a terminal in order to make deposits, transfer funds, or withdraw cash.

Because almost all modern business systems depend extensively upon the use of computers, they also are computer information systems. For these systems, computer *hardware* and *software* are examples of system resources. Hardware refers to the physical components of a computer system, such as input, storage, processing, and output devices. Hardware is an example of an equipment resource. Software is the collection of programs that facilitates the use of a computer. Typically, software resides on a magnetic medium, and it is an example of a material resource.

Business information systems usually are composed of smaller components that are themselves systems. Because they are parts of a larger system, these components are called *subsystems*. Figure 1.5 illustrates the subsystem concept for a product-oriented enterprise, such as a manufacturer. Major systems usually present in such enterprises include marketing, product development, finance, and administration. As this figure illustrates, major systems are made up of subordinate systems. These are subsystems, each of which performs a specific function. For example, a marketing system may contain distribution and sales subsystems. A subsystem may be made up of lower-level subsystems. Thus a sales subsystem might be composed of mail order and retail sales subsystems. Many subsystems are very large, and it is not uncommon to hear them referred to as "systems."

Similarly, it is not unusual to use the term *computer system* to refer to the entire computer information system. In this text, we will consider the computer system (the computer hardware and software) to be a resource. It is an important resource—one that may support one or more computer information systems. However, it is not the entire computer information system. In most such systems, many system functions are performed outside of the computer component. These also rely upon personnel, material, equipment, and facilities resources. Everyday examples of computer information systems that contain noncomputer elements are airline ticketing and baggage handling systems, sales presentations, and long-distance business conferences.

■ Figure 1.5   Systems and subsystems. Business information systems usually are large systems, themselves composed of subordinate systems, called subsystems. A marketing system (a), a product development system (b), a finance system (c), and an administrative system (d) are typical major systems that are made up of subsystems.

a. **marketing system**
   sales subsystem
   distribution subsystem

b. **product development system**
   purchasing subsystem
   receiving subsystem
   inventory subsystem
   production subsystem

c. **finance system**
   billing subsystem
   collection subsystem
   paying subsystem

d. **administration system**
   personnel subsystem
   contracts subsystem

The Systems Development Life Cycle

The Life-Cycle Phases

A step-by-step, structured process for the development of computer information systems has emerged. This process draws upon the engineering approach to the analysis and solution of complex problems. It is based upon the concept of a sequence of necessary activities through which all business information systems must pass during the period of their creation and existence, or **life cycle.** Within the life cycle, significant series of related activities are combined into phases, called the *life-cycle phases.* The concept of the life cycle of a computer information system is widely accepted and has led to the adoption of a project-oriented approach to the design and development of computer information systems. This approach is referred to as the *life-cycle methodology,* commonly referred to as the **systems development life cycle,** or **SDLC.**

   In general the activities that must be performed throughout the systems development life cycle and the sequence in which they are to be performed are well identified, however the number of activities assigned to a phase and, hence, the number of phases considered to make up the systems development life cycle is not standardized. In this text we divide the life cycle of a computer information system into four major phases. As shown in figure 1.6, we identify the four phases of the SDLC as: study, design, development, and operation. We will study each phase of the SDLC and its associated activities in detail in subsequent chapters. For the present, we can briefly define each as follows:

study phase   The life-cycle phase in which a problem is identified and analyzed, alternate solutions are evaluated, and a system solution is recommended at the general design level. Acceptance of the recommendation by the user of the system involves the commitment of the resources needed to complete the detailed design of the system.

■ Figure 1.6   Systems development life-cycle phases. Significant sequences of activities are associated with the life cycle of a computer information system. These activities can be collected into four phases: study, design, development, and operation.

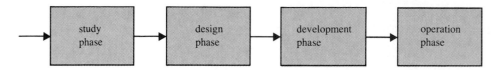

design phase   The life-cycle phase in which the detailed design of the system selected in the study phase is accomplished. In this phase the technical specifications are prepared for all tasks that must be performed in order to develop the computer system. The resources needed to complete equipment tasks, personnel tasks, and computer program tasks are allocated.

development phase   The life-cycle phase in which the system is constructed according to the design phase specification. Computer programs are written. All manuals, software specifications, and other documentation are completed. Users and support staff are trained, and the developed system is tested for operational readiness.

operation phase   The life-cycle phase in which the system is installed, operated, and maintained. The performance of the new system is reviewed, and necessary changes to the system are managed throughout the remainder of its life cycle.

The Life-Cycle Flowchart

The Life-Cycle Activities

Figure 1.7 is a flowchart that provides us with a more detailed pictorial overview of the systems development life-cycle process. This figure identifies three important types of activities that must be performed concurrently as a business information system progresses through its life cycle. These are (1) management of the entire life-cycle process, (2) performance of the tasks characteristic of each life-cycle phase, and (3) documentation of the system. In the previous section, we briefly described the characteristics of each of the life-cycle phases. At this point it is appropriate to provide a similar overview of the management and documentation activities.

Life-Cycle Management and Documentation

Management of all of the activities that make up the major life-cycle tasks is of major importance. As is true of other projects, the goal of life-cycle management is to complete the job on time and within budget and to deliver a quality product that meets the needs of the business. Throughout the SDLC, an important management responsibility is the frequent review of the project. Reviews may occur at any time throughout the life-cycle process; however, the conclusion of each phase is a natural and appropriate time for a major management review. These are formal, scheduled reviews that must occur before a SDLC phase can be considered complete. They

■ **Figure 1.7** Life-cycle activities. Management review, performance of tasks, and preparation of documentation are parallel activities that occur throughout the systems development life cycle. As the feedback paths indicate, return to an earlier point in the life-cycle process may occur at any time.

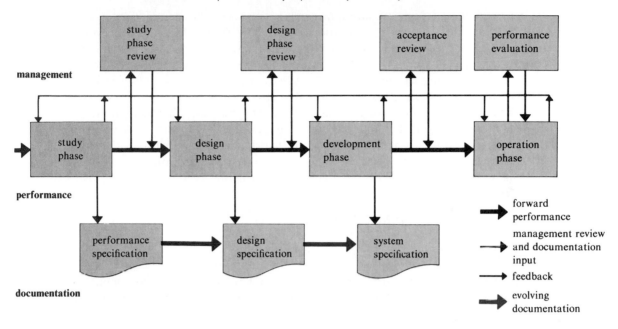

ensure that the principal users of the computer information system are involved at critical decision points. Three types of decisions can result from management reviews: (1) proceed to the next phase; (2) cancel the project; or (3) redo certain parts of the current or a preceding phase.

Activities that are redone must be reviewed before the project can proceed to a subsequent phase. Management review often is the mechanism that triggers "cycling back," or feedback, to an earlier stage in the life cycle to remedy performance deficiencies or to respond to changes in requirements. An important benefit of a successful review is the renewal of management commitment to the project.

The preparation and accumulation of documentation parallels the project management and task performance life-cycle activities. The three most essential SDLC documents are called **baseline specifications** because they are specifications to which changes can be referred. They are as follows:

performance specification Completed at the end of the study phase, the performance specification describes in the language of the user exactly what the system is to do. It is a general "design-to" specification.

design specification Completed at the end of the design phase, the design specification describes in the language of the programmer (and others actively involved in constructing the system) how to develop the system. It is a detailed "build-to" specification.

system specification   Completed at the conclusion of the development phase, the
    system specification contains all of the essential system documentation. It is the
    basis for all manuals and procedures, and it is a complete "as-built" specification.

Actually, documentation is continuous and cumulative. The design specification
evolves from the performance specification, and the system specification evolves
from the design specification. The life-cycle methodology is a modular, *top-down* process. It is called top-down because in successive phases the major modules are expanded into additional, increasingly detailed modules. Fortunately, powerful
computer-based tools have been developed to assist the project team to overcome
complexity, perform the life-cycle tasks, create and maintain documentation, and
manage the entire project. In many ways, these tools make it possible both to speed
up the life-cycle process and to improve the performance and quality of the information system. Before introducing these aids, it is appropriate to define systems analysis and describe the role of the systems analyst in relation to the SDLC and the users
of the information system.

Systems Analysis and the Systems Analyst

Systems Analysis

Systems analysis is a general term that refers to a structured process for identifying
and solving problems. In this text we are concerned with computer information
system problems and with the SDLC as the process for identifying and solving them.
Strictly speaking, *analysis* implies a process of breaking something down into its parts
so that the whole may be understood. Actually, systems analysis includes not only the
process of analysis, but also that of *synthesis,* which is the process of putting parts
together to form a new whole.

The Systems Analyst

A **systems analyst** is a person who performs systems analysis during any, or all, of
the life-cycle phases of a business information system. The systems analyst not only
analyzes business information system problems, but also synthesizes new systems to
solve those problems or to meet other information needs of an enterprise. In doing
so, a senior systems analyst often is responsible for managing all of the activities associated with the four phases of the SDLC. In this sense, a systems analyst may be
considered to be a *life-cycle manager.*

Careers in Systems Analysis

Performing Systems Analysis
The principal functions performed by systems analysts date back to the period before
the use of computers became widespread. These were, and still are, the following:

1. To analyze business systems with problems and to design new or modified
   systems to solve those problems.
2. To develop business systems to meet new information or operational needs.

3. To prepare and maintain documentation needed to communicate company policies and procedures.
4. To design the various business forms used to collect data and to distribute information.
5. To perform records management, including the distribution and use of reports.
6. To establish standards for and to participate in the selection of information processing equipment.
7. To prepare and maintain business organization charts.

Although the basic functions performed by systems analysts have not changed, the manner in which they are performed has undergone great change. The introduction of computers led to a phenomenal growth in the number and complexity of business information systems. Also, because of the importance of computer information systems to the success of an enterprise, systems analysts have benefited, and continue to benefit, from expanded career opportunities.

Opportunities and Compensation

The job outlook for systems analysts is promising. The U.S. Department of Labor projects continuing growth in this field for the remainder of the century as advances in technology and competition among industries lead to new applications for computers. By the mid-1990s there will be more than 400,000 systems analysts. Besides the opportunity to display leadership and to exercise creativity, two important factors that make a career as a systems analyst rewarding are the reporting level of the systems analysis group and the compensation relative to other information service careers.

Increasingly, the senior information systems executive is a vice-president who reports directly to the president of the corporation. Meaningful titles for this executive are vice-president of information services, vice-president of information resources, or vice-president of information systems. Typically, the systems analysis staff is headed by a director of corporate systems who reports to the vice-president of information services. As displayed in figure 1.8, the salaries paid to information system professionals relate to the point in the systems development life cycle where they begin to apply their skills. Salaries are the highest for those positions requiring the most creativity and responsibility. Because systems analysts often act as life-cycle managers from the beginning of a project, it is not surprising to find that their compensation is at the upper end of the salary scale.

Personal Qualifications

As actual, or potential, life-cycle managers who may be assigned the responsibility for managing complex computer information system projects, systems analysts must possess leadership and human relations skills. Because much of their work is of a service nature, they must be able to secure cooperation. Also, they must be able to speak and write well in order to communicate effectively with people at all levels in an organization. They must possess not only technical skills, but also the ability to translate technical terms and ideas into nontechnical language that users and others can understand.

■ Figure 1.8   Salaries and the computer information system life cycle. As compared with those of other information systems professionals, salaries for systems analysts are highest because analysts apply their creative skills and experience early in the life-cycle process. Also, systems analysts have major responsibilities throughout all of the life-cycle phases.

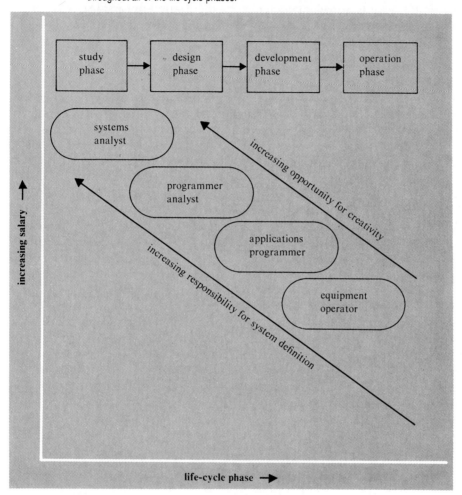

As computer information systems continue to increase in scope and complexity, the background that analysts must possess becomes more important and more demanding. Most systems analysts entering the field have a bachelor's degree or higher. The most common college majors for systems analysts are computer information systems (CIS) and management information systems (MIS). The two curricula overlap, with the difference being the relative emphasis upon computers and management. Of course, other fields of study, such as business administration and accounting, may enable persons to begin a career as a systems analyst because computers and their applications are almost universally integrated into these curricula.

Because of the rapidly changing CIS technologies, many companies hold seminars and training programs designed to keep analysts' knowledge current. Often there are opportunities to attend courses at local colleges or classes sponsored by information product vendors. Professional organizations such as the Association for Systems Management, the Data Processing Management Association, and the Association for Computing Machinery also provide opportunities for individuals to keep up to date and to exchange information with professionals in the same field.

Although education is important, with a four-year degree usually required for an entry-level position, actual on-the-job seasoning is essential. It is unlikely that an individual could become a systems analyst without first serving an apprenticeship to gain job experience. This experience usually includes some computer programming and acquiring a detailed knowledge of one or more major business areas. Both are gained by starting in a junior or trainee position and working on small projects or as a member of a large-project team under the direction of a senior analyst.

The User and the SDLC

Information Resource Management

Among businesses of all types, we are witnessing the rapid convergence of the data processing, automated office, and communications technologies. This convergence is graphically illustrated in figure 1.9. At the center of this figure is a region of overlap labeled *information resource management*, which pertains to a centralized responsibility for selecting, distributing, and managing information resources of the type listed in figure 1.9. This responsibility greatly increases the complexity of the tasks that the corporate information services support staff must perform. As a result many information services organizations have established *information resource centers* in order to inform and assist users of information resources. Most often the information resource center works with users to select the most appropriate microcomputer or personal workstation. Because of the ongoing trend to distribute computing power to users, increasing numbers of these workstations are remote from the location of the central information services organization. Consequently, communicating with and working with remote users will become an increasingly important aspect of the role of the systems analyst.

Distributed Data Processing

From the mid-1950s and throughout the 1960s, literally the dawn of the computer age of business data processing, most information systems were under the complete control of a centralized computer services organization that served the entire enterprise, and information received by users of those services usually was in the form of printed reports. Since this information was based upon input information that was submitted to the computing center in batches for later processing and manual distribution, reports were periodic and, in most instances, did not reflect current situations. Beginning in the 1970s, computer systems were developed that were able to place computing power wherever and whenever it was needed. Initially, these were centralized enterprise or department-level systems; but, with the increasing power and widespread use of microcomputers, computing power quickly spread to the workstations of CIS users. The number of personal computing systems, often referred to as workstations, is continuing to increase without seeming limit because they provide the flexibility and fast response time required to meet the needs of local

Convergence of information technologies. The importance of information resource management is emphasized by the area of overlap in the center of the figure, which emphasizes the merging of the data processing, automated office, and communications technologies.

small computer systems
large computer systems
distributed data processing
terminals
peripherals
graphics

word processing
micrographics
intelligent copier/printer
dictating systems

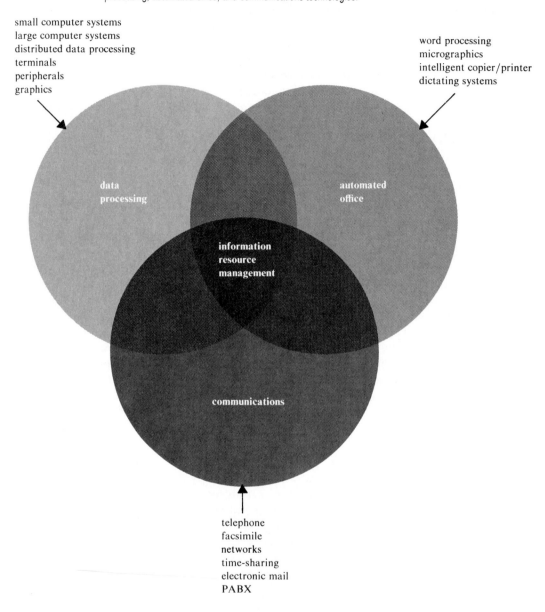

data
processing

automated
office

information
resource
management

communications

telephone
facsimile
networks
time-sharing
electronic mail
PABX

operations. Communications networks are proliferating at all levels within corporations. Local area networks provide department-level connectivity and access to other networks throughout the enterprise. As a result, increasing numbers of users' microcomputers are being linked electronically to create, access, and process information in the manner pictured in figure 1.10. Throughout the foreseeable future, newer and more powerful information resources will become available to users, and communications networks will continue to grow in size and complexity. These trends will provide new opportunities to enhance productivity; also they will continue to emphasize the necessity for cooperative relationships between information services organizations and the users of their services.

The Concept of Usability

In this text, we will discuss many tools and techniques for systems analysis and design. However, more important than any particular tool or technique is the necessity that the analyst follow the systems development life-cycle road map *and* involve the user every step of the way. The greatest mistakes that systems analysts can make are to assume (1) that they know better than their users what those users need, and (2) that the users will be satisfied with what someone else believes is the best solution to their problem. In the final analysis, the acceptance or rejection of a systems analyst's product will be based upon its **usability,** which is the worth or quality of the system as perceived in the value system of its principal users. Users who feel a sense of ownership can compensate for the defects in a less than adequate system and will work to improve it. Users who feel that a system, however good it may be, has been thrust upon them can find a way to make it fail.

Fortunately, the same engineering-based approach that led to the life-cycle methodology also led to the introduction of powerful tools that systems analysts can use to communicate with the users of the system and to manage increasingly complex computer information system projects. These tools, which we will introduce in the next section and revisit throughout this text, have an additional benefit: they require that analysts and end-users work together as members of a team.

Evolution of Information Systems Engineering

Classical Life-Cycle Methodology

The *classical life-cycle methodology,* which was introduced in the early 1970s, uses special flowchart symbols that emphasize the physical attributes of a system. In many cases the symbols resemble the operations to be performed or the objects themselves. Figure 1.11 is an example of a classical system flowchart that is drawn to represent the inputs and outputs for a portion of a sales subsystem. The three systems flowcharting symbols used in this figure are the manual input symbol, which represents the keyboard entry of data; the rectangle, which is a generalized symbol for a processing operation; and the document symbol, which resembles a portion of a report. The classical method still is in common use in industry, and it has many features that are of continuing value at appropriate stages of the SDLC.

■ **Figure 1.10** Distributed data processing. In a typical department-level work environment, a minicomputer may act as a dedicated processor that supports peripheral devices, such as printers, and a local area network (LAN). The LAN uses a satellite link to communicate with a large network connected to a remote mainframe. The local microcomputers function as (1) *user* personal workstations, (2) *servers* that provide resources, such as data files, to user stations, or (3) *masters* that act as both server and user workstations.

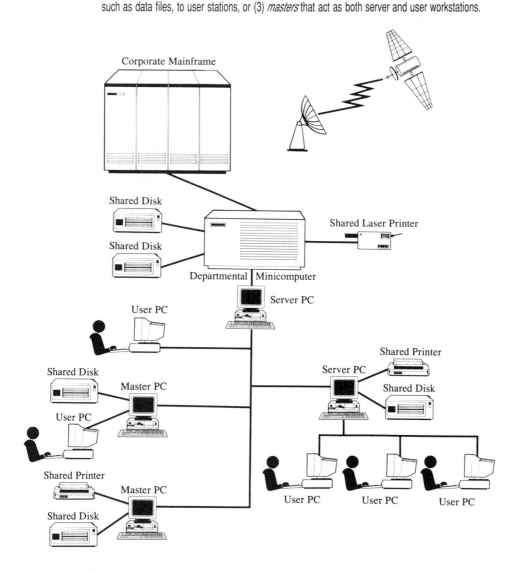

■ Figure 1.11   Classical methodology. The special flowchart symbols used to draw this systems flowchart represent the processes by which data are entered manually at a keyboard as inputs to an order processing system. Outputs are produced as printed customer invoices and shipping orders.

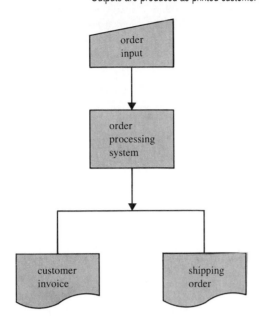

Structured Analysis and Design Methods

The *structured methods,* which have found increasing use and acceptance since the early 1980s, evolved from successful efforts to improve the productivity of programmers and the quality of software end-products. The structured methods use flowchart symbols that identify the data flows within a system. They are an effective, free-form means of creating and working with a logical model of a system, and of communicating with users without implying a premature commitment to specific physical components. Figure 1.12 illustrates a structured method for flowcharting the logical model of the portion of the sales subsystem shown in figure 1.11. The lines arc labeled to represent data flows (as indicated by a data-carrier, such as a sales order) without any indication of a physical implementation. The circle, or "bubble," identifies the process that transforms input data flows into output data flows.

Unlike the symbols for the classical methodology, those used for the structured methods are not standardized, and there are variations in the methods by which data flow diagrams are represented. The symbols used in this text are representative, and you should experience no difficulties when encountering slightly different versions of data flow diagrams. As contrasted with the classical systems symbols that represent

Structured method. The flowchart symbols in this data flow diagram show sales-order data as the input to a process that creates the data that appears on the customer-invoice and shipping-order. The "bubble" is the process that transforms the input data flow into the output data flows.

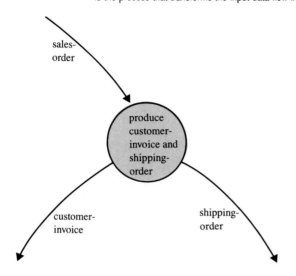

the "how," the structured symbols represent the "what" of an information system. A systems analyst should be familiar with both types of symbols. The symbol sets should not be considered to be exclusive but complementary. Each has a best use at appropriate points in the systems development life cycle.

Prototyping

Definition of Prototyping

Adapted from the engineering world, the practice of working with a model, or prototype, of an information system has proved to be an effective means of improving the life-cycle process. With respect to computer information systems, we can define **prototyping** as a technique for speeding up the development of a computer information system by working with a model of that system that evolves into a final design specification. An engineering analogy is the long-time practice of using wind tunnels to determine the aerodynamic properties of reduced-scale models before committing to the expense of constructing a full-size airplane.

Prototyping Version of the SDLC

A principal reason that prototyping enables analysts to speed up the SDLC is that a continuous evaluation can be made by the analyst and users working together throughout the critical study and design phases. If the model does not perform as expected, changes can be made without the commitment of large time and money

■ Figure 1.13   Prototype version of the SDLC. A prototype, or small-scale model, makes possible rapid recycling, or iteration, of study and design phase activities until an acceptable computer information design specification is created. The process benefits from strong user involvement and participation.

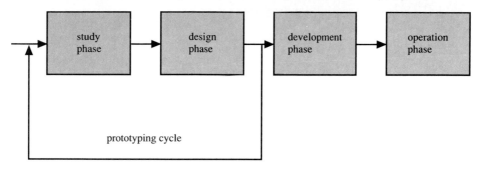

resources. Prototyping is particularly suitable in situations in which there is a high degree of user interaction with the information system, such as on-line queries. Where applicable, it can greatly reduce the time and cost of the development phase, which is the phase in which the major project resource and time expenditures usually occur. The prototyping version of the SDLC is shown in figure 1.13, which illustrates the process of rapid cycling through design alternatives before beginning undertaking the development of a full-scale system. Often, this process is referred to as *rapid prototyping,* or *rapid applications development (RAD).*

The true power of prototyping lies in extensive user involvement at the beginning of the SDLC. Often users are not able to visualize or express their information needs clearly. However, most users can recognize what they want when they actually can see it, and, hence, prototyping makes possible the rapid exploration of alternative versions of major information system input, processing, and output attributes. Increasingly, companies are recognizing that better systems can be created at a lower cost if the front-end investment in planning is increased. Figure 1.14 illustrates how the additional time that users and analysts may spend in analysis and design is more than recovered by the payoff at the end of the development phase. Additionally the cost of maintenance and change will be minimized for a well-designed system.

Even with the support of powerful information system engineering aids such as prototyping, computer information system design and development is a very complex process. Fortunately, the application of engineering principles to computer information systems has evolved to a point at which we are witnessing the development and increasing use of software tools designed to provide system developers with a means of performing rapid prototyping and automating almost all of the life-cycle activities. We will introduce these tools in the section that follows.

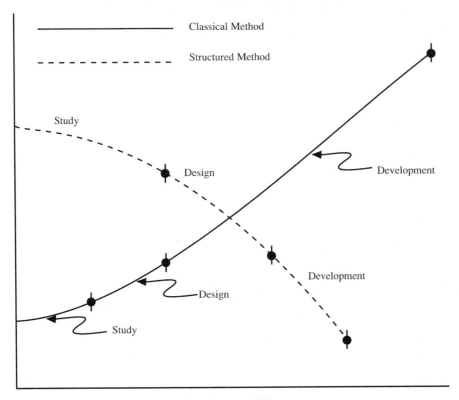

■ Figure 1.14   Prototyping payoff. A front-end investment in a sound design pays off by reducing the length of the SDLC and, therefore, the cost of developing and operating a computer information system.

Time Spent per Phase

Automating the Systems Development Life Cycle

The Forces of Change

In the future, information systems will continue to undergo dramatic change. The forces causing this change will be: (1) increasingly complex users' needs, (2) advances in the information processing technologies, and (3) the introduction of new methodologies for system design. A three-dimensional interaction among these forces is shown in figure 1.15. The presence and use of computers will become ever more commonplace as the present workforce is replaced by persons now in school or in training. Computers will be so embedded in our culture and education that "computer literacy" will no longer need to be singled out as a unique need. Figure 1.16, which shows the trend in the growth of the information services market, and figure 1.17, which projects user spending trends, underscore the magnitude of

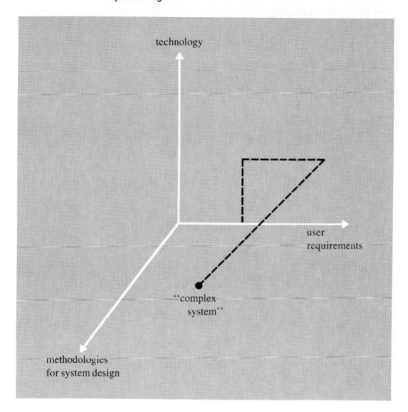

ongoing change. The projections in these figures are probably conservative, with the automated office market alone expected to increase at a rate of forty percent per year over the next five years.

Automated Systems Development Life-Cycle Tools

Task-Oriented Tools

The magnitude of all but the smallest SDLC projects is such that manual methods are not adequate. Wherever possible, there is a need to provide automated support. This support ranges from computer programs that perform specific tasks to very comprehensive, integrated software packages designed to support activities throughout all of the life-cycle phases. We refer to programs designed to support specific tasks or functions as *task-oriented tools*. Examples of these are: programs for project management; business graphics packages; and personal workstation-based productivity software, such as spreadsheets, word processors, and data base management systems for microcomputers.

■ Figure 1.16   Market growth in information processing. Worldwide revenues for U.S. firms involved in three major market segments—communications, the automated office, and data processing—will continue to increase, doubling approximately every five years. Conservatively, total revenues are projected to increase to approximately $600 billion by 1995.

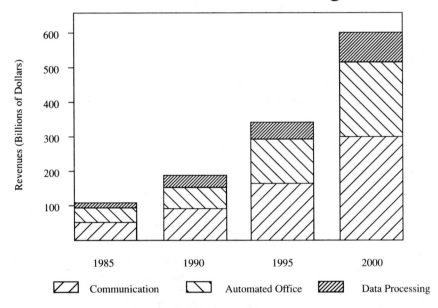

Market Growth in Information Processing

Computer-Assisted Systems Engineering (CASE)

Currently we are witnessing the development and introduction of major software packages designed to build rigor into the life-cycle process in order to increase the productivity of system developers and to reduce the cost of computer information systems. Because these software packages represent an engineering approach toward automating all phases of the life-cycle process for developing software, they often are referred to as **computer-assisted systems engineering,** or **CASE,** tool kits. Simply put, CASE tools are software for developing software. Examples of CASE tools are flowcharting tools, screen display tools, data repositories, documentation generators, and computer program code generators.

The most complete CASE tool kits support all four phases of the SDLC: study, design, development, and operation. They provide prototyping support and include powerful graphics capabilities that enhance user interaction by making much of the analysis and design process a visual activity that can take place at a user workstation.

■ Figure 1.17   User spending for information processing. As a percent of the gross national product, user spending for
information processing in the United States is projected to increase from a level of approximately 13
percent in 1990 to over 30 percent by the end of the decade.

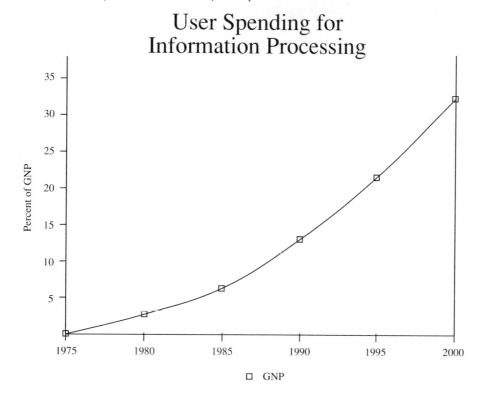

CASE tools will continue to evolve and will become increasingly comprehensive and powerful means for fully automating and managing all aspects of the computer information system life cycle. As such, they will contribute to the emergence and economic dominance of computer-integrated enterprises.

Summary

The productivity of modern business systems depends upon the use of computer information systems. These systems use resources, such as personnel, facilities, materials, and equipment, to convert raw data into usable information. Computer hardware and software are examples of such resources. Business information systems are computer information systems that use resources to convert data into the information needed to accomplish the purposes of the business. Business information systems are made up of components, called subsystems, that exhibit all of the characteristics of systems.

Because of the complexity of modern business information systems, a structured, project-oriented process has evolved for their design and development. This process, called the systems development life cycle (SDLC), is based on the concept of four phases through which all business systems must pass, as follows:

1. The study phase, in which a problem is identified and analyzed, alternate solutions are evaluated, and a systems solution is recommended at the general design level.
2. The design phase, in which the detailed design of the system selected in the study phase is accomplished.
3. The development phase, in which the system is constructed according to the design phase specification.
4. The operation phase, in which the developed system is installed, operated, and maintained.

Performance of the life-cycle tasks must be accompanied by effective project management and comprehensive documentation. Three important, baseline documents are the performance specification, created during the design phase; the design specification, created during the design phase; and the system specification, created during the development phase.

Systems analysis is a general term that refers to a structured process for identifying and solving problems. We define a systems analyst as a person who performs systems analysis during any, or all, of the life-cycle phases of a business information system. Because of the importance of systems analysis, career opportunities and compensation are promising. Qualifications for the field include not only education and experience, but also effective leadership and communications skills. In the final analysis, a system will be judged by its usability, which is its worth, or quality, as perceived in the value system of its principal users. Increasingly, these users are working in a distributed data processing environment, one in which communications networks place computing power at remote locations. Supporting these remote users will become an important role for systems analysts.

Information system engineering has evolved from a classical to a structured methodology. The former emphasizes the ''how'' of a process and the latter the ''why'' of data flows. Both have appropriate uses throughout the SDLC. The practice of working with a model, or prototype, of a computer information system is proving to be an effective means of improving the quality of system design, speeding up the SDLC process, and producing a better, less costly, and more easily maintained information system product. Because of the increasing complexity of information systems, it is necessary to automate the SDLC methodology. Fortunately, software designed to produce software is becoming available. These packages are called computer-assisted systems engineering (CASE) tool kits. Many major corporations, often referred to as computer-integrated enterprises, are adopting CASE products for the design of corporatewide, integrated computer information systems, and it is anticipated that the scope and capabilities of CASE tools will continue to increase and that they will contribute to the emergence of and economic dominance of computer-integrated enterprises.

For Review

systems analysis	task-oriented tools
system	computer information system
information	data
software	hardware
computer system	subsystem
life-cycle phases	life cycle
systems development life cycle	life-cycle methodology
design specification	performance specification
top-down design	system specification
analysis	systems analysis
life-cycle manager	synthesis
information resource center	information resource management
classical life-cycle methodology	usability
prototyping	structured methods
rapid prototyping	computer-assisted systems engineering
rapid applications development	computer-integrated enterprise
business information system	

For Discussion

1. What do you perceive to be the effect of computers and computer-based information systems on the well-being of our economy and upon future jobs?
2. Distinguish between the general definition of a system and the definition of a business information system.
3. What are the similarities and differences between a business system, a computer information system, and a computer system?
4. Identify the types of business information system resources, and give examples of each.
5. What is the systems development life cycle? What are the four life-cycle phases, and what occurs in each?
6. What two major activities must parallel the performance of the SDLC tasks? Of what does each consist?
7. Name and briefly describe each of the three baseline documents.
8. Define and relate the terms "systems" and "systems analyst" to the SDLC.
9. What types of functions are performed by systems analysts, and how have they been affected by the increasing use of computers?
10. Why are job opportunities promising and compensation high for systems analysts?
11. What are the education, experience, and personal qualifications necessary for success as a systems analyst?
12. How is the environment of the users of computer information systems changing? What is the impact of this change upon the services provided by the corporate information services staff?
13. Define "usability," and discuss its importance to systems analysts.

14. Discuss "information resource management" and "information resource center" in terms of (1) the resources to be managed and (2) the responsibilities of the corporate systems staff to information system users.
15. Describe the classical and structured methods for developing computer information systems. What are their similarities? Differences?
16. Define "prototyping" as it relates to the SDLC. Describe the prototyping version of the SDLC, and explain why prototyping is an important advance in the evolution of information system engineering.
17. What forces of change are contributing to the increasing complexity of computer information systems? Briefly discuss these as they relate to automating the SDLC.
18. What are the two classes of tools used to automate the SDLC?
19. What is CASE? How can it increase the productivity of information system developers and decrease the cost of maintaining operational systems?
20. Distinguish between "rapid prototyping" and CASE.

For Exercise: Quality Management and Computer Information Systems

The design, development, and marketing of quality products is a frequently stated goal of most enterprises engaged in global competition. Also, the information systems upon which these enterprises depend are becoming increasingly computer dependent. Many of the themes introduced in the preface to the text and in this chapter relate to the link between a quality service or product and computer information systems. Examples are: the systems development life cycle, the concept of usability, computer-assisted systems engineering, and the computer-integrated enterprise. As a mini-research project, locate an article in a newspaper, book, magazine, or trade journal that you feel links quality management to computer information systems, and, in writing, briefly relate your findings to the key concepts presented in this chapter. Be aware that commonly encountered terms for quality management are total quality management (TQM), continuous improvement (CI), and continuous quality improvement (CQI).

2

■ ■ ■

A Business as an Information System

Preview

Businesses may be viewed as systems of systems since they are made up of major units that are themselves systems. The management of a business determines the organizational structure that best meets the goals and objectives of the business. Organization charts display this structure and identify areas of responsibility and lines of authority. Behind the organization chart, there is a constant flow of product-oriented and information-oriented activities. These are due to internally and externally generated information needs. There are four levels of business information needs. In addition to an operational level, there are three management information levels: supervisory, tactical, and strategic. All of the latter rely on feedback and control to assist managers in decision making. Total Quality Management (TQM), a set of quality management principles that focuses on both external and internal customer satisfaction and continuous process improvement, is being used increasingly by industries to increase their productivity and competitiveness.

Objectives

1. You will be able to describe the principal characteristics of businesses as information systems.
2. You will be able to identify the shared characteristics of systems and subsystems.
3. You will be able to interpret and prepare organization charts.
4. You will be able to relate business information needs to product-flow and information-flow activities.
5. You will be able to describe and distinguish between the four information levels in a corporation.

Key Terms

goal a broadly stated purpose of a business.

objective a concrete, specific accomplishment necessary to the achievement of a goal.

organization chart a flowchart that identifies organizational elements of a business and displays areas of responsibility and lines of authority.

organization function list a document that describes the major activities performed by each organization shown on an organization chart.

product flow flow of raw materials into finished goods.

information flow the network of administrative and operational documentation.

information generator a business information need, either external or internal in origin.

feedback the process of comparing an actual output with a desired output for the purpose of improving the performance of a system.

control the actions taken to bring the difference between an actual output and a desired output within an acceptable range.

TQM a set of quality management principles that focuses on customer satisfaction and continuous improvement.

Business System Characteristics

Business Goals and Objectives

In chapter 1 we defined a business information system to be a system that uses resources to convert data into information in order to accomplish the purposes of the business. We classified these resources as personnel, facilities, materials, and equipment. Also, we introduced the concept of systems and subsystems. In this chapter, we will add to this foundation. We will consider the entire *business* to be an information system.

The purposes of a business can be defined in terms of goals and objectives. A **goal** is a very broadly stated purpose. Examples are the goal of making profit and the goal of educating students. **Objectives,** on the other hand, are concrete and specific accomplishments necessary to the achievement of goals. For example, an automobile manufacturer must have as an objective the production of a competitive product in order to achieve a profit goal; a college must have as an objective relevant curricula in order to achieve its educational goal. Major objectives are composed of lower-order objectives. Accordingly, before a car can be made, subassemblies must be produced and, before that, proper tools must be designed. Goals are relatively long term, and objectives are relatively short term.

Most business enterprises fall into one of two broad categories: production or service. Examples of *production enterprises* are manufacturing, farming, construction, and agriculture. *Service enterprises* include transportation, communications, medicine, and education. Each enterprise, whether production or service, has its particular goals and goal-supporting objectives. Certain system concepts are applicable to all business enterprises. Systems analysts must be familiar with them to understand how businesses are structured and organized. This chapter presents important concepts that will sharpen your perceptions of business systems.

A Business: A System of Systems

As we learned in chapter 1, business systems are composed of smaller elements, which also are systems. These systems transform or convert inputs into outputs. The transformation process was shown in figure 1.4. It is also shown in figure 2.1. Additionally, figure 2.1 introduces the idea of constraints. A business functions within a set of constraints, which generally it cannot alter significantly. Examples of such constraints are federal laws, social environment, total market, raw materials limitations, and scientific principles. The resources that affect the transformation of inputs into outputs are also shown in figure 2.1.

Principal functional systems associated with most product-oriented enterprises are shown in the flowchart of figure 2.2. In order to emphasize the relationship between these functional systems, management and administrative systems, although present in all enterprises, are not included in figure 2.2. Customers, employees, and

■ Figure 2.1   The system environment. The ability of a system to convert data into useful information is affected by limitations on resources and by environmental constraints that are external to the system.

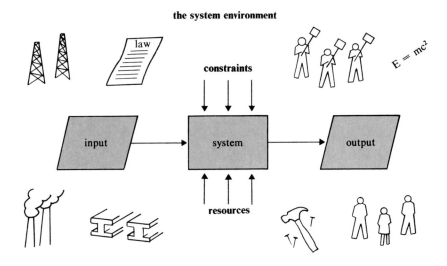

■ Figure 2.2   Functional business systems. Nine principal systems are associated with most product-oriented businesses: purchasing, receiving, inventory, production, sales, distribution, billing, collection, and paying. Persons who interact with these systems include customers, vendors, and employees.

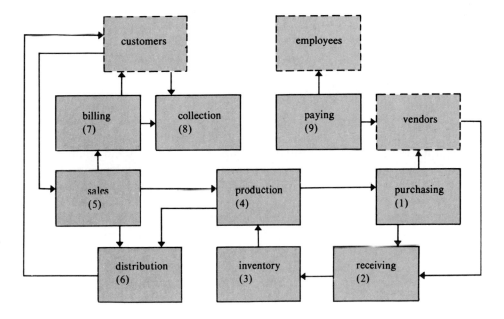

vendors, indicated by dashed-line rectangles, are shown to provide continuity to the illustration. The nine basic functional systems shown in this figure are as follows:

purchasing   Procuring from the vendors the goods and materials needed by the business.

receiving   Inspecting and accepting delivered goods and materials.

inventory   Storing the received goods and materials.

production   Designing and manufacturing the goods to be sold.

sales   Marketing the goods produced.

distribution   Supplying the customer with the goods sold from a produced-goods inventory.

billing   Sending statements of the amount owed to customers.

collection   Receiving payments from customers.

paying   Making payments to those whom the business owes money, such as vendors and employees.

Each of these functional systems produces one or more outputs in the form of products or documents. These outputs establish the relationship of each system to other systems and to the business as a whole. Since systems are assigned their own necessary resources they are, to a degree, relatively independent elements of a business. This is why we have defined a *system* as a combination of resources (personnel, materials, facilities, and equipment) working together to convert inputs into outputs. Again, we note that the definition of a system is similar to the definition of a business. However, whereas a system produces outputs, a business integrates the outputs of its component systems to accomplish objectives and to achieve goals. Often a system is thought of in terms of its mechanics, such as the methods, techniques, and procedures by which it achieves its purpose. The above definition of a system, by inference, includes such mechanics. For example, a distribution system is defined to include not only its functions, but also the associated written methods and procedures for processing shipping orders.

Because systems are its major elements, a business may be considered to be a *"system of systems."* This concept is illustrated in figure 2.3, which depicts the nine operational systems and a central complex of management and administration systems. By extension of this concept, most systems may be considered to be composed of *subsystems,* with the same transformation characteristics as systems. For example, as is shown in the first part of figure 2.4, a production system may be composed of subsystems such as engineering, production planning, manufacturing, and quality control. In practice, the distinction between systems and subsystems is fluid. It depends on the size, field of enterprise, objectives, and goals of the particular business. Thus the other example in figure 2.4 shows the billing, collecting, and disbursing systems of figure 2.3 assembled as subsystems of an accounting system.

■ Figure 2.3   The business: A system of systems. A business may be considered to be a large system composed of smaller, operational systems. This "system of systems" is integrated, through management and administration, to meet its objectives and goals.

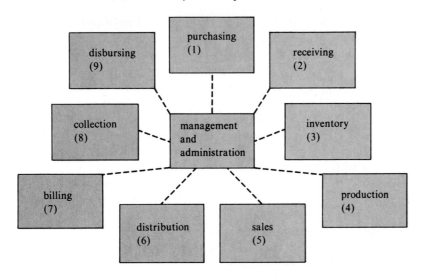

■ Figure 2.4   Systems and subsystems. Most large systems are made up of subsystems that also transform inputs into outputs. Two examples of such large systems are a production system and an accounting system.

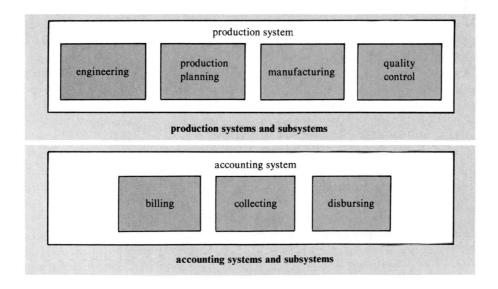

Describing the Business Organization

The Organization Chart

The owners of a business decide on the type of management and organizational structure that best meets their goals and objectives. The owners, or their legal representatives, the board of directors, hire managers and other employees. Each employee from the president on down occupies a position that must be defined with respect to those of all other members of the organization. This definition is necessary to control activities and channel the flow of information within the business organization.

The **organization chart** is a flowchart that identifies the organizational elements of a business and displays areas of responsibility and lines of authority. It is the responsibility of top management to define and to update the organization chart. However, a continuing effort is required to prepare organization charts and modify them as organizational plans are altered to cope with changes in the business environment. Hence, the responsibility for the preparation and maintenance of organization charts usually is assigned to the systems staff. This is an important systems activity because it stimulates management to keep its organizational plan up to date.

Management has many uses for current organization charts. These include (1) reviewing functions performed by major elements of the company; (2) aligning the corporate structure with business opportunities; and (3) comparing salaries, authority, and organizational size at equivalent and subordinate levels.

As useful as they may be to management, organization charts are essential to the systems analyst. In all aspects of work the systems analyst deals with individuals who have a specific position in the organization. Therefore, the analyst must understand the organization chart—not only what is printed on it, but also the personalities who are behind it. Without an understanding of the latter, the analyst may be unaware of real but unwritten authority.

The structure of the typical modern business organization chart has evolved from concepts of authority and responsibility handed down from the governments of Greece and Rome and from the feudal period of history. These concepts have been formalized in more recent times by religious and military organizations as a series of *superior-subordinate relationships,* as illustrated in figure 2.5. The standard means for presenting an organization chart is a flowchart that uses lines to connect rectangles identifying individuals and functions. As is indicated in figure 2.5, authority can be delegated downward, but responsibility must flow upward. When expanded, this type of organization chart displays vertical overlapping group linkage. Figure 2.6 is a segment of a typical organization chart for a modern business enterprise. It clearly depicts the superior-subordinate relationship. It also displays the characteristic aspect of this type of organization—the expansion into successively subordinate levels, using the connecting elements as *link pins.* Thus, to the extent that the organization is shown, the vice-presidents, the directors, and the managers are link pins.

There is considerable evidence that an organization like the one in figure 2.6 functions more effectively if its operating characteristics are participative rather than authoritarian. For example, organizations in which departmental goals are established by group participation tend to have superior motivation and to outperform those in

■ Figure 2.5   Basic superior-subordinate relationship. Most business organization charts are structured as a series of superior-subordinate relationships. Rectangles identify positions and functions; lines and arrowheads indicate the downward flow of authority and the upward flow of responsibility.

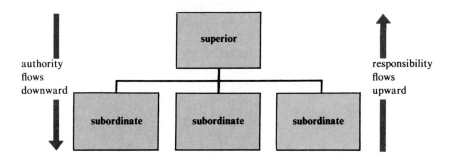

■ Figure 2.6   Organization chart. Organization charts can be expanded to display linkages between successive levels. Positions for which both a superior and subordinate reporting relationship are shown are called link pins. On this chart, the link pin positions are president, director, and manager.

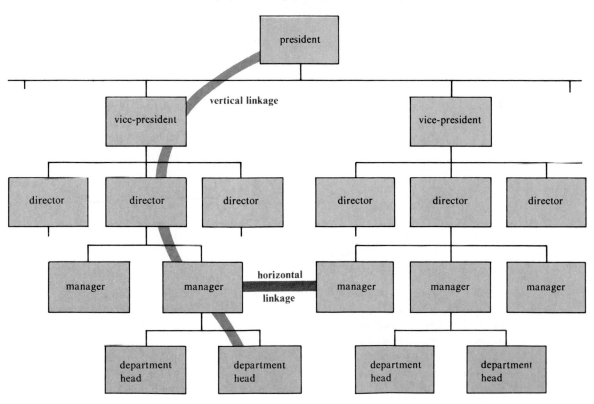

■ Figure 2.7 Organization chart symmetry. There are many ways of laying out symmetrical organization charts. The three methods shown are equivalent, since the superior-subordinate relationships are the same.

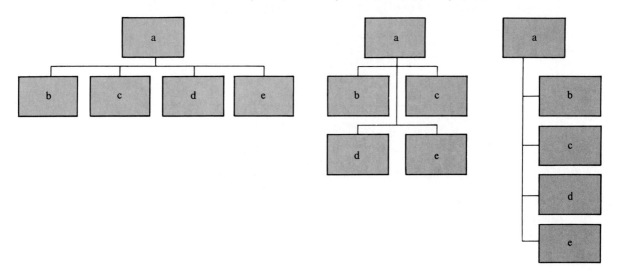

which goals are rigidly set by "orders from above." Also, in most organizations there are meaningful requirements for horizontal as well as vertical linkages. One area in which such a requirement is strikingly evident is systems analysis. Systems analysts work with information systems, and these systems often flow across organizational boundaries. Horizontal linkages permit systems activities to cross organization chart boundaries. This need is particularly accentuated in the case of computer-based business systems, since many of these generate outputs for the use of more than one organizational group and derive their inputs from many different groups.

There are no universal standards for the construction of organization charts. However, certain general principles apply. Above all, it is important when considering what to put on a chart and what to leave off to realize that the organization chart is the picture of the company seen not only by its management and employees, but also by its general business environment. Therefore, this chart should properly reflect to important vendors, customers, and agencies the picture the company wishes them to see. With this in mind, some general guidelines for organization charts are suggested:

1. *Layout* The layout of the chart should be attractive. The picture should be made up of rectangles and lines. It should be centered, with margins and white space selected to make the chart pleasing to the eye. The structure of the chart should be symmetrical. As figure 2.7 illustrates, there is more than one way of displaying equivalent relationships. In the three sections of this figure the same relationship is shown in different ways. In all cases B, C, D, and E are at the same level and report to A. A general guideline is to make balanced use of the space available.

2. *Title and approvals* The organization chart should have a meaningful title. A standard position should be provided for approvals, date, and other identifying information.

3. *Scope* One organization chart giving an overview of the organization's main elements is required. The chart shown in figure 2.8 is an example of an overview organization chart. This chart illustrates the use of the "dashed line" convention to represent a *staff position* as contrasted with a *line position*. The latter is a direct authority relationship, and the former is a service relationship. Some executives—the president of the United States for example—have large staffs. In the example of figure 2.8 the staff person is a full-time employee of the corporation. In other instances, the individuals may be consultants, "on-call," or members of the board of directors. For these cases, one convention is to also represent the position rectangle with dashed lines.

The information services organization appears as a line organization in figure 2.8. However, because it has no direct authority over the other line organizations that it services, the information services organization is also a type of staff activity. This organization does derive authority indirectly from the specifics of its assignments however, and from a line of command that commonly leads to the president through a senior executive, such as a vice-president of information services.

Figure 2.8 also illustrates the use of a special area for title, approvals, and date. In this case the only approval required is that of the president. Usually, lower-level organization charts bear the signature of the highest-level person shown on the chart and the signature of that person's supervisor.

The detail on an overview organization chart should fit easily on an 8½ by 11-inch page, viewed from the 11-inch edge. This type of layout is common. The amount of information presented on an organization chart should not exceed that which can be conveniently shown on a standard page. The overview picture of the entire organization is like a long-range photograph. Some closer-range pictures are required also.

A medium-range picture should be prepared for each of the organizational elements shown on the overview organization chart. Figure 2.9 is an example of a medium-range organizational picture.

Some close-up pictures also may be required for lower-level organizational elements. For example, organization charts often are prepared in detail by managers responsible for particular projects or activities. Such charts are necessary for assigning and monitoring tasks.

The systems group should exercise restraint with respect to the number of organization charts they prepare, because these charts must be maintained. However, the availability and increasing capabilities of group, or department, *desktop publishing* systems is of invaluable assistance to analysts responsible for maintaining organization charts and keeping other documentation current. Desktop publishing systems are relatively inexpensive microcomputer systems

■ Figure 2.8   Overview organization chart. The overview organization chart is one that provides a long-range picture of the corporation. The information presented in an overview organization chart should be limited, with detail left to lower-level charts.

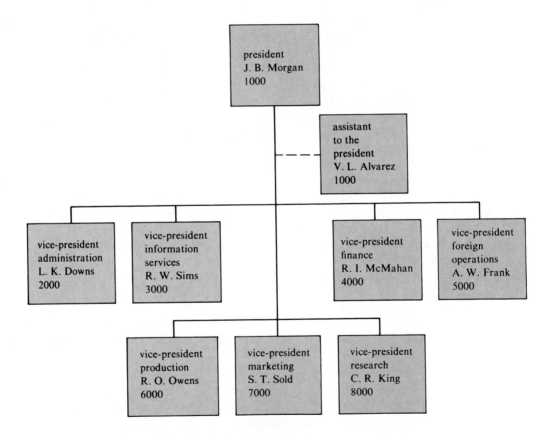

■ Figure 2.9   Information services organization chart. The information services organization chart is an example of a medium-range picture for a major element of a corporation. Two principal functions shown are corporate systems and data processing, the directors of which report to a corporate vice-president.

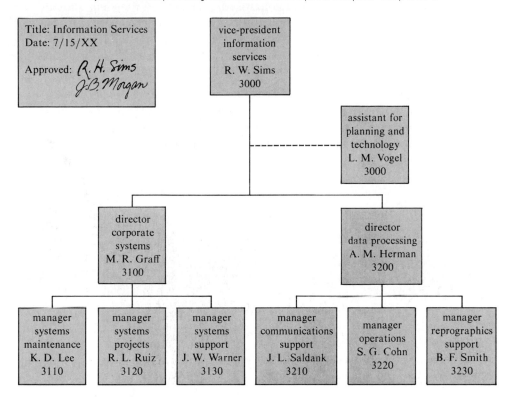

capable of combining text and graphics to produce output of almost professional typographic quality. Typically, these systems consist of a powerful microcomputer, large-capacity, hard-disk storage, a laser printer, and special purpose software for page design. Figure 2.9 is an example of an organization chart prepared by a desktop publishing system.

Restraint should be exercised also in deciding on the amount of detail to be presented on an organization chart. For example, figure 2.9 shows only significant individual staff positions, such as the assistant to the person occupying the key position on the organization chart.

4. *Organization chart distribution*   The overview organization chart should be distributed to top management and to all operating officers of the business. It should be available to customers and to employees who express an interest in the general organization of the company. Normally, new employees are provided with a copy of the top view organization chart as part of their indoctrination. Other organization charts should be distributed to individuals who have their responsibilities shown on the chart, to their superiors, and to any other persons, such as systems analysts, who have a legitimate need for the

information. Of course, a file should be maintained of all current and past organization charts. These should be available to the president and to other authorized persons upon request.

5. *Information provided*   Each organizational rectangle on the chart should contain a title with functional significance (for example, vice-president, information services), the name of the individual in that position, and an identifying organization number. Figures 2.8 and 2.9 illustrate a typical format.

Other kinds of information, such as salaries and number of individuals supervised, can be added to charts for the use of managers who wish to review their organizational plan. This type of information usually is confidential and is not for general distribution. The organization chart identifies the major functions of the organizations shown. Additional details are supplied by supporting documents known as organization function lists.

The Organization Function List

An **organization function list** is a document prepared for each organization shown on an organization chart to describe the specific major activities performed by that organization. It is keyed to the organization chart by use of the organizational titles and numbers shown on the organization chart. Figure 2.10 is an organization function list for the systems support department of the information services organization shown in figure 2.9. Note that the functions are described briefly in the present tense using action verbs (*controls, performs,* and so forth).

Systems analysts who understand the organization chart and its associated function list are better equipped to improve the efficiency of business systems for which they are responsible. Analysts can use the organization chart as a means of increasing their knowledge of operational processes, job responsibilities, and information flow.

Information Structure of a Business

Product Flow and Information Flow

The organization chart is only a one-dimensional picture of a business. Behind it there is a constant flow of information-oriented and product-oriented activities. All these activities involve individuals with differing levels of responsibility and authority. In order to examine the information structure of a business, let us start by distinguishing between information flow and product flow. We will use a manufacturing company as an example.

Product flow, which is relatively easy to visualize, is the flow of raw materials into subassemblies, then into assemblies, and finally into finished goods. **Information,** or data, **flow** consists of the creation and movement of the administrative and operational documentation necessary for product flow. Information flow is more difficult to visualize than product flow because its physical manifestation is a vast

■ Figure 2.10 Organization function list. An organization function list provides information about the major activities performed by an organization. A separate organization function list is prepared for each element shown on an organization chart.

Organization Function List
Systems Support Department
Department Number: 3130
Date: 6/15/XX
Approved:

J. W. Warner
J. W. Warner

M. R. Graff
M. R. Graff

1. designs and controls forms

2. manages and retains records

3. performs work measurement studies

4. prepares and maintains organization charts

5. analyzes reports

6. writes policies and procedures

network of data carriers such as forms, electronic communications, and visual displays. Yet it is this network that the analyst must understand. Although their actions must be governed by the physical reality of the goods that the company is producing, systems analysts deal primarily with the creation and management of data in its many forms. Therefore, it is necessary that the information flow be known in those segments of the business for which the analyst has assigned responsibilities.

To bring information flow into sharper focus, we can redraw figure 2.2, which depicts functional business systems, to emphasize the distinction between product flow and information flow. This is done in figure 2.11. In this figure, the heavy flow lines trace the product flow path. The lighter lines indicate paths by which information flows among the nine major functional business systems.

Product flow and information flow. Product flowlines trace the flow from raw materials to end-product. Information flowlines not only parallel product flow; they also link functional systems not directly related to production.

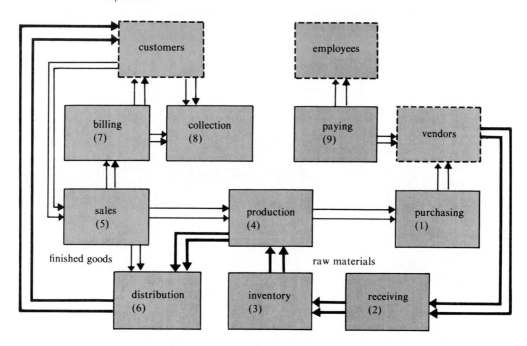

If we identify the principal documents associated with these information flow paths, the relative complexity of information flow can be depicted. This complexity is illustrated in figure 2.12. The documents shown in figure 2.12 can be defined, in context, as follows:

1. The *purchase order* is prepared by Purchasing, which sends the original to the vendor, retains a copy, and sends a copy to Receiving.
2. When the materials ordered arrive, Receiving verifies the order against its copy of the *purchase order,* inspects the material, and informs the Purchasing department of its arrival and acceptance by means of a *receiving report.* The material is transferred to Inventory accompanied by an *inventory transfer.*
3. By means of a *purchase requisition,* Inventory requests Purchasing to order those materials that are not on hand in sufficient quantity.
4. Production designs and develops the product. The components that are built in-house are combined with the components or subassemblies that are procured out-of-house. Production uses a *material requisition* to request needed materials from Inventory. Inventory notifies Production of the availability of the requisitioned materials by returning a copy of the *material requisition.*

Principal information flow documents. Information flow documents illustrate the complexity of the network of information carriers in a business. Information carriers may be "softcopy," for example, a visual display, as well as the "hardcopy" documents shown here.

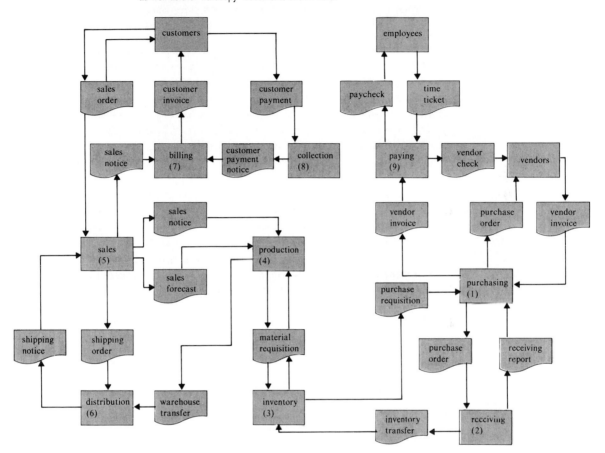

5. Sales contacts the customer, sells the product, and prepares the *sales order*. The customer is provided a copy of the *sales order*. A copy of the sales order, entitled *sales notice,* is sent to Billing and to Production. An additional copy, the *shipping order,* is sent to Distribution.

6. Distribution receives the finished goods from Production accompanied by a *warehouse transfer notice*. Distribution ships the product to the customer and informs Sales by means of a *shipping notice*.

7. Billing prepares and mails the *customer invoice*.

8. Collection receives *customer payments* from the customer and sends updated information to Billing by means of a *customer payment notice*.

9. Paying makes payments to vendors by means of a *vendor check*. This check is prepared after the vendor has submitted a *vendor invoice* and after that invoice has been verified and forwarded by Purchasing. Paying also distributes *paychecks* to employees. The amounts of the *paychecks* are based upon *time tickets* submitted by employees.

As complicated as the network shown in figure 2.12 may appear, it is a necessary oversimplification of the real volume of information flow in a typical corporation. Every major functional system is composed of complex subsystems, each of which has its documentation needs. In most enterprises, the production of printed reports (hardcopy) is reduced through use of visual displays, or screen images (softcopy). Usually hardcopy is available on demand, and it is convenient to use the document symbol, as in figure 2.12, to display information flow. However, where appropriate, other symbols, such as that for a screen display, could be used to represent data carriers.

Information flow exists for service enterprises as well as for product enterprises, and it exists in different forms at different reporting levels within an organization. We will describe the information needs and uses at these levels; however, there are two other factors that add to the complexity of the information network: (1) there are external as well as internal generators of information; (2) information must be reported with different emphasis and formats according to the needs of different levels of management. Each of these factors deserves discussion.

Information Generators

A company must develop information systems to meet not only its internal reporting needs, but also the external reporting needs that arise from its general business environment. Figure 2.13 distinguishes between the two information needs that act as **information generators.** The internal information needs are represented by the nine functional business systems discussed previously. Externally generated needs are represented by agencies such as federal, state, and local governments, shareholders, vendors, advertising, lenders, unions, and customers. Often information generators are the external entities that establish the scope, or contents, of an information system.

Not all the information generated externally is useful to the corporation. That which is useful is most likely to be of use to the upper levels of management. Also, in its "raw" form not all the internally generated information is useful at all levels within the corporation. Different types of outputs must be prepared to meet the information needs of each level of user. Because of these differing user needs, we must distinguish between levels of information systems.

Management Uses of Information

Information System Levels

Figure 2.14 depicts the four levels of information systems that exist in a typical business of moderate to large size. These are (1) operational; (2) lower management; (3) middle management; and (4) top management.

Information generators. The information that a company must provide to meet its business needs is generated not only by its internal reporting requirements, but also by its external reporting environment.

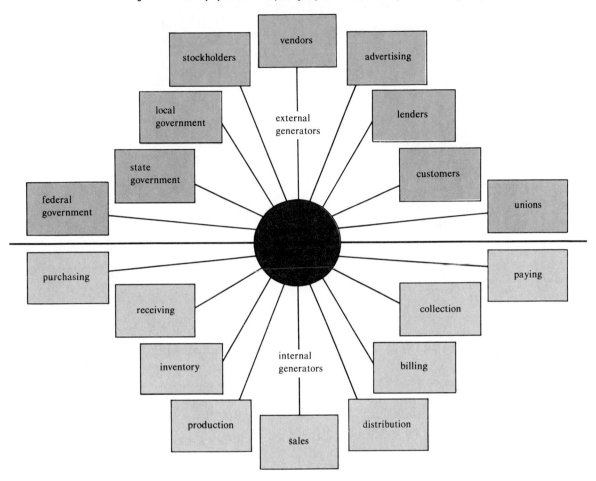

At the operational level, routine production or clerical operations are performed. Operational systems provide little feedback directly to the employee. For example, the materials clerk receives a material requisition, fills the requisition, and files a report of action taken. A supervisor evaluates the employee's performance. However, records of transactions occurring at the operational level constitute data that, when collected, organized, and processed, becomes information that is the basis for higher-level management actions.

Lower management performs supervisory functions that are short term relative to the higher levels of management. They deal with day-to-day job scheduling, checking the results of operations, and taking the necessary corrective actions.

Middle management functions are tactical in nature. This level is responsible for allocating and controlling the resources necessary to accomplish objectives that support the strategic goals of the business. Planning occurs; authority is delegated to the supervisory level; and performance is measured.

■ Figure 2.14   Information system levels. Information systems meet not only operational needs, but also three levels of management needs. Both horizontal and vertical integration exists among all four information levels.

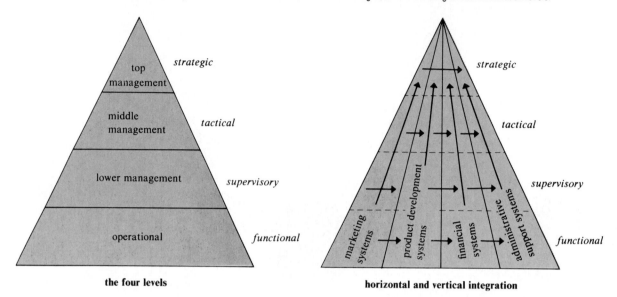

the four levels   **horizontal and vertical integration**

Top management functions are strategic. They include establishment of the goals of the business, long-range planning, new market and product development, mergers and acquisitions, and major policy decisions. Appropriate authority is delegated to middle management.

Figure 2.14 also shows that there are both horizontal and vertical information system structures. In this figure, for illustrative purposes, the nine functional systems of figure 2.2 are collected, vertically, as four major systems. Marketing systems include Sales and Distribution; product development systems include Purchasing, Receiving, Inventory, and Production. Financial systems include Billing, Collection, and Paying. Support operations, such as personnel and contracts, are grouped as administrative support systems.

Horizontal integration may occur within or between major systems. An example of horizontal integration, internal to a major system, is the combination of Purchasing, Receiving, and Inventory (within product development) into a procurement system on the basis of a shared data base. An example of horizontal integration, between major systems (in this case between finance and administrative support), is a personnel-payroll system based on employee-related data elements common to both Personnel and Payroll.

The following is an example of a possible vertical integration of an information system within Production:

1. Machine assignment and job time reporting—functional
2. Machine scheduling—supervisory
3. Make (in own shop) or buy (from vendor) decision—middle management
4. New product decision—top management

All management-level positions require that decisions be made. These decisions range from the routine to the complex. However, effective management decisions require two elements:

1. A process that includes objectives, measurement of performance against objectives, and corrective action
2. The availability of appropriate information on which to base decisions

The first of these elements establishes management as a feedback and control process. The second leads to distinctions between the characteristics of information required at each management level. Feedback and control and management-level information characteristics are described in the next sections.

Feedback and Control

Feedback and control are essential to the design of any management system. **Feedback** is the process of comparing an actual output with a desired output for the purpose of improving the performance of a system. **Control** is the action taken to bring the difference between an actual output and a desired output within an acceptable range. These concepts are illustrated in figure 2.15. Part A depicts a system in which there is no feedback and control. This system does transform an input into an output; however, because it lacks feedback, it is called an open loop system.

From part A of figure 2.15, it is evident that the output depends solely on the characteristics of the input and of the system. If the output is not satisfactory, there is no provision for modifying either the input or the system. Operating such a system is analogous to driving a car while blindfolded. If, however, the driver compares the position of the car with the location of the white line in the middle of the road, corrective action is possible. In this case, the feedback is visual, and the corrective action is initiated by manually turning the steering wheel. Because there is feedback, this type of a system is called a closed loop system. The elements of a closed loop system are shown in part B of figure 2.15. This flowchart demonstrates that the comparison of desired and actual outputs results in management action, which may modify the inputs, the system, or both. The result is a modified system that will produce altered outputs. Many operational systems are open loop systems. All true management systems are closed loop systems.

Because management information systems are feedback systems, they are more complex to design than are open loop operational systems. Feedback systems are effective only if they can respond quickly enough for the necessary corrective action to take place when needed. Otherwise, the time lapse may be so great that belated management action only makes the situation worse. Such systems are said to be unstable. Instability may also result if information is fed back at such a rate that it cannot be absorbed or if management action is premature.

All information systems that assist managers in decision-making display two characteristics: (1) at least one level of vertical integration; and (2) feedback and control. Of course, at each management level, the specific requirements for information (and hence for the design of the feedback system) vary significantly. The different uses and requirements for information at each management decision level are summarized in

■ Figure 2.15   Feedback and control. (a) An open loop system provides no opportunity for management control. (b) A closed loop system provides managers with both a comparison of actual and desired outputs (feedback) and a means of taking action to bring them into correspondence (control).

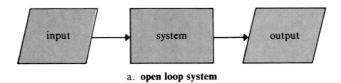

a. **open loop system**

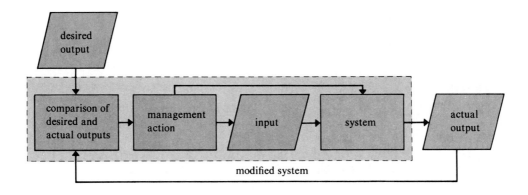

b. **closed loop system**

figure 2.16. Note that all management systems rely upon exception reporting. The lower-level exception reports are closely related to day-to-day operations. Some other significant observations are as follows:

1. The higher the decision level, the greater the reliance on externally generated information and the less the reliance on internally generated information.
2. The higher the decision level, the greater the emphasis upon planning and the use of longer-term trend information.
3. The higher the decision level, the greater the necessity to ask "what if" questions as part of the decision process.

Information systems at the operational level can provide immediate payback, usually measurable in dollars. The continuing development of such systems is a meaningful activity not only because they pay off in dollars, but also because they provide the necessary foundation on which to base higher-level systems. Although the payoffs for higher-level systems may be less tangible than dollars, there is increasing management acceptance of such other benefits. Intangible payoffs include (1) improved internal control; (2) better management awareness of problems and opportunities; (3) long-term profitability; and (4) faster response to changes in the business environment.

At the higher decision levels in a company, information needs and uses are future-oriented and depend to a greater extent upon external sources of information. This

Management decision levels: Information use and requirements. Information uses and, therefore, information requirements differ at each management decision level. At the higher decision levels more emphasis is placed upon external information, long-term trends, and "what if" considerations.

MANAGEMENT LEVEL	INFORMATION USE	INFORMATION REQUIREMENTS

TOP MANAGEMENT	1. GOAL SETTING
	2. LONG-RANGE PLANS
	3. STRATEGY
	4. RETURN ON INVESTMENT
		1. EXTERNAL INFORMATION, e.g.
		   Competitor actions
		   Government actions
		   New markets
		   Resource availability
		2. INTERNAL INFORMATION, e.g.
		   Financial reports
		   Key exception reports
		3. LONG-TERM TRENDS
		4. "WHAT IF" INFORMATION

MIDDLE
 	
MANAGEMENT
	1. OBJECTIVES DEFINITION
	2. MEDIUM-RANGE PLANS
	3. TACTICS
		1. INTERNAL INFORMATION, e.g.
		   Financial reports
		   Exception reports
		2. SHORT-TERM TRENDS
		3. SOME "WHAT IF" INFORMATION

LOWER
 	
MANAGEMENT
	1. OBJECTIVES ATTAINMENT
	2. SHORT-RANGE PLANS
	3. SUPERVISION
		1. INTERNAL INFORMATION, e.g.
		   Recent historical information
		   Detailed operational reports
		   Appropriate exception reports

type of information is difficult to quantify and must be coupled with the experience and judgment of the decision maker. At these levels, computer-based information systems often are referred to as *decision support systems (DSS)* because they provide information to support the particular decision processes practiced by senior managers. Increasingly, personal computers supported by productivity software, such as electronic spreadsheets and data base managers, are adding flexibility to decision-making at all managerial levels.

Information must be prepared in the manner that best meets the operational and management needs of the business. In addition to the operational level, there are three management levels, each with its own information needs: (1) lower management, which is supervisory; (2) middle management, which is tactical; and (3) top management, which is strategic. All management information systems rely on feedback and control to accomplish their purposes.

Quality Management

Total Quality Management (TQM)

Within the last decade a set of quality-based management principles referred to as **total quality management (TQM)** has been embraced by an increasing number of companies throughout the United States. Although "quality" is an elusive concept, it requires only an examination of the competition in the marketplace for products and services of all kinds, from automobiles to rest homes, to realize that quality is the worth of a service or product as perceived by the user of that product, the *customer*. It also is something for which consumers will pay. When successfully practiced, TQM is a management approach based on understanding and perfecting the systems by which an organization operates, with an unrelenting emphasis on continuous improvement and customer satisfaction.

Actually TQM began shortly after World War II, when the management ideas of Dr. W. Edward Deming and other disciples of "quality management" were adopted by the Japanese. The focus on quality and the use of statistical techniques for production-process control has enabled Japanese manufacturers to win a large market share in industries such as automobile manufacturing and industrial electronics. Evidence of consumer belief in the quality of these products is present in the often-heard phrases "getting it right the first time" and "zero-defect manufacturing." The annual Deming Award for quality is the most prestigious in Japanese industry. A similar award, the Malcom Baldrige Award, is now offered in the United States, and recipients include such well-known corporations as IBM, Motorola, and General Motors.

Associated with TQM are Dr. Deming's now famous fourteen points for quality management that are listed in figure 2.17. The major TQM components common among industries that have focused upon quality are as follows:

1. A commitment by top management to participate and lead by example.
2. Emphasis upon prevention of problems and improvement of processes rather than upon inspection and correction.
3. Emphasis upon total customer satisfaction, which includes internal (to the firm) as well as external customers.
4. Involvement by everyone in the enterprise, a concept extending to suppliers and other business partners.
5. Creation of "quality" teams to identify problems and to improve processes of all kinds, including not only manufacturing processes, but all work performed in the organization.
6. Acceptance of the doctrine that quality improvement is a continuous, never-ending process.

In sum these points require a shift from a quick-fix, short-term results approach to problem solving and a long-term commitment to employee involvement and training—with rewards coming in the form of continuous improvements that, over time, lower costs, improve productivity, and create profit.

In the United States, an award similar to the Deming Award was initiated in 1987 under the Malcom Baldrige National Quality Improvement Act. Named after Malcom Baldrige, the former Secretary of Commerce, this award blends Deming's fourteen-point philosophy with specific, measurable results. As shown in figure 2.18, which summarizes the Baldrige Award scoring system, key criteria for this award are evidence that:

1. Top executives incorporate quality values into day-to-day management.
2. Products are as good as or better than those of competitors.
3. The corporation is working with its suppliers to improve the quality of their services or products.

QUALITY MANAGEMENT

1. Create a constancy of purpose toward improvement of product and service.

2. Adopt the new philosophy.

3. Cease dependence on inspection to achieve quality.

4. Do not award business on the basis of price tag alone. Instead, minimize total cost. Move toward a single supplier for any one item based on a long-term relationship of mutual loyalty and trust.

5. Improve constantly and forever every process for planning, production, and service.

6. Introduce training on the job.

7. Adopt and institute leadership.

8. Drive out fear.

9. Break down barriers between departments.

10. Eliminate slogans, exhortations, and targets for the work objective. Substitute leadership.

11. Eliminate quotas on the factory floor and management objectives. Substitute leadership.

12. Remove barriers that rob people of pride of workmanship. Eliminate the annual rating or merit system.

13. Institute a vigorous program of education and self-improvement for everyone.

14. Put everybody in the company to work to accomplish the transformation.

Scoring the 1991 Baldrige Award

1.0 Leadership (100 points)
1.1 Senior Executive Leadership (40)
1.2 Quality Values (15)
1.3 Management for Quality (25)
1.4 Public Responsibility (20)

2.0 Information and Analysis (70 points)
2.1 Scope and Management of Quality Data and Information (20)
2.2 Competitive Comparisons and Benchmarks (30)
2.3 Analysis of Quality Data and Information (20)

3.0 Strategic Quality Planning (60 points)
3.1 Strategic Quality Planning Process (35)
3.2 Quality Goals and Plans (25)

4.0 Human Resource Utilization (150 points)
4.1 Human Resource Management (20)
4.2 Employee Involvement (40)
4.3 Quality Education and Training (40)
4.4 Employee Recognition and Performance Measurement (25)
4.5 Employee Well-Being and Morale (25)

5.0 Quality Assurance of Products and Services (140 points)
5.1 Design and Introduction of Quality Products and Services (35)
5.2 Process Quality Control (20)
5.3 Continuous Improvement of Processes (20)
5.4 Quality Assessment (15)
5.5 Documentation (10)
5.6 Business Process and Support Service Quality (20)
5.7 Supplier Quality (20)

6.0 Quality Results (180 points)
6.1 Product and Service Quality Results (90)
6.2 Business Process, Operational, and Support Service Quality Results (50)
6.3 Supplier Quality Results (40)

7.0 Customer Satisfaction (300 points)
7.1 Determining Customer Requirements and Expectations (30)
7.2 Customer Relationship Management (50)
7.3 Customer Service Standards (20)
7.4 Commitment to Customers (15)
7.5 Complaint Resolution for Quality Improvement (25)
7.6 Determining Customer Satisfaction (20)
7.7 Customer Satisfaction Results (70)
7.8 Customer Satisfaction Comparison (70)

1,000 Total Points

Source: National Institute of Standards and Technology

■ Figure 2.19   TQM cycle illustrating explicit customer feedback. The customer is not only an integral part of the feedback and control system, but becomes the driver of the process by which the enterprise is continuously and dynamically modified to reflect the changing needs of the consumer.

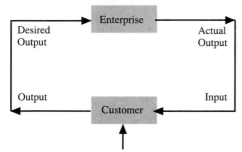

Perturbation in Customer Environment

4. Customer needs are being met and customer satisfaction ratings are as good or better than those of competitors.
5. Workers are trained and being trained in quality techniques, with systems in place to ensure that high quality is achieved.
6. The quality management system yields concrete results, such as increased market share and reduction in product-development-cycle time.

In a model TQM environment, managers become less authoritarian and function more like facilitators whose main task is to guide and support empowered employees. In this respect, the pyramid structure of figure 2.14 is up-cndcd, and roles are reversed.

As shown in figure 2.18, references to "quality" and to "customers" of all types, such as employees, customers, and support services, appear throughout the scoring system. Also, 300 points, out of a total of 1000 quality-oriented points, are directly assigned to customer satisfaction. In the context of computer information systems, the term "usability," introduced in the first chapter of this book, is synonymous with "customer satisfaction."

As are all true management systems, TQM is a feedback and control system. Figure 2.19, which is the feedback model for TQM, differs from the closed loop system of figure 2.15 in one significant respect. The customer is shown in the feedback loop, and customer output (i.e. the "voice of the customer") becomes the input to (i.e. the desired output of) the system. Thus, the changing needs of the customer and not a preconceived plan for product development and marketing that might not be sensitive to customer needs drives the system, and the system continuously adjusts itself to meet those needs.

Enterprises establishing a TQM program must take care not to confuse *process* with *progress.* It is not sufficient to introduce a comprehensive training program and a wide range of "total quality" activities with the expectation that performance and productivity improvements will automatically materialize. The training and problem-solving activities themselves may be mistaken for actual results. A reasonable approach is to identify a small number of important, customer-focused areas and to achieve and build upon successes supported by measurable results. Thus Mt. San Antonio College, a California Community College, was able to reduce the number of on-campus registration days from fourteen to four through telephone registration, greatly increasing customer (student) satisfaction by eliminating long on-campus waiting lines. A by-product benefit to the college was a reduction in annual registration-related costs from $26,840 to $3,150. Satisfied customers will pay for perceived quality. As an example, hardware and software mail order firms that cater to owners of personal computers provide overnight delivery for all orders via Airborne Express. Customers gladly pay the $3.00 charge.

TQM and Information Systems: The Agile Enterprise

The principles of TQM are consistent with the concept of the systems development life cycle (SDLC) and the perception of a business as an information system. Without a quality enterprisewide information system infrastructure, no management system can succeed, and TQM is highly dependent upon information dissemination and feedback at and across all levels of an enterprise. As examples, market research must know which engineering designs are feasible; engineering manufacturing corporations will be replaced by "agile" enterprises capable of a quick response to rapid, often unexpected, changes in consumer needs and wants. An agile enterprise will be able to build-to-order a virtually defect-free product that will delight the customer over the full life of the product. Agile enterprises, whether in the manufacturing or service sector, will be distinguished from others by two characteristics: (1) an unrelenting commitment to customer satisfaction, and (2) a SDLC methodology for the design and development of information systems that make effective use of current hardware, software, and communications technologies.

Summary

The purposes of a business can be defined in terms of broad goals and specific objectives. Businesses not only use resources to achieve their purposes; they also are governed by constraints, which they cannot alter. Businesses may be considered to be systems of systems, since their major elements are systems that transform inputs into outputs. The relationships between these systems can be displayed by flowcharts that exhibit both product flow and information flow. The information flow network is complex because the objectives of the business and the constraints of its environment act as information generators.

The management of a business decides on the organization structure that best meets the goals and objectives of the business. This structure is represented by a series of organization charts that provide both an overview of the entire organization, and medium- and short-range detail. These charts, which have evolved from historic concepts of authority and responsibility, display vertical superior-subordinate linkages. Horizontal linkages are also necessary. Thus systems analysts usually have staff instead of line positions, and they work with information systems that often flow across organizational boundaries. Organization function lists are prepared to accompany organization charts. They describe the major activities for which each organization on the chart is responsible.

Behind the organization chart, there are constant flows of product-oriented and information-oriented activities. Product flow is the flow of raw materials into subassemblies, and then into assemblies and finished goods. Information flow is caused by the need for hardcopy and softcopy documentation of product flow.

The principles of quality management, often referred to as total quality management, or TQM, have evolved from the theories of Dr. Edward Deming. TQM has been used successfully by Japanese industries for many years. Now, an increasing number of leading companies in the United States have adopted TQM principles as a means of improving their productivity and competitiveness. TQM requires top management commitment, an emphasis on customer satisfaction, and acceptance of continuous improvement as a way of doing business. Agile industries combine a commitment to TQM with recognition of the need for effective computer information systems.

For Review

business	staff position
goal	line position
objective	desktop publishing
production enterprise	total quality management (TQM)
service enterprise	organization function list
system	product flow
system of systems	information flow
subsystem	information generator
organization chart	feedback
superior-subordinate relationship	control
link pin	decision support system

For Discussion

1. Distinguish between goals and objectives. Name some businesses and identify typical goals and objectives.
2. Why can a business be considered to be a system of systems?
3. What are the principal purposes of organization charts?
4. Who is responsible for defining the business organization chart? Who is responsible for preparing and maintaining the chart?
5. Relate the flow of authority and responsibility to the superior-subordinate relationship.
6. What is the difference between an authoritative and a participative organization?
7. What is an organization function list? How does it relate to the organization chart?
8. Distinguish between product flow and information flow.
9. Distinguish between external and internal information generators. Give some examples of each.
10. What are the differences between open loop and closed loop systems?

11. Distinguish between feedback and control. How do they relate to the concept of exception reporting?
12. Identify the three levels of management and explain why their information needs differ.
13. What is a desktop publishing system? How could it be used by systems analysts?
14. What is a decision support system? How might a DSS assist the vice-president of sales in decision-making?
15. How do customer satisfaction and continuous improvement relate to total quality management (TQM)? Who is the customer?
16. How do the principles of TQM relate to the successful application of the SDLC process?

For Exercise: Organization Chart for NEWDREAM Corporation

As a result of a prolonged takeover battle, your company, MYDREAM has been acquired by a group of investors led by Howard Leverage. At a meeting with Howard and the new owners, you learn that you are no longer president but are now a member of the Finance Committee, which serves in an advisory capacity to the board of directors of a new corporation, NEWDREAM.

You also have been informed of some of the details of the plan for a new, top-level organization. Your notes read as follows:

1. The board chair will be Howard Leverage, who also will occupy your former position.
2. Sidney Urban, your manager of manufacturing, will retain the same position, but he will report to Howard's brother, Mason, who is to be vice-president of operations.
3. Sidney will be at the same level as Grace Vasquez and Sam Roberts, who, respectively, will be responsible for purchasing and product distribution.
4. The new vice-president of finance is to be Sylvia Moreno, who will bring with her two subordinates to fill the positions of controller and treasurer. Sylvia also is to be chair of the finance committee.
5. William Tell will retain the position of manager of data processing, but he now will report to Susan Smothers, the new vice-president of information services.

You are to construct an organization chart for NEWDREAM, including names and positions to the extent known to you.

2

Managing the Computer Information Systems Project

The goal of this unit is to describe the approaches, tools, and techniques that a systems analyst needs to effectively communicate with users and managers. This essential communication may take the form of either verbal or written media. To be effective communicators, analysts must be familiar with the basic principles of communication, the different forms of technical writing, and an appropriate approach to making presentations. The two chapters in Unit 2 introduce these communication concepts which are used throughout the systems development life cycle.

Chapter 3, "Communication and Documentation," presents the elements of effective communication and the application of those communication elements in interviews, technical writing, and presentations. Effective communicators use these methods to enhance the likelihood that their communications will not only be received but also understood. Interviewing techniques that allow the analyst to get the most information and cooperation from those being interviewed are presented. Each of the five common forms of technical writing will be presented, and the scheduling of and preparing for oral presentations are discussed. In addition, the most common tools for developing documentation and presentations are identified. These tools include word processing, presentation graphics, and desktop publishing.

Chapter 4, "Project Management," introduces the concepts of the system team and project reviews. The purpose of the system team is to provide a variety of inputs from systems analysts, users, and technical people. The objective is to develop an effective system that will meet the needs of the users. One approach to the system team concept is called the Joint Application Design (JAD) team. This approach emphasizes the importance of close, concentrated efforts by the designers of the system with the users of the system. The purpose of project reviews is to keep users and managers informed about the progress of the project. This chapter specifically addresses planning, scheduling, and tracking the progress of a project by using a series of charting techniques. The techniques presented include Gantt charts, cost charts, and performance charts. In addition, critical path networks and PERT charts are introduced as an approach to scheduling multiple-activity projects.

3

∎ ∎ ∎

Communication
and
Documentation

A systems analyst must be able to communicate effectively. To do so, the analyst must understand the elements of communication and be able to apply techniques for effective communication. Particularly important are oral communication and technical writing, since the reviews that occur within each phase of the life-cycle process require the preparation of reports and oral presentations to managers and users. It is also important that the analyst be aware of the approaches to generating the documentation that makes up the reports and supports effective oral presentations. This documentation includes not only text but also the graphics that illustrate the points to be communicated.

Objectives

1. You will be able to describe the components of effective communication.
2. You will be able to apply the guidelines for conducting interviews.
3. You will be able to name the types of technical writing used by systems analysts.
4. You will be able to describe the techniques for making effective presentations.
5. You will be able to identify the major functions of word processing packages.
6. You will be able to identify the basic types of charts and describe how they are used.
7. You will be able to explain the SDLC-related uses of desktop publishing.

Key Terms

communication   the process of transferring information from one point to another.

interview   a one-on-one, two-way oral communication for the purpose of collecting information.

technical writing   a document written for the purpose of communicating facts.

presentation   oral communication of plans or results made in order to influence people and to obtain decisions.

word processing   the entering, editing, and formatting of text using a computer terminal or a personal computer.

presentation graphics   high-quality charts and graphs used as illustrations within printed documentation and as visual supplements to oral presentations.

desktop publishing   the use of a formatting program that allows text and graphics to be combined into a single, high-quality printed output.

The Elements of Communication

The Communication Process

Communication is the process of transferring information from one point to another. This transfer may involve both people and machines. In this chapter, however, we are not concerned with the machine aspects of data communication. Our purpose is to present the elements of effective person-to-person communication and to relate them to technical writing and presentations, two of the most essential ways in which systems analysts must be trained to communicate.

Communication consists of sending and receiving messages. Effective communication requires that the sender send the message accurately and that the receiver receive it without distortion. Distortion may occur because of the characteristics of the transmission medium or because of filtering by the receiver. Figure 3.1 illustrates the dynamics of communication. Note that feedback is included in this communication model. All the elements of the communication process must function effectively; if not, information will not be transferred without error. Here are some examples of defective communication elements that the analyst should avoid:

1. The sender's message is not clear because the vocabulary used is not understood by the receiver.
2. The transmission medium is incorrect because the situation calls for a face-to-face meeting instead of a memorandum.
3. The receiver has "tuned out" the message because of preoccupation with another matter.
4. There is no feedback because the sender only "gives orders."

The ability to communicate is an essential skill that must be acquired because the systems analyst is sending and receiving information constantly during interaction with managers, programmers, users, and fellow team members. The analyst should, therefore, work continuously toward more effective communication.

■ Figure 3.1   The communication process. The communication process consists of sending and receiving messages. Effective communication requires that the sender send the message accurately and that the receiver receive it without distortion. The medium carries the message.

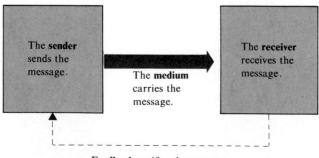

■ Figure 3.2   Tips for senders and receivers. Communication becomes more effective if the sender and receiver are sensitive to each other, if an effort is made to seek feedback, and if the appropriate transmission media are selected.

tips for the sender	tips for the receiver
organize your thoughts	be alert and attentive
know your receiver	analyze the message
use facts and evidence	be open-minded

Toward More Effective Communication

Communication becomes more effective if the sender and the receiver are sensitive to each other, if an effort is made to seek feedback, and if the appropriate transmission media are selected. Figure 3.2 lists some simple guidelines for the transfer of information.

The sender's thoughts should be organized to stress the purpose of the message. The message should be receiver-oriented, not sender-oriented. The sender should gauge the ability of the receiver to understand the message. The sender should be sensitive to both the status of the user within the organization and the user's attitudes. The sender should use facts and evidence to support the objectives of the message; unsupported opinions must be avoided.

The receiver should try to remain alert and attentive. Attention spans must be adjusted to the requirements of the message. The message must be analyzed and its main points noted as it is presented. The receiver should set aside personal attitudes and be open-minded in order to comprehend the sender's objectives.

In previous chapters, the importance of feedback in information systems has been emphasized. Examples of feedback in an information system are the life cycle of a computer-based business system, management information systems, and the total quality management process. On a person-to-person basis, the analyst not only reports to a supervisor but also often supervises the work of others. Analysts should be aware that if they encourage and react positively to feedback, they will increase their own effectiveness as managers.

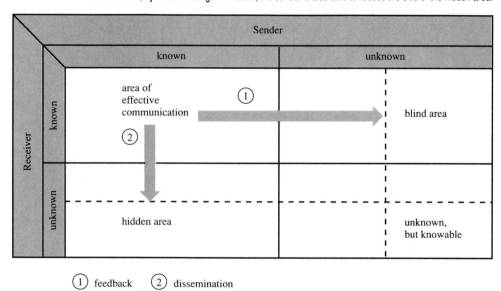

■ Figure 3.3   Effective communications. This chart shows four areas, each representing an information-based relationship between a sender and receiver. By encouraging feedback, a sender is able to reduce the size of the blind area and, by disseminating information, the sender is also able to reduce the size of the hidden area.

Figure 3.3 depicts the importance of feedback and dissemination (of information) in communication effectiveness. Four areas are shown, each representing an information-based relationship between a sender and receiver:

1. Area of effective communication—known both to the sender and to the receiver.
2. Blind area—known to receiver, but not known to the sender; may be reduced through feedback.
3. Hidden area—known to the sender, but not known to the receiver; may be reduced through dissemination of information.
4. Unknown, but knowable area—not known to the sender or to the receiver, but potentially knowable.

The sender is able to reduce the size of the blind area by encouraging feedback; by disseminating information the sender is able to reduce the size of the hidden area. As shown by the dashed lines in figure 3.3, the result of these actions is an enlargement of the sender's area of effectiveness and a reduction of the area representing information not known to either the sender or the receiver. Thus communication is not an event in time, but a continuous process. The effectiveness of this process depends on both present communication and past actions.

As figure 3.1 shows, the remaining element of the communication process is the medium. It should be selected with both the message and the receiver in mind. The two primary media for transferring information are audio and visual. Effective communicators both show and tell. All the tools of the system analyst that are discussed in this unit and the next (for example, interviewing techniques, presentation graphics, and data flow diagrams) can be used to enhance communication.

Interviewing Techniques

Interviews are one-on-one, two-way oral communications. They are vital for collecting information. Without the information from users gained through interviews, the system analyst's job would be impossible. Enough could never be learned about an existing system, the relationships between users, or the requirements for a new or upgraded system to allow the analyst to do the job.

An analyst arriving in a user area represents change and as such may not always be a welcome sight to the users. In addition, the analyst will be asking users to spend some of their working time in interviews. To gain as much useful information as possible, the user has to want to cooperate and want to be involved. Appropriate interviewing techniques can motivate the user to give you the needed information—even when you don't ask the right questions.

Psychologists know that one of the most powerful motivators for an individual is the feeling of importance. If the users are convinced that their opinions are important, and that they are a vital part of an important project, the analyst will probably have little problem getting information. If there is a feeling that their opinions are not important, the users will feel that they are wasting their time. The analyst will get only the briefest of answers and the users will not volunteer any information not specifically requested.

The following guidelines will help the users feel that the interview is important enough to justify their time and effort:

1. Know the users' names. If it isn't possible to know their names prior to meeting them, ask for their names at the beginning of the interview. Call them by name often during the interview. It shows that you think they are important.
2. Make sure that they know what problem is to be solved. Explain the benefits of solving the problem.
3. Explain that they know much more about the details of the problem system than you do and that their input is vital in finding a solution to the problem.
4. Always take notes during the interview. Write a note about everything they say, even if you already knew the information—It shows that what they say is important.
5. Keep the interview to twenty minutes or less. Don't make it appear that you are using a lot of their time.
6. Interview users more than one time. They will be thinking about the interview long after it is over. When you return for follow-up interviews, you will often find that the users have remembered additional information. Many times the most important information is gained during these follow-up interviews.
7. Always thank users for their time. Remind them that you appreciate their help.

Interviews are a powerful tool for gaining information from others. Make people feel that they are contributing and that they are important to the project, and interviews can be the best fact-gathering technique available to you.

Technical Writing

Technical Writing Defined

The written word is the most common conveyor of business information. For example, we have identified cumulative documentation as the key to the successful development of computer-based information systems. Throughout the life cycle of a business system, the systems analyst writes many different types of technical documents. **Technical writing,** as contrasted with many forms of nontechnical writing, is direct and to the point. Its purpose is to communicate facts. Therefore, easily understood words and short sentences are used to transmit information from the sender to the receiver. Some of the more important technical documents are policies and procedures, narratives, specifications, manuals, and reports.

As the list implies, the analyst must be qualified to prepare many types of documents. Brief descriptions of these documents illustrate their use as communication media. Examples of the first three types of documents (policies, procedures, and narratives) are included in this chapter because, although we will encounter and use them, we will not describe them in further detail in this book. The remaining three documents (specifications, manuals, and reports) are described in this chapter; however, examples are not provided at this time. In later chapters we will discuss in more detail the specifications, manuals, and reports that are of particular importance to the life-cycle process for developing computer-based business systems.

Types of Technical Writing

Policies and Procedures

Policies are broad written guidelines for conduct or action. They are the result of top-level decision-making. Policies should be readable; that is, they should use clear sentences, tell who has authority, and state any exceptions. (Occasionally the systems analyst will encounter—and so should be sensitive to—"unwritten" policies.)

Procedures are subordinate to policies. *Procedures* are specific statements that tell how policies are to be carried out. They provide the series of logical steps by which repetitive business operations are performed. They state the necessary action, who is to perform it, and when it is to be performed.

Policies are collected in manuals called policy manuals; procedures are collected in procedure manuals. Since procedures relate to policies, a common practice is to include the policy statement in the procedure. When this is done, the policy appears at the top of the first page and is followed by the procedure, as shown in figure 3.4. The particular format in which the example policy and procedure statement is laid out is called playscript. Although other formats, such as outlines and narratives, are used for policy and procedure statements, playscript is one of the most effective

■ **Figure 3.4** Policy and procedure statement. This example policy and procedure statement illustrates the format called playscript. Playscript is one of the most effective formats for this type of technical writing.

ABCO CORPORATION	POLICY AND PROCEDURE	
SUBJECT: COMPUTER-BASED BUSINESS SYSTEMS: STUDY PHASE	DATE: 3/17/XX	NUMBER: CS-300-0
	PAGE: ⊥ OF ⊥	SUPERCEDES: NEW *J. Worth*
	APPROVED:	*J. Worth* PRESIDENT

POLICY: All Study Phase Activities for computer-based business
                    systems shall be completed prior to the authorization
                    of a Design Phase.

RESPONSIBILITY: ACTION:

User   1. Prepares an Information Service Request, Form C-6-1.

Information Service   2. Performs an initial investigation.
                                           3. Prepares a Modified Information Service Request,
                                                Form C-6-1.

User   4. Reviews Modified Information Service Request.
                                           5. Issues a Project Directive, Form C-6-1.

Information Service   6. Prepares a formal definition of system performance.
                                           7. Evaluates candidate systems.
                                           8. Prepares a Performance Specification, Form C-9-3.
                                           9. Prepares a Project Plan and Status Schedule, Form C-9-1.
                                         10. Prepares a Project Cost Estimate, Form C-10-0.
                                         11. Prepares a Study Phase Report, Form C-10-1.

User   12. Reviews Study Phase Report.
                                         13. Issues Approval to Proceed, Form C-10-1.

formats. The actors (that is, the doers) are shown clearly on the left side of the page; the steps of the procedure are numbered in sequence; and the actions are expressed in simple sentences using action verbs. The allowance for white space adds to the statement's readability

Narratives

The *narrative* tells a story and is the most informal type of technical writing. Technical reports frequently contain many passages that are best communicated in a storytelling fashion; for example, introductions, summaries, problem statements, and background discussions. The narrative technique also may be used to describe charts and diagrams and to define words or concepts in context. The paragraph you are reading is an example of a narrative description.

Specifications

Specifications are reference documents that contain basic detailed data. They are the most formal and rigid type of technical document and may even include technical drawings. Specifications may accompany procedures or narratives. For example, if we consider the step-by-step process for rebuilding an automobile engine to be a procedure, the technical description of the engine and its component parts is a specification.

As was illustrated in figure 1.7 of chapter 1, the process of managing the life cycle of computer-based business systems depends upon the creation of three critical specifications: the performance specification, the design specification, and the system specification. We shall describe these specifications in chapters 10, 15, and 18, respectively.

Manuals

Manuals are printed and assembled pages of instructional material. Manuals usually are written for the use of a homogeneous group of people, and so most corporations have many different manuals. They are of four basic types, as follows:

1. Employee manuals introduce the employee to the company, to its rules, and to company benefits.
2. Policy and procedure manuals are used to present policies and procedures.
3. Organization manuals contain organization charts and organization function lists.
4. Specialty manuals are prepared in order to meet the needs of different occupational groups.

The manuals with which we will be most concerned are the three types of specialty manuals required before a computer-based business system can be considered operational. These are (1) the programmer's reference manuals; (2) the operator's reference manuals; and (3) the users' reference manuals. We shall discuss the format and content of these reference manuals in chapter 18, "Development Phase Report and Review."

Reports

A *report* is a formal communication of results and conclusions due to a particular set of actions; it summarizes work that has been performed. The types of reports of most importance to us are the decision-oriented reports prepared at the conclusion of each phase of the computer-based business system life cycle. In particular, these are the study phase report, the design phase report, and the development phase report. These reports are described in chapters 10, 15, and 18, respectively.

Presentations

Preparing for the Presentation

Presentations of plans or results are made in order to influence people and to obtain decisions. Because they are decision-oriented, presentations are a form of selling. Analysts are expected to do more than just present facts; they are expected to have opinions. After all, by the time an analyst has been immersed at length in a problem, some conclusions and recommendations have to have been developed that the analyst believes to be in the best interest of the company. They are what must be "sold."

All the principles of good communications discussed in this chapter should be applied to the preparation of presentations. The analyst should use both verbal and visual techniques. Following are some pointers:

1. *Participate in the selection of people to attend the presentation.* Attempt to have there the individuals who will benefit most from the project and who are most involved in it at present.
2. *Know the names, titles, and attitudes (prejudices?) of all of the attenders.* Prepare to counter anticipated objections. *Above all, know which person is the decision-maker.*
3. *Select a title for your subject that is easy to remember.* For example, call it the "Inventory Cleanup Project" instead of "Project 13A."
4. *Keep your presentation simple.* Use words that will be understood. Organize your main points step-by-step so that they lead to your conclusion.
5. *Make the intangible tangible.* Before-and-after comparisons are effective. Examples are comparisons of the number of required inventory items; reductions in out-of-inventory items; and reductions in cost, time, and personnel.
6. *Use visual aids.* Visual aids that can be used in most conference rooms are flip charts, chalkboards, overhead projectors, computer screen projections, and multimedia presentations.
7. *Keep an eye on the clock.* Do not overstay your welcome. Complete your presentation within the allocated time. Allow approximately 25 percent of your time for discussion.
8. *Rehearse your presentation.* Almost nothing is more disconcerting than not being able to operate equipment. Be particularly aware of unintentional nonverbal communication. You will be communicating to the audience by your dress and manners, by your vocabulary, by your posture, by your sense of humor, and by your enthusiasm.

Scheduling the Presentation

The analyst is frequently faced with the prospect of presenting material to several different groups. These groups may have different interests and represent different levels of management. The analyst must decide whether to start the presentations at the top level or at a lower level. The top level is determined by the scope of the application. A department head is the top-level manager for systems affecting only that department; the president of the company may be the top-level manager for a system with corporatewide impact. It is advantageous if the material to be presented is familiar to top management and if there is genuine top-level interest in the system. A top-level presentation can result in formal management backing, giving the analyst an aura of authority. Also, if the project is rejected at the top management level, there is no need to schedule other meetings.

The advantage of starting at lower levels is the opportunity to inform and to "sell" the system to operational people. Often managers consult with their subordinates after hearing a presentation and before making a decision. Subordinates who feel that they have been left out can "poison" the mind of a supervisor against a good system. Most managers are realists; they know that a poor system may be made to work if accepted and that a good system will not work if not accepted.

A recommended approach is to work with the supervisor who is most directly involved with the system and who has the most to gain from its success. This supervisor can assist the analyst in gaining the support of subordinates and can help to presell management. The supervisor and the analyst, jointly, can decide when and how to present the project to top management.

Sometimes it is desirable to make informal presentations. These provide opportunities to presell and to get valuable feedback without actually seeking a decision. Informal presentations, particularly to senior management, are valuable. However, a word of caution is in order. The analyst should plan for an informal presentation no less carefully than for a formal one. Because an informal presentation is less structured than a formal one, the analyst must be prepared to be responsive to a broad range of topics and questions.

The Presentation Outcome

There are many possible outcomes from a management-level presentation. Some typical outcomes are:

1. The analyst's recommendations are accepted.
2. The analyst's recommendations are accepted with modification.
3. Some recommendations are accepted and others are rejected.
4. A decision is deferred on all recommendations.
5. The project is terminated.

In the case of the first two outcomes, the analyst is free to move forward. The second two usually mean that additional work must be done and another presentation must be scheduled. These outcomes are not necessarily bad. The analyst may have received valuable feedback and direction; in any event, many system projects have to be sold in increments.

One of the most important storm signals that an analyst can sense during a presentation is lack of user identification with the system. If the managers who will be most affected by the system refer to it as "your (their)" system and not as "my (our)" system, the analyst knows that the system will not be accepted or successful until those attitudes are changed. This is the most important reason why it is necessary to work with a user-manager who identifies the system as "ours."

Management interest and commitment patterns. Management interest normally is highest during the study phase and when the system first becomes operational. Reviews are a means of reminding management that a significant activity is underway; they are also a means of sustaining interest and support.

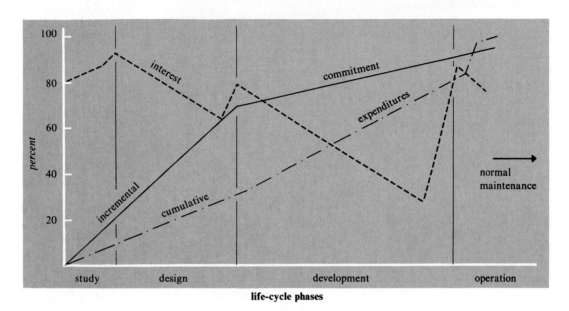

life-cycle phases

   If the project is terminated, the action the analyst should take is clear: update the documentation and file the project, analyze (and rationalize) the failures, smile, and look forward to the next assignment.

   Within the context of this book, the outcomes of certain presentations are critical. These are the outcomes of the reviews held at the conclusion of each of the first three major phases of the computer-based business system life cycle: (1) the study phase review; (2) the design phase review; and (3) the development phase review. These reviews are critical because they are a structured interaction with management for the purpose of obtaining a renewed commitment to the system.

   Management interest normally is highest when a project is launched and when the system first becomes operational. (Of course, problems encountered as the system is being designed and developed may result in periods of intense management interest.) The interim reviews are a means of reminding management that a significant activity is underway. They also are a means of sustaining interest and support during periods when large expenditures of resources are being made for activities that are not wholly comprehensible to management because of their detailed or technical nature. The importance of these reviews is portrayed in figure 3.5. In this figure the phases of the computer-based business system life cycle are spaced to simulate realistic time spans. Note that management interest is high at the onset of a program and then tends to decay as the project enters the design and development phases. It is high again as the system approaches operational status and drops off after the initial

■ **Figure 3.6**   Incremental commitment and cumulative documentation in the life cycle of a computer-based business system.

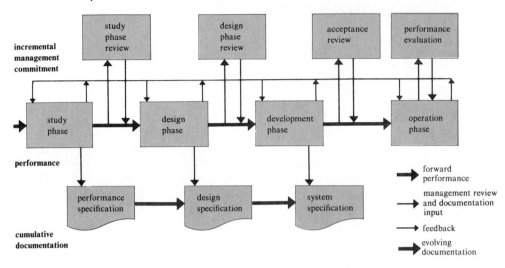

operational problems have been overcome and the system qualifies for normal maintenance. The peaks shown in the graph of management interest are due to the scheduled study, design, and development phase reviews. As the commitment and expenditure graphs indicate, commitment tends to outstrip expenditure. Note that at the end of the study phase, when the cumulative expenditures are only 10 percent, the commitment is 25 percent. Similarly, the commitment is 70 percent at the beginning of the development phase, when expenditures are only 30 percent. Thus the key management reviews rekindle and peak management interest and generate a new increment of management commitment at the end of each phase.

The communications-oriented concepts of *cumulative documentation* and *incremental commitment* are related in figure 3.6 which is the familiar systems development life cycle. However in this figure, the incremental commitment and cumulative documentation are identified to the ongoing processes of management and documentation.

Generating the Documentation

Documentation is a vital part of any system. Without documentation it is not possible to prevent or identify the unofficial changes to the system that always seem to happen. The documentation provides the standard against which official changes are made. One reason documentation is often not completed or is out-of-date is the tedious nature of manually generating it. With the common access to computer terminals, personal computers, and workstations, automated tools for the generation and maintenance of documentation are widely available. Three of these tools are word processing, presentation graphics, and desktop publishing software packages.

Word Processing

Word processing is automated typing and more. **Word processing** is the entering, editing, and formatting of text using a computer terminal, personal computer, or workstation. It allows you to "type" using the keyboard, much as you would use a typewriter, and then to manipulate the text within the computer system prior to printing the text.

The entering of text (into a computer) using a word processor is very much like using a typewriter except that you need not worry about returning the carriage at the end of each line. The keyboard placement of the alphabetic, numeric, and most of the special symbol keys is the same as a standard typewriter keyboard.

The biggest difference between word processing and typing is in the editing abilities of the word processor. Editing the text means that any changes you wish to make to the text can be done by retyping just the text that needs to be changed. In other words, after the first rough draft of the document has been entered, any text that is not being changed from the original text never has to be retyped. If one word on a page is changed using a typewriter, the entire page must be retyped. Using a word processor, only the word or words being changed need to be typed. If necessary, the word processor will make space on the line for the new text. In addition, most word processing packages include features such as spelling correction and thesauruses with both synonyms and word definitions for greater ease in editing the text. The editing features of word processors not only allow you to make changes in the text as you go from draft to draft of the original documentation, they also allow a much easier way of keeping the documentation up-to-date as changes to systems are made. The easier it is to update the documentation, the more likely it is to be kept up-to-date.

A third important feature of a word processor is its ability to format the text without retyping. That is, the margins (top, bottom, left, and right), line spacing, type size, and type style can be changed by entering a simple command—no retyping of the text!

Presentation Graphics

In describing presentations earlier in this chapter, it was noted that they can be much more effective if visual aids are used. If analysts use attractive, well-thought-out visuals with their presentations and within documentation, the communication task can be made much easier and certainly more effective. The old saying of "A picture is worth a thousand words" can be true if the correct picture is used. **Presentation graphics** are high-quality charts and graphs used as illustrations within printed documentation and as visual supplements to oral presentations.

Types of Basic Charts

Charts inform, compare, emphasize, and, in some cases, predict. Charts inform by displaying relationships or changes in relationships. They compare by relating items of information to an index, or scale. They emphasize significant changes or patterns of movement by accenting them visually. To the degree that past performance is an indicator of future performance, charts can predict by displaying trends.

■ **Figure 3.7**   Best use of basic charts. Bar and pie charts are best used to show relationships. Line and step charts best show movement over time or trends.

type / display	bar chart	line chart	pie chart	step chart
relationship	✔	0	✔	0
movement	0	✔		✔

✔ = best use
0 = other use

■ **Figure 3.8**   Bar charts. Bar charts depict relationships between elements better than any other type of chart. They may also be used to show a pattern of movement.

relationship

pattern of movement

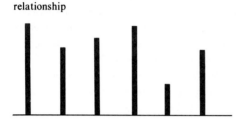
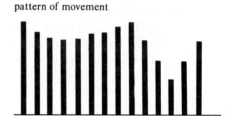

There are four types of basic charts: bar charts, line charts, pie charts, and step charts. Most of these charts can be used to display relationships and motion. However, some are more suitable than others for each type of display. Figure 3.7 relates each basic chart to the display for which it is best suited. An alternate, less frequent use is identified as "other use." Each of the four basic types of charts is described in the sections that follow.

Bar Charts.   **Bar charts** depict relationships among elements better than any other type of chart. For this reason, and because they are easily understood in a variety of arrangements, bar charts often are used for management displays. When the bars are separated, the chart displays relationships. When they are spaced closely together, the chart creates an impression of a pattern of movement. Figure 3.8 depicts the appropriate use of bar charts to emphasize a relationship and to emphasize movement. The individual bars may be shaded to enhance the visual impact.

Line Charts.   **Line charts** are the most common type of chart. Line charts are often called graphs because they usually are constructed by connecting a set of previously plotted points. Line charts communicate movement better than any other type of chart. They can display trends, curves, or any relationship where rate of change is important. Two or more lines may be used to compare trends. If more than one line is shown on a line chart, different types of lines (solid, broken, dotted, and so forth) or colors may be used to provide contrast. However, care must be taken not to display too many lines. When more than three or four lines are plotted on a single chart, the

■ **Figure 3.9** Line charts. Line charts communicate movement better than any other type of chart. Multiple plots on a single chart can show relationships. Care must be taken to avoid having too many plots and confusing the chart message. Line charts are also called graphs.

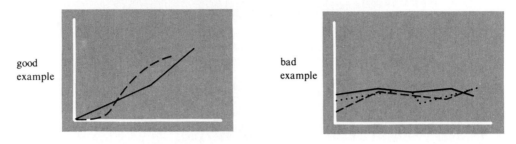

good
example

bad
example

plots can overlap and obscure the message of the chart. Several lines can be on a single chart as long as they do not overlap. If the lines overlap, the chart may confuse the viewer. Figure 3.9 demonstrates both a good and a bad example of the use of line charts. Note that the first part of the figure not only compares the two lines, but also lets the viewer extrapolate a change in relationship on the basis of the pattern of motion shown. The second part is too cluttered to be an effective graph.

Pie Charts.   *Pie charts* are excellent charts for presenting relationships as percentages. A pie chart is divided up into slices of various sizes. Since the total number of degrees in a circle is 360°, each slice represents a percentage that is the ratio between the angle of its arc and 360°.

Two pie charts also may be used to good effect for comparisons. Both charts should be the same size unless the total quantity that is sliced up has changed. For example, if the sources of funds for a fiscal year were presented on one pie chart, the applications of those funds could be presented on another pie chart of the same area. When the total quantity to be presented has changed in size, as might be the case at different points in time, the areas of the charts should be adjusted. When making this type of comparison, it is important to remember that the area increases as the square of the radius. For example, if ten-year data for annual sales were presented as two pie charts, with sales increasing by a factor of four in the interval, the representation would be as shown in figure 3.10. Note that a 4:1 increase in surface area is obtained by doubling the radius. Generally, this type of comparison is not recommended due to the difficulty of "seeing" the magnitude of change implied by the relative sizes of the pie charts.

Step Charts.   *Step charts* often can be used in the place of line charts to convey patterns of motion when relatively few points are plotted and when individual levels are to be emphasized. The first part of figure 3.11 is an example of a common type of step chart. This chart, sometimes called a "staircase chart," is an alternative to the line chart for showing movement. This chart does not convey a "flow" of movement to the same degree as does the line chart. However, it also possesses some of the characteristics of a bar chart. It can display even minor differences in relationships between small increments.

■ Figure 3.10 Pie charts. Pie charts are excellent charts for presenting relationships as percentages of the whole. They should not be used to show movement with multiple pies as in this example.

trends in sales by product

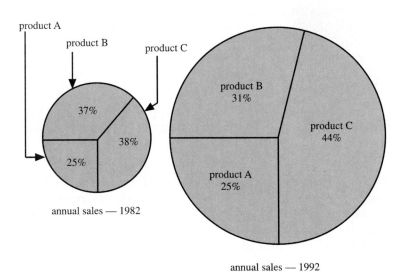

annual sales — 1982

annual sales — 1992

■ Figure 3.11 Step charts. Step charts often can be used in the place of line charts to convey patterns of motion when relatively few points are plotted and when individual levels are to be emphasized.

staircase   histogram

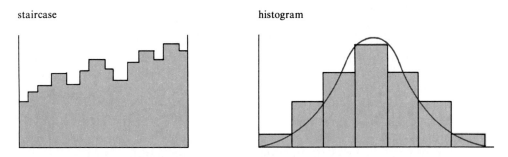

In many cases step charts can be used effectively in lieu of line charts. An interesting example, which brings together the step and line charts, is the histogram. The histogram is used by statisticians to plot the relative frequency of the occurrence of events over definite intervals. The step chart in the second part of figure 3.11 is a typical histogram. The histogram can be used to develop a mathematical approximation to a continuous distribution. This is illustrated by the "equivalent" normal distribution curve that is superimposed on the pictured histogram.

Effect of scale selection. The choice of vertical and horizontal scales on a chart has a major impact on the chart message. It is important to emphasize the message without distorting it.

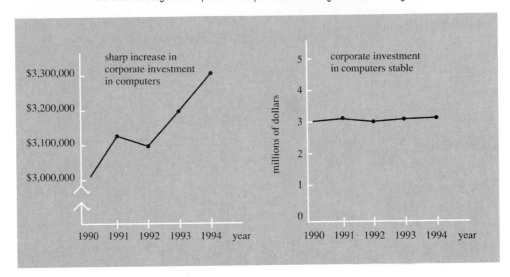

Development of Effective Charts

There are six basic steps in the development of effective charts, as follows:

1. Decide upon the message for the chart.
2. Decide upon the best type of chart (for example, line, pie, bar, or step) to communicate the message.
3. Make an initial layout of the chart.
4. Analyze the layout to be sure that the chart stresses its message.
5. Modify the chart to eliminate unnecessary words and distracting detail.
6. Prepare the final chart.

This step-by-step procedure will result in the development of effective and useful charts. An important thing to remember when preparing a chart is to "keep the chart honest." Charts can be misleading. For example, comparisons between quantities can be distorted by the improper selection of scales for the abscissa (horizontal axis) and the ordinate (vertical axis). Figure 3.12 illustrates how the choice of scale can alter the emphasis of a graph. Both graphs present the same data about corporate computing costs. Each reveals a 10 percent increase in computing costs from 1990 to 1994. The first graph accents the increase in cost; the second graph deemphasizes it. Whether or not the increase is alarming depends upon factors that are not presented in either graph. However, an alert person would be suspicious of the motive behind such obvious "chartmanship."

Graphics Software

Every systems analyst wants to have high-quality visual aids and illustrations for their presentations and documentation. The problem generally has been one of not enough time to develop the desired high-quality graphics. The lead-time required to have your requirements communicated to an artist and then to allow the artist to create the visual is often more time than you have available.

Computer-generated charts: (a) line chart, (b) bar chart, (c) pie chart. Presentation graphics software to generate charts is common and easy to use. These charts were generated and printed in a matter of minutes using a microcomputer.

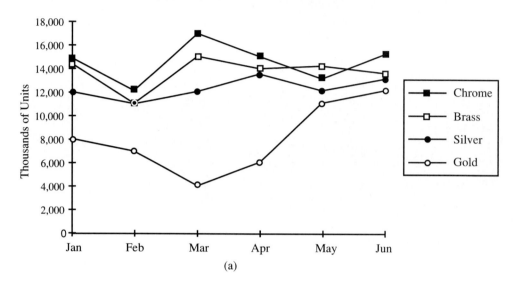

Widget Sales (First Six Months)

(a)

A solution to the time problem is in the form of presentation graphics software packages that run on personal computers. These software packages allow the analyst to prepare professional-quality presentation and documentation materials that catch and hold the audience's attention, and do it in a minimum of time. Full-featured packages include the ability to draw free-style pictures as well as generate standard charts.

When drawing free-style pictures, several predefined graphic elements are available for use. Examples of these elements include arcs, boxes, circles, wedges, and straight lines. These graphic elements may be placed on the screen and then modified to reduce the workload of drawing everything free-style. Modifications to the graphic elements are generally quick and easy to accomplish. Examples of the modifications that are possible include copying, rotating, moving, sizing, and stretching the element shape. Of course the finished drawing can also have titles and labels in a variety of styles and sizes. Many packages also allow for special effects such as color, 3-D effects, spiraled text, and the like.

The standard charts include bar, line, and pie. The bar charts may be horizontal or vertical, stacked or grouped, with or without a 3-D effect. Line charts may be drawn with solid or dotted lines of variable widths. Pie charts may be displayed as a solid pie, or with one or more "slices" pulled out from the pie, flat or with a 3-D effect. Figure 3.13 illustrates computer-generated bar, line, and pie charts. Each of these charts was generated in a few minutes.

Widget Sales (First Six Months)

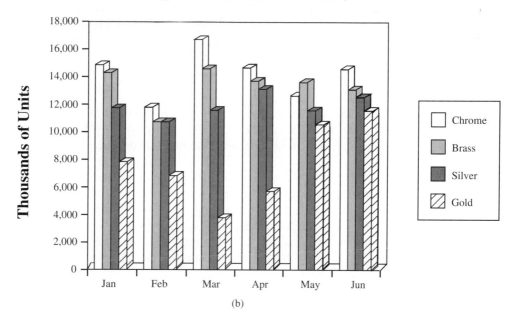

(b)

Widget Sales (First Six Months)

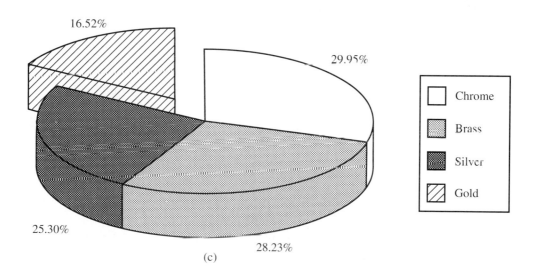

(c)

Being able to generate terrific graphics on a computer screen doesn't really satisfy most graphics needs. You need the graphic on paper, or as a transparency or a 35mm slide. Presentation graphic software packages support laser printers (including color ones), plotters, and 35mm camera devices. If none of these output devices is available, several graphics service companies provide hardcopy output from diskettes or the graphic data may be transmitted to them via a modem. These graphics services are very reasonable in price considering the high-quality results.

Desktop Publishing

Word processors provide an effective means to enter, manipulate, and print text. Presentation graphics software allows us to create, revise, and print graphics. The required system documentation commonly requires both text and graphics in the same document.

In the past, the only way to achieve the desired combination of text and graphics was to manually "cut and paste." Today, programs called desktop publishing packages will electronically combine the text and graphics into a single document. **Desktop publishing** is the use of a formatting program that allows text and graphics to be combined into a single, high-quality printed output. The "desktop" part of the term comes from the fact that these programs run on personal computers.

Word Publishing

Several of the full-featured word processing packages allow the user to add graphics to their documents. The source of the graphic can be any of several popular graphics packages, scanned images, or purchased artwork. The purchased artwork is usually available on diskette and is called clip art.

Word processing packages with a graphics insert capability can certainly be useful in the creation of system documentation. In addition, these word processors typically include some line drawing capability. In many cases, these word processing packages provide all the features required to create the desired results. They are, however, not as powerful or as flexible as a true desktop publishing package.

Text/Graphics Formatting

Desktop publishing packages usually are not used to create the text or the main graphics of a document. A word processing system is used to create the text and a graphics package, scanner, or drawing/painting program is used to generate the graphics. The desktop publishing software then combines the text and graphics outputs into a single document.

The process starts with the selection of a standard or user-defined style sheet. The style sheet describes the "look" of the combined output by describing the number and width of columns, margins, and so on. The second step is to place the text and graphics onto the style sheet. If the graphics are placed on the style sheet first, the text will wrap around the graphics when it is placed onto the style sheet. If the text is placed first, the text will be reformatted around the graphic as each graphic is placed. Figure 3.14 is an example of a two-column style sheet with both text and a graphic image.

THE TEAM MEMBERS

The membership of the systems team must be chosen carefully. The objective in selecting team members is to get people who are enthusiastic about getting the problem solved, have a background in the user area, have appropriate technical expertise, and/or can assist in the tasks of systems analysis.

At least one member of the team should be a user of the problem system. This person is familiar with the current system and knows what works well and not so well. This user representative also will be familiar with the unique vocabulary that every department seems to use. Before the analyst recommends someone from the user group to serve on the systems team, the analyst should be sure that the user's attitudes about the system and making changes to it are known. The best team member is someone who is enthusiastic about making the system better than it is, not someone who is afraid of change. If the problem system has users in more than one department, get a representative from each department.

It is wise to have someone from general management as a team member. A manager can bring the philosophy of management to the team. There is no point to designing a system approach which will not be acceptable to management. Preferably, this manager should have input into the budgeting process and be familiar with company resource availability.

Most systems today involve the use of computers. If the analyst does not have a current technical background in computer systems, a member needs to be added to the team that has the technical expertise. Computer technology is changing so rapidly that it is not unusual for the systems analyst to be unaware of the latest computer hardware capabilities. If the systems team is to analyze system choices, it has to know what is possible and what is not. This technical member of the team would most likely come from the Information Services Department of your company.

Depending upon the size and scope of the problem system, the analyst may need assistance in completing the required systems analysis tasks. If so, an additional analyst, or more, should be added to the system team. The additional systems analyst will not only help get the job done, but will also serve as a backup to the primary analyst in case of illness or other unforeseen problems. Many organizations team an experienced analyst with one who is new to systems analysis to provide the latter with systems experience.

One warning! Try not to make the systems team any larger than necessary

to get the appropriate input and help. A team with too many members can easily develop problems in communication and cooperation.

THE PRINCIPAL USER

The systems team has the task of developing a system that will meet the needs of the user organization. The analyst must remember that the benefits of a new or modified system are not measured by the value system of the analyst, but by the value systems of users. The users, however, are most likely a group of people. It is not likely that any system solution is going to be exactly what every person in the user organization wants. If you can't please every user, you must at least please the principal user. The **principal user** is the person who, in practice, will accept or reject the computer-based information system. The early identification of the principal user is critical to the success of the computer-based business information system.

In addition to combining text and graphics, desktop publishers also have considerable line drawing and editing capabilities. The editing of text placed on the style sheet includes font style and size changes, the addition of titles and headings, and the repositioning of text. Graphic images may be edited by cropping, positioning, and controlling the brightness and contrast of the image.

Summary

Communication is the process of transferring information from one point to another. Effective communication has four components: a sender, a receiver, a medium, and feedback. A systems analyst must understand the communications process and be skilled in techniques for effective technical writing and oral presentations.

An important one-to-one communication process is the interview. If the person being interviewed feels that she or he is making a valuable contribution, the interview can be one of the best fact-gathering techniques available to the analyst.

Technical writing involves the creation of several different types of documents, each with a different purpose. These documents include policies and procedures, narratives, specifications, manuals, and reports. All communicate facts as directly and concisely as possible.

Presentations may be either formal or informal. Even informal presentations require careful planning. Particularly important is the communication that occurs during the reviews at the end of each life-cycle phase. Oral presentations and technical reports affect management commitment to the project. Hence, they should be carefully prepared and directed toward the supervisor who has the most to gain from the success of the system.

Documentation that is easy to create and maintain is more likely to be complete and up-to-date. Word processing, presentation graphics, and desktop publishing packages are common tools to make the task of documentation easy. Word processing systems aid in creating and editing the text portion of the documentation. Presentation graphics packages make it easy to create high-quality bar, line, pie, and step charts. Desktop publishing software combines the text and graphics on a style sheet for a professional-looking documentation product.

For Review

communication
technical writing
policy
procedure
narrative
specification
manual
report
presentation

chart
bar chart
line chart
pie chart
step chart
presentation graphics
word processing
word publishing
desktop publishing

For Discussion

1. Give an example of communication, and identify each of the four elements (or lack thereof). Why is feedback necessary for effective communication?
2. Name some situations that may distort a message.
3. Is "body language" a part of communication feedback? Give some examples.
4. What can senders and receivers do to increase the area of effective communication?
5. Why do the authors state that "communication is not an event in time, but a continuous process"?
6. It has been estimated that communication is 80 percent visual. What visual communication processes were described in this chapter? Can you name some others?
7. Distinguish between policies and procedures. What purposes do narratives, specifications, manuals, and reports serve?
8. Discuss different approaches to scheduling presentations. How can an analyst sense a lack of user identification?
9. What are the differences and similarities between formal and informal presentations?
10. What is meant by the terms "cumulative documentation" and "incremental commitment"? How do they relate to effective communication? To the life cycle of computer-based business systems?
11. What are possible presentation outcomes? What is the appropriate action to be taken by the analyst for each outcome?
12. What is word processing? How does it compare to typing?
13. What are presentation graphics? Name and relate each of the four basic types of charts to its best use.
14. Name the major function of desktop publishing software. How does this function compare to the functions of word processing?
15. What is the difference between word processing and desktop publishing?

For Exercise: Communicating with Charts

Presentation graphics can be excellent media for the communication of the meaning behind the data. Trend and/or relationship information is commonly presented in media such as magazines and newspapers.

Locate and present examples of three of the four basic chart types (line, bar, pie, and step) found in the media available to you. For each of these three charts:

a. Include the original (or copy) of the chart. Identify the chart type of this example and where the chart was found.
b. Describe the message that the chart maker is trying to communicate.
c. Evaluate the effectiveness of the chart by explaining why (or why not) the chart type was the best choice to communicate the message.

Chapter

4

■ ■ ■

Project
Management

Preview

The design and development of a computer-based business information system is accomplished through the efforts of many people doing tasks for the very first time. Each new system is unique—no one has designed and developed anything exactly like it. Though they are dealing with the unknown, users, managers, and systems analysts have three common goals: they all want a system that works properly, is within budget, and is completed on time. These three goals can be met by using a system team, careful project planning and reporting, and a series of project reviews.

Objectives

1. You will be able to describe the purpose of the systems team and the team's typical membership.
2. You will be able to identify the roles and responsibilities of the system team.
3. You will be able to list the purposes of project reviews and be able to describe the project review package.
4. You will be able to define and explain JAD and usability engineering as they relate to the SDLC.
5. You will be able to use charts for the planning and status reporting of system progress and costs.
6. You will be able to summarize the status of a project by using performance indices and charts.
7. You will be able to describe the critical path methods for managing complex projects.

Key Terms

systems team   a group of people from user areas, management, and information services to assist the systems analyst.

principal user   the person who, in practice, will accept or reject the computer-based information system.

joint application design (JAD)   a series of intensive meetings with users for the purpose of the analysis and design of a system.

progress plan   a schedule of milestones over the duration of the project.

Gantt chart   a horizontal bar chart most often used to show the progress plan and actual progress in meeting the plan.

project cost report   a line chart with a plot of the estimated costs (the plan) and a plot of the actual costs as they are incurred.

performance indices   a set of three indices to show the actual performance as compared to the planned performance for the time schedule, costs, and an overall project status.

critical path networks   a management tool that uses a graphical format to depict the relationships between tasks and schedules.

project reviews   a series of reviews or meetings with users and management to apprise them about the progress of the project.

The Systems Team

The performance of systems analysis and design requires a great deal of insight to understand the problem to be solved and creativity to develop effective solutions to the problem. The systems analyst needs the input and ideas of others. The synergy of a systems team can produce far more than any one person. The **systems team** is a group of people from user areas, management, and information services who assist the systems analyst. The team is usually formed as soon as the analyst is familiar with the people in the user area or areas that work with the system. This is most likely to be at or near the end of the initial investigation activities, the first major task of the study phase.

The Team Members

The membership of the systems team must be chosen carefully. The objective in selecting team members is to get people who are enthusiastic about getting the problem solved, have a background in the user area, have appropriate technical expertise, and/or can assist in the tasks of systems analysis.

At least one member of the team should be a user of the problem system. This person is familiar with the current system and knows what works well and not so well. This user representative also will be familiar with the unique vocabulary that every department seems to use. Before the analyst recommends someone from the user group to serve on the systems team, the analyst should be sure that the user's attitudes about the system and making changes to it are known. The best team member is someone who is enthusiastic about making the system better than it is, not someone who is afraid of change. If the problem system has users in more than one department, get a representative from each department.

It is wise to have someone from general management as a team member. A manager can bring the philosophy of management to the team. There is no point to designing a system approach which will not be acceptable to management. Preferably, this manager should have input into the budgeting process and be familiar with company resource availability.

Most systems today involve the use of computers. If the analyst does not have a current technical background in computer systems, a member needs to be added to the team who has the technical expertise. Computer technology is changing so rapidly that it is not unusual for the systems analyst to be unaware of the latest computer hardware capabilities. If the systems team is to analyze system choices, it has to know what is possible and what is not. This technical member of the team would most likely come from the Information Services Department of your company.

Depending upon the size and scope of the problem system, the analyst may need assistance in completing the required systems analysis tasks. If so, an additional analyst, or more, should be added to the system team. The additional systems analyst will not only help get the job done but will also serve as a backup to the primary analyst in case of illness or other unforeseen problems. Many organizations team an experienced analyst with one who is new to systems analysis to provide the latter with systems experience.

One warning! Try not to make the systems team any larger than necessary to get the appropriate input and help. A team with too many members can easily develop problems in communication and cooperation.

The Principal User

The systems team has the task of developing a system that will meet the needs of the user organization. The analyst must remember that the benefits of a new or modified system are not measured by the value system of the analyst, but by the value systems of users. The users, however, are most likely a group of people. It is not likely that any system solution is going to be exactly what every person in the user organization wants. If you can't please every user, you must at least please the principal user. The **principal user** is the person who, in practice, will accept or reject the computer-based information system. In keeping with the principles and practices of TQM, the early identification of the principal user is critical to the success of the computer-based business information system.

The system project is usually initiated by someone in the user group area by sending a memo or information service request to the Information Services Department. While the person signing the request is usually the principal user, that is not always the case. The principal user may be a superior or a subordinate of the person signing the request. The principal user may delegate the task of sending the request to the subordinate, or the principal user might not have the authority to sign the information service request and it is therefore initiated by someone higher in the organization. In some cases, this individual may be a member of a different department or area. For example, the head of the purchasing department may request a copy of a report that identifies vendors by amount of money subcontracted and by geographic location. This report may not be designed by the purchasing department, but by the director of contracts who uses it to demonstrate to the federal government that the company subcontracts a certain percentage of its work with local small businesses.

Identifying the principal user aids the analyst in another important way. It helps to establish the scope of the project, which should not extend beyond the level of responsibility of the principal user. Thus if the individual who is to accept or reject the system is the manager of the accounts receivable department, the scope of the system is different than if the principal user is the manager of accounting. In the one case, the scope would be limited to the accounts receivable department and its immediate interfaces. In the other case, the scope might include several other accounting subsystems and might interface with many other elements of the company.

Roles and Responsibilities Throughout the SDLC

Each member of the systems team represents a user area or management, or brings technical expertise to the systems analysis and design process. This representative role requires each team member to ensure that they are fully aware of the concerns and requirements of their respective areas. The technical experts must be up-to-date in their knowledge of the current and planned technical capabilities of the organization. Managers must be knowledgeable about organizational goals and the availability of company resources. Each member of the systems team must openly communicate with all other members throughout the systems development life cycle.

Joint Application Design (JAD)

The **joint application design (JAD)** approach is a series of intensive meetings with users for the purpose of the analysis and design of a system. JAD is mostly used in the design phase, but it may also be used in parts of the study phase. These intense JAD meetings are often scheduled as half-day sessions. As a meeting with both business users and system developers, JAD is an excellent approach for assuring that appropriate user input occurs. The JAD team membership is usually the system team plus additional users.

The use of JAD has many benefits. These include faster definition of requirements, greater involvement of users, improved communication between users and analysts, and more accurate system specifications. The common outcomes of the JAD effort are: data flow diagrams, data flow definitions, data element identification, process specifications, screen layouts, and report layouts.

Usability Engineering

Human-computer interfaces are becoming an increasingly important component of information system development methods, such as a JAD process. Before businesses began to focus on TQM and when options were limited and often linked to cumbersome interactions with a mainframe computer, users often had to settle for anything they could get. Now, however, because of the personal computer revolution and the abundance of specialized software, users are not willing to tolerate complex or difficult-to-learn computer interfaces. Systematic efforts to provide users with comfortable links to a machine have led to emergence of an engineering field called *usability engineering*. Usability engineering spans the entire systems development life cycle and encompasses the total user interface—not only computer screens and keyboards, but also items such as manuals and training. Differences among users and variations among tasks to be performed are key usability engineering concerns. Research indicates that the most important usability engineering techniques that a systems analyst can employ to anticipate and avoid interface frustrations are:

1. Visits to customer locations before the start of a project to learn, first-hand, how the system is going to be used and follow-up visits when the system becomes operational.
2. Involvement of real users in iterative and participatory design and testing, including the use of software tools for prototyping.[1]

---

[1] J. Nielson, "The Usability Engineering Life Cycle," *Computer,* a publication of the IEEE Computer Society, March 1992, pp. 12–22.

Gantt-type chart. Gantt-type charts are used to schedule the major events of a project and to record actual progress in completing those events. The open bar shows scheduled progress. The filled-in bar shows actual progress. The uppermost bar is for the total project.

reporting date: Week 5	reporting period in weeks											
activity	1	2	3	4	5	6	7	8	9	10	11	12
project	▓	▓	▓	▓	▓	▢	▢					
activity 1	▓	▓	▓									
activity 2		▓	▓	▓								
activity 3		▓	▓	▓	▓							
activity 4			▓	▓	▓▢							
activity 5				▓	▓	▢						
activity 6						▢	▢					

Project Planning and Reporting

All projects are made up of significant events, or milestones, that must occur in some time sequence in order for the project to be completed. Each of these events will require time and dollar resources. Users always want to know "how long?" and "how much?" before they make a commitment to the system. Plans must be made and progress relative to these plans must be measured if these questions are to be answered.

Progress Planning and Status Reporting

A **progress plan** is a schedule of milestones over the duration of the project. Charts are an effective means of depicting a project schedule and of reporting progress (or lack of progress) as it occurs. The type of chart most often used to show the progress plan and actual progress in meeting the plan is called a **Gantt chart.** It is in the form of a horizontal bar chart. In figure 4.1, a Gantt-type chart illustrates the principles of a project planning and reporting chart. In this chart a project made up of six activities is scheduled over a time period of seven weeks. The length of the horizontal bar corresponds to the duration of the activity. Initially, activities are scheduled by means of an open bar to show the plan. Then, the bar is "filled in" to show how much of the activity has been completed. In the example of figure 4.1 the reporting date is the end of the fifth week. Activities 1, 2, and 3 have been completed at this point in time. Activity 4 appears to be lagging about one-half week behind schedule. Activity 5 is slightly ahead of schedule, and Activity 6 has not yet been started.

■ Figure 4.2 Project plan and status report. The project plan and status report is an example of a more complex Gantt-type chart. In addition to the major activities, it shows the project title, programmer/analyst name, committed date, completed date, and the percent of completion and status for each of the activities.

PROJECT PLAN AND STATUS REPORT						

PROJECT TITLE

PROJECT STATUS SYMBOLS
O Satisfactory
□ Caution
△ Critical

PLANNING/PROGRESS SYMBOLS
□ Scheduled Progress   V Scheduled Completion
■ Actual Progress   ▼ Actual Completion

PROGRAMMER/ANALYST

COMMITTED DATE	COMPLETED DATE	STATUS DATE

ACTIVITY/DOCUMENT	PERCENT COMPLETE	STATUS	PERIOD ENDING (Week)														

There are many techniques for managing projects. Among the more innovative and effective of these is "management by objectives." This technique depends on the development of a cooperative rather than an authoritative environment, one within which individuals participate in defining their responsibilities and have the opportunity to achieve results and earn recognition for a project (or for a phase of a project). In a joint discussion, the employee and their superior arrive at mutually understood and accepted objectives, results, and criteria for measuring results. Figure 4.2 is an example of a Gantt-type chart that can be used to manage projects in this type of an environment. This chart reports the following items:

1. Project title: the name of the project.
2. Programmer/analyst: the name of the responsible individual.
3. Committed date: the date the project is scheduled for completion.

4. Completed date: the date the project actually is completed.
5. Status date: the date of the status report.
6. Activity/document: a line entry for each major activity or document to be completed.
7. Percent complete: the analyst's interpretation of the percentage already completed of a scheduled line entry.
8. Status: the analyst's evaluation of the status of each line entry. Status is reported by means of the following symbols:
   ○ Project status satisfactory
   ☐ Caution: problem encountered but not considered critical
   △ Critical condition: completion of project could be endangered
9. Period ending: the end dates of selected reporting intervals (for example, weeks or months).
10. Project planning/progress symbols:
    ☐ Scheduled progress
    ■ Actual progress to date
    ∨ Scheduled or rescheduled completion date
    ▼ Actual completion date

Figure 4.3 is an example of the use of management by objectives. In this figure the principal activities that constitute the study phase for a computer-based business system appear as line entries. The report, which has a status date corresponding to the eighth week of the project, is interpreted as follows:

1. Initial investigation: 100 percent complete; completed one week ahead of schedule (as indicated by the appearance of the actual completion date, ▼, ahead of the scheduled completion date, ∨); status is satisfactory.
2. Project directive: 100 percent complete; completed approximately one-half week ahead of schedule; status is satisfactory.
3. Performance definition: 100 percent complete; completed on schedule; status is satisfactory.
4. Candidate system evaluation: 50 percent complete; approximately one-half week behind schedule; rescheduled for completion a week later; status is caution because slippage has occurred.
5. Performance specification, study phase report, and study phase review: not started, but all have slipped a week because of the rescheduled completion date for the feasibility analysis.
6. The study phase: the overall project is 45 percent complete; status is caution because the completion date has been rescheduled. (In this reporting scheme a major line entry, for example, study phase, must not be given a more satisfactory rating than its least satisfactory element, in this case, the candidate system evaluation.)

The percentage complete and status ratings shown in figure 4.3 represent the analyst's personal evaluations. For example, even though the shaded-in part of the study phase bar is more than 50 percent of the total area, the analyst feels that only 45 percent has been completed. This could be due to the fact that additional resources

■ **Figure 4.3** Study phase plan and status report. The study phase plan and status report shown is an example of a completed project plan and status report. Note that, as of the eighth week, the project is slightly behind schedule.

PROJECT PLAN AND STATUS REPORT																						
PROJECT TITLE STUDY PHASE FOR PAYROLL AND PERSONNEL SYSTEM (PAPS)	**PROJECT STATUS SYMBOLS** O Satisfactory □ Caution △ Critical									P. H. Eagle PROGRAMMER/ANALYST													
	PLANNING/PROGRESS SYMBOLS □ Scheduled Progress ▽ Scheduled Completion ■ Actual Progress ▼ Actual Completion									COMMITTED DATE 6/3/xx			COMPLETED DATE				STATUS DATE 4/29/xx					
ACTIVITY/DOCUMENT	PERCENT COMPLETE	STATUS	PERIOD ENDING (Week)															
			1	2	3	4	5	6	7	8	9	10	11	12	13	14	15	16	17	
STUDY PHASE	45	□																		
Initial Investigation	100	0																		
Project Directive	100	0																		
Performance Definition	100	0																		
Candidate System Evaluation	50	□																		
Performance Specification	0	0																		
Study Phase Report	0	0																		
Study Phase Review	0	0																		

have been scheduled for the latter part of the project. The evaluation of caution and the analyst's apparent acceptance of a week's lag in completion of the project may not be concurred with by the analyst's supervisor. However, in a project environment in which it is safe for an individual to report openly, many possible actions may be taken before temporary difficulties become insurmountable problems. We also should realize that plans and schedules will change, since no one can forecast the future without error. A major advantage of a plan, however, is that it provides a good reference on which to base necessary changes.

Cost Planning and Status Reporting

Project progress reporting, as described in the previous section of this chapter, does not by itself provide a complete status picture. Costs must be reported as well as progress. All projects operate within the constraints of a budget. A project might be on schedule in performance but at the same time be seriously overexpended. Therefore, a project cost report is required as well as a project plan and status report. A **project cost report** is a line chart with a plot of the estimated costs (the plan) and

■ Figure 4.4   Project cost report. The project cost report is a line chart used to show both estimated and actual system costs. The dashed line represents estimated costs, while the solid line is the actual cost to date.

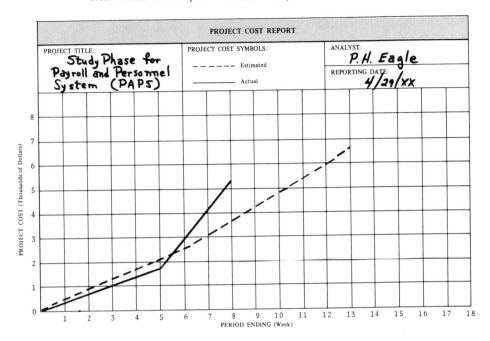

a plot of the actual costs as they are incurred. With both the planned and actual costs on the same line chart, it is easy to judge the accuracy of the original cost estimate. Figure 4.4 is an example of a cost report that might accompany the project plan and status report of figure 4.3. In this example, the project is approximately $1,700 over-expended at the end of the eighth week. This overexpenditure, coupled with the schedule slippage shown in the project plan and status report, is reason for a reappraisal meeting between the analyst and supervisor. In fact, this meeting should have taken place at least one week earlier. When appropriate, as in this instance, the analyst should submit an explanatory memorandum along with the project plan and status report and project cost report.

Performance Indices and Charts

The project plan and status report and the project cost report always present a current picture of project performance. They do not present historical or trend information. Although this type of information can be obtained by referring to previous reports, it is more desirable to extract the required information from reports as they are presented and to maintain a management control chart. This chart should contain only the data essential to summarizing past performance and to predicting future performance. The following discussion of performance indices is based upon this technique.

We can define three performance indices as follows:

1. *Cost Index* (CI): The ratio of actual costs to planned costs.

$$CI = \text{actual costs} / \text{planned costs}$$

2. *Achievement Index* (AI): The ratio of actual achievement to planned achievement.

$$AI = \text{actual achievement} / \text{planned achievement}$$

3. *Status Index* (SI): The ratio of the achievement index to the cost index.

$$SI = AI / CI$$

The cost index measures the expenditure of money. The information for calculating cost index is obtainable from the project cost reports. A value of CI greater than 1.00 represents overexpenditure.

The achievement index measures results. It can be calculated from the project plan and status report as the ratio between the estimates of actual percentage complete and planned percentage complete. A value of AI less than 1.00 represents underachievement.

The status index is a single measure of effectiveness that is calculated from the other two indices. It may be viewed as a "rate of return" on expenditure. Note that the status index alone cannot indicate schedule slippage or cost overrun. We still have to refer to either the achievement index or the cost index for this information. For example, a project with an achievement index of 0.80 and cost index of 0.60 would have a status index of 1.33. This means that the rate of return on dollars expended is very high. However, the achievement index indicates that accomplishment is behind schedule.

Let us make some sample calculations showing the value of the three performance indices in reporting trends. Let us assume that the data summarized in figure 4.5 was extracted from the status and cost reports as they were received by management. Note that the cost and achievement entries are cumulative and relate to the overall project. The last entry (week 8) corresponds to the data shown in figures 4.3 and 4.4. Note that we were able to obtain all of the cost data from figure 4.4; however, we would have to rely on previous status reports for the historical achievement information. Figure 4.6 is a graph of the three indices summarized in figure 4.5.

As figure 4.6 dramatically illustrates, costs begin to increase and achievement decreases rapidly by the end of the fifth week. Management action should have been triggered by the declining SI and AI no later than the end of the sixth week. By the end of the eighth week the project is badly out of control.

Status index graphs for some potential performance situations are shown in figure 4.7. The left part of this figure shows a project that is going out of control; the center part a project that appears to be outperforming the plan; and the right part a project that appears to be performing consistently as planned. We say "appears" because we must remember to check the achievement index or cost index also.

- Figure 4.5   Project trend summary data. This project summary status report worksheet is a convenient form to record data used to calculate performance indices. The performance chart was generated from the worksheet data.

Project Summary Status Report Worksheet							
	Achievement (%)		Cost ($)		Performance Indicies		
Week	Actual	Planned	Actual	Planned	AI	CI	SI
1	8	8	450	500	1.04	0.90	1.16
2	15	15	800	900	0.98	0.89	1.10
3	23	23	1,000	1,300	1.00	0.77	1.30
4	30	31	1,300	1,700	0.98	0.76	1.28
5	33	38	1,650	2,100	0.86	0.79	1.09
6	37	46	3,000	2,550	0.80	1.18	0.68
7	41	54	4,150	3,100	0.76	1.34	0.57
8	45	62	5,300	3,750	0.73	1.41	0.52
9		69		4,200			
10		77		4,900			
11		85		5,450			
12		92		6,000			
13		100		6,700			
14							
15							
16							
17							
18							

- Figure 4.6   Performance indices for a typical out-of-control project. This performance chart shows that the project has gone badly out of control. Management should have been alerted to the problem when the status index started to decline. Control should have been exercised by no later than the sixth week of the project.

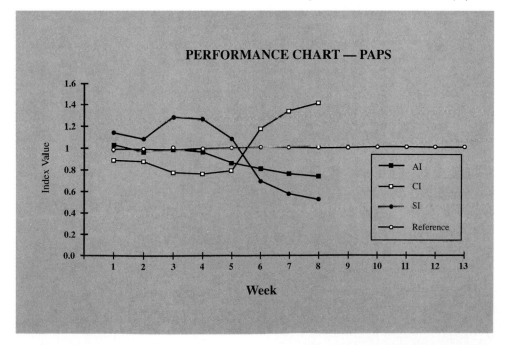

Illustrative status index graphs. Projects performing as planned will have a status index that remains near the on-schedule reference line (1.0). Projects whose status index continues to move away from the on-schedule reference line require management attention.

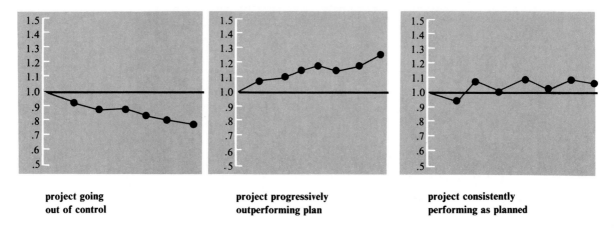

project going
out of control

project progressively
outperforming plan

project consistently
performing as planned

The following "rules of thumb" apply to the use of the status index:

1. SI between .9 and 1.1: normal range.
2. SI between 1.1 and 1.3 or between .7 and .9: management attention, perhaps action.
3. SI greater than 1.3 or less than .7: management action usually required.

The project management techniques we have discussed thus far usually can be applied without the aid of a computer. More sophisticated techniques are available, but they usually require the assistance of a computer. Among the more powerful and widely used of these techniques are critical path networks, described in the following section.

It should be noted that it is not necessary to spend large amounts of time to prepare Gantt-type and cost charts for effective project management. There are several varieties of project management software that run on personal computers. While different programs provide slightly different-looking charts, they all provide an easy means to update and print the charts as often as is desired. Figure 4.8 is a computer-generated example of a Gantt chart. The activity schedule data shown is the same as that for figure 4.3. Cost charts may be developed using any graphics program that produces line charts. Figure 4.9 was generated using Microsoft Excel®.

Critical Path Networks

Critical path networks are planning and management tools that use a graphical format to depict the relationship between tasks and schedules. They differ from conventional scheduling methods in two major respects: (1) they do not use a single time scale; and (2) they facilitate the analysis of many interdependent tasks, some of which must be performed in sequence and some of which should be performed parallel with other tasks.

■ Figure 4.8　Computer-generated Gantt chart. This Gantt chart was generated quickly and easily using a microcomputer with a laser printer. The dashed vertical line shows the current date. The Candidate System Evaluation task is a little behind schedule.

ID	Name	Duration	February 2	February 9	February 16	February 23	March 1	March 8	March 15	March 22	March 29
1	OARS Study Phase	43.38ed							60%		
2	Initial Investigation	1w	100%								
3	Modified ISR	1d		100%							
4	User Review	1d		100%							
5	Project Directive	0d		◆							
6	System Perf. Definition	2w			100%						
7	Cand. Sys. Eval.	2w					60%				
8	Study Phase Report	2w						20%			
9	Study Phase Review	1w							0%		

Project: OARS Study Phase
Date: 2/28/XX

Planned
Critical
Critical Progress

Noncritical
Noncritical Progress
Planned Milestone

Milestone
Planned Summary
Summary

Computer-generated cost report using Microsoft Excel spreadsheet software. The chart was printed using a laser printer.

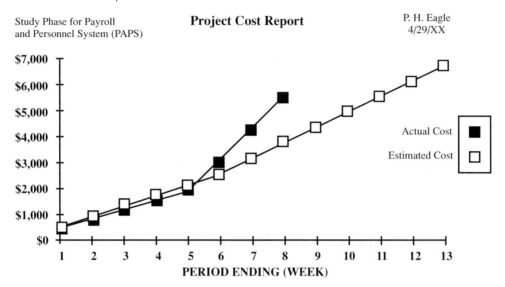

The two most common critical path network techniques, which are the same in all essential aspects, are CPM (critical path method) and PERT (program evaluation review technique). The PERT network is a more sophisticated approach than CPM.

Critical Path Method (CPM)

As in all critical path networks, the CPM technique uses a diagram of activities. Some of these activities must be done in sequence, and some may be done in parallel with other tasks. The objective is to determine the overall project schedule time. Figure 4.10 is a simplified example illustrating the principles that underlie this powerful management tool. A network such as that shown in figure 4.10 is constructed from two basic elements:

1. Activity: the application of time and resources to achieve an objective.
   Activities are measured in units of time, usually weeks.
2. Event: the point in time at which an activity begins or ends.

Network management techniques are based upon calculation of the time required to proceed from start (S) to finish (F) along each possible path in order to determine the path that requires the longest overall time.

The longest network path from start to finish is called the *critical path.* In figure 4.10 all the possible paths from start to finish and their respective times are as follows:

Path	Start to Finish Time
S-1-F	6 Weeks
S-1-2-F	12 Weeks
S-3-F	14 Weeks

■ Figure 4.10   Critical path network. Critical path networks are planning and management tools that use a graphical format to depict the relationships between tasks and schedules. The longest network path from start to finish determines the total time to complete the project. This path is known as the critical path.

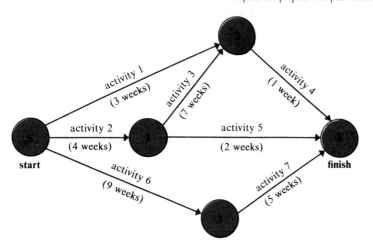

Note that S-2-F is not an allowable path because the activities along S-1-2, which take 11 weeks, must be completed before it is possible to proceed from 2 to F. The critical path is S-3-F.

Events along paths other than the critical path can be delayed without causing the time from start to finish to exceed the critical path time. Critical path information is valuable to the project manager because it gives an opportunity to shift resources from activities associated with events not on the critical path to activities that are.

As is apparent from inspection of figure 4.10, a critical path network could become quite complex for even a moderate sized project. Computer programs that perform critical path network analysis are available. In fact, computer programs called PERT-COST programs have been devised to relate network schedules and cost. Nevertheless, the manual construction of critical path networks is of value on small projects or on segments of larger projects. Also, many project planning and monitoring programs are available to use with microcomputers.

Critical path method networks have been used most successfully on applications for which all the tasks are well understood and where estimates of times can be based upon valid past experience. For example, the construction industry makes excellent use of critical path techniques. As another example, networks are useful in scheduling the flow of work through computer centers. CPM networks also are of value in scheduling the many activities in the process of converting from an old system to a new system.

■ Figure 4.11   Elementary PERT network. A critical path network, such as PERT, is a management planning and analysis tool. The building blocks of a PERT network are activities and events.

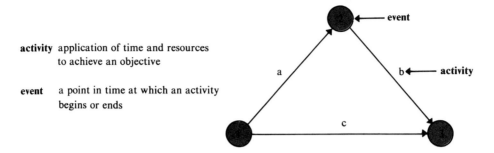

activity application of time and resources
            to achieve an objective

event a point in time at which an activity
          begins or ends

Program Evaluation and Review Technique (PERT)

PERT is a management planning and analysis tool that uses a network to show relationships between tasks that must be performed to accomplish an objective. PERT is a means of creating a master plan for the control of complex projects. Developed by the United States Navy, Lockheed Aircraft Corporation, and the consulting firm of Booz, Allen, and Hamilton for use on the Polaris submarine program, PERT has been applied widely to both civil and military projects.

PERT is a management tool. It provides a manager with an orderly approach to planning. By forcing the manager to construct a network, PERT points out relationships between tasks that might otherwise be overlooked. It also brings about coordination of effort, since it requires that participants in a project communicate with each other in order to establish and review the network. In short, PERT is a technique that helps managers answer questions such as these:

1. What work is to be done?
2. How will the work be done?
3. When is the work to be done?
4. What management actions can be taken?

To answer the question "What is to be done?" objectives must be specified and a plan developed to identify the tasks to be completed to achieve these objectives. In PERT, the plan is represented by a network such as that in figure 4.11, which displays related activities and events. A network is a graphical representation of related activities and events. An *activity* is the application of time and resources to achieve an objective. It is measured in units of time, usually weeks, and is represented on the PERT network by an arrow. The arrows labeled *a, b,* and *c* in figure 4.11 represent activities. These activities are similar to horizontal bars on a Gantt chart; however, they differ in that elapsed time is not necessarily proportional to the length of the arrow.

An *event* is a point in time at which an activity begins or ends. It is represented on a PERT network by a circle. Thus in figure 4.11, event 2 represents the end of activity *a* and the start of activity *b*. That is, each internal activity has a predecessor and a successor event. Events are similar to milestones on a Gantt chart, but the relationships between events are expressed much more explicitly than are those between milestones. Typically, events are identified by phrases such as "training manuals prepared," "training completed," and "equipment installed."

The PERT network helps to answer the question "How will the work be done?" by displaying the sequences in which activities must occur if specified events are to be reached. For example, the network of figure 4.11 tells us that three separate jobs, *a*, *b*, and *c*, must be performed in order to achieve the end objective denoted by event 3. Further, it identifies two independent paths along which activities must be completed. Along one path, activities *a* and *b* must be performed in sequence. Along the other path, activity *c* must be performed concurrently with activities *a* and *b*. PERT networks also help to answer the question "When is the work to be done?" This is accomplished by estimating an expected time for each activity. The expected activity time is based upon three estimates: optimistic, pessimistic, and most likely. It is calculated according to the following formula:

$$t_e = (O + 4M + P) / 6$$

where

t_e = Expected activity time (in weeks)
O = Optimistic estimate (how long the activity would take if everything went well)
M = Most likely estimate (the normal time the activity should take)
P = Pessimistic estimate (how long the activity could take under adverse conditions)

The expected activity time formula is the essential difference between PERT and CPM. CPM uses only one estimate to obtain a value for t_e. The time to reach any event along a network path can be calculated as the sum of the activity times along the path. However, since more than one path may lead to an event, it is necessary to select the largest sum of activity times, that is, the longest path, as the determining time. This time is defined as the expected event time, T_E. Thus

T_E = The sum of all expected activity times (t_e's) along the longest path leading to an event

The longest T_E is the time needed to proceed by the longest path from the first to the last event in the network. This is the minimum amount of time that must be scheduled for the project represented by the PERT network. The path along which the longest T_E is measured is called the *critical path*. Slippage along the critical path can cause the scheduled completion date, which usually corresponds to the end of the longest T_E, to be missed.

There is time to spare along all other paths in the network leading from the first event to the last event (unless there are multiple critical paths). This time to spare is called slack (s). Slack is calculated for each event by subtracting the T_E for that event from the latest allowable time, T_L, which is the latest time that an event can be reached without causing any path on which the event lies to exceed the critical path. Thus

$$s = T_L - T_E$$

We will use the network previously presented in this chapter to illustrate the basic calculations performed to obtain values for t_e, T_E, T_L, and s. This network is redrawn as the first part of figure 4.12. The values of the optimistic, most likely, and pessimistic expected activity times are shown above each activity line. For example, for the activity extending from event S (start) to event 2,

$$t_e = (1 + 4(3) + 5) / 6 = 18 / 6 = 3 \text{ weeks}$$

The second part of figure 4.12 is a useful format for a table for calculations. We will illustrate its use as we proceed with our example. The procedure for the use of the table is as follows:

1. All events are entered in the event column in sequence, from first to last.
2. The numbers of all events that immediately precede each event are entered in the predecessor events column. Note that an event may have more than one predecessor.
3. The values of the expected event time, T_E, are calculated and entered in the expected event time column. All T_E's are calculated by starting with the first event and continuing until the last event is reached. The successive values are cumulative and are calculated from the following relationship:

$$T_E = T_E \text{ (predecessor)} + t_e \text{ (activity)}$$

Thus

$$T_E \text{ (event S)} = 0$$
$$T_E \text{ (event 1)} = 4$$
$$T_E \text{ (event 2)} = 4 + 7 = 11, \text{ or } 3$$

Event 2 has two predecessor events. Hence, there are two possible values for T_E. The larger is used, in this case, 11.

$$T_E \text{ (event 3)} = 9$$
$$T_E \text{ (event F)} = 4 + 2 = 6, \text{ or } 11 + 1 = 12, \text{ or } 9 + 5 = 14$$

The largest is used, which is 14. To illustrate the results, the values for all T_E's on the PERT network have been entered.

4. The values for the latest allowable time, T_L, are calculated by subtracting t_e from the T_L for its successor event. T_L is calculated by working from the last event toward the first event. The equation for calculating T_L is

$$T_L = T_L \text{ (successor)} - t_e \text{ (activity)}$$

Example of PERT calculations. PERT network calculations are based upon optimistic, most likely, and pessimistic estimates of activity times. Because there is no slack along the path S-3-F, this path is the critical path.

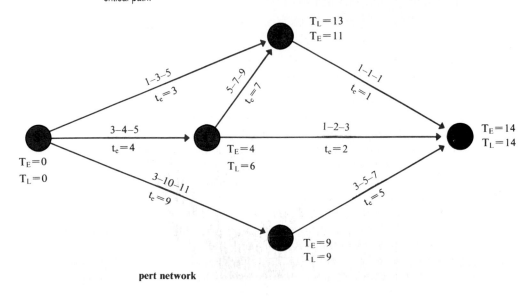

pert network

event	predecessor events	expected event time T_E	latest allowable time T_L	slack $s = (T_L - T_E)$
S	–	0	0	0
1	S	4	6	2
2	S, 1	11	13	2
3	S	9	9	0
F	1, 2, 3	14	14	0

table of pert calculations

Whenever there are multiple paths leading back to an event, there is more than one possible value for T_L. The smallest value is used. Thus

T_L (event F) = T_E (event F) = 14

T_L (event 3) = $14 - 5 = 9$

T_L (event 2) = $14 - 1 = 13$

T_L (event 1) = $13 - 7 = 6$, or $14 - 2 = 12$, and we use 6

T_L (event S) = $13 - 3 = 10$, $6 - 4 = 2$, or $9 - 9 = 0$, and we use 0

Again, for illustrative purposes, the values of T_L have been entered on the PERT network. The reason why there is no slack along paths that contain events S, 3, and F is that each of these events appears on the critical path, which is S-3-F.

It is important to note that slack applies to an entire path and not to each event on the path. Also, the value of slack is not always obvious. For example, it would be incorrect to assume that there is a slack of 10 weeks along path S-2-F by observing that the expected times from event S to event 2 and from event 2 to event F are 3 weeks and 1 week, respectively. Subtracting 4 weeks from the critical path time of 14 weeks would, in this case, result in an erroneous result. Event 2 cannot be completed in 3 weeks. It requires the prior completion of event 1. The path S-1-2 (which is the T_E for event 2) is 11 weeks long. The identification of slack time by inspection is very difficult for complex networks. In such cases, the use of a computer is warranted.

Now the question "What management actions can be taken?" can be considered. The PERT network lends itself to "exception" reporting. This means that the manager need focus attention only on those activities and events that are not proceeding according to schedule. The PERT network can be expanded to provide more detailed coverage in areas requiring management attention. Also, conventional Gantt-type charts may be prepared from the PERT networks.

PERT provides the manager with an early warning of possible difficulties. The manager has many ways of reacting to problems if made aware of them with sufficient time for action. For example, the manager may:

1. Add new resources along a path with zero or negative slack. (Negative slack occurs when the slippage is such that the path length exceeds that of the critical path.)
2. Trade off resources by shifting them from less critical to more critical activities.
3. Extend the scheduled completion time.

The manager may utilize PERT networks to answer "What if?" questions. This is an effective technique for exploring the implications of alternative actions when complex PERT networks are maintained on a computer. The PERT network becomes a model that can be used to simulate the effect of changes of allocations of time and other resources.

To further illustrate the value of PERT, consider a PERT network for implementing a computer-based system. Figure 4.13 is a PERT network that displays the major implementation activities that must be planned prior to the actual implementation of a new system. This network illustrates some of the management options made possible

■ Figure 4.13   Implementation network. PERT networks are useful in managing complex tasks, such as the implementation of a computer-based information system. The complexity of the network is due to the number of activities that must be completed. In this example, the critical path is S-4-5-6-10-11-12-F.

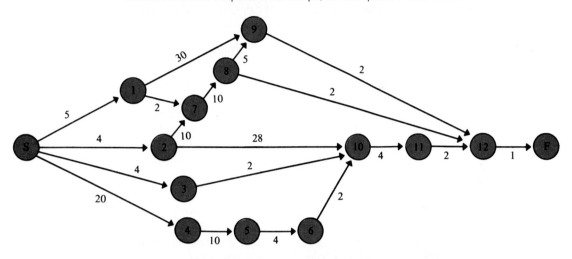

event	description
S	start of development phase
1	implementation plan prepared
2	interim system specification prepared
3	equipment installed
4	computer programming and testing completed
5	system tests completed
6	test reports prepared

event	description
7	training manuals prepared
8	completion of training
9	changeover plan prepared
10	final system specification completed
11	development phase report completed
12	acceptance review completed
13	approval to proceed received

event	predecessor events	T_E	T_L	S
S	—	0	0	0
1	S	5	10	5
2	S	4	8	4
3	S	4	18	14
4	S, 3	20	20	0
5	4	30	30	0
6	5	34	34	0

event	predecessor events	T_E	T_L	S
7	1, 2	14	25	11
8	7	24	35	11
9	1, 8	35	40	5
10	2, 3, 6	36	36	0
11	10	40	40	0
12	8, 9, 11	42	42	0
F	12	43	43	0

critical path   S-4-5-6-10-11-12-F

TABLE OF PERT CALCULATIONS FOR IMPLEMENTATION NETWORK

by PERT. The events are numbered and described in the table accompanying the network. The expected activity times (t_e) have been calculated and appear beneath each activity line. The second part of figure 4.13, the table of PERT calculations for this network, presents the results of the significant calculations. Examination of this table leads to the following observations.

1. The critical path is the path along which the computer program development takes place (S-4-5-6-10-11-12-F). The length of this path is 43 weeks. The next longest path is that along which the interim and final system specifications are prepared (S-2-10-11-12-F). This path has a slack of 4 weeks. The manager may be able to reduce the longest path by several weeks by diverting resources from other paths and applying them to computer program development and testing.
2. The path along which training occurs (S-2-7-8-12-F) has a slack of 11 weeks. This may present both a problem and an opportunity. The problem is that the expected event time, T_E, for event 8, completion of training, is 24 weeks. Personnel training will be completed too soon, and people may forget their training. The opportunity is the possibility of rescheduling the training program and using the available resources to accelerate progress along the critical path and along other paths with little slack.
3. Along the critical path (S-4-5-6-10-11-12-F) the longest T_E is associated with event 4, complete system tests. The manager may wish to review all program development and test plans. They may already be represented by subordinate PERT networks. If they are not, the manager may request that such networks be constructed to aid in the review.

The above network example illustrates some of the possible uses of PERT as a management tool. For actual management control of a project of moderate size, the network would be expanded to at least one additional level of detail. In this practice the manager would probably want to use a computer to maintain and analyze the detailed PERT network. PERT computer programs and other software tools are available to aid in the design, construction, and implementation of computer-based systems.

Project Reviews

Project reviews are a series of reviews or meetings with users and management to apprise them about the progress of the project. These reviews may be quite informal and, in fact, may actually be accomplished by way of a memo. The intent is to keep users and managers informed.

Purposes of Project Reviews

Systems analysts, managers, and users understand, or should understand, that plans are estimates. They represent the best educated guess about schedules and costs that can be made based upon the information that is available. As the project progresses, the schedule and costs become accomplished fact rather than plans. One purpose of the project review is to let users and managers know how close reality is to the plan. A second purpose is to give users and managers alternatives if the planned schedule and/or planned costs are not being met.

We all seem to be optimistic rather than pessimistic in formulating our plans. If the plans are not accurate, it is most likely that the project is behind schedule and over cost estimates. If the analyst waits until the project is supposed to be completed before informing the user that the project will be late, the users have no alternatives. Even if the completion date is critical to the users, there is nothing they can do if the scheduled completion time has arrived and the project is not finished. If the analyst waits until the project is completed before disclosing that the project is over cost, the users again have no alternatives.

If you as the systems analyst review the project progress and costs with management and users on a one or two week basis, you give them choices. In the case of a project that is still in its early stages and is behind schedule, the alternatives may be: (1) be late, or (2) bring in more people to get the project back on schedule. In the same case, a project that is obviously going to be over budget offers the choices of: (1) reduce the size of the project with the plan of adding the other functions at a later date, (2) cancel the project if the new estimated cost is too high, or (3) begin to justify a larger budget. None of these options is a great choice, but at least the users have choices.

The Project Review Package

The simplest way to keep the users and management informed about the project progress is to give them a copy of the project plan and progress report (Gantt chart), cost report (line chart), and performance chart, and a memorandum giving the analyst's interpretation of the charts. If the reviews are on a weekly basis, the most that the analyst has to explain is the progress and costs of one week. The memo does not have to be lengthy or time-consuming to write.

Summary

The formation of the systems team is a critical activity that can lead to the success or failure of the systems project. The team is a major source of input for the systems analyst if the membership of the team is appropriate. The team membership should consist of representatives of each user group affected by the system, a representative of management, and someone with the appropriate background to advise the team on technical matters. One very important task for the team is to identify the principal user.

An extension of the system team concept is the joint application design (JAD) team. It is a team with heavy user involvement for the purpose of the analysis and design of a system. The approach consists of a series of intensive meetings with users, often half-day sessions at a time. JAD is mostly used in the first two phases of the systems development life cycle.

Project planning allows the systems analyst to answer the questions that every user group will ask: "How long will the project take?" and "How much will it cost?" Project reporting can provide the answer to the question "How is the project doing relative to the plan?" Project planning and reporting of schedule progress is often accomplished with the use of a Gantt-type chart. Usually open bars on the Gantt chart show scheduled progress (the plan) and a filled-in bar shows the actual progress on the project as tasks are completed. The cost report usually takes the form of a line chart with two plots on it—one to show the planned expenditures and one to show the actual expenditures as the project progresses.

Achievement on the schedule and the actual spending can be compared with the plan through the use of performance indices. The achievement index (AI) is computed as the actual progress divided by the planned progress, both expressed as a percentage of the overall project. The cost index (CI) is the actual costs divided by the planned costs. Both the achievement and costs affect the overall performance of the project. The combined effect of the achievement and spending can be shown with a third index value called the status index. The status index (SI) is computed as the AI divided by the CI. An index value of 1.0 for any of these three indices means "on plan." Usually, all three index values are plotted on a single line chart that includes an "on plan" reference line.

Critical path networks are also planning and management tools and use a network format to depict time and progress relationships. The two most common forms of critical path networks are the critical path method (CPM) and program evauation review technique (PERT). Critical path networks are very useful for planning projects that have many interrelated tasks, some of which must be done in series and others that may be done in parallel.

Project reviews provide the systems analyst the opportunity to report the progress and status of the project to the appropriate users and managers. By keeping users and managers informed about the project, the analyst allows choices of actions if the project should become behind schedule or over in costs.

For Review

systems team	project plan and status report
principal user	critical path network
joint application design (JAD)	program evaluation review technique
usability engineering	(PERT)
progress plan	critical path method (CPM)
Gantt chart	event
usability engineering	activity
project cost chart	project review
performance indices	

For Discussion

1. What should be the membership of the systems team?
2. What does JAD stand for?
3. What is the purpose of a JAD team?
4. Who is the principal user? Why is it important to identify the principal user?
5. What is meant by "management by objectives"?

6. What information is contained on the project plan and status report? On the cost report?
7. What correlations should be made between the project status and project cost reports?
8. What are the three performance indices, and what do they show?
9. What are the two most common types of critical path networks?
10. When would you use a critical path network to plan a project?
11. What are the two main purposes of the project reviews?
12. What is contained in the project review package?

For Exercise: Critical Path Network for the Janis Corporation

The Janis Corporation is in the design phase of a system project. The project manager wants to develop a critical path network to plan the activities of designing the system outputs. The activities and their times are as follows:

Event	Description	Time (weeks)	Predecessor Events
S	Start Output Design	—	—
1	Develop Sample Data Base	1	S
2	Plan Screen Layouts	2	1
3	Plan Report Layouts	2	1
4	Prototype Screens	2	2
5	Prototype Reports	3	3
6	Review Outputs with Users	1	4, 5
F	Complete Output Design	—	6

After drawing the required CPM, answer the following questions:

a. What is the critical path?
b. How many weeks in length is the critical path?
c. A new screen prototyping tool is available for purchase. It would allow event 4 to be completed in 1 week rather than 2 weeks. Should the Janis Corporation purchase the new tool? Please explain why or why not.

U N I T

3

Information Systems Engineering

Unit One provided a general framework of contemporary systems analysis and design concepts, and Unit Two described the communications and project management skills required of an effective systems analyst. Unit Three, "Information Systems Engineering," adds to this background by describing the tools and techniques essential for structured systems analysis and design.

Chapter 5, "Data Flow Diagrams and the Data Dictionary," presents data flow diagrams and the associated data dictionary and process specification as powerful tools for the top-down, structured design of computer-based business information systems. The chapter provides a comprehensive introduction to these tools and their use in analyzing data flows within existing information systems, and in designing new or modified systems. An important related topic related to the data dictionary is identification codes. The importance and use of a code plan is explained, and the four most commonly used codes are described.

Chapter 6, "Computer-Assisted Systems Engineering (CASE)," focuses on computer-assisted methods that make possible the automation of the systems development life cycle (SDLC) and increase user involvement throughout the SDLC. The chapter describes the hardware and software developments that led to CASE, including the increase in microcomputer capabilities, micro-to-mainframe links, and developments in programming languages. It distinguishes among upper CASE, lower CASE, and full-function CASE products and identifies and explains the functions performed by the basic and advanced tools that are integrated into full-function CASE products.

Chapter

5

■ ■ ■

Data Flow Diagrams and the Data Dictionary

Preview

The structured method for systems analysis and design is based on the concept that "what" a system does can be separated from "how" it is done. Data flow diagrams are an essential tool for this method because they are a means of preparing and analyzing a logical abstract of what has to be done before committing to a specific form of physical implementation. They provide systems analysts with a network that displays system data flows, data stores, and the transformation processes that change data flows from one form to another. This network can be subdivided into a set of data flow diagrams with as many levels of detail as is necessary to accurately and completely specify the system performance. The set of data flow diagrams, accompanied by a data dictionary that defines all data flows and stores data by specifications for the transformation processes that are not further subdivided, provides documentation that is essential to the description and development of a computer information system. Entity-relationship diagrams are introduced as a means of identifying entities and the linkages between them as they relate to data dictionary entries. Also, codes, which are used to identify and retrieve information, are presented as an effective means for making data dictionary entries. The importance and use of a code plan is described, as are the four most commonly encountered identification codes: sequence, group classification, significant digit, and alphanumeric.

Objectives

1. You will be able to explain what data flow diagrams are and describe their importance as tools for structured analysis and design.
2. You will be able to construct multilevel data flow diagrams.
3. You will be able to explain why a data dictionary is needed to document data flow diagrams and demonstrate how to make data dictionary entries.
4. You will be able to define a process specification and describe its uses.
5. You will be able to define and distinguish between decision trees and structured English and will be able to convert one to the other.
6. You will be able to relate the terms "entity" and "attribute" to data dictionary entries.
7. You will be able to describe the elements of an entity-relationship diagram and explain how it can be used to assist in constructing a data dictionary.
8. You will be able to describe the purposes of a code plan and will be able to distinguish among the four principal types of identification codes.

Key Terms

data flow diagram (DFD) a network that describes the flow of data throughout a system, data stores, and the processes that change, or transform, data flows.

decomposition subdivision of a high-level data flow diagram into a hierarchy of lower-level data flow diagrams.

context diagram a diagram that identifies the domain of a system; it identifies the net input and output data flows between the system and the external entities with which it interacts.

data element the smallest unit of data that is meaningful to a system.

data structure refers to a structured relationship between data elements; data structures are composed of data elements and other data structures.

data dictionary a central repository that contains the definitions and descriptions of all of the system data structures.

process specification the rules by which a process transforms input data flows into output data flows.

decision table a table used to describe logical rules.

decision tree a network-type chart that is the logical equivalent of a decision table.

structured English a method for displaying a logical process in an outline format.

entity any object, physical or abstract, about which data are stored.

attribute any property that describes an entity.

identification code a means of uniquely and concisely describing the characteristics of an object.

entity-relationship diagram a diagram that uses predefined symbols to identify entities and the relationships among them.

Structured Analysis and Design

Separating the What From the How

In the first chapter we identified the structured method for systems analysis and design as one that is rapidly gaining acceptance in industry because it is an effective means of communicating with users about "what" a system must do before a decision is made about "how" it is to be done. Data flow diagrams, which provide a logical map of a problem before suggesting a specific solution, have proved to be a fast and efficient method of communication among systems analysts and are an effective means of conducting dialog with users.

Also, data flow diagrams are the basis for the essential documentation that defines the data stores and the processes that operate on and transform streams of data as they flow throughout a computer information system. Therefore, our principal purpose in this chapter is to familiarize you with data flow diagrams. With the understanding you will get in this chapter and in later chapters as we apply this powerful tool to a systems development life cycle-case study, you will acquire proficiency in preparing and using data flow diagrams.

Documentation Needs

Systems analysis cannot be performed without complete supporting documentation. All methods of analysis and design used to develop computer information systems according to the systems development life-cycle roadmap must provide both text and graphic documentation every step of the way. In addition to meeting a number of other communication needs, this documentation must:

1. Describe the relationships between data and the processes that transform data.
2. Define all data structures.
3. Specify the essential transformation processes.

A set of data flow diagrams meets the first documentation requirement. A data dictionary, which is prepared to accompany the set of data flow diagrams, meets the second requirement; a set of process specifications, derived from subdivided, or decomposed, DFDs, satisfies the third. These documents are included in the *performance specification,* which is the general design specification completed at the end of the study phase. They become important components of the cumulative documentation process that continues throughout the design and development phases and results in a complete system specification.

Data flow diagram symbols. Data flow diagrams are constructed from four basic symbols. Using these symbols, a systems analyst can construct a logic network that traces data streams throughout a system.

A square represents a data source or destination.

A directed line respresents a flow of data, that is, a data stream.

A circle, or a "bubble," represents a process that transforms data streams.

Two parallel lines represent a data store.

Data Flow Diagrams

Definition of a Data Flow Diagram

A **data flow diagram (DFD)** is a network that describes the flow of data throughout a system, data stores, and the processes that change, or transform, data flows. The DFD network is a formal, logical abstract of a system that may have many possible physical configurations. For this reason, a set of symbols that do not imply a physical form is used to represent data sources, data flows, data transformations, and data storage. In practice, a standardized set of symbols for data flow diagrams has not been adopted. In this text we will use the four commonly encountered data flow diagram symbols shown in figure 5.1.

As illustrated in figure 5.2, the circle, or "bubble," represents a *transformation process,* and the label inside the bubble describes the process, using an active verb to do so. *Data flows* are directed lines that identify the input data flows and output data flows at each process bubble. *Data storage* is represented by two parallel lines with a label that identifies the data store, or *file.* The square is labeled to identify an *external entity* that is a *source* or *destination* of a data flow.

Figure 5.3 shows how a data flow diagram can be prepared early in the study phase to derive the current logical system, which is a logical extract, or model, of the current physical system. Subsequently, another DFD would be developed to represent a logical model of a new system. Thereafter, alternative physical systems that could satisfy the logical requirements of the new system would be evaluated in order to select the most cost-effective and usable form of physical implementation.

■ Figure 5.2   Data flow diagram. This diagram illustrates the use of the four data flow diagram symbols: data source, data flow, process bubble, and data storage.

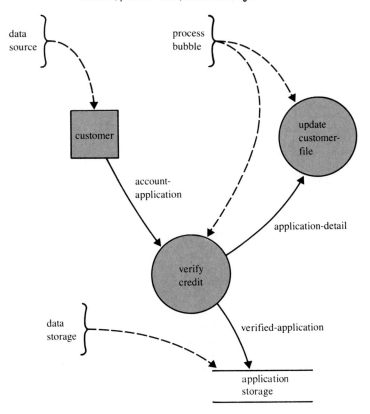

Data Flow Diagram Transformations and Decomposition

The three principal types of data stream transformations that take place at the processing bubbles are shown in figure 5.4. These are combining, splitting, or modifying data streams. Most data flow diagram networks prepared by systems analysts to assist in the solution of real problems exhibit many combinations of the three basic transformations, and they can become very complex. When studying complex situations, we must keep in mind the limitations of human data processors. Data flow diagrams would become much too confusing for analysts to understand and to work with if all of the significant data flows were drawn as a single network.

It is best to prepare one data flow diagram that provides an overall picture of what is occurring and, then, to break the picture down into a hierarchy of smaller pictures—much in the manner that we have learned to prepare organization charts.

Example of the derivation of a current logical model from a current physical model. Figure 5.3a repeatedly uses the system flowchart symbol that represents a printed document. In figure 5.3b, there is no suggestion of a specific physical form; instead, data streams are emphasized.

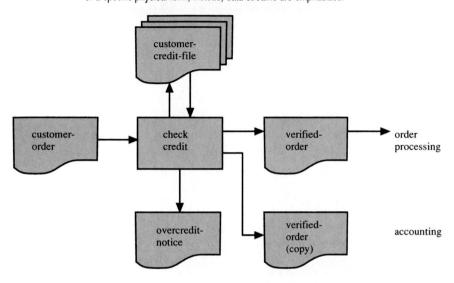

a. **current physical system**

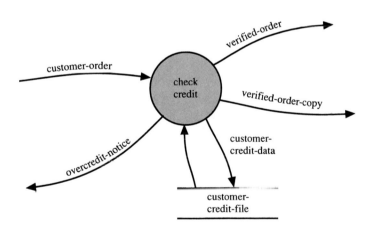

b. **current logical system**

■ **Figure 5.4** Data flow diagram transformations. The principal processes that take place at a process bubble are combining, splitting, and modifying data streams.

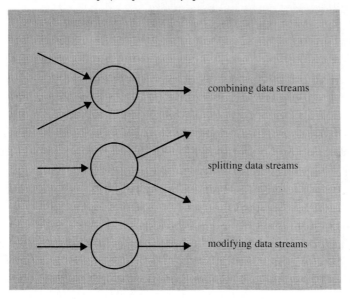

Thus high-level DFDs are subdivided, or *partitioned,* into a hierarchy of lower-level DFDs through a procedure called **decomposition,** which is illustrated in figure 5.5.

The big-picture data flow diagram that is prepared before decomposition begins identifies the *domain,* or boundaries, of the system that is being studied. This DFD is called a **context diagram,** and it identifies the net input and output data flows between the system and the external entities with which it interacts. When processes are partitioned into sets of subprocesses, there is a link pin relationship between successive levels of detail. When working with data flow diagrams, systems analysts refer to this type of linkage as a *parent-child* relationship, and it is necessary to label all processes in a manner that identifies the parent and child.

Figure 5.6 is a series of schematic drawings that illustrate the context diagram and parent-child concepts. Figure 5.6a is a context diagram, and it identifies a system domain. The context diagram is not considered to be a level of a DFD. The initial data flow diagram that is drawn within the boundaries established by the context diagram is called a level-0 DFD, and it is a graphic picture of the major system data flows and the processes that transform them. Figure 5.6b depicts a level-0 DFD, and figure 5.6c shows a level-1 DFD that is the result of a partial decomposition of the level-0 DFD. At each level, the net inputs and outputs of the child must correspond exactly to those of the parent. For example, the net input and outputs of the level-1 child are F, G, and H, and they correspond to the input and outputs of the level-0 parent. As figure 5.6c also illustrates, when a data store is first drawn, it is customary to show all of its inputs and outputs.

■ **Figure 5.5** Hierarchy of data flow diagrams. High-level data flow diagrams (DFDs) can be decomposed into lower-level DFDs, each of which is a network of more elementary processes.

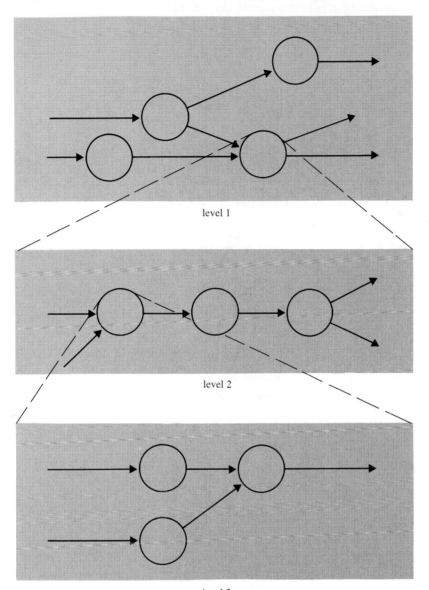

level 1

level 2

level 3

Context diagram and parent-child concepts. The context diagram establishes the domain of the system. The highest-level DFD is level-0, and this parent can be decomposed into subordinate levels; however, each child must exhibit the same net input and output data flows as its parent.

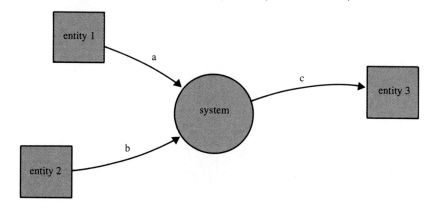

a. context diagram

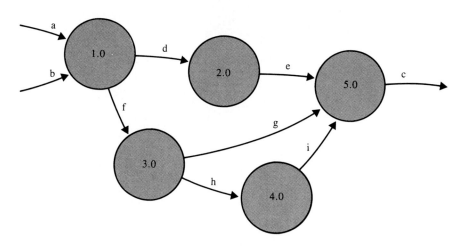

b. level-0 DFD

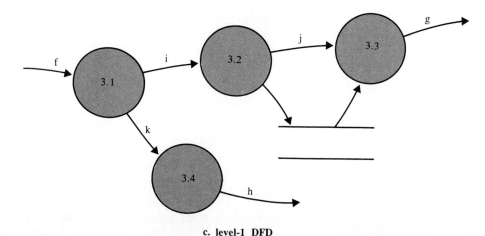

c. level-1 DFD

Context diagram and data flow diagram example. Part a of this figure is a context diagram for an accounts receivable, A/R, system. Part b illustrates the expansion of the context diagram into a level-0 DFD for the A/R system. Part c shows the decomposition of an element of the level-0 DFD into a level-1 DFD.

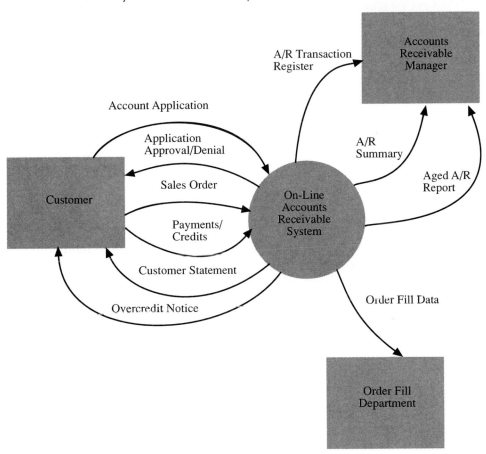

Figure 5.7 shows, in part, how a context diagram and DFDs might appear as a result of a decision to analyze an accounts receivable (A/R) system. Figure 5.7a is a context diagram, and figures 5.7b and 5.7c illustrate two levels of decomposition for the current logical system. If the process of decomposition were continued, it would become evident that all high-level processes could not be decomposed to the same degree. Some could be expanded into many subordinate levels and others, perhaps, not at all. Decomposition should be continued until a bottom set, called the *set of leveled DFDs,* is arrived at for each major transformation process. Each bubble in the set of leveled DFDs is called a *primitive* because it is not further decomposed.

A reasonable question to ask is: "How many levels of decomposition are required?" The answer to that question is that it depends upon the complexity of the problem and upon the knowledge and abilities of the systems analyst and of the project team members and users working with that person. Decomposition should

■ Figure 5.7b

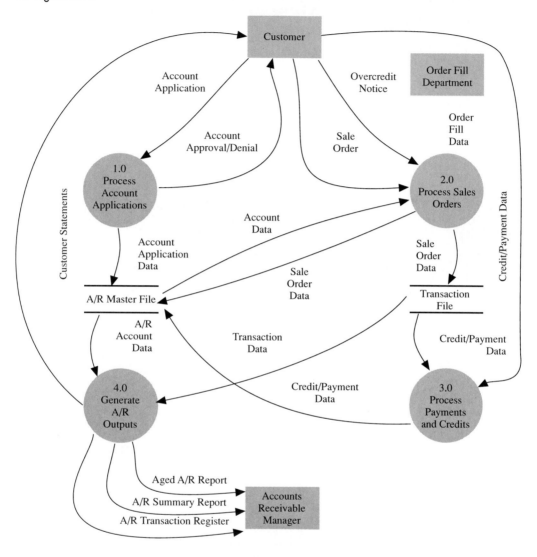

continue until the meaning, origin, and use of every data flow and store is understood and can be explained. Also, the team should be prepared to define the functional requirements for each primitive in the set of leveled DFDs. This is equivalent to specifying the functional requirements for the entire system because of the parent-child relationship between processes and subprocesses.

It usually is not practical to expand DFDs beyond six or seven levels. This means that the less significant processes, of which minor editing of some input data might be an example, would have to be dealt with later in the systems development life cycle. Also, because analysts work most of the time with the higher-level DFDs, our goal, as we proceed in this text, will be to provide you with opportunities to gain

■ Figure 5.7c

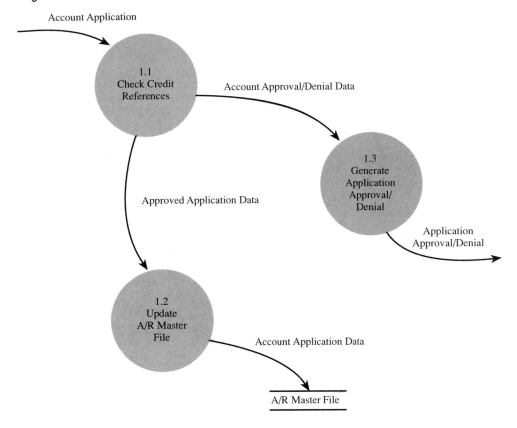

Account Application

1.1
Check Credit
References

Account Approval/Denial Data

1.3
Generate
Application
Approval/
Denial

Approved Application Data

Application
Approval/Denial

1.2
Update
A/R Master
File

Account Application Data

A/R Master File

experience by applying the principles emphasized in this chapter to system models that do not require the number of levels of decomposition that might be characteristic of actual business systems.

Guidelines for Drawing Data Flow Diagrams

As the foregoing discussion indicates, data flow diagrams can easily become quite complex; therefore, it often is helpful to follow a set of general guidelines. There are eight general rules that can be of assistance in most cases after the systems analyst has carefully studied the problem. These rules are stated and illustrated in figure 5.8.

The Data Dictionary

Data Elements and Data Structures

Most of the activities undertaken by a systems analyst in analyzing a problem and designing a system to solve that problem relate to data. The analyst must learn all about all of the data that an existing system uses or generates. Additionally, the analyst must carry forward to a new system data that are usable and add other data required

Rule 1. Establish the context of the data flow diagram by identifying all of the net input and output data flows.

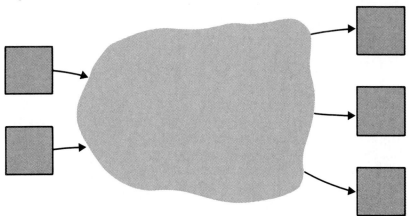

Rule 2. Select a starting point for drawing the data flow diagram.

from inputs to outputs:

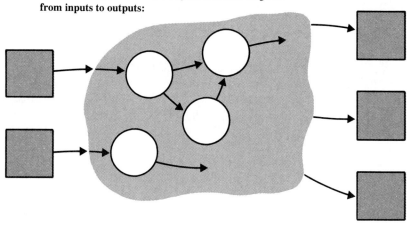

backwards from outputs to inputs:

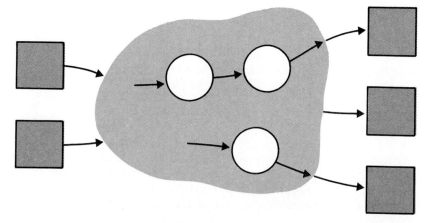

or from the center out:

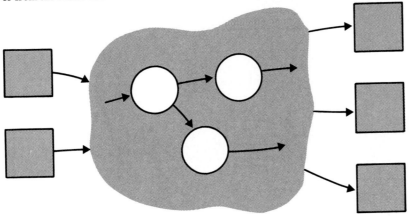

Rule 3. Give meaningful labels to all data flow lines.

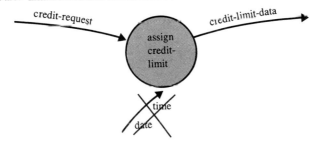

Rule 4. Label all processes with action verbs that relate input and output data flows.

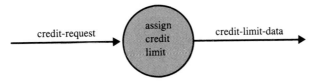

Rule 5. Omit insignificant functions routinely handled in the programming process.
Examples are: **initialization and termination details**

■ Figure 5.8   Continued.

details of minor error paths:

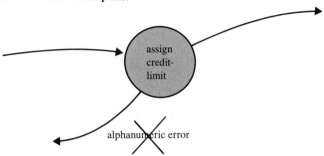

Rule 6. Do not include control or flow of control information.

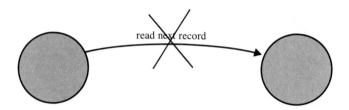

Rule 7. Do not try to put too much information in one data flow diagram. Try to plan for the number of levels.

Rule 8. Be prepared to start over. Often the data flow diagram does not begin to "flow" without several false starts.

by the system. Before the design of a new system can begin, all of the data elements used by the system and the relationships between them must be defined and explained. We start by defining a **data element** to be the smallest unit of data that is meaningful to the system in which it is used. Often there are structured relationships between data elements. These relationships, called **data structures,** are characteristic of the data streams and data stores that appear on data flow diagrams. Data structures are composed of data elements and other data structures. For example, "Name-Address" might be a data structure composed of:

1. The data structure "Name," which includes the data elements "Last-Name," "First-Name," and "Middle-Initial," and
2. The data structure "Address," which includes the data element, "Street," and the data structure "State-Zip."

When analyzing data flow diagrams, we may consider data flows to be data structures in motion and data stores to be data structures at rest. A data flow that could not be further subdivided would be considered to be a data element. Data stores are places in a system where data are stored between processing transactions. They include files and data bases—topics that we will consider in greater detail when we study the design phase.

Clearly, a data flow diagram would be of very limited use if we were not able to describe fully all of the data structures that appear on it. Also, the method used previously to describe the data structure "Name-Address" could become awkward and unwieldy if we were to deal with other than very small systems. The need for documenting DFDs in a compact and workable manner can best be satisfied by maintaining a data dictionary.

Data Dictionary Definition and Entries

A **data dictionary** is a central repository that defines and describes all of the data structures (i.e., data elements, data flows, and data stores) within a system. A data dictionary entry should contain at least the following four elements:

1. Name of the data structure.
2. Identification of the data structure as a data flow, a data store, or a data element.
3. Other names by which the data structure is called.
4. Definition of the content of the data structure.
5. Significant comments.

Each data dictionary entry should be defined completely, concisely, and correctly. A set of symbols that can be used to define data dictionary entries without ambiguity is illustrated in figures 5.9 through 5.11, using examples taken from figure 5.7. Figure 5.9 illustrates a data dictionary entry for a data flow labeled account-application. Note that the data flow is defined in terms of its subordinate data structures and that the relationships are presented in the format of an equation, with the data flow equated to its component data structures, which are linked by + signs. Other useful symbols are:

Braces { }, which indicate that an item may be repeated.

Underlines, which identify the item as a key field by which a record may be accessed.

Parentheses ( ), which indicate that the data is optional.

Appropriate comments might relate to data flow sources and destinations and to the frequency and volume of transactions. When the data dictionary entry form is first prepared, all of the information required to complete the entry may not be known. However, if the need is identified, the entry can be completed at a later stage of the systems development life cycle.

Figure 5.10 is an example of a data dictionary entry for a data store labeled A/R file. In this instance, identification of the type of file structure could be an appropriate comment.

Figure 5.11 shows a data dictionary entry for a data element named account-number. Since a data element is the smallest meaningful unit of data and one that cannot be further subdivided, it is appropriate to explain the meaning of any particular codes or values that might be assigned to it.

■ Figure 5.9   Illustration of a data dictionary entry for a data flow. This example shows the data structure for an account-application, which is part of an accounts receivable (A/R) system.

```
                    Data Dictionary Entry

  Name of Data Structure:    Account-Application

  Type of Data Structure:    Data Flow

  Other Names:    Customer-Account-Application

  Content:
     Account-Application= Firm-Name +
                          Wholesale/Retail Code +
                          Date +
                          Telephone +
                          Street Address +
                          City-State-Zip Code +
                         ⎧ Reference Name +        ⎫
                         ⎪ (Branch) +              ⎪
                         ⎨ Telephone +             ⎬
                         ⎪ Street Address +        ⎪
                         ⎩ City-State-Zip Code +   ⎭

                          Account-Number +
                          Effective-Date +
                          Credit-Code +
                          Discount-Code +
```

```
  COMMENT:    If reference is a bank, branch
  should be identified: Else, this item
  may be omitted. Firm name is included as a
  key field in order to produce an alphabetic
  listing of customer accounts.
```

Illustration of a data dictionary entry for a data store. This example shows the data elements in an accounts receivable (A/R) master-file.

```
                    Data Dictionary Entry

Name of Data Structure:    A/R-File

Type of Data Structure:    Data Store

Other Names:    A/R-Master-File

Content:
    A/R-File=                Firm-Name +
                             Street-Address +
                             City-State-Zip Code +

                             Account Number +
                             Amount-Paid +
                             Previous-Balance +
                             Total-Purchase +
                             Total-Payments-and-Credits +
                             Purchases-Month-to-Date +
                             Credits-Month-to-Date +
                             Balance-30-Days +
                             Balance-60-Days +
                             Balance-90-Days +
                             Balance-Over-90-Days +
                             Credit-Code +
                             Discount-Code
```

```
COMMENT:    Key fields are account-number and
firm-name, which is included in order to
produce an alphabetic listing of customer
accounts.
```

Illustration of a data dictionary entry for a data element. This example describes a data element that is part of an A/R system. It is account-number, and it is a key field by which customer account information may be accessed.

```
                    Data Dictionary Entry

Name of Data Element:        Account-Number

Other Names:    Customer-Number

Format:     X X - X X X X X

Size:       10 Character

Code:           X X - X X X X X X
                ⏜      ⏜
            Region  Six-Digit Sequence

Source:     Account-Application
```

```
COMMENTS: All account numbers are assigned
and maintained as block sequence codes.
The first block is a region, numbered from
01 to 99. The second block is a six-digit
alphanumeric sequence code. The first two
characters are alphabetic and the last four
are numeric. File should be index-sequential.

            Example:
                12-AA1243
```

All data flows and data stores are made up of data elements. However, these data elements may not be unique to a particular data flow or data store. For example, in a sales order system, customer-account-number could appear as a data element on the sales order, in the customer credit file, on the customer invoice, and in a number of other data structures. Therefore, it is necessary to prepare a data dictionary entry for each data element as it is encountered or created. Figure 5.11 also is an example of a form that could be used for this purpose. Comments that clarify the description of the data element should be included. For example, customer-order-number might be referred to elsewhere in the system as order-number, and this other name should be noted. Other appropriate comments might explain the format, size, meaning, and range of values characteristic of a particular data element.

In practice, the processes that transform data need to be specified, and these, too, are considered to be part of the data dictionary. Even for a system of moderate size, data dictionaries can quickly become complex and difficult to maintain. Often a project librarian is assigned this task. Fortunately, software packages designed to provide automated data dictionaries are available. Thus as the design of a computer information system proceeds, selected information can be retrieved from the data dictionary. For example, a list of data elements, described by format and size, could be created as an aid to file or data base design.

Entities and Attributes

In this chapter, as illustrated in figure 5.7a, we used the term *external entity* to describe a source or destination of the data flows that established the context of the information system project. As this context is decomposed into successively more detailed DFDs, additional entities become evident. Actually, an **entity** is any object, physical or abstract, about which data are stored. Entities are described by nouns. In figure 5.7b, for example, customer, order-fill department, and A/R manager are entities—as are the A/R data base and the data flows. Any property that describes an entity is called an **attribute.** Thus the data structure named account-application is an entity, and the attributes that describe this entity are recorded in the "content" section of figure 5.9.

In chapter 12, "Data Modeling," we will examine entities and their attributes in considerably more detail. You will learn how to use entity-relationship diagrams (E-R diagrams) as a design phase tool for creating a data-driven model of the computer information system.

Entity-Relationship Diagrams

The data structures cataloged in the data dictionary may not only be large in number but also may exhibit many types of linkages. One method for displaying these linkages and for identifying and modeling the data structures stored in the data dictionary is by means of an **entity-relationship diagram (E-R diagram, or ERD).** Entity-relationship diagrams use predefined symbols to identify entities and to display the

■ Figure 5.12   Entity relationship diagram (ERD) for an accounts receivable system. This ERD displays the one-to-one (1:1) and one-to-many (1:m) relationships that can occur between entities. In this example: each customer places many orders; many orders generate a customer statement; and each customer pays one customer statement.

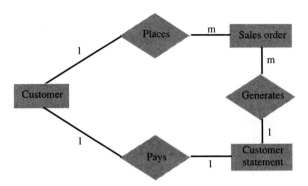

relationships among them. As shown in figure 5.12, which is a simple ERD, "rectangles" represent entities, and "diamonds" depict the relationships among entities. Lines are drawn to connect the entities, and each entity is identified by a (singular) noun. The relationships among entities are described by verbs. The occurrences of entities may be one or many, with the latter represented by the letters "m" and "n." They are identified on an ERD as one-to-one (1:1), one-to-many (1:m), or many-to-many (m:n).

Entity-relationship diagrams often differ significantly among systems that appear to be similar. The relationships and occurrences can be defined only through analysis and understanding of the specific nature of the enterprise to which the design of the information system pertains. For example, the meaning of figure 5.12 is as follows:

1. One customer places many orders.
2. Many orders generate one customer statement.
3. One customer pays one customer statement.

Next, the data structures that define pertinent attributes must be developed for each entity. In practice, systems professionals often annotate ERDs with data structure descriptions. Thus the data dictionary entries that appear in figures 5.9 through 5.11 could have been derived from notations on ERDs. Also, a m:n entity relationship usually indicates the existence of a data store, such as a master file. In chapter 12, "Data Modeling," we will examine ERDs in further detail.

Identification Codes

The Code Plan

A knowledge of and the ability to work with codes and coding techniques are essential skills required of systems analysts, who must deal with data in its many forms. As you may have noticed, in figure 5.11, the illustration of a data dictionary entry for a data

■ Figure 5.13   Simple sequence code dictionary. This example was developed by listing employee names alphabetically and then assigning employee numbers in sequence.

code	employee name
1	Addington, Horace R.
2	Aquilar, Maria
3	Conrad, Robert L.
4	Crane, James M.
5	Custer, George G.
6	Dawson, Helen R.
7	Duncan, Suzanne A.
8	Eckel, Lisa T.
*	****
*	****
*	****

element, a code is assigned to each account-number. This code, called an **identification code,** was developed in accordance with a *code plan* prepared by the analyst. The purpose of a code plan is to provide brief and usable descriptions of particular attributes of entities with which the system must deal. Five important considerations involved in the preparation of a code plan are as follows:

1. Expansion: The code must allow for a reasonable growth in the number of objects to be coded.
2. Precision: The code must uniquely identify an object.
3. Conciseness: The code should be as brief as possible and still conform to the code plan.
4. Meaningfulness: The code must be useful to the people who must work with the coded object; if possible, it should identify some meaningful attribute of the object.
5. Operability: The code should be compatible with current and anticipated methods of data processing.

After completing the code plan, the analyst selects the type of code most appropriate for identifying the particular characteristics of each object selected for coding.

Common Types of Codes

The four most common identification codes are: sequence, group classification, significant digit, and alphanumeric. In practice, combinations of these codes often are found.

Sequence Codes

Simple Sequence Code

A sequence code has no relation to the characteristics of an item. The assignment of consecutive numbers, for example, 1, 2, 3, . . . , to a list of items as they occur is called a *simple sequence code.* Figure 5.13 is an example in which employees' names

■ Figure 5.14   Block sequence code dictionaries. Block sequence codes assign a block of numbers to a characteristic
of the items to be encoded. In these examples, the first letter of the last name and the furniture material
are the selected characteristics.

code	employee name	code	data item
1	Addington, Horace R.	1	Chair, Wood — Table
2	Aquilar, Maria	2	Chair, Wood — Folding
20	Conrad, Robert L.	3	Chair, Wood — Rocking
21	Crane, James M.		
22	Custer, George G.	10	Chair, Plastic — Table
30	Dawson, Helen R.	11	Chair, Plastic — Folding
31	Duncan, Suzanne A.	12	Chair, Plastic — Rocking
40	Eckel, Lisa T.		
*	****	20	Chair, Chrome — Table
*	****	21	Chair, Chrome — Folding
*	****	22	Chair, Chrome — Rocking

are listed alphabetically and then assigned an employee number in sequence as they appear on the list. The alphabetic order of the items is for the purpose of aiding in the decoding process. However, if a new item were added, it would be assigned the next sequential number. Thus if "Allen, James" joined the company, he would be assigned the next available number, and the effectiveness of the alphabet sequence would be diminished.

The advantage of the simple sequence is that it lets one code a large number of items with the least number of code digits. Its principal disadvantage is the limited amount of information it can convey. However, the simple sequence code often is used as a component of more complex codes.

Block Sequence Code

This code is a modification of the sequence code that makes possible a more homogeneous collection of related items. In a *block sequence code,* a series of consecutive numbers and/or letters is divided into blocks, each one reserved for identifying a group of items with a common characteristic.

As in the simple sequence code, a list is prepared of items to be coded. The difference is that, in assigning the codes, "blocks" of sequence numbers are set aside for items with some common characteristics. As an example, the simple sequence codes assigned to employees in figure 5.13 could be changed to a block sequence code in which the common characteristic of the items in a block is the first letter of the employee's last name. As shown in the first part of figure 5.14, a "block" of numbers (1-9) is assigned to the A's, another block of numbers (10-19) assigned to the B's, and so on. With this block code we can add new employees and assign them a code from their alphabetic block. Although we cannot maintain the original alphabetic sequence, we can keep the employees grouped by the first letter of their last name.

A common use of the block sequence code is shown in the second part of figure 5.14. In this example of a furniture inventory, blocks of code numbers are assigned by basic characteristics—in this case, the material used in the furniture's construction.

Note that, in this example, we could have used the type of chair as the major characteristic just as easily as the construction material. Table chairs could have been assigned numbers 1–10; folding chairs, numbers 11–19; rocking chairs, numbers 20–29; and so on. The characteristics the analyst should select are those that are most meaningful to the users of the code.

Like the simple sequence code, the block sequence code often appears as part of more complex codes.

Group Classification Code

Another common code type, the *group classification code,* designates major, intermediate, and minor data classification by successively lower orders of digits. This code type is useful when the item or information to be coded can be broken down into subclassifications or subdivisions. The ZIP code is a familiar example of a group classification code. For example, the U.S. Postal Service has recently modified the ZIP code to one called the ZIP + 4. The ZIP + 4 code 91791-0344 relates to major through minor classifications as follows:

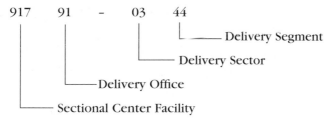

The code provides for 1,000 (000–999) Sectional Center Facility (SCF) numbers. This number identifies a relatively large geographic area. The lowest numbers are on the East Coast and the largest numbers are in the West. The next two digits identify one of 100 (0–99) delivery offices within the SCF. The four digits to the right of the hyphen represent the expansion of the original ZIP code to the ZIP + 4 code. The delivery sector identifies an area within the delivery office. This area can be several blocks, a group of streets or large buildings, or a small geographic area. The delivery segment divides the delivery sector into even smaller areas. A segment can be one side of a city block or both sides of a particular street, one floor in a large building, a cluster of mail boxes, one post office box or a group of boxes, or other similar limited geographic locations. Each element of the code is a sequence code. Code directories are available for the interpretation of each code including a national directory stored on magnetic tape to assist businesses in changing to the ZIP + 4 system.

In another example, shown in figure 5.15, the primary objective is to uniquely identify a salesperson within a large department store chain. In addition to the identification of the individual, we want to be able to determine the store and the department where the salesperson works. The highest level of classification is the store, and so the store number becomes the "major" classification. The second subdivision is the department within the identified store; the department number becomes an "intermediate" classification. The number of the employee within an identified department is the "minor" classification. We form the group classification code by combining the numbers of the major, intermediate, and minor classifications. In

■ Figure 5.15 Group classification code. Group classification codes designate major, intermediate, and minor data classifications by successively lower orders of digits. In this example, the salesperson group (minor) is within the department group (intermediate), which is within the store group (major).

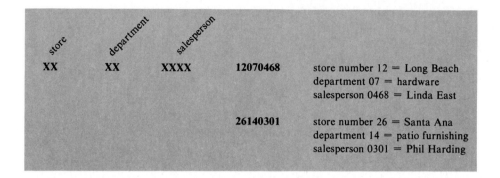

this example of a code, each salesperson has a unique identification number. Furthermore, we have coded additional valuable data about the workstation of the employee.

Note that the store, department, and salesperson numbers are probably simple sequence or block sequence codes. The code is called a group classification code, however, since the dominant part of the code plan is the use of major, intermediate, and minor classifications.

Significant Digit Code

A third common code is the *significant digit code,* a numeric code in which the numbers describe a measurable physical characteristic of the item. The characteristic may be weight, size, length, capacity, time, or any other physically measurable attribute that is part of the code plan. Figure 5.16 gives as an example the code plan for tire size. It has three elements: the tire profile, the ratio of the tire height to its width, and its rim size. This code describes two of the elements as significant digits. These are "ratio of tire height to width" and "rim size." The tire profile is indicated by a letter rather than the actual numerical measurement. A dictionary is required to interpret the profile. As in this example, it is not unusual to see a mix of code types. However, in this case, the tire code is predominantly a significant digit code.

Significant digit codes and group classification codes are often confused with one another. Remember: In a significant digit code, the digits are a measurement of one or more physical characteristics.

Alphanumeric Codes

A fourth common type of code is the *alphanumeric code,* which describes items by the use of letter and number combinations. There are two categories of alphanumeric codes: mnemonic codes and alphabetic derivation codes.

■ Figure 5.16 Significant digit code. Significant digit codes are numeric codes in which the numbers describe a measurable physical characteristic of the item. In this example, the physically measurable attributes are the ratio of tire height to its width and rim size.

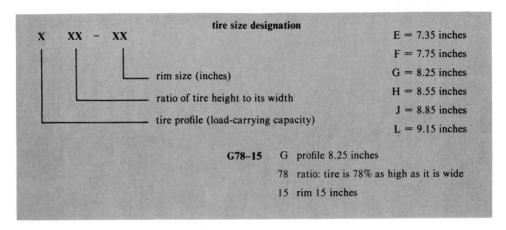

■ Figure 5.17 Mnemonic codes. Mnemonic codes are letter and number combinations obtained from descriptions of the coded item. A mnemonic is a memory aid, or reminder, of the name or description of an item.

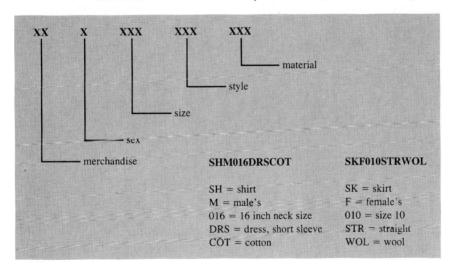

Mnemonic Codes

Mnemonic codes are letter and number combinations obtained from descriptions of the coded item. A mnemonic, or memory aid, is a reminder of the name or description of an item. Often it is a severe abbreviation of the item's name. Figure 5.17 shows two examples of mnemonic merchandise codes. With a little experience, most people using the code can decode it without reference to a dictionary.

■ Figure 5.18   Alphabetic derivation code. Alphabetic derivation codes are made up of characters taken or derived from the name or description of the coded item according to a set of rules. A very common use of this code type is to identify subscribers of magazines.

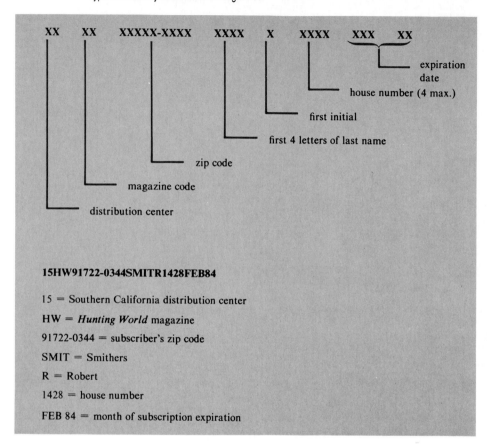

15HW91722-0344SMITR1428FEB84

15 = Southern California distribution center

HW = *Hunting World* magazine

91722-0344 = subscriber's zip code

SMIT = Smithers

R = Robert

1428 = house number

FEB 84 = month of subscription expiration

Alphabetic Derivation Codes

These codes are characters taken or derived from the name or description of the coded item according to a set of rules. *Alphabetic derivation codes* are used to handle large volume lists that must be maintained and processed in sequence. These codes are used because it is not practical to encode and decode full descriptions or numeric codes. Figure 5.18 is an example of a magazine subscriber's code. The code not only uniquely identifies the subscriber but also provides information about the distribution center, the ZIP code, the magazine's name, and the expiration date of the subscription. Mailing labels can be printed in ZIP code sequence within the distribution center for ease of handling for shipment. Renewal notices can be sent within selected time periods based on the subscription's expiration date. The magazine name may identify special interests of the subscriber to which direct mail advertisers can appeal.

There are other forms of alphabetic derivation codes. These are based on relatively elaborate sets of rules for the use of consonants and phonetic characteristics of the item to be coded.

Often, an analyst may encounter or elect to develop codes that are combinations of the four basic types of codes. These may be predominantly a single type of code or a combination of several types. However, the analyst should be able to identify the underlying code types. As an example, the account-number code in figure 5.11 is a combination of a simple sequence code, used to identify a region, and an alphanumeric code, used to identify a customer account within a region. The alphanumeric code is made up of both a two-character, alphabetically derived code (in this case AZ, for Arizona) and a four-digit simple sequence code. For these reasons the analyst decided to describe the six-digit sequence component of the entire code as an alphanumeric-sequence code.

Process Specification

From a process viewpoint, data flow diagrams can be viewed as networks of processes in which data travel from one process to another through data streams. Also, as you have learned, the decomposition of data flow diagrams leads to the preparation of sets of leveled DFDs. In order to proceed with the design and development of the computer information system, the analyst must specify the functions performed by each primitive in the set of leveled DFDs.

It is appropriate to write a narrative description of processes at any level. However, a specification that is more precise than a narrative alone is required for the primitive processes. This specification is called a **process specification,** and it is one in which the rules by which processes transform input data flows into output data flows must be stated without any possibility of misunderstanding or ambiguity. Among the tools most suitable for this purpose are decision tables, decision trees, and structured English.

Decision Tables

Decision tables are a tabular technique for describing logical rules. Most people tend to associate decision tables with the logic of computer programs. However, decision tables also are an important tool of the systems analyst because they are an effective means of expressing the logic of administrative rules and procedures. The first part of figure 5.19 depicts the basic format of a decision table. The table has four parts:

1. Condition stub—lists all conditions to be considered
2. Condition entries—make up the rules to be followed
3. Action entries—point to actions that may be taken
4. Action stub—identifies the action to be followed

The decision table is read in the direction indicated by the heavy line and arrowheads. The condition stub is read as an "if" statement, and the action stub is read as a "then" statement. These statements are connected by a rule, which is a combination of the condition entry, usually indicated by a Y(yes) or an N(no), and the action pointed to, usually indicated by X.

■ Figure 5.19   Decision tables. Decision tables are a tabular technique for describing logical rules. They may be used in both manual and automated systems. This example describes the rules for cashing a customer's check at a retail store.

basic format

check cashing policy		1	2	3	4
conditions	valid store identification card	Y	N	N	N
	purchase > $20.00		N	N	Y
	two other identifications		Y	N	
actions	allow purchase + $25.00	X			
	allow purchase amount		X		
	call store manager			X	X

example: check cashing policy

We will use a simple example to exhibit the use of a decision table to condense and display systems logic. Consider the following check-cashing policy in a supermarket:

If the customer has a valid store identification card, a check may be cashed for the amount of the purchase plus $25.00. If a customer does not have a valid credit card but can show two other identifications, a check may be cashed for the amount of the purchase, not to exceed $20.00. Otherwise, the store manager must be called to authorize the acceptance of the check.

The "check-cashing policy" decision table appears in the second part of figure 5.19. A typical rule reads: "If a customer does not have a valid credit card, and if the purchase is not greater than $20.00, and if the customer has two identifications, then allow acceptance of the check for the amount of the purchase." Note that, in order to avoid redundancies, it is not necessary to fill in all the spaces in the condition entry section with *Y*s and *N*s. In rule 4, for example, if the amount of the purchase is greater than $20.00, the store policy is that the manager must approve the customer's check if the customer does not have a valid card. Therefore, it would not be necessary to include a *Y* or *N* entry corresponding to the condition stub "two identifications."

Systems analysts often use decision tables as a means of communicating the systems logic, embedded in policies and procedures, to the programmer. When this type of logic is made available, the programmer is able to do a more effective job of developing the detailed computer program logic. Decision tables, then, are a technique that is useful in eliminating one of the major pitfalls that has impeded past efforts to develop effective computer-based business systems. This is the pitfall of forcing programmers, through default, to develop logical rules that may not reflect the true procedure that the computer program is intended to implement.

A decision tree. The branches of a decision tree form a network that represents the logical rules by which a number of conditions are related. Lower-level relationships are nested within higher-level relationships.

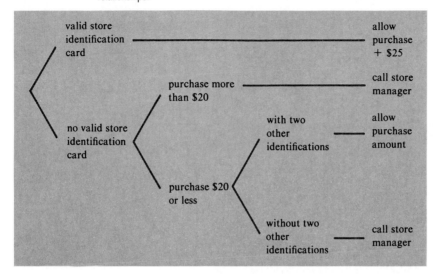

In summary, the decision table has the following major values for the systems analyst:

1. The structure of the table lends itself to a concise and correct statement of decision logic.
2. The table is an effective means of communicating with the computer programmer because it is easily understood.

These examples are only an introduction to the uses of tables. We have encountered and will continue to encounter many kinds of tables in this text. What must be emphasized here is the value of tables as powerful tools for collecting, analyzing, and reporting relationships among data.

Decision Trees

A **decision tree** is a network-type chart that is equivalent to a decision table. Like a decision table, it describes logical rules, showing all of the actions that result from various combinations of conditions. Figure 5.20 shows how network branches are drawn to handle combinations of conditions. This particular network is the logical equivalent of the decision table of figure 5.19.

A decision tree is less compact than a decision table and, in some cases, may be less suitable for presenting complex branching relationships. However, a decision tree provides a very easily understood picture since the branches can be read to show how all of the major and minor logical components go together. Like decision tables, decision trees can represent both system and computer program logical relationships.

An example of structured English. Structured English uses standard logical terms, such as IF, THEN, and ELSE. It also follows rules, such as successive levels of indentation, for expressing logical relationships.

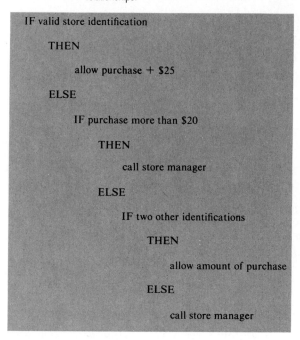

IF valid store identification

    THEN

        allow purchase + $25

    ELSE

        IF purchase more than $20

            THEN

                call store manager

            ELSE

                IF two other identifications

                    THEN

                        allow amount of purchase

                    ELSE

                        call store manager

Structured English

Decision tables also lend themselves to the use of **structured English,** which is a method for displaying logical processes in an outline format. The "structure" of structured English results from the use of an accepted structured-design terminology for describing the logical operations that computers can perform and from the manner in which the logic is expressed. Figure 5.21 presents the structured English equivalent to the decision tree of figure 5.20. Although structured English, in this instance, describes systems-level logic, this "pseudo language" technique also is used to describe the logic of computer programs. When this is done, the logic is said to be written in *pseudocode,* since it is a "pseudo-programming language." Pseudocode often is used as an alternative to computer program flowcharts.

The creation of process specifications marks the transition from the study phase to the design phase, and subsequently, to the preparation of computer programs, which occurs in the development phase. As we proceed in this text, you will become familiar with other process specification tools, such as structure charts and system flowcharts, that can assist with the detailed design phase activities that are required to produce a complete design specification.

Summary

The structured method for system analysis and design emphasizes the determination of "what" has to be done before a commitment is made about "how" it will be done. The structured method has three essential documentation needs:

1. Descriptions of the relationships between data and the processes that transform data.
2. Definitions of all data structures.
3. Specifications for all essential transformation processes.

Data flow diagrams satisfy the first documentation need. A data dictionary, which is prepared to accompany the data flow diagram, meets the second need, and process specifications, which are derived from decomposed data flow diagrams, meet the third.

A data flow diagram (DFD) is a network that describes the flow of data throughout a system, data stores, and the processes that change, or transform, data flows. The symbols selected to represent data flow diagrams do not imply a specific physical form, hence DFDs are used to prepare logical abstracts of current physical systems and logical models for new systems. Thereafter, alternative physical systems that meet the new logical requirements can be evaluated.

Because data flow diagrams for all but the most simple systems would become very complex, there is a need to simplify them so they can be understood and worked with within human limitations. This is accomplished by decomposition, which is a process for expanding a high-level data flow diagram into a hierarchy of lower-level data flow diagrams. The preparation and decomposition of data flow diagrams adheres to the following procedures:

1. A context diagram is drawn. This diagram shows the domain of the system and its net input and output data flows.
2. A level-0 DFD is drawn. This network shows the principal data flows, data store, and data transformations.
3. Lower-level DFDs (i.e., level-1, level-2, etc.) are drawn.
4. The decomposition process is continued until a bottom set of DFDs is arrived at for each processing node.

The bottom set is called the set of leveled DFDs, and the process bubbles in this set are called primitives. It is the level at which the analyst must describe clearly and unambiguously the meaning, origin, and use of each data flow and data store.

A data dictionary is prepared to accompany the data flow diagrams for a system. It is a central repository that contains the descriptions and definitions of all of the system data structures (i.e., data elements, data flows, and data stores). The data dictionary also should contain specifications for the functions performed by each process shown on the leveled set of DFDs. Because of the volume of information that must be stored, data dictionaries quickly become complex and difficult to maintain for all but the smallest computer information systems. Fortunately, automated aids for preparing and maintaining data dictionaries have become available.

Important terms used in association with data structures and data dictionary entries are entity and attribute. The former refers to any object about which data are stored, and the latter refers to any property that describes an entity.

Entity-relationship diagrams are predefined symbols to identify entities and the relationships among them. They aid the systems analyst to develop data dictionary entries.

Codes are important tools used by systems analysts to identify entities. They are based upon a code plan which leads to the selection of the most appropriate type of code. The four most common types of codes are: sequence, group classification, significant digit, and alphanumeric.

The rules by which a process transforms input data flows into output data flows are called process specifications, and one is required for each primitive process that is part of the set of leveled DFDs. The process specification is an essential systems development life cycle link between the study phase and the design and development phases. Tools that are of value in developing process specifications include decision tables, decision trees, and structured English.

Decision tables and decision trees are methods for describing logical rules, showing actions that result from combinations of conditions. Structured English is a method for presenting the same logical relationships in an outline format. It is a structured design tool.

For Review

performance specification
data flow diagram (DFD)
transformation process
data flow
data storage
file
entity-relationship diagram
external entity
source
destination
partition
decomposition
domain
context diagram
parent-child
set of leveled DFDs
primitive
data element

data structure
data dictionary
process specification
decision table
structured English
entity
identification code
simple sequence code
group classification code
alphanumeric code
alphabetic derivation code
decision tree
psuedocode
attribute
code plan
block sequence code
significant digit code
mnemonic code

For Discussion

1. What is a data flow diagram, and what types of symbols are used to construct one?
2. What is the meaning of the concept of separating the "what" from the "how?" How do data flow diagrams relate to this concept?
3. Which, if any, of the following statements are true? Explain your answers.
   a. Data flow diagrams are used to construct a logical model of a current system.
   b. Data flow diagrams are used to construct a logical model of a new system.
   c. Data flow diagrams are a logical abstract of a physical system.
4. Identify and describe the three items that are essential to the documentation of computer information systems.
5. In what manner do data flow diagrams relate to each of the three essential documentation items?
6. What is decomposition? Why is it necessary to decompose data flow diagrams?
7. What is the purpose of a context diagram?
8. Distinguish between a context diagram, a level-0 DFD, a level-1 DFD, a set of leveled DFDs, and a primitive.
9. How many levels of decomposition are necessary? Explain your answer.
10. Define and distingush between a data element, a data store, and a data structure.
11. What is a data dictionary? What is its relationship to a data flow diagram?
12. What elements should a data dictionary contain? What comments might be appropriate?
13. What is a process specification and why is it needed?
14. At what level of decomposition are process specifications prepared? Why?
15. Why is it often necessary to consider automating a data dictionary?
16. Define the terms "entity" and "attribute," and relate these to data dictionary entries.
17. What is an entity-relationship diagram, and how is it used? Give an example.
18. What considerations affect the development of a code plan?
19. Describe, including an example of each, the four types of identification codes. Why are many codes combinations of these basic types?

For Exercise

For Exercise 1: Data Flow Diagram Representation of the Systems Development Life Cycle

Using the appropriate symbols, prepare a level-1 data flow diagram representation of the systems development life cycle. Refer to figure 1.6 in chapter 1. The principal transformations are:

study the problem

design the system

develop the system

operate the system

Refer to the baseline documents described in chapter 2 to identify the principal data flows. Include the project management reviews in your DFD.

Compare the data flow diagram you have constructed with figure 1.6. Briefly describe the similarities and differences in the information conveyed to a user.

For Exercise 2: Understanding Codes

Obtain and describe in writing examples of the four basic types of codes, and for each:

a. Describe the purpose of the code.
b. Explain and identify (by code type) each element of the code.
c. Name the type of code that best describes the overall code.

Chapter

6

■ ■ ■

Computer-
Assisted
Systems
Engineering
(CASE)

Preview

Computer-assisted systems engineering (CASE) products are receiving increasing attention as a means of automating the systems development life cycle. CASE is based upon the application of engineering principles to the development of computer information systems. CASE has been made possible by the emergence of structured techniques for systems analysis and design; the development of nonprocedural languages; and the widespread distribution of computer power to microcomputer workstations, linked by communication networks to mainframe data bases. Full-function CASE workbenches include tools for diagramming, error checking, maintaining a central repository, code generation, and prototyping.

Objectives

1. You will be able to explain why we define CASE to be computer-assisted systems engineering.
2. You will be able to describe the developments that made CASE feasible.
3. You will be able to explain the importance of extensive user involvement in the SDLC.
4. You will be able to distinguish between upper, lower, and full-function CASE workbenches.
5. You will be able to identify the basic CASE tools and to describe their significant attributes.
6. You will be able to describe the effect of CASE on the SDLC and its significance in relation to the computer-integrated enterprise.
7. You will be able to describe and compare the process-oriented, data-oriented, and object-oriented models for developing computer information systems.

Key Terms

computer-assisted systems engineering (CASE) an engineering approach toward automating all phases of the systems development life cycle methodology.

workbench an integrated assembly of CASE tools.

upper CASE workbenches integrated assemblies of tools that apply to the analysis and design phases of the SDLC.

lower CASE workbenches integrated assemblies of tools that apply to the development and operation phases of the SDLC.

full-function CASE workbenches integrated assemblies of tools that apply to all phases of the SDLC.

Pathways to CASE

Search for Productivity and Quality

The search for improved productivity and quality in the products developed by information service organizations has been continuous since the mid-1960s, when the business uses of computers were initiated. Yet today's reality in most corporations is that the backlog of new applications is growing, delivery times are increasing, budgets are overspent, and overall quality is poor. In the first chapter of this text, we emphasized the magnitude of the productivity challenge and the dependence of our economy upon increasingly complex computer-based business information systems. The chapter identified a methodology, called **computer-assisted systems engineering (CASE)** that had great potential for improving the information system design and development process. We defined CASE to be an engineering approach toward automating all phases of the systems development life cycle (SDLC) methodology. Because CASE is a means of using software to develop software, a common definition of CASE is computer-assisted (or aided) software engineering. However, full-function CASE products include many elements that relate to the entire computer information system, not just the software end-product.

Examples are project management, program reviews, and training media. Hence, as do many others, we prefer to refer to CASE as computer-assisted systems engineering. CASE products are steadily increasing in capability and number. As shown in figure 6.1, the major factors contributing to the emergence of these products are those that enhance the interactions between analysts and users. Four such factors are: (1) hardware and software developments, particularly in microcomputers and local area networks, leading to the distribution of computer power to users; (2) increasing user involvement in all phases of the SDLC; (3) the development of nonprocedural languages; and (4) the introduction of structured and related methodologies for systems analysis and design.

Hardware and Software Developments

Microcomputers
Few persons could have anticipated that, in the period between their introduction in the mid-1970s and the present, advances in the performance of microcomputers would, in many cases, outstrip those in mini and mainframe computers. Hundredfold increases in the power of microcomputers and their distribution to millions of desktops forever changed the relationships between the conventional centralized information services organizations and their user/customers. As measured by speed and storage capacity, the microcomputers of today have processing capabilities that rival the mainframes of a few years ago, and they have made inroads into the market for

Factors contributing to the emergence of CASE products. This figure identifies the major technology-dependent events that have contributed to the development of CASE tools and techniques.

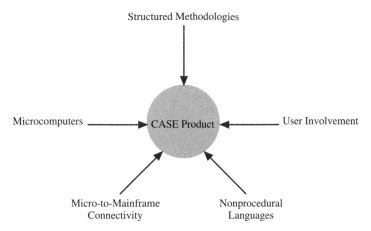

minicomputers. Even more powerful workstations are on the near horizon. They will greatly enhance user-computer interaction and improve upon already available desktop capabilities that include:

1. The power to perform many computations formerly within the domain of larger computers.
2. *Multitasking,* which is the ability to run multiple applications and to serve many users concurrently.
3. High-capacity internal memories and external storage devices.
4. Displays designed for high-resolution graphics.
5. Power to support multiple users, working concurrently.

Micro-to-Mainframe Link

Performance improvements in microcomputers, such as those listed above, now make it possible to meet the needs of information system users who require on-line access to centrally maintained corporate data bases. Consequently, a major thrust in the computer industry is for improved connectivity not only within a single vendor's product line, but also between the products of different vendors.

Local area networks, called *LAN,* exist at several levels within organizations. Typically, there is a "backbone" corporate network with both external and internal communication links. Internally, several levels of LAN are linked to service departmental and individual needs. Figure 6.2 is an example of a department-level network within a corporate environment.

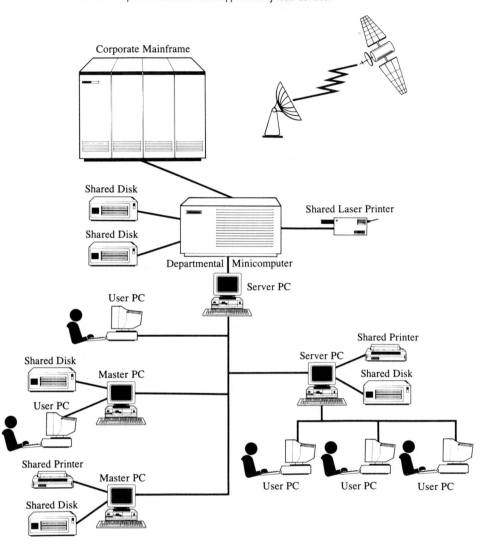

Standards for data communications and connectivity are continuing to evolve. Many of these are designed to support the use of personal computers as elements of information system networks. Important information system uses of personal computers include the following:

1. To emulate terminals in order to utilize the storage capabilities of a large computer system and to share data.
2. To process on-line transactions, with the capability to collect and transmit data to a mainframe computer for further processing.
3. To process department-level data that are down loaded from a mainframe computer.
4. To share messages, mail, programs, data files, and peripheral devices as part of a corporate communications network.
5. To develop and test new programs without dependence on a central-site computer, which reduces mainframe workload and makes possible downsizing.

As a consequence of the above developments, both microcomputer and mainframe versions are being developed for many CASE products. There will be many opportunities for users and information system professionals to improve their productivity as they work, jointly, to design and develop usable computer information systems.

User Involvement in the SDLC

Emphasis in contemporary systems analysis and design is upon the role of the user. Regardless of the quality of the tools used to develop a computer information system, its evaluation depends on its usability, i.e. quality, as perceived by its principal users. The acceptance of the systems development life cycle methodology, along with the distribution of desktop computing power to users, has resulted in increased opportunities for user involvement in the SDLC process. Because it also is a technique for project management, the SDLC establishes important control points, such as the transition from one life-cycle phase to the next. When these points are reached, user/manager review and decision-making are required. Less evident, however, are the specific activities throughout the SDLC in which user participation can improve the end-product, which we call a computer information system.

Figure 6.3 identifies many activities in which direct user participation should be encouraged as an information system project progresses through the phases of the SDLC. The relative magnitudes of the information services organization and user efforts shown in this figure are more representative of goals than current practice. Fortunately, powerful information system development tools are available to facilitate user involvement and to lead toward the achievement of these goals. Also, these tools are incorporated in many CASE products. Among them are nonprocedural languages and structured methodologies for systems analysis and design. Nonprocedural languages provide a friendlier user environment than conventional programming languages that directly reflect logical steps, or procedures, that computers must follow. Nonprocedural languages include: applications generators, query languages, report generators, and fourth-generation languages (4GLs). Structured methodologies rely on powerful diagramming tools and graphics displays that help users and analysts to communicate.

■ Figure 6.3   Relative information services and user efforts throughout the SDLC. This figure identifies some significant
activities that illustrate the importance of user participation throughout the systems development life cycle.
An important and continuing systems analysis goal is to increase user participation in all phases of the
SDLC.

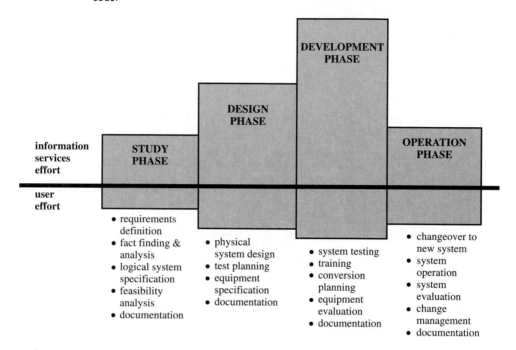

Nonprocedural Languages

Applications Generators

An *applications generator* is a type of nonprocedural command language that can be
used in conjunction with a data base to minimize programming tasks that would be
very tedious and repetitive if they were performed using a third-generation language
such as COBOL. With relatively few commands, an applications generator might generate a major percentage of the COBOL instructions required for a particular application. As an example, a typical applications generator command might read
somewhat like the following: "add 20 percent to the salaries of all faculty who teach
computer information systems." This type of statement is equivalent to a dozen or
more lines of COBOL code.

Query Languages and Report Generators

Query languages enable users to access data bases and to answer questions quickly
without having to write computer programs. Query languages components are: an
application-specific vocabulary, a utility program that creates an information retrieval

Attributes of a comprehensive fourth-generation language (4GL). The features of a 4GL are integrated into comprehensive CASE products.

attributes of a fourth-generation language (4GL)
- a data base management system, including a data dictionary
- a user-friendly query language
- a user-friendly report writer
- an interactive utility program for developing screens
- a nonprocedural language for complex applications
- software support for "what if analysis," financial modeling and statistical computations

file, and a query module that accepts and responds to user requests. Similarly, *report generators* enable users and programmers to access a data base and create reports formatted to user specifications without requiring the use of a programming language.

Fourth-Generation Languages (4GLs)

The first three computer generations are considered to have evolved from machine-oriented languages to powerful procedure-oriented languages, such as COBOL. Hence, the term *4GL* was coined to describe languages that need not conform directly to the rules and procedures for computer program coding. A 4GL differs from a query language or report generator although it incorporates features of both. The attributes of a comprehensive 4GL are shown in figure 6.4. An example of a widely used 4GL is SQL (Systems Query Language), which was developed by IBM and introduced in the mid-1980s.

Although 4GLs originally were developed for mainframe computers because of their processing and storage requirements, versions are available for microcomputers. A popular 4GL for microcomputers is dBASE IV, developed by Ashton-Tate Corporation. Oracle, developed by Oracle Corporation, is an example of a 4GL product for which there are both mainframe and microcomputer versions.

Structured Methodologies

Evolution of Structured Methodologies

For many years efforts have been underway to improve the quality of computer information systems with highly structured, graphics-based diagramming and presentation techniques. Modern structured analysis and design methods have their roots in structured programming, which, in the 1970s, introduced logically consistent rules for improving the writing, testing, and maintenance of computer programs. Structured programming is an SDLC development phase activity and, by itself, does not ensure that an adequate front-end systems analysis and design job has been performed. Subsequently, many structured methodologies were developed to improve the analysis and design processes by focusing on the "what" before attempting the "how." Most employ a top-down, hierarchical series of modules. Data flow diagrams, which we studied in the previous chapter, are an example of a widely used technique for structured analysis and design.

Specific advantages of the structured methodologies are as follows:

1. A better understanding of the system.
2. Fewer errors.
3. Ease of revision.
4. Improved delivery schedule.
5. Efficient use of hardware.
6. Improved communication between users, analysts, and managers.

Classification of Structured Methodologies

We can approach the design of a computer information system from different, but equally valid, perspectives. These perspectives, often referred to as models, are not necessarily exclusive, and they often provide useful design options. Currently, the two major design approaches are the *process-oriented model* and the *data-oriented model.* A third design approach, which builds upon the structured methodologies, is the *object-oriented model.* All require comprehensive data dictionaries such as those incorporated in powerful CASE products.

Process-Oriented Model

The process-oriented model identifies the desired outputs and describes the processing operations that must be performed on inputs in order to convert them into the desired outputs. Then, the process-supporting data requirements are determined. As we have previously described them, data flow diagrams, accompanied by hierarchical decompositions, are an example of a process-oriented model because they focus on the processes that transform data flows. In this approach, entity-relationship diagrams are a supporting tool used to develop detail descriptions of the attributes of the data structures stored in the data dictionary.

Because the process-oriented model most closely resembles traditional methods of systems analysis, it is, at present, the most popular and widely used model. This approach works best when the performance needs of a system (outputs) are relatively well known and when relationships between data elements are not particularly complex. Most conventional business systems, such as payroll, accounts payable, and customer billing, are sufficiently stable for this model to work well. The process-oriented model has several variations, named after its principal proponents. Examples are the Yourdon-Constantine-DeMarco and Gane-Sarson methodologies.

Data-Oriented Model

As contrasted with the process-oriented model, the data-oriented model focuses upon data at rest and the optimum structure of data bases. It is becoming the preferred approach to information system design under conditions of uncertainty and where input, output, and processing requirements are not well defined.

Recall that we have identified the decade of the 1990s as one that will be dominated by agile industries that are able to respond quickly to changes in competition and customer demand. In this environment, business decisions will be based on data as it is obtained, and input, processing, and output requirements will follow. This is an appropriate environment for the data-oriented model.

Development of the data-oriented model begins with the identification of the decisions to be made and, hence, requires a close working relationship between the systems analyst and users for whom the information system is intended. Entity-relationship diagrams are constructed to identify decision criteria and to record the attributes of the data structures related to those criteria. For example, if vendor past performance were a criterion, attributes might include price, date ordered, date promised, and date delivered. As another example, in a total quality management (TQM) environment, the criterion for an effective supplier-manufacturer relationship might be based on attributes such as response time and the nature and frequency of flaws in materials and components delivered.

The data structures that define these attributes are used to create data flow diagrams and the data dictionary. Subsequently, inputs, outputs, and required processing operations are derived. Examples of the data-driven approach are methodologies developed by Peter Chen, Michael Jackson, and James Martin. Information Engineering, developed by Martin, is an example of a data-oriented CASE tool.

Object-Oriented Model

The object-oriented model exhibits characteristics of both the process-oriented and data-oriented approaches. However, the goal of this approach is not to define and develop an information system to solve a single problem. Instead, the goal is to develop a library of reusable software modules, called *objects,* from which systems analysts can make selections when there is a need to create a new system. Like an entity, an object is represented by a noun and can be anything that is pertinent to the domain, or context, of an information system about which data are stored. However, an object encapsulates not only attributes, represented by data structures, but also the operations performed on data that cause a certain behavior. For example, in an accounts receivable system, "retail customer" could be an object that encapsulates both billing data and the processing operations performed on that data. This object could, then, be reused for other customers in other applications. Objects are invoked by messages that need only specify what should be done, since the how (that is, the processing operations to be performed) is already a part of the object. Objects not only respond to messages, but they also may send messages to other objects.

The concepts of *class* and *inheritance* are important in dealing with objects. A class is a group of objects that have the same structure and behave in the same way. Thus "retail customer" and "wholesale customer" could be objects that comprise the class "customer." Inheritance pertains to a hierarchy of classes that share attributes and operations. For example, the subclasses "customer-domestic" and "customer-foreign" could inherit operations and attributes from the superclass "customer," and, like most subclasses, they could add attributes of their own. In this case, common attributes might be "customer name," "customer number," and "customer address." An added or modified attribute might be a field called "ZIP code," which would pertain to domestic customers only.

All three of the methodologies that we have described are consistent with the SDLC and may be used in conjunction with techniques such as prototyping for rapid applications development. Like the process-oriented and data-oriented approaches that depend upon top-down decomposition to generate a leveled set of data flow diagrams and process specifications, object-oriented design may also be considered to be a top-down process the first time that the classes of objects are created. However, as contrasted with the other two approaches, the object-oriented approach thereafter becomes a "bottom-up" process in which reusable components are assembled to create a whole. In the object-oriented universe, the object-oriented design (OOD), created in the design phase, specifies the functions to be performed by the reusable computer program code generated by an object-oriented programming (OOP) language in the development phase.

In summary, the ongoing evolution from a process-oriented to an object-oriented approach to systems analysis is driven by and consistent with the need to speed up the design and development of information systems so that they can better meet the quick response needs of agile, competitive industries.

CASE Products

Tools and Workbenches

For all except small systems, the structured techniques frequently lead to humanly unmanageable levels of complexity. Complex data flow diagrams, data base descriptions, and hierarchical charts and structure diagrams cannot effectively be handled by manual methods. This situation gave impetus to efforts to develop CASE products. Most of the system development tools and structured methodologies described above are parts of one or more CASE products. These products range from single, stand-alone tools that automate a specific SDLC task to integrated software environments designed to cover the complete life-cycle process. An integrated assembly of CASE tools is called a CASE system, or **workbench.** The term *tool kit* often is used to describe a collection of CASE tools. CASE workbenches go beyond fourth-generation, nonprocedural languages in two significant respects. First, they store all information about a system, not just its data base, in a central repository where it can be accessed and shared. Second, the final product is a usable and fully documented computer information system.

■ Figure 6.5   Upper CASE tools focus on analysis and design, resulting in a set of design specifications. Prototyping is a useful preliminary and detailed design tool. Lower CASE products convert a detailed design specification into usable computer programs. 4GLs interface with the central repository to generate program source code.

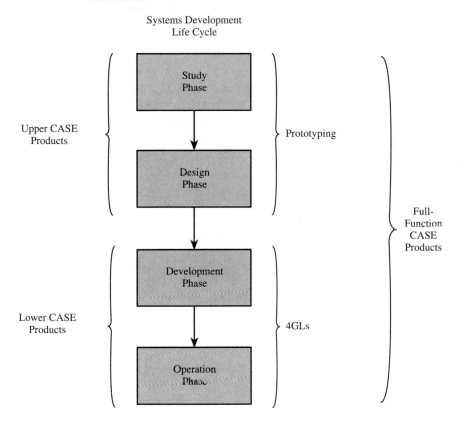

Categories of CASE Products

At present there are three major categories of CASE workbenches, distinguished by the phases of the systems development life cycle to which they are applied. These distinctions are shown in figure 6.5, which also relates prototyping tools and 4GLs to the SDLC. The categories are as follows:

1. **Upper CASE workbenches** are integrated assemblies of tools that apply to the analysis and design phases of the SDLC. They are used to identify computer information system requirements and to develop a complete set of design specifications. Upper CASE products also are referred to as *front-end* systems, and the largest number of CASE products are of this type. Prototyping is an example of a tool that is supported by upper CASE products.

2. **Lower CASE workbenches** are integrated assemblies of tools that apply to the development and operation phases of the SDLC. They are used to convert detailed design specifications to complete computer programs. Additionally they assist in maintaining the computer information system after it becomes operational and in responding to change. Lower CASE products also are referred to as *back-end* systems. Typically, 4GLs are among the tools supported by CASE products of this type.

3. **Full-function CASE workbenches** are integrated assemblies of tools that apply to all phases of the SDLC. Also referred to as *integrated CASE (ICASE)* systems, these workbenches combine the attributes of both upper and lower CASE products. Although full-function CASE systems are complex and expensive, some systems of this type have been developed, and more are becoming available.

Two other types of CASE workbenches are *redevelopment-engineering CASE workbenches* and *real-time system CASE workbenches.* Redevelopment engineering is used to analyze operational systems and to redevelop their specifications in structured form. This is an area of great importance if the use of CASE tools is to become widely adopted, because most corporations have a large number of poorly documented computer applications. More often than not, these have been developed without the benefit of structured methods, and they are the operational systems that must be improved before CASE techniques can be applied elsewhere. The two principal forms of redevelopment engineering are reverse engineering and reengineering, and these are described in chapter 19, which deals with the operation phase of the SDLC.

Real-time system CASE workbenches are used to design and develop systems that must respond to external inputs in a time-sensitive manner. Often these are referred to as *event-driven* systems. Examples are manufacturing process control systems, aircraft guidance and control systems, and surveillance and activity reporting systems. Real-time information systems span both the computer information system and engineering control system fields. The dynamics of real-time systems adds an additional level of complexity to their design and development.

An example of a full-function CASE product is an announced IBM applications development architecture called *AD/Cycle.* Four important goals of AD/Cycle are:

1. To provide a software development management methodology that ensures a quality product.
2. To reduce the long lead times associated with computer applications development.
3. To reduce the time and effort required to maintain the application after its development.
4. By coordinating and controlling the flow of information among many applications and users groups, to implement the enterprise model required for the effective sharing of data.

Accordingly, AD/Cycle provides a framework for an integrated set of applications development tools. At the front end of the SDLC these tools focus on enterprise modeling and analysis and design. An enterprise modeling capability enables business

■ Figure 6.6 A full-function CASE product contains five basic tools. Among these is a central repository, which is the hub about which all CASE functions revolve.

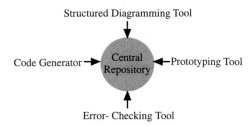

professionals working in areas such as payroll, order entry, inventory management, and production planning to participate, early in the SDLC, in the specification and development of a prototype for a system that meets their requirements.

AD/Cycle will use IBM and other-vendor-supplied tools to support both front-end and system development activities, including coding and testing. To achieve the goals set for AD/Cycle, IBM has entered into relationships with leading CASE product developers, including Index Technology Corporation, KnowledgeWare, Inc., and Bachman Information Systems, who will supply both basic and advanced components for CASE systems.

Components of CASE Products

Basic CASE Tools

The basic tools that must be integrated into a full-function CASE system are shown in figure 6.6. They are as follows:

1. A *structured diagramming tool* that enables analysts to create, verify, and modify system analysis and design diagrams in an interactive mode. Clear and explicit graphical representations are a necessity, as they are invaluable for documentation and for considering various design alternatives. Examples of essential diagrams are data flow diagrams, data model diagrams, and tree structure diagrams. High-quality graphics greatly enhance communication between analysts and users and are an effective means for involving users in the project.

2. An *error-checking tool,* which is needed because, without detection, errors can greatly increase development costs and cause unwelcome surprises when the system enters the operation phase. Flaws and omissions must be identified and corrected as they occur throughout the SDLC, without being allowed to propagate throughout the computer information system. Examples of error checking are: data flow diagram completeness and consistency checking, among and across levels; functional decomposition checking of hierarchical tree structures; and syntax checking to ensure that diagramming rules are not violated.

3. *A central repository* that is the very core of the workbench. The repository stores all of the information related to the computer information system, including the data base. It includes a comprehensive data and process specification dictionary. Also, the repository must contain all of the tools needed to manage the information system project and to maintain the developed system. It is the means by which the integrity of the system is preserved; thus automatic change analysis and control must be included. With an import-export capability, the central repository is able to interface with dictionaries and data bases external to the system. For good reason, the central repository is referred to as an *encyclopedia* in some CASE methodologies.

4. *A computer program code generator* to create applications software directly from the detailed design specification. Object code can be created for programming languages, such as COBOL, by application generators included in CASE workbenches. Not only the program but also its complete documentation can be generated. Code generators are available for both mainframe and microcomputer environments.

5. *A prototyping tool* to stimulate the emerging system and to answer "what if" questions. Prototyping, sometimes referred to as *rapid prototyping* because the prototyping process involves many rapidly performed iterations, is an important technique for speeding up the analysis and design phase activities. Prototyping makes use of tools such as screen painters, report generators, forms designers, and menu builders to communicate with users in a friendly environment. Prototyping is primarily an analysis and design phase tool. However, in some instances, with the use of an application generator and through successively detailed iterations, the information system model can evolve into the actual system.

Advanced CASE tools

The CASE technologies are relatively new, and much progress remains to be made in truly integrating collections of tools into "seamless" products. This is an important focal point for the near future. In addition to redevelopment engineering capabilities, advanced CASE environments will include tools that provide extensive project management and expert system capabilities. Needed project management features include: the ability to schedule in hourly, daily, or weekly intervals; critical path analysis; cost and performance integration; cost and budget reporting; contract management; and "what if" analyses for situations beyond problem context.

Expert systems, sometimes referred to as *knowledge-based systems,* are systems that can diagnose problems and propose solutions. These systems are becoming elements of computer information systems. Expert systems access special data bases that enable them to act as consultants in specific areas of knowledge. For example, prototyping environments that now focus on system externals such as screens and reports will evolve to accommodate models based upon interviews with user "experts" who are familiar with the functions to be performed by the system. Prototypes based on interviews with experts are called *functional prototypes.* Beyond expert systems, there are potential applications of ongoing research in fields such as artificial intelligence and natural language processors.

■ Evolution of software technology. The trend in software aids for the design and development of computer information systems shows a transition from programmer-oriented tools to increasing use of higher-level languages and user-friendly tools. The latter are the tools that will be embedded in the full-function CASE products that will support the computer-integrated enterprises of the future.

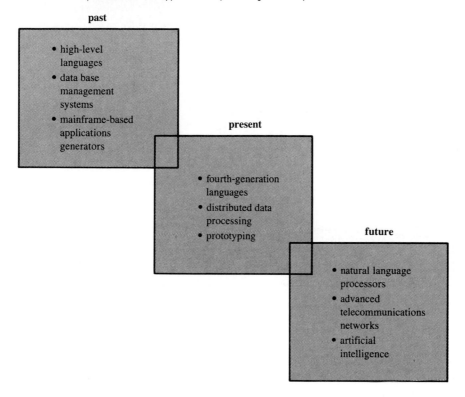

Figure 6.7 displays the evolution of software technology, from high-level programming languages to artificial intelligence, which goes beyond expert systems as we now know them. Even though labeled "past," "present," and "future," all of these have current uses in the design of business information systems. However, the trend is toward increased use of the leading edge tools, which will usher in the era of the computer-integrated enterprise.

CASE and the SDLC

The trends shown in figure 6.8 illustrate the effect that structured techniques and CASE products have had on the systems development life cycle. The phases that make up the SDLC have not changed, however the distribution of effort among them has changed dramatically, with much more of the effort taking place at the front end of the cycle. The result of this front-end investment is systems that can be developed more quickly and for less cost. Although this figure does not display the operation phase, a major benefit is the creation of more reliable and more easily maintained information systems than were possible with traditional information system design and development techniques.

■ **Figure 6.8**   The effect of CASE on the SDLC. The introduction of structured and CASE techniques has shifted the major life-cycle effort away from the development phase, in which coding and testing occur, to the front-end life-cycle phases. The most significant shift is the increase in study phase effort, which reduces development time and cost and produces a more usable system.

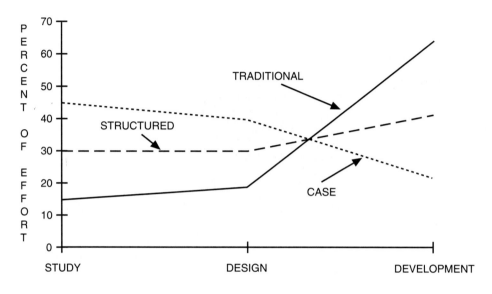

EFFECT OF CASE ON SDLC

SYSTEMS DEVELOPMENT LIFE CYCLE

Summary

Computer-assisted systems engineering (CASE) tools, although relatively new, are receiving increasing attention as methodologies for improving the productivity of information system developers and the quality of the software that they produce. Factors contributing to the emergence of CASE products have been and will continue to be the following:

1. Hardware and software developments, particularly the distribution of processing power to microcomputer workstations supported by multilevel local area networks.
2. Increasing opportunities for user involvement in all phases of the SDLC as a result of a more friendly, graphics-oriented environment.
3. Development of powerful nonprocedural languages to minimize time-consuming programming tasks and to automate the generation of computer program code.
4. Introduction of structured methodologies for the top-down, orderly implementation of the analysis and design phases of the SDLC. Selected methodologies allow analysts to view a computer information system as process-driven or data-driven.

The principal types of nonprocedural languages are applications generators, query languages, report generators, and fourth-generation languages, called 4GLs. All are data base oriented, with 4GLs having the most comprehensive attributes and capabilities.

CASE-based methodologies support products called workbenches, or tool kits, and they consist of integrated sets of specialized tools. These products are classified as upper CASE, lower CASE, or full-function CASE, depending upon the phases of the SDLC that they support. Upper CASE workbenches support the analysis and design phases, and lower CASE workbenches support the development and operation phases. Full-function CASE workbenches support the entire SDLC. They are broader in scope and content than 4GLs because they store all information about a system, not just a data base, in a central repository. These workbenches provide support for process-oriented, data-oriented, object-oriented, and event-driven methodologies for systems analysis, design, and development.

In addition to a repository, a full-function CASE system must provide: (1) a structured diagramming tool, (2) an error-checking tool, (3) a computer program code generator, and (4) a prototyping tool. Advances in CASE technology will allow CASE systems to incorporate features such as redevelopment engineering, functional prototyping, and expert system capabilities.

CASE tools will continue to evolve, and, by shifting effort from the latter to the earlier life-cycle phases, they will make possible the development of more usable and more easily maintained computer information systems—in less time and for less cost. Hence, their contribution to the success of computer-integrated enterprises also will increase.

For Review

computer-assisted systems engineering (CASE)
CASE workbench
upper CASE workbenches
lower CASE workbenches
full-function CASE workbenches
multitasking
LAN
applications generator
query language
report generator
process-oriented model
data-oriented model
tool kit
redevelopment-engineering CASE workbench
real-time system CASE workbench
front-end CASE workbench

back-end CASE workbench
AD/Cycle
structured diagramming tool
error-checking tool
central repository
real-time system
event-driven system
object
class
inheritance
object-oriented model
computer program code generator
prototyping
rapid prototyping
expert system
knowledge-based system
functional prototype

For Discussion

1. Why do you think that CASE is described as an engineering approach to the development of computer information systems?
2. Which do you think better fits the "S" in CASE, "systems" or "software"? Why?
3. What developments made CASE possible? What is the significance of each?
4. Why is user involvement in the SDLC process important?
5. What do you feel the role of a centralized corporate information services center ought to be in implementing CASE in a distributing data processing environment?
6. What is a nonprocedural language?
7. What do application generators, query languages, report generators, and 4GLs have in common? What are their differences?
8. In what ways is a CASE workbench more comprehensive than a 4GL?
9. Is a 4GL an upper, lower, or full-function CASE tool?
10. What is prototyping? Rapid prototyping?
11. How does the prototyping version of the SDLC differ from the conventional SDLC?
12. Is prototyping considered to be an upper CASE tool? Explain.
13. Distinguish among process-oriented, data-oriented, and object-oriented models for information system analysis, design, and development. Under what circumstances would you use each?
14. Why would a CASE workbench be more complicated for a production-line control system than for an accounting system?
15. Why would a redevelopment engineering capability be a desirable feature for a CASE product?
16. Discuss the relationship between an advanced CASE product, such as AD/Cycle, and the computer-integrated enterprise.

For Exercise: Potential for CASE

With more than one hundred vendors offering CASE products, CASE is widely heralded as a panacea that promises to improve productivity in building computer information systems through a better understanding of requirements, reduction of errors, ease of revision, on-schedule delivery without cost overruns, and efficient use of staff and hardware resources. At present, however, CASE is a relatively new methodology with much of its potential for supporting the computer-integrated enterprise yet to be realized.

For exercise, respond in writing to the following questions:

1. What do you perceive to be the major obstacles to the successful implementation of CASE in a business?
2. How do you perceive these obstacles being overcome (if at all), now and in the future?

Note: You may wish to refer to current periodicals and journals, for example, publications of the Data Processing Management Association (DPMA), the Association for Computing Machinery (ACM), and the *Harvard Business Review,* as background research before answering these questions. Some considerations might be: high front-end costs, need for top management support, unrealistic expectations, staff training and readiness, users' aversion to change, and total quality management (TQM) considerations.

4

The Study Phase

The **study phase** is the first *life-cycle phase* in the process of creating a business information system, either a new system or a modification of an existing system. During the study phase a preliminary analysis is carried out in sufficient depth to permit a technical and economic evaluation of the proposed system. At the conclusion of the study phase, a decision is made whether or not to proceed with a design phase. A formal project may not be established until a design phase is initiated. However, the study phase is conducted in an organized, projectlike manner. The principal study phase activities are depicted and numbered in figure U4.1. Chapter 7, "Initial Investigation," includes activities one through three shown in this figure. Chapter 8, "System Performance Definition," is depicted by activity four, and chapter 9, "Candidate System Evaluation," by activity five. Activities six and seven are described in chapter 10, "Study Phase Report and Review." Following is a brief overview of each of the activities that comprise the study phase.

1. *User Need*

    The creation of a computer-based business information system begins with a stated *user need.* This need may be a requirement for new information or for the solution of a problem. The statement of need is a written request for information systems service, which we shall refer to as an **information service request.** The information service request may define the user's needs completely and may be sufficient for an analyst to proceed with the system design. In this case, it would be accepted as a "contract" between the sponsor and the information services organization. However, normally an **initial investigation** must be completed before a fully informed response can be made. When this is the case, the request for service is identified as a limited information service request, and a systems analyst is assigned to conduct an initial investigation.

■ Figure U4.1   Study phase activity flowchart. The principal activity sequences of the study phase are the identification of user need, documented as a project directive; system performance definition; and feasibility analysis. A study phase report is prepared and reviewed prior to proceeding with the design phase.

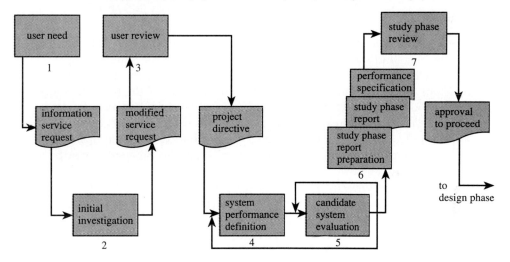

2. *Initial Investigation*

The first steps in the initial investigation are directed toward clarifying the problem and strengthening the analyst's background in the problem area. If there is an existing system that is performing some or all of the functions the new system is to perform, the analyst must study this system. After becoming familiar with the system, the analyst can investigate specific operations, particularly problem areas, in detail.

Two major activities are fact-finding and fact-analysis. Fact-finding activities include reviewing existing manuals and procedures, preparing questionnaires, and conducting personal interviews. Fact-analysis is accomplished by techniques such as data element analysis; input-output analysis, including data flow diagrams; recurring data analysis; and report use analysis. After completing the initial investigation, the systems analyst presents the results and a recommendation to the principal users of the system as a modified information service request.

3. *User Review*

The modified information service request reflects the analyst's understanding of the problem and states that person's understanding of the system's objectives. The modified request is discussed with the user-sponsor, and additional revisions are made if necessary. With the concurrence of the user, the modified information service request becomes the formal contract between the user-sponsor and the systems analyst. This contract is called a **project directive.** The project directive establishes the scope, or context, of the information system project, and it authorizes the systems analyst to proceed to complete the study phase.

4. *System Performance Definition*

System performance definition is the transition from a logical performance requirement to a physical one. The process includes the statement of general constraints, identification of specific objectives, and description of the outputs to be provided.

5. *Candidate System Evaluation*

Candidate System Evaluation is the identification of candidate systems and the selection of the most feasible. It is accomplished by evaluating alternative methods for converting available input data into the information outputs needed to meet the objectives of the system. Each of the alternative physical systems is called a *candidate system,* and each must be described uniquely.

Candidate systems are evaluated by identifying factors that significantly affect system cost and performance and by ranking each candidate in terms of these factors. Typical factors are development costs, operating costs, response time, development time, accuracy, and reliability. The candidate system evaluation is concluded by the selection of the most suitable candidate.

As shown in figure U4.1, two major *feedback* loops can occur during the study phase. The loop around the candidate system evaluation block indicates the consideration of more than one system variation, or candidate. The loop around the system performance definition block indicates that the process of selecting a feasible system could include modification of the initially desired outputs. The feasibility analysis processes are described in chapter 9, "Candidate System Evaluation."

6. *Study Phase Report Preparation*

   After the candidate system evaluation has been completed, a **study phase report** is prepared for the user-sponsor of the system. It contains a summary of the candidate system evaluation and presents recommendations related to proceeding with the design phase. An essential part of the study phase report is a user-oriented *performance specification.* This specification is a general design specification; it is the first of the three major baseline specifications. If the recommendation is to proceed with a design phase, a project plan and a cost schedule are prepared, and they are included as part of the study phase report. These schedules provide detailed estimates for the design phase and gross estimates for the development phase of the system project. They also serve as bases for continuing and expanding the project control functions.

7. *Study Phase Review*

   The study phase report is reviewed with the user-sponsor and other affected management. If the recommendations of the report are accepted, the user issues a written approval to proceed. This approval includes an authorization for staffing and other resource expenditures required for the design phase.

Chapter

7

■ ■ ■

Initial
Investigation

Preview

The initial investigation begins with a written information service request (ISR) and includes as its principal activities background analysis, fact-finding, and fact-analysis. The ISR usually is modified in the course of the initial investigation. At the end of the initial investigation, the ISR becomes a written contract, called a project directive, between the principal user of a computer information system and the information services organization, and it authorizes the continuation of the study phase activities.

Objectives

1. You will be able to distinguish among and explain each of the major study phase activities.
2. You will be able to discuss the principal purposes of an initial investigation.
3. You will be able to prepare an information service request (ISR).
4. You will be able to describe and apply fact-finding and fact-analysis techniques.

Key Terms

study phase the life-cycle phase in which a problem is defined and a system recommended as a solution.

information service request a written request for information services support.

initial investigation an investigation performed to clarify the business information system problem and to develop a project directive.

project directive the final version of an information services request; the written contract between the user and the information services organization. It establishes the scope of the information system project.

system performance definition the transition from a logical performance requirement to a physical one. It includes the statement of general constraints, the identification of specific objectives, and the description of outputs.

candidate system evaluation a procedure for identifying system candidates and selecting the most feasible.

study phase report a comprehensive report prepared at the conclusion of the study phase activities.

Problem Identification

Need Identification

Either a user or a systems analyst may identify the need for a new or improved system. Users must react to external information requirements, such as government regulations; they must respond to their own management's request for additional information; they may become aware of the unsatisfactory performance of systems for which they are responsible. For instance, the manager of an accounts receivable department may become concerned about the repeated late billing of customers or about an increase in the percentage of delinquent accounts.

Similarly, a systems analyst who is familiar with an operational or administrative area may suggest improvements. Frequently an analyst is able to view systems and their interactions with a perspective that individuals involved in daily operations lack. Often problems come into focus after joint discussions between users and an analyst, each of whom provides an individual expertise and viewpoint.

The Information Service Request

For illustrative purposes, we will assume a typical industrial systems environment, one in which the systems analysis department is part of a larger information organization, which we will call information services. Information services also is responsible for programming support and for information resource management, including communications, data processing, and office automation equipment and operations. We will identify the formal request for information services support as an information service request (ISR). Figure 7.1 is our ISR form. As a typical document of this type, it provides for the following:

1. *Job title:* Name assigned by user to the work requested.
2. *New or rev:* Identifies the request as a new job or a revised job.
3. *Requested date:* Date the request is submitted.
4. *Required date:* Date the job should be completed.
5. *Objective:* Briefly states the principal purposes of the job.
6. *Labor:* Authorization to expend labor hours and dollars (amount).
7. *Other:* Authorization to expend nonlabor (for example, computer time) hours and dollars (amount).
8. *Anticipated benefits:* Lists the principal benefits (for example, cost savings, faster response) the company will derive from the system.
9. *Output description:*
   Destination—the external entity that receives the output.
   Comments—describe significant attributes of the output.
10. *Input description:*
    Source—the external entity that provides the input.
    Comments—describe significant attributes of the input.
11. *To be filled out by requestor:*
    Requested by—name, department, title, telephone.
    Approved by—name, department, title, telephone.

Information service request. An information service request is a formal request from a user group for support from the information services organization. It provides for statements of objectives and anticipated benefits, and for the description of outputs and inputs.

INFORMATION SERVICE REQUEST		Page ___ of ___

JOB TITLE:	NEW ☐ REV. ☐	REQUESTED DATE:	REQUIRED DATE:

OBJECTIVE:	AUTHORIZATION			
	LABOR		OTHER	
	HOURS	AMOUNT	HOURS	AMOUNT

ANTICIPATED BENEFITS:

OUTPUT DESCRIPTION	INPUT DESCRIPTION
TITLE:	TITLE:
DESTINATION:	SOURCE:
COMMENTS:	COMMENTS:
TITLE:	TITLE:
DESTINATION:	SOURCE:
COMMENTS:	COMMENTS:

TO BE FILLED OUT BY REQUESTOR			
REQUESTED BY:	DEPARTMENT:	TITLE:	TELEPHONE:
APPROVED BY:	DEPARTMENT:	TITLE:	TELEPHONE:

TO BE FILLED OUT BY INFORMATION SERVICES			
FILE NO:	ACCEPTED ☐	NOT ACCEPTED ☐	
SIGNATURE:	DEPARTMENT:	TITLE:	TELEPHONE:
REMARKS:			

FORM NO: C-6-1	ADDITIONAL INFORMATION: USE REVERSE SIDE OR EXTRA PAGES

12. *To be filled out by information services:*
    File number—identifier assigned to request by information services.
    Accepted or not accepted—explained, as necessary, in remarks.
    Signature—name, department, title, telephone.
    Remarks—filled in by information services as appropriate, for example, explanation of nonacceptance, indication of limits on the ISR, request for additional information, or identification of an analyst assigned to the job.
13. *Additional information:* The requestor may use the reverse side of the form, additional pages of the form, or other supplemental pages, as appropriate, to describe more fully any part of the information service request.

As it evolves, the ISR becomes the basis for a context diagram that defines the external entities that form the boundaries of the proposed modified or new information system. Also, it leads to the development of data flow diagrams and a data dictionary, which, in turn, provide the systems developer with process-oriented and data-oriented views of the system. Therefore, it is important that the initial investigation be as complete as possible and that the findings be recorded. Normally, extensive user involvement is required throughout the initial investigation. In order to produce a meaningful ISR, the analyst must fully understand the existing system, if there is one, and work closely with the principal users of the new or revised system. This is an opportunity to apply the principles of quality management by forming a joint applications development (JAD) team to focus on problem identification—and to establish a foundation that extends that team relationship throughout the entire SDLC.

The ISR initiates a process that can greatly benefit from the tools and techniques, many of which are computer based, that the analyst is able to bring to the team. For example, the ISR need not be the printed form shown in Figure 7.1. This form, as well as other forms and diagrams introduced in this chapter, could be produced and modified as computer-screen displays. As another example, most CASE tools are able to generate documentation, support prototyping, and store information about data entities and data flows in their encyclopedias.

Unquestionably automated tools can be powerful aids throughout the initial investigation that leads to a final ISR. However, it is important for the analyst to be aware of and avoid the "tool trap"—which is to lose sight of the real problem by becoming overly engrossed in the detailed application of the tool. Remember that tools, however sophisticated, do not analyze requirements or perform systems analysis and design; humans who exercise insight and judgment do. Tools only aid the team, making it possible for analysts and others to understand and work effectively with complex systems.

There are two types of affirmative responses to an ISR. The first response is a "can do" response. If all of the data and other resources required to perform the task within the authorized expenditure and time limits are available, the ISR can be accepted without modification as a project directive. This may be the case for an existing system with which both the user and systems analyst are very familiar as a result of having worked together in the past.

However, if the job is new, if the system is large, or if many factors are unknown, another type of response usually is made. The ISR is identified as a *limited ISR* in the remarks section of the request form, and authorization is limited to an initial investigation. This enables the analyst to study the problem and to develop a more definitive ISR before additional expenditures are authorized to complete the study phase. After the initial investigation is completed, a *modified ISR* is prepared by the systems analyst and reviewed with the user-sponsor. The modified ISR is the project directive suggested by the analyst. During review it may be accepted without change or further modified. If the result of the review is to proceed with the job, a final ISR is drafted. When approved by the appropriate user and information service managers, the final ISR becomes a contract between the user and the analyst.

This contract, the project directive, as distinguished from less comprehensive or intermediate information service requests, is the formal, mutual commitment that binds the user and the analyst throughout an information system project. Thus the iterative revision of the ISR is a feedback process that structures a goal-oriented and documented interaction between the user and systems analyst. As illustrated in figure U4.1, the purpose of steps 1 through 3 and the feedback path to the user is more to depict this iterative process than to imply a rigid set of steps that must be followed in all instances.

The Initial Investigation

Project Initiation

The analyst commences an initial investigation armed with a limited ISR. Figure 7.2 is an example of one page of a limited ISR. This ISR authorizes an initial investigation for an accounts receivable system. The systems analyst must contact individuals in the user's organization and in other organizations that may be affected by the system. These individuals will be concerned (and often with cause) about the analyst's activities. Therefore, it is a good practice for a senior user-manager to issue an information memorandum stating the general purpose of the investigation and establishing the identity and responsibilities of the systems analyst. This memorandum should originate at the managerial level, at which responsibility lies for all activities the system may affect. Figure 7.3 shows an information memorandum related to an initial investigation of an on-line accounts receivable system. This system has been given the acronym of OARS.

The scope of the initial investigation may vary from a brief one-person effort to an extensive series of activities requiring the participation of many individuals. Regardless of the size of the initial investigation, the analyst should perform the investigation within a project management framework. This framework should include (1) a project file; (2) a project plan and status report chart; and (3) a project cost report chart.

Limited information service request—partial. A limited information service request enables the analyst to study the business problem and to fully define an information systems project.

INFORMATION SERVICE REQUEST		Page _1_ of _3_	

JOB TITLE: Initial Investigation of an On-line Accounts Receivable System

NEW ☑
REV. ☐

REQUESTED DATE: 9/1/XX

REQUIRED DATE: 9/22/XX

OBJECTIVE: To improve the efficiency of customer billing and account collection

AUTHORIZATION

	LABOR		OTHER	
	HOURS	AMOUNT	HOURS	AMOUNT
	100	$2,000	0	0

ANTICIPATED BENEFITS: 1. Faster customer billing and collection
2. Reduction of cash flow problems

OUTPUT DESCRIPTION	INPUT DESCRIPTION
TITLE: Customer Statement	TITLE: Sales Order
DESTINATION: Customer	SOURCE: Customer
COMMENTS: Currently, 6000/month	COMMENTS: Currently, 20,000/month
TITLE: A/R Transactions	TITLE: Payments/Credits
DESTINATION: A/R Management	SOURCE: Customer
COMMENTS:	COMMENTS:

TO BE FILLED OUT BY REQUESTOR

REQUESTED BY: *G. Davis*	DEPARTMENT: 310	TITLE: Head, A/R Dept.	TELEPHONE: X3250
APPROVED BY: *Ben Franklin*	DEPARTMENT: 300	TITLE: Manager, Acct. Division	TELEPHONE: X3208

TO BE FILLED OUT BY INFORMATION SERVICES

FILE NO: ISR-310-1   ACCEPTED ☑   NOT ACCEPTED ☐

SIGNATURE: *C. Hampton*	DEPARTMENT: 200	TITLE: Manager, Info. Serv. Div.	TELEPHONE: X2670

REMARKS: This is a limited ISR. All output and input descriptions

are tentative. J. Herring, Senior Systems Analyst,

is assigned to conduct an initial investigation.

FORM NO: C-6-1   ADDITIONAL INFORMATION: USE REVERSE SIDE OR EXTRA PAGES

■ **Figure 7.3** Information memorandum. An information memorandum gives the purpose of the system, defines the role of the systems analyst, and demonstrates user-management support.

MEMORANDUM

TO: All Department Heads and Supervisors, Accounting Division.

COPIES TO: Vice President, Finance; Vice President, Sales; Division
               Managers; Head, Systems Analysis Department, J. Hering; File.

FROM: Manager, Accounting Division.

SUBJECT: Study of an On-line Accounts Receivable System (OARS).

DATE: September 1, 19XX

I have requested that the Systems Analysis department of our Information Services Division initiate a study of the feasibility of modifying our present accounts receivable system. As you are aware, we are currently experiencing delays in collecting account payments. One reason is the overload and obsolescence of the batch-oriented computer system installed five years ago. An additional reason, stemming from our business success, is an anticipated accelerated growth in the number of new accounts and in the daily volume of invoices. Another is the corporate plan to establish regional cost centers.

Ms. J. Herring has been assigned the responsibility for conducting an initial investigation. She will be working most closely with Mr. G. Davis, head of the Accounts Receivable department. However, I have asked that Ms. Herring visit with each Accounting Division department head preparatory to beginning her investigation in order to explain her approach to this assignment. I will appreciate your cooperation in aiding her to familiarize herself with all of the current accounting operations and documentation related to accounts receivable.

Please inform your personnel of Ms. Herring's assignment and solicit their participation in an area that can contribute significantly to the profitability of our corporation.

Ben Franklin

Ben Franklin
Manager, Accounting Division

Approved:

Alex Hamilton

Alex Hamilton
Vice President, Finance

A project file is essential to the management of systems projects because of the volume of data that must be collected, organized, digested, and summarized. The major elements of a project file are as follows:

1. The information service request and other directives and memoranda received by the project.
2. Plans and schedules.
3. Collected documentation and working papers.
4. Memoranda and reports produced by the project.

Of course, the scope and depth of the initial investigation and of the project management framework must be scaled to the size of the assignment. Regardless of project size, effective project management is required in order to provide documentation of completed work and a sound basis for continuing the study phase.

The principal activities managed and performed during an initial investigation are background analysis, fact-finding, fact-analysis, and the organization and presentation of results. Their purpose is to lead to an understanding of the existing physical system and the development of a logical model for a proposed new or improved system.

Background Analysis

The analyst performs background analyses related to the proposed application in order to become familiar with the organization environment and the physical processes related to the new or revised system. The analyst must understand the structure of the organization within which the current system is operating and within which (often after considerable alteration) the new system will be expected to operate. It is necessary to determine the interactions between procedures and organization. Often, complex procedures are the result of inefficient organization. The analyst may have occasion to recommend organizational changes. Therefore, the systems analyst should (1) obtain or prepare organization charts; (2) obtain or prepare organization function lists; and (3) learn the names and duties of the people shown in the organization charts.

Since product flow deals with the movement of material and with the physical operations performed upon that material, the analyst observes these physical processes to acquire a "feel" for them. This feel is important if a person expects to conceive and implement systems that will perform in an actual working environment. As an example, the manufacturing processes for producing a large volume of small components, such as integrated circuits, are quite different from those for producing a relatively low volume of large items, such as computers, although each computer contains large quantities of integrated circuits. The systems for controlling each of these types of operations are different. The former may be highly repetitive and component-oriented, while the latter may be nonrepetitive and system-oriented.

After acquiring the necessary background knowledge, the systems analyst investigates the information environment in which the proposed system is to operate. To do this, the analyst finds and analyzes facts and then organizes and summarizes them.

Fact-Finding Techniques

The analyst collects data from two principal sources: printed documents and personnel who are knowledgeable about or involved in the operation of the system under study. The analyst selects the fact-finding techniques judged to be most appropriate to the situation. Some systems are well documented; others are not. In some instances, interviewing all operating personnel may be effective; in others, interviews should be conducted on a very selective basis.

Fact-finding techniques that analysts often employ include: (1) *data collection*, (2) *correspondence* and *questionnaires*, (3) *personal interviews*, (4) *observation*, and (5) *research*.

Data Collection

In this first fact-finding step, the analyst gathers and organizes all documentation related to the system under investigation. Examples are forms, records, reports, manuals, procedures, and CRT display layouts. The analyst must be cautious in relying upon the validity of collected documents. Procedures, for example, may not have been updated to include recent changes to the system. Day-to-day problems may have introduced changes that are not reflected in the system documentation. And, of course, some people have a tendency to ignore procedures. Therefore, unless recently familiarized with the system and with its operating personnel, the analyst must have current information. This information can be obtained through correspondence, including questionnaires, through personal interviews, and by direct observation.

Correspondence and Questionnaires

One method by which the systems analyst can determine if a particular procedure is current and being followed is to request that the individuals responsible for specific activities verify the procedure. The analyst may accomplish this by marking or reproducing appropriate sections of manuals or procedures and sending them to the responsible persons along with an explanatory letter.

Correspondence enables the analyst to explain the purpose of the investigation activities and to inform people of what is expected from them. It is particularly important that interviews be preceded by correspondence defining the subject area and the specific topics to be reviewed.

The questionnaire is an important and often effective type of correspondence. For example, it may be the only efficient method of obtaining responses from a large number of people, particularly if they are widely scattered or in remote locations. Questionnaires should be brief in order to increase the promptness and probability of response. The questionnaire can also be used to solicit responses to specific questions from individuals. However, because of the possibility of misinterpretation, questionnaires should be followed up by personal interviews whenever possible. Figure 7.4 is an example of question-oriented correspondence between an analyst and an individual, in this case, an accounts receivable department manager. Note that an effort has been made to make the questions straightforward and unambiguous.

■ **Figure 7.4**   A questionnaire. A questionnaire helps the systems analyst to perform a background investigation. It supplements personal interviews.

TO: George Davis, Head, Accounts Receivable Department

FROM: Judy Herring

SUBJECT: On-line Accounts Receivable System (OARS)

DATE: October, 1, 19XX

I have used the manuals and procedures that you sent me to prepare an input-output analysis sheet and data flow diagrams. These reflect my understanding of the flow of documents between the customer, the Shipping department, and the Accounts Receivable department. A copy of my flowchart and accompanying input-output analysis sheets are attached to this memorandum. I would like to discuss the chart with you and will call you for an appointment in a few days. I also would appreciate it if, at the same meeting, you could provide me with answers to the following questions:

1.   Have you observed an increasing delay in receipt of customer payments? If so, to what do you attribute the delay?

2.   Do the customer statements contain all of the information you need? If not, what changes would you suggest?

3.   How will the proposed regional cost center concept affect your operations?

4.   What is the delay between date of sale and date of customer billing?

5.   Why are. . .

Personal Interviews

The personal interview is one of the most fruitful methods of obtaining information. An interview is a person-to-person communication. Hence, the guidelines for effective communications described in chapter 3, "Communication and Documentation," should be observed. The analyst is more of a receiver than a sender when conducting an interview. Although it is appropriate for analysts to use interviews to explain their projects and to "sell" themselves, they are primarily seeking information. Therefore, they must remember to be good listeners.

Interviews are critical because people are the most important ingredient of any system. The success or failure of a system often depends upon the acceptance of the analyst by the personnel who are affected by the system. These personnel determine its usability. The following are some interview guidelines:

1. Plan the interview just as carefully as you would plan a presentation.
2. Adhere to your plan by keeping the interview pertinent. However, be flexible. Do not force the interview to follow a preconceived pattern.
3. Be informed, but do not attempt to present yourself as "the expert."
4. Arrange for a meeting time and place free from interruptions and other distractions.
5. Be punctual.
6. Know the name and position of the person you are interviewing.
7. Be courteous at all times.
8. Avoid the use of potentially threatening devices, such as tape recorders and cameras.

These guidelines are intended to help the analyst to create an atmosphere of co-operation, confidence, and understanding. This type of atmosphere is conducive to effective communication; however, it is difficult to create because the factors by which individuals are motivated are complex. Abraham Maslow defined a widely accepted ascending hierarchy of the needs of individuals in his classic book, *Motivation and Personality*.[1] These needs are:

1. Physiological needs
2. Safety needs
3. Belonging and love needs
4. Need for self-esteem and the esteem of others
5. Self-actualization needs
6. Cognitive needs
7. Aesthetic needs

Except for self-actualization and cognitive needs, the list is self-explanatory. Self-actualization refers to a self-started growth that encourages people to be what they are best suited to be. Cognitive needs refer to one's impulse to understand and to explain. Higher-order needs usually emerge only after the lower-order needs are satisfied. Thus it is unlikely that cognitive needs could be gratified by an individual who perceived himself or herself to be deprived of physiological or safety needs.

When it is likely that the solution to a problem will involve the use of a computer, many individuals become fearful. They sense a threat to the fulfillment of basic needs, such as physiological needs and safety needs. Unfortunately, their fears often are justified because computers can introduce major changes. However, most companies do not want to lose the services of skilled and loyal employees. Very often these employees are or can become qualified to perform important functions in the new

---

1. Abraham Maslow, *Motivation and Personality* (New York: Harper and Brothers, 1954).

system. Also, it usually is less expensive (and more humanitarian) to retrain employees of proven worth to the company than it is to recruit and indoctrinate new employees.

As an analyst, you should attempt to motivate individuals to work toward the success of the new system. Frederick Herzberg,[2] a psychologist who devoted many years to the study of motivation, developed foundational insights that should be of value to the analyst. Professor Herzberg distinguishes between *motivating factors* and *hygiene factors*. The motivators are the primary cause of job satisfaction; they relate to job content. The hygiene factors do not motivate, but cause dissatisfaction if they are absent. They relate to job environment. Motivators include achievement of something useful, recognition of achievement, meaningful work, responsibility for decisions, advancement, and growth.

Hygiene factors include relationship with supervisors, salary, status, security, and working conditions. Unhappiness results if these factors are not present. However, their presence does not contribute nearly as much to job satisfaction as does the presence of motivators. Hence, a systems analyst should describe the roles of individuals in the new system in terms of motivators whenever possible.

It is good professional practice for the analyst to schedule the first interviews with management personnel. The analyst should solicit their aid in scheduling interviews with employees under their supervision. The analyst should attempt to enlist user-managers as allies in quieting the concerns of their subordinates and in encouraging support for the new system.

If successful in the conduct of interviews, the systems analyst will have not only obtained information, but also gained the support and confidence of the people who can make the project succeed or fail. This support is essential throughout all the phases of the life cycle of the business system.

Observation

In the course of data collection, interviewing, and other fact-finding activities, an experienced analyst observes the operation of the ongoing system and begins to formulate questions and draw conclusions on the basis of what is observed. Skilled analysts are able to discipline their powers of observation and recall. By "walking through" operations and seeing for themselves, they are able to correlate work flow and data flow and identify anomalies.

Observation is a continuous process. It usually is informal. However, there also are formal observation techniques that analysts may employ. For example, they may sample operations at predetermined or random times. They may perform statistical analyses. One observation technique that often is effective as a means of communication is the construction of data flow diagrams. For example, a data flow diagram might identify faulty customer billing procedures. From this, the analyst might conclude that one possible reason for delays in account collections had been identified.

2. Frederick Herzberg, "One more time: How do you motivate employees?" *Harvard Business Review* (Jan.–Feb. 1986).

Research

The final fact-finding technique we will mention is research. Research is of particular importance when a new application is being considered because it is a means of stimulating creative approaches to problem solving. All the fact-finding methods we have discussed are forms of in-house research. However, there are many out-of-house sources of information. These include trade and professional journals, computer-oriented news publications and magazines, government publications, and, of course, libraries.

A potential problem with much of the literature available to an analyst is that it may be out of date by the time it is in print. Two relatively time-current research resources are vendors and personal contacts. Vendors, such as the IBM Corporation, have found that by providing "applications" assistance to their customers, they can increase the effectiveness of and enlarge the market for their products. An analyst who can distinguish between real system needs and the possible overenthusiasm of a vendor can tap this rich research resource. Also, membership and participation in professional organizations can lead to a wealth of personal contacts within special interest groups.

Analysts should establish and maintain contacts with their counterparts in other companies. One highly recommended method for making such contacts is membership and active participation in a professional society, such as the Association for Systems Management or the Data Processing Management Association. These organizations conduct many professional seminars related to current topics. Also, visits to companies with similar problems and the exchange of ideas with their analysts can be rewarding.

Fact-Analysis Techniques

Fact-finding and *fact-analysis* are related activities. As they collect information, efficient analysts organize, analyze, and use it to identify additional information needs. There are many useful techniques for the organization and analysis of collected documents. These techniques provide the analyst with insight into the interaction among organizational elements, personnel, and information flow. Four general techniques we will discuss and provide examples of are:

1. Data element analysis
2. Input-output analysis
3. Recurring data analysis
4. Report use analysis

■ Figure 7.5 Document numbered for data element analysis. The first of two steps in data element analysis is to assign a number to each data element on a document.

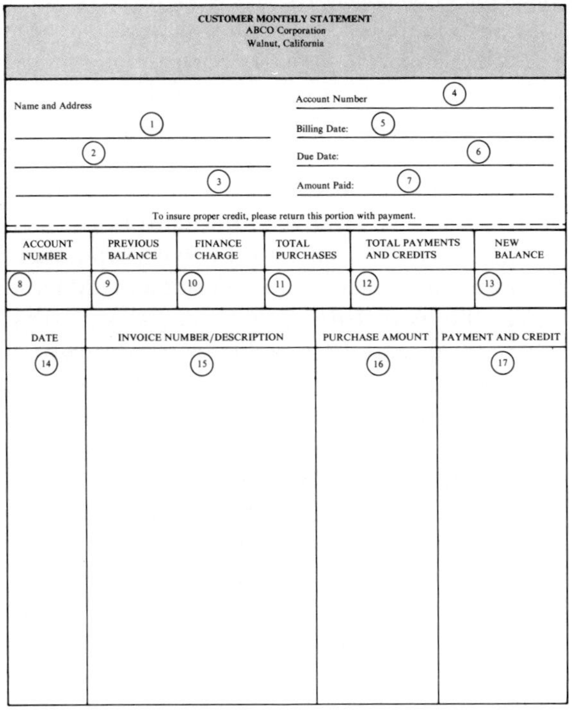
CUSTOMER MONTHLY STATEMENT
ABCO Corporation
Walnut, California

Name and Address (1) (2) (3)

Account Number (4)
Billing Date: (5)
Due Date: (6)
Amount Paid: (7)

To insure proper credit, please return this portion with payment.

ACCOUNT NUMBER	PREVIOUS BALANCE	FINANCE CHARGE	TOTAL PURCHASES	TOTAL PAYMENTS AND CREDITS	NEW BALANCE
(8)	(9)	(10)	(11)	(12)	(13)

DATE	INVOICE NUMBER/DESCRIPTION	PURCHASE AMOUNT	PAYMENT AND CREDIT
(14)	(15)	(16)	(17)

Data Element Analysis

By analyzing data elements and data structures, systems analysts assure themselves that they understand the meanings of the data names and the codes that appear in the manuals, procedures, charts, and other forms of documentation they have collected. One method of *data element analysis* has two steps:

1. Assign a number to each data element or code that appears upon a data carrier, such as a document or a CRT screen display.
2. Head a separate piece of paper with the title or other identification of the data carrier and write the meaning of each numbered data element or code.

Figure 7.5 is an example of a document, in this case a customer monthly statement, taken through the first step. Figure 7.6 is a partial analysis of the same document. Analysts employ their knowledge of code planning and construction in data element analysis. This knowledge is essential if the analyst is to recommend improvements to a system or to perform a data flow-related activity, such as the preparation of a data dictionary.

Data element analysis. The second and final step in data element analysis is to record the meaning of each data element, in order to be certain of a common understanding by the user and the analyst.

DATA ELEMENT ANALYSIS

DOCUMENT: Customer Monthly Statement

DATA ELEMENT:

1. Company Name

2. Address: Number and Street

3. Address: City, State, Zip Code

4. Account Number: Customer Account Code, 6 digit simple sequence code.

5. Billing Date: Closing date of billing cycle--month, day, and year

6. Due Date: Date after which account becomes delinquent.

7. Amount Paid: Filled in by customer to correspond to amount of check.

8. Account Number: Same as item 4

9. Previous Balance: Balance on previous month's statement.

10. Finance Charge: charge on unpaid balance.

11. Total Purchases: Total amount of purchases covered by this statement.

12. Total Payments & Credits: Total amount of payments and credits covered by this statement.

13. New Balance: Amount due equal to previous balance and total purchases--total payments and credits.

14. Date: Date of each transaction--month and day.

15. Invoice Number/Description: Invoice number or transaction description (e.g., credit)

16. Purchase Amounts: Net amount of reference purchases.

17. Payments & Credits: Amount of payment or credit.

Similarly, analysts use their knowledge of forms analysis and design to determine whether a form is adequate. Very often a systems analyst will recommend the redesign of forms as a means of reducing error and improving information flow.

Input-Output Analysis

Input-output analysis is a general term for all analysis techniques based upon the perception of a system as a process that converts inputs into outputs. Information-oriented system flowcharts, process-oriented system flowcharts, and data flow diagrams are excellent tools for input-output analysis. Figure 7.7 is an example of an input-output analysis sheet prepared for an accounts receivable department. In dealing with complex information systems the systems analyst should prepare similar sheets for each organization affected by the system. These sheets provide the systems analyst with documentation that describes relationships among inputs, processing operations, outputs, and data files. Additionally, they serve to pinpoint areas that are not completely understood and that may require additional study. They are valuable research tools that assist the analyst in preparing flowcharts such as data flow diagrams and entity-relationship diagrams.

Input-output analysis sheet for an accounts receivable system. Input-output analysis sheets are high-level charts that describe the relationships between inputs, processing functions, outputs, and data files among organizational entities.

INPUT-OUTPUT ANALYSIS SHEET		
ORGANIZATION: Accounts Receivable Dept. SYSTEM: Accounts Receivable Date: 9/3/XX		
INPUT	PROCESSING FUNCTIONS/FILES	OUTPUT
Account Application	Customers submit account applications, which are processed by the Accounts Receivable/Credit department. If an application is accepted, it is sent to Data Processing for entry into the system. Data Processing returns the application for filing. Application approval/denial is sent to the customer.	Application Approval/ Denial
Sales Order	Sales orders are sent directly to Data Processing for order processing. The customer retains the carbon copy. Order fill data are sent to the Order Fill department.	Order Fill Data
Payments/Credits	Payments are sent to the Accounts Receivable department. The payment/credit data are sent to Data Processing. An aged A/R report is sent to the Accounts Receivable manager from Data Processing each month. Data Processing sends overcredit notices to a credit clerk whenever a new order would exceed the customer's credit limit. Unless additional credit is extended, the notice is sent to the customer. Customer statements are sent to Accounts Receivable in duplicate. The original copy is sent to the customer; the duplicate is filed. One-third of the statements are produced each ten days of the month, that is, on the 1st, 10th, and 20th. An A/R transaction register is sent to the Accounts Receivable manager. The accounts receivable summary report is prepared weekly and sent to the Accounts Receivable manager for distribution.	Aged A/R Report Overcredit Notice Customer Statement A/R Transaction Register A/R Summary

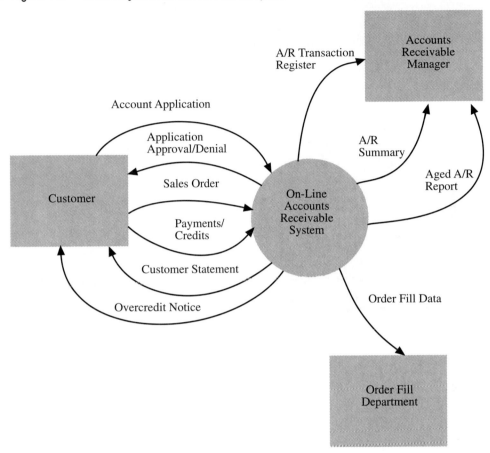

A dramatic input-output analysis technique that analysts sometimes employ is to mount actual forms and reports on a wall of a room. Information flow can be displayed by colored tape or string. The values of this technique are that it provides the analyst with a life-size model; it keeps all of the data carriers in view; and it provides impact for presentations and group discussions.

Data flow diagrams are powerful tools for relating and displaying facts about the logic of the current physical system. As contrasted with figures 7.8 and 7.9, which are particularly useful in documenting the characteristics of the existing physical system, the data flow diagrams of figures 7.6 and 7.7 are an effective means of communicating with users and become a basis for developing a conceptual model of a new or improved information system. Figure 7.8, which is the same as figure 5.7a, is an example of a context diagram for an existing accounts receivable system; figure 7.9, which is the same as figure 5.7b, is a level-0 data flow diagram for the same system. In the course of the initial investigation, the latter would be decomposed into as many levels as necessary to identify all of the significant data flows and processes that transform them.

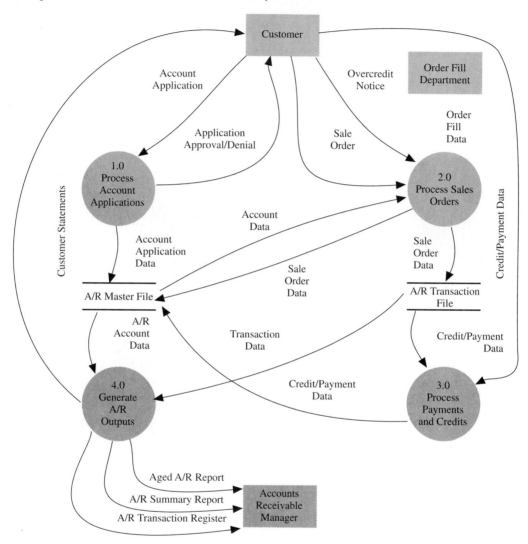

Recurring Data Analysis

After becoming familiar with the content and meaning of the principal system documents, the systems analyst may analyze recurring data. For this purpose a form is prepared like the one in figure 7.10. Document names and identifying numbers are entered across the top of the sheet. All the data elements associated with the first form are listed in the column headed Data Element. This process is continued for each form, moving from left to right across the sheet. Only previously unlisted data elements are added to the Data Element column. A check mark is entered at the intersection of corresponding forms and data elements. The analyst must be familiar with the forms being analyzed to avoid being deceived by the same name appearing with different meanings. An example might be the term "quantity," which could mean quantity ordered on a sales order or quantity shipped on an invoice. Similarly, the analyst should be able to distinguish between different names with the same meaning. For example, "employee number" and "badge number" might have the same meaning.

The significance of *recurring data analysis* is twofold: (1) Unnecessary input and output data duplication can be detected. This leads to form simplification, consolidation, and elimination. (2) Redundant data elements and files can be located. This leads to clarification of data dictionary entries and to more efficient use of storage media.

Report Use Analysis

Reports and copies of reports tend to proliferate. Many individuals are collectors of reports, more because of fear of being left out than because of any legitimate need for information. A useful technique for dealing with reports that are suspect because of a lengthy distribution list is a *report use analysis.* A form of the type shown in figure 7.11 is prepared and the data elements are associated with identified users of the report. A completed report use analysis sheet can be correlated with information obtained from other sources, such as user interviews. It may disclose data elements (and possibly entire reports) not required by many of the individuals or groups on the distribution list. It is not unusual to find reports that no one uses. The report use analysis sheet can provide insight into the true information needs of an organization and can help the analyst to develop more meaningful reports for the new or revised system.

Having concluded the fact-finding and fact-analysis, the analyst is at this point prepared to organize and summarize the results of these activities.

Results of Analysis

The systems analyst usually collects and analyzes large amounts of data. In the course of the initial investigation, the analyst has to discard data that is irrelevant and organize and summarize that which is relevant. After completing the process of organizing and

■ Figure 7.10 Recurring data analysis sheet. Recurring data analysis sheets are used to identify data duplication in order to eliminate, or consolidate, forms and files.

RECURRING DATA ANALYSIS SHEET													
FORM NAME / DATA ELEMENT	Sales Order	Shipping Order	Shipping Invoice										
Customer Name	✓	✓	✓										
Customer Address	✓	✓	✓										
Invoice No.	✓	✓	✓										
Account No.	✓	✓	✓										
Date	✓	✓	✓										
Quantity Ordered	✓	✓	✓										
Description	✓	✓	✓										
Unit Price	✓		✓										
Amount	✓		✓										
Customer Signature	✓												
Salesperson	✓												
Total Amount	✓		✓										
Ship to		✓											
How Shipped		✓											
Quantity Shipped			✓										

Report use analysis sheet. Report use analysis sheets assist the systems analyst in identifying data elements not used by individuals on the report distribution list. This leads to reduced distribution, consolidation, or elimination of reports.

REPORT USE ANALYSIS SHEET						
REPORT DESCRIPTION: Customer Monthly Statement						
USER NAME/FUNCTION / DATA ELEMENT	Customer	Customer Account Credit Clerk	Accounts Receivable Department (File copy)			
Customer Name	√					
Customer Address	√					
Account No.	√	√				
Billing Date	√	√				
Due Date	√	√				
Amount Paid	√	√				
Previous Balance	√	√				
Total Purchase	√	√				
Total Payments & Credits	√	√				
New Balance	√	√				

summarizing data, the analyst should have a file of current information and a thorough knowledge of the current system. The information file should include the following:

1. Updated system documentation, including copies of all pertinent forms and reports.
2. Correspondence and completed questionnaires.
3. Interview records.
4. Results of fact-analysis, including data flow diagrams, fact analysis sheets, and other important information recorded during the investigation.

The file should document the knowledge that the analyst has acquired in the course of the initial investigation. This knowledge should include:

1. A comprehensive understanding of how the current system operates, including its cost.
2. Familiarity with the names, positions, and personalities of personnel operating in or affected by the system.
3. Identification of the good and bad features of the current system.
4. Correlation of actual system problems with the problems listed on the ISR that initiated the investigation.

With respect to correlation between actual system problems and those listed in the ISR, the analyst should be able to distinguish between those problems that can be solved by a new or revised system and those that cannot. For example, a new system might be completely ineffective if the problem is an uncontrollable executive personality.

User Review

Modified Information Service Request

The analyst presents both the results of the initial investigation and recommendations to the user-sponsor. (We will assume that the user-sponsor is the principal user. If not, it is vital that the principal user also attend the review.) If the analyst has concluded that the project should be continued, a modified information service request is included in the presentation. The modified ISR may suggest modifications to the objectives, benefits, output descriptions, and input descriptions from those put forth in the original ISR. Figure 7.12 is an example of a modified ISR for an accounts receivable system. It is identified as a modified ISR in the remarks section of the bottom of the form. Differences from the limited information service request of figure 7.2 are as follows:

1. Identification of an additional benefit
2. Recommendation of an integrated data base solution
3. Labor authorized to complete the study phase

However, the initial investigation produced no essential changes in the concept of the on-line system.

The analyst should provide all those invited to the presentation with copies of the modified ISR and other pertinent documents, such as preliminary data flow diagrams, beforehand. This affords them a chance to familiarize themselves with the material and to prepare questions. The user review typically includes the user-sponsor, the analyst, the analyst's supervisor, and other appropriate management and operational personnel.

Modified information service request—partial. At the conclusion of the initial investigation the systems analyst may present the user with a modified information service request, based on findings that occur during the initial investigation.

INFORMATION SERVICE REQUEST		Page 1 of 3			
JOB TITLE: Study Phase for an On-Line A/R System (OARS)	NEW ☑ REV. ☐	REQUESTED DATE: 9/1/XX		REQUIRED DATE: 12/19/XX	
OBJECTIVE: To improve the efficiency of customer billing and account collection		AUTHORIZATION			
		LABOR		OTHER	
		HOURS	AMOUNT	HOURS	AMOUNT
		600	$18,000	0	0

ANTICIPATED BENEFITS: 1. Faster customer billing and collection
2. Reduction of cash flow problems
3. Improved A/R controls

OUTPUT DESCRIPTION	INPUT DESCRIPTION
TITLE: Customer Statement	TITLE: Sales Order
DESTINATION: Customer	SOURCE: Customer
COMMENTS: Currently, 6000/month Anticipate growth to 20,000/mo.	COMMENTS: Currently, 20,000/month Anticipate growth to 100,000/mo.
TITLE: A/R Transaction Register	TITLE: Payments/Credits
DESTINATION: A/R Management	SOURCE: Customer
COMMENTS:	COMMENTS:

TO BE FILLED OUT BY REQUESTOR			
REQUESTED BY:	DEPARTMENT:	TITLE:	TELEPHONE:
APPROVED BY:	DEPARTMENT:	TITLE:	TELEPHONE:

TO BE FILLED OUT BY INFORMATION SERVICES			
FILE NO: ISR-310-1	ACCEPTED ☐	NOT ACCEPTED ☐	
SIGNATURE:	DEPARTMENT: 210	TITLE: Senior Systems Analyst	TELEPHONE: X2675

REMARKS: This is a modified ISR prepared by J. Herring and recommended as a project directive.

Except for identifying an opportunity to improve A/R system controls and recommending

the study of an integrated A/R data base, the modified ISR does not differ from the intial ISR.

FORM NO: C-6-1   ADDITIONAL INFORMATION. USE REVERSE SIDE OR EXTRA PAGES

The analyst should discuss the key elements of the initial investigation. The analyst should be able to support the recommendations, whatever their nature. If the recommendation is to proceed with the study phase, the resources required should be identified and a project plan and a cost schedule should be presented for the remainder of the study phase.

As a result of the user review, the project may be terminated, modified, or continued. If the decision is to proceed, it is documented by the issuance of a project directive.

Project Directive

The modified ISR really is a draft of a proposed project directive. The project directive is an authorization document issued by the user after the review of the initial investigation has been completed; it reflects the results of discussions and decisions made during that review. It may or may not be identical to the modified ISR prepared by the analyst.

When the project directive is signed by the user and accepted by information services, it becomes a contract under which both organizations are accountable for performance. The format and content of the project directive are similar to those of the ISR. Often the same form is used for both. This is the practice that we will follow in this book. Figure 7.13 is based on the modified ISR of figure 7.12. Note the following changes: The requested date has been advanced, and the labor allocation has been increased slightly. In the remarks section, this ISR is designated a project directive. Also, the requestor is to be informed when 90 percent of the authorized funds have been spent. This is a safeguard against an unauthorized cost overrun.

The project directive is the first of many incremental commitments made by management in the course of the life cycle of a computer-based business system. At this time, the project directive may authorize all the resources required to develop the new system. Usually it authorizes only the resources required to complete the study phase. Additional resources are authorized after successful reviews of the study phase and of subsequent phases. In figure 7.13, as the job title indicates, the analyst is authorized to complete the study phase.

The project directive formally establishes the scope, or context, of the information system, and it initiates a comprehensive study of the feasibility of the proposed system. This study is preceded by the development of a detailed user-oriented definition of expected new system performance. The process by which the expected system performance is arrived at is described in chapter 8, "System Performance Definition." This process involves the evaluation of alternative physical systems and the selection of the one that best meets the detailed system performance requirements. This process is discussed in chapter 9, "Candidate System Evaluation."

■ Figure 7.13 Project directive—partial. The final version of the information service request (ISR), based upon discussions between the user and the analyst of the modified ISR, is called a project directive. It is the "contract" between the user and the systems analyst.

INFORMATION SERVICE REQUEST		Page 1 of 3	

JOB TITLE: Study Phase for an On-Line A/R System (OARS)	NEW ☑ REV. ☐	REQUESTED DATE: 11/7/XX	REQUIRED DATE: 12/19/XX

OBJECTIVE: To improve the efficiency of customer billing and account collection	AUTHORIZATION			
	LABOR		OTHER	
	HOURS	AMOUNT	HOURS	AMOUNT
	600	$18,000	0	0

ANTICIPATED BENEFITS: 1. Faster customer billing and collection
2. Reduction of cash flow problems
3. Improved A/R controls

OUTPUT DESCRIPTION	INPUT DESCRIPTION
TITLE: Customer Statement	TITLE: Sales Order
DESTINATION: Customer	SOURCE: Customer
COMMENTS: Currently, 6000/month Anticipate growth to 20,000/mo.	COMMENTS: Currently, 20,000/month Anticipate growth to 100,000/mo.
TITLE: A/R Transaction Register	TITLE: Payments/Credits
DESTINATION: A/R Management	SOURCE: Customer
COMMENTS:	COMMENTS:

TO BE FILLED OUT BY REQUESTOR			
REQUESTED BY:	DEPARTMENT: 310	TITLE: Head, A/R Dept.	TELEPHONE: X3250
APPROVED BY:	DEPARTMENT: 300	TITLE: Manager, Acct. Division	TELEPHONE: X3208

TO BE FILLED OUT BY INFORMATION SERVICES			
FILE NO: ISR-310-1	ACCEPTED ☑	NOT ACCEPTED ☐	
SIGNATURE:	DEPARTMENT: 200	TITLE: Manager, Info. Serv. Div.	TELEPHONE: X2670

REMARKS: This is a project directive. J. Herring is appointed project leader. Advise requestor when
funds are 90% expended.

FORM NO: C-6-1	ADDITIONAL INFORMATION: USE REVERSE SIDE OR EXTRA PAGES

Summary

The study phase is the first of the four life-cycle phases. It is the phase in which the business information system problem is identified, the system performance defined, alternate solutions evaluated, and the most feasible solution recommended for system design. The study phase begins with a written statement of the user's need, called an information service request. Usually this is a limited information service request since the problem is not completely defined and since the systems analyst requires a familiarization period. An initial investigation is performed for these purposes. At the conclusion of the initial investigation, the analyst prepares a modified information service request for review with the user. The result of this review is a written contract, called a project directive, between the user and the information services organization.

The initial investigation is initiated by a written request for information services support, called an information service request (ISR). The ISR may undergo several modifications before it becomes a written contract, called a project directive, between the user and the information services organization. Four major activities that are performed during the initial investigation are: (1) background analysis; (2) fact-finding; (3) fact-analysis; and (4) organization and presentation of results. Some useful fact-finding techniques are: data collection, correspondence and questionnaires, personal interviews, observation, and research. Fact-analysis techniques include: data element analysis, input-output analysis, recurring data analysis, and report use analysis. Data flow diagrams and other flowcharting techniques are of value throughout fact-finding and fact-analysis.

After completing the fact-analysis activities, the systems analyst will have identified the principal user of the computer-based business information system. This is the person who, in practice, will accept or reject the system. Also, after fact-finding, the analyst will be able to prepare a modified ISR for review with the user. The result of this review is the final version of the ISR—the project directive. It establishes the scope, or context, of the information system, and it initiates a formal definition of expected system performance and a comprehensive analysis of the feasibility of the proposed information system.

For Review

study phase

life-cycle phases

user need

information service request

initial investigation

user review

project directive

system performance definition

candidate system evaluation

candidate system

feedback

fact-finding

data collection

correspondence and questionnaires

personal interviews

observation

research

data carrier

motivating factor

hygiene factor

fact-analysis

data element analysis

study phase report
performance specification
study phase review
limited information service request
modified information service request

input-output analysis
recurring data analysis
report use analysis
principal user
data flow diagram

For Discussion

1. Define and explain the purpose of each of the following:
   a. information service request
   b. initial investigation
   c. project directive
   d. candidate system evaluation
   e. system performance definition
2. What is a candidate system, and how does it relate to the candidate system evaluation?
3. What is the purpose of the study phase report?
4. Why should a user's need be stated in written form?
5. How does the initial investigation benefit the user? The systems analyst?
6. What is the significance of the authors' reminder to "avoid the tool trap"?
7. With reference to figure 7.1, identify some instances when feedback might occur during the study phase. What might cause this feedback?
8. Describe several ways in which a business system information problem might be identified.
9. Distinguish between the terms information service request, modified information service request, and project directive.
10. Why should an information memorandum be issued at the time an analyst begins an initial investigation?
11. Why does an analyst perform a background analysis? Under what conditions might such an analysis not be necessary?
12. What tentative conclusions can you draw from the recurring data analysis and report use analysis sheets of figure 7.10 and figure 7.11?
13. How does an analyst apply skills in coding and forms design during an initial investigation?
14. Discuss "motivators" and "hygiene factors" as they relate to personal interviews.
15. What should an analyst's information file contain, and what knowledge should the analyst have at the conclusion of an initial investigation?
16. What type of data flow diagram can be developed directly from the project directive? From an input/output analysis sheet?

For Exercise: The Hollerith Card Company

The Hollerith brothers, Harry and Herman, are co-owners of the Hollerith Company, a mail-order greeting card business founded by their grandfather. In recent years the business has grown, and there are three strong product lines: (1) seasonal cards, (2) standard occasion cards (birthday, anniversary, illness, etc.), and (3) custom cards.

The brothers are very computer literate and have immersed themselves in introducing the use of microcomputers with high-quality graphics capabilities in the card business. This gave them the opportunity to benefit from an inexpensive, quick-turnaround design capability. Their enthusiasm for the technology led them to hire an advertising agency, and the resulting advertising campaign was very successful. It created a strong customer demand for custom cards, almost doubling the normal volume of business. To the surprise of Harry and Herman, the new technology and growth in sales brought with them a sudden increase in customer complaints. Most of these were directed toward orders that were lost, late, or incorrectly filled and toward billings for orders that were wrong or never received.

As the systems analyst hired to identify and solve the order-handling problem, your approach was to spend time with the Hollerith brothers and other key personnel to learn about the product flow and to conduct an initial investigation. As a result of your preliminary fact-finding and fact-analysis activities, you learned that:

1. Customer orders are received by mail and phone by order-entry clerks who maintain a customer file and whose task is to validate each order as it is received. A request for further information is sent to customers for whom order information is incomplete.

2. The order-processing clerks sort validated orders by product line and send them to the appropriate order-filling department. At the same time a copy of each order is sent to the billing department, which proceeds to bill the customer. All custom orders are routed by company mail to the fast-turnaround, custom-card design group, which, as necessary, designs and makes the card before sending the order on to the custom-card order-filling department.

3. Upon further investigation you also learned that each order-filling department maintains its own customer file and physical inventory, sending order-pickup-and-ship requests to the shipping department.

4. In speaking with the advertising firm executive in charge of the special-card campaign, you learned that the creative design suggestions that appeared in advertisements were approved by Harry, who assumed that any quantity of orders of any kind could be handled by Herman because Herman was personally in charge of the custom-card operation.

Your assignment in this exercise is to complete the following steps:

1. Record the details of your initial findings by preparing input-output analysis sheets for the order-entry system, the custom-card design system, and the three order-filling systems.

2. Prepare a context diagram and a first draft of a level-0 data flow diagram. You have determined that the entities external to the domain of the order-handling system are: (1) the customer, (2) the advertising agency, and (3) the billing department.

3. In writing, identify some potential problem areas that you feel you should discuss with the Hollerith brothers and investigate promptly as you continue the initial investigation. Explain why you selected these areas.

8

■ ■ ■

System
Performance
Definition

In the preceding chapter we discussed the fact-finding and fact-analysis activities that take place as an initial investigation is performed. The initial investigation concludes with a project directive, which establishes the scope and the logical context of the computer information system. The next step is to initiate a formal transition from the logical model of the new system to a physical model. This model defines the performance required of all physical systems that might be considered as candidates for implementing the information system. System performance definition is accomplished in the following four steps:

1. Developing a logical model of the new system.
2. Stating as general constraints the limitations placed on any candidate system considered.
3. Ranking and listing the specific objectives of the information system.
4. Describing the system outputs as they will appear to its users.

Subsequently, a system candidate evaluation can be performed to select the most cost-effective of the physical systems that qualify as candidates for meeting the information needs of the system.

Objectives

1. You will be able to demonstrate data flow diagram techniques.
2. You will be able to formulate and state general constraints.
3. You will be able to rank and state specific objectives.
4. You will be able to describe outputs using output specification sheets and data element lists.

Key Terms

system performance definition the transition from a logical performance requirement to a physical one. It includes the statement of general constraints, identification of specific objectives, and description of outputs.

constraint a condition, such as time or money, that limits the solutions that an analyst may consider.

specific objective a measurable performance outcome.

Transition from the Logical to the Physical Model

The formal transition from the "what" of the logical model of a new or improved information system to the "how" of a physical model begins as soon as the initial investigation is completed. The project directive, created at the end of the initial investigation, is used to prepare a context diagram, which is expanded into a set of leveled data flow diagrams for the new system. This ensures that all of the significant data flows and transformation processes that characterize the new system are understood and recorded in a data dictionary.

The context diagram, then, can be used to initiate the **system performance definition**, which is the transition from the logical system performance requirement to a physical one. The system performance definition process includes a statement of general constraints and the identification of specific objectives. The process concludes with a user-oriented description of all of the physical outputs that the system provides to the external entities that form its boundaries. All proposed physical solutions must satisfy the system performance definition. In the study phase, the data flow diagrams are also useful as a means of distinguishing between manual and computer data processing operations. In the design phase, the set of leveled DFDs and its accompanying data dictionary are used to create a design specification that includes a detailed set of structured processing requirements. Analysts and users usually work closely together throughout the initial investigation, and it would be ignoring reality to assume that no discussions about, or considerations of, physical implementations occur. Similarly, it would not be realistic to assume that thinking about or discussing some physical components would not take place as a logical model of a new system is developed during system performance definition. After all, information systems are created by real people working in a real world, one in which there often are evident physical constraints, for example the necessity for remote access to a data base maintained on a specific mainframe computer. The important principal to keep in mind is that it would be premature to make final physical decisions before the logical requirements of a system are fully understood. Data flow diagrams are a powerful aid to the understanding of logical requirements, for communicating with users in an open-minded manner, and for keeping decisions about actual system components in the background until that decision process becomes a formal performance definition task.

Example System—ABCO Corporation: On-Line Accounts Receivable System (OARS)

ABCO History

In order to illustrate the activities that occur during system performance definition, we will continue to work with the accounts receivable system used as an example of an existing system in chapter 7, "Initial Investigation." We will add to the information presented in that chapter, and we will associate the new on-line accounts receivable system (OARS) with the ABCO corporation. Also, we will continue to work with OARS as we proceed to discuss each of the life-cycle phases.

The ABCO corporation is a small business that designs and manufactures specialty household items. It does not sell to the public, but is a nationwide wholesale and retail supplier. It currently has three regional sales divisions through which merchandise is supplied to its customers. Currently, the ABCO corporation has 10,000 customer accounts distributed over the three regional divisions. This level of accounts appears to be the maximum capacity of the present accounts receivable system. The number of accounts is expected to increase by approximately 2,000 accounts each year for the next five years. The current system cannot meet this projected growth and satisfy the corporate goal of distributing information processing resources to regional profit centers. In addition, the number of regions is expected to grow to five from the current three regions to better serve ABCO customers. Specific problems that have been identified are:

1. Saturation of the capacity of the present computer system, causing difficulties in adding new accounts and in obtaining information about the status of existing accounts.
2. Processing delays in preparing customer billing statements because of the batch-oriented design of the current accounts receivable system.
3. Excessive elapsed time between mailing of customer statements and receipt of payments, which creates a high-cost, four-day float (the time that the money is not in use, even though the customer has sent a check).
4. Inadequate control of credit limits.
5. Inability to provide the regional centers with timely customer-related information.

The ABCO corporation has a midrange size computer that is being used to its capacity. In addition, its design is not oriented toward on-line systems. Mr. B. Franklin, manager of the accounting division, felt that the best way to reduce the time required to process orders and customer statements, and provide a faster response to requests for customer information to the regions, is through a distributed data processing system. By placing computer terminals within each region, ABCO regions would have fast access to the data base and customer orders could be entered locally, rather than mailed or faxed to a central site. Entering sales data through terminals would also eliminate a source of delays and errors due to paperwork handling.

Accordingly, Mr. Franklin instructed Mr. G. Davis, head of the A/R department, to ask the information services division to study the feasibility of an on-line accounts receivable system. The initial request for service was accepted as a limited information service request. Ms. J. Herring was assigned the responsibility for conducting the initial investigation.

ABCO Corporation—partial organization chart. This chart depicts the reporting relationships between the major organizations affected by the A/R system.

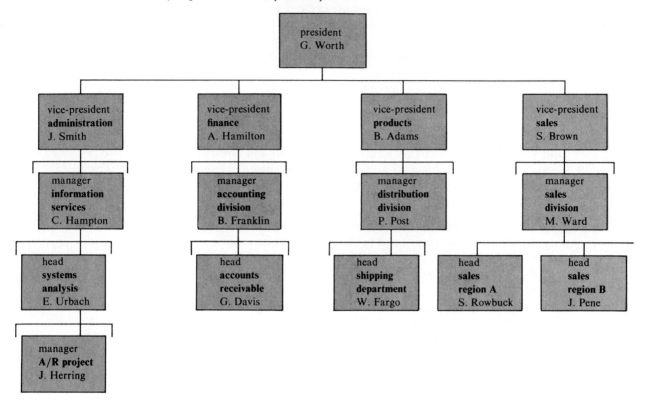

OARS Initial Investigation

Figures 8.1 through 8.4 summarize pertinent information collected and analyzed during the OARS initial investigation. The material is presented as follows: a partial organization chart, the existing system context diagram, the current system costs, and the existing system input-output analysis sheet.

Partial Organization Chart.   Figure 8.1 depicts the reporting relationships between the major organizations affected by the A/R system. This is a working chart used by the analyst to record background information pertinent to the organizational environment. Other useful information, such as department numbers and telephone numbers, also can be indicated.

To show additional detail, such as the organizational breakdown within the accounts receivable department, the analyst can prepare additional charts. These charts should identify by name and function the individuals with whom the analyst expects to come into contact. Organizational function lists for each department shown on the organization chart should also be developed. This additional detail is not included as part of the example; however, it is implicit to the development of the detail presented in the subsequent figures that describe the example company's existing A/R system.

Context Diagram.   Figure 8.2 is the context diagram for the existing system. It identifies the flow of data from the customer through the shipping, accounts receivable, and data processing departments and back to the customer.

Current System Costs.   The direct operating costs of the current A/R system were found to be a combination of computer, data entry, and clerical costs. These costs are summarized in figure 8.3. The total current operating cost is $25,100 a month ($2.51 per account for 10,000 accounts).

Input-Output Analysis Sheet.   Figure 8.4 is an input-output analysis for the accounts receivable department. The narrative content was prepared from organizational background information and from information gathered during fact-finding and analysis.

Project Directive

The project directive prepared at the conclusion of the initial investigation identified the following three major system inputs:

1. Account application
2. Sales order
3. Payments/credits

It also identified seven major outputs:

1. Customer statement
2. Overcredit notice
3. A/R transactions
4. A/R summary
5. Aged accounts receivable
6. Order fill data
7. Application approval/denial

The complete project directive for OARS appears as figure 8.5.

■ Figure 8.2   A/R system context diagram. This data flow diagram identifies the major data flows of the A/R system.

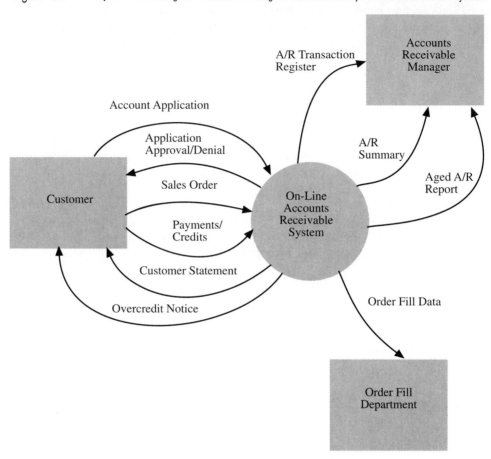

■ Figure 8.3   Current A/R system costs. These direct operating costs of the current A/R system were collected during the initial investigation activities.

Accounts Receivable Operating Cost Summary
(monthly cost per account at 10,000 accounts)

computer time	$ .44
personnel	1.23
data entry	.38
supplies	.46
total	$2.51

Total monthly cost is $25,100.00

A/R system Input-Output Analysis Sheet. This chart summarizes the processes and their inputs and outputs as determined during the initial investigation activities.

INPUT-OUTPUT ANALYSIS SHEET		
ORGANIZATION: Accounts Receivable Dept. SYSTEM: Accounts Receivable Date: 9/3/XX		
INPUT	PROCESSING FUNCTIONS/FILES	OUTPUT
Account Application	Customers submit account applications, which are processed by the Accounts Receivable/Credit department. If an application is accepted, it is sent to Data Processing for entry into the system. Data Processing returns the application for filing. Application approval/denial is sent to the customer.	Application Approval/ Denial
Sales Order	Sales orders are sent directly to Data Processing for order processing. The customer retains the carbon copy. Order fill data are sent to the Order Fill department.	Order Fill Data
Payments/Credits	Payments are sent to the Accounts Receivable department. The payment/credit data are sent to Data Processing. An aged A/R report is sent to the Accounts Receivable manager from Data Processing each month. Data Processing sends overcredit notices to a credit clerk whenever a new order would exceed the customer's credit limit. Unless additional credit is extended, the notice is sent to the customer. Customer statements are sent to Accounts Receivable in duplicate. The original copy is sent to the customer; the duplicate is filed. One-third of the statements are produced each ten days of the month, that is, on the 1st, 10th, and 20th. An A/R transaction register is sent to the Accounts Receivable manager. The accounts receivable summary report is prepared weekly and sent to the Accounts Receivable manager for distribution.	Aged A/R Report Overcredit Notice Customer Statement A/R Transaction Register A/R Summary

■ **Figure 8.5** Project directive for OARS (On-line A/R System). The inputs and outputs listed on the project directive reflect the conclusions reached by the analyst and principal user during the initial investigation, and they establish the context of the system. Along with the system objectives and anticipated benefits, they assist in completing the system performance definition.

INFORMATION SERVICE REQUEST		Page 1 of 4	

	NEW ☑ REV. ☐	REQUESTED DATE: 11/7/XX	REQUIRED DATE: 12/19/XX

AUTHORIZATION

OBJECTIVE: To improve the efficiency of customer billing and account collection	LABOR		OTHER	
	HOURS	AMOUNT	HOURS	AMOUNT
	600	$18,000	0	0

ANTICIPATED BENEFITS: 1. Faster customer billing and collection
2. Reduction of cash flow problems
3. Improved A/R controls

OUTPUT DESCRIPTION	INPUT DESCRIPTION
TITLE: Customer Statement	TITLE: Sales Order
DESTINATION: Customer	SOURCE: Customer
COMMENTS: Currently, 6000/month Anticipate growth to 20,000/mo.	COMMENTS: Currently, 20,000/month Anticipate growth to 100,000/mo.
TITLE: A/R Transaction Register	TITLE: Payments/Credits
DESTINATION: A/R Management	SOURCE: Customer
COMMENTS:	COMMENTS:

TO BE FILLED OUT BY REQUESTOR

REQUESTED BY: *J. Davis*	DEPARTMENT: 310	TITLE: Head, A/R Dept.	TELEPHONE: X3250
APPROVED BY: *Ben Franklin*	DEPARTMENT: 300	TITLE: Manager, Acct. Division	TELEPHONE: X3208

TO BE FILLED OUT BY INFORMATION SERVICES

FILE NO: ISR-310-1	ACCEPTED ☑ NOT ACCEPTED ☐		
SIGNATURE: *C. Hampton*	DEPARTMENT: 200	TITLE: Manager, Info. Serv. Div.	TELEPHONE: X2670

REMARKS: This is a project directive. J. Herring is appointed project leader. Advise requestor when

funds are 90% expended.

FORM NO: C-6-1	ADDITIONAL INFORMATION: USE REVERSE SIDE OR EXTRA PAGES

INFORMATION SERVICE REQUEST	Page 2 of 4

JOB TITLE: Study Phase for an On-Line A/R System (OARS)

NEW ☑
REV. ☐

REQUESTED DATE: 11/7/XX

REQUIRED DATE: 12/19/XX

OBJECTIVE: To improve the efficiency of customer billing and account collection

AUTHORIZATION

	LABOR		OTHER	
	HOURS	AMOUNT	HOURS	AMOUNT
	600	$18,000	0	0

ANTICIPATED BENEFITS:
1. Faster customer billing and collection
2. Reduction of cash flow problems
3. Improved A/R controls

OUTPUT DESCRIPTION

INPUT DESCRIPTION

TITLE: Overcredit Notice

TITLE: Account Application

DESTINATION: Customer

SOURCE: Customer

COMMENTS:

COMMENTS:

TITLE: A/R Summary

TITLE:

DESTINATION: A/R Management

SOURCE:

COMMENTS:

COMMENTS:

TO BE FILLED OUT BY REQUESTOR

REQUESTED BY: *J. Davis*	DEPARTMENT: 310	TITLE: Head, A/R Dept.	TELEPHONE: X3250
APPROVED BY: *Ben Franklin*	DEPARTMENT: 300	TITLE: Manager, Acct. Division	TELEPHONE: X3208

TO BE FILLED OUT BY INFORMATION SERVICES

FILE NO: ISR-310-1	ACCEPTED ☑ NOT ACCEPTED ☐		
SIGNATURE: *C. Hampton*	DEPARTMENT: 200	TITLE: Manager, Info. Serv. Div.	TELEPHONE: X2670

REMARKS: This is a project directive, J. Herring is appointed project leader. Advise requestor when

funds are 90% expended.

FORM NO: C-6-1   ADDITIONAL INFORMATION: USE REVERSE SIDE OR EXTRA PAGES

INFORMATION SERVICE REQUEST		Page 3 of 4	

JOB TITLE: Study Phase for an On-Line A/R System (OARS)	NEW ☑ REV. ☐	REQUESTED DATE: 11/7/XX	REQUIRED DATE: 12/19/XX

AUTHORIZATION

OBJECTIVE: To improve the efficiency of customer billing and account collection	LABOR		OTHER	
	HOURS	AMOUNT	HOURS	AMOUNT
	600	$18,000	0	0

ANTICIPATED BENEFITS: 1. Faster customer billing and collection
2. Reduction of cash flow problems
3. Improved A/R controls

OUTPUT DESCRIPTION	INPUT DESCRIPTION
TITLE: Aged Accounts Receivable	TITLE:
DESTINATION: A/R Management	SOURCE:
COMMENTS:	COMMENTS:
TITLE: Order Fill Data	TITLE:
DESTINATION: Order Fill Dept.	SOURCE:
COMMENTS: To maintain a perpetual inventory	COMMENTS:

TO BE FILLED OUT BY REQUESTOR

REQUESTED BY: *J. Davis*	DEPARTMENT: 310	TITLE: Head, A/R Dept.	TELEPHONE: X3250
APPROVED BY: *Ben Franklin*	DEPARTMENT: 300	TITLE: Manager, Acct. Division	TELEPHONE: X3208

TO BE FILLED OUT BY INFORMATION SERVICES

FILE NO: ISR-310-1	ACCEPTED ☑ NOT ACCEPTED ☐		
SIGNATURE: *C. Hampton*	DEPARTMENT: 200	TITLE: Manager, Info. Serv. Div.	TELEPHONE: X2670

REMARKS: This is a project directive. J. Herring is appointed project leader. Advise requestor when

funds are 90% expended.

FORM NO: C-6-1	ADDITIONAL INFORMATION: USE REVERSE SIDE OR EXTRA PAGES

INFORMATION SERVICE REQUEST	Page _4_ of _4_

JOB TITLE: Study Phase for an On-Line A/R System (OARS)	NEW ☑ REV. ☐	REQUESTED DATE: 11/7/XX	REQUIRED DATE: 12/19/XX

OBJECTIVE: To improve the efficiency of customer billing and account collection		AUTHORIZATION			
		LABOR		OTHER	
		HOURS	AMOUNT	HOURS	AMOUNT
		600	$18,000	0	0

ANTICIPATED BENEFITS: 1. Faster customer billing and collection
2. Reduction of cash flow problems
3. Improved A/R controls

OUTPUT DESCRIPTION	INPUT DESCRIPTION
TITLE: Application = Approval	TITLE:
DESTINATION: Customer	SOURCE:
COMMENTS:	COMMENTS:
TITLE: Application - Denial	TITLE:
DESTINATION: Customer	SOURCE:
COMMENTS:	COMMENTS:

TO BE FILLED OUT BY REQUESTOR

REQUESTED BY: _J. Davis_	DEPARTMENT: 310	TITLE: Head, A/R Dept.	TELEPHONE: X3250
APPROVED BY: _Ben Franklin_	DEPARTMENT: 300	TITLE: Manager, Acct. Division	TELEPHONE: X3208

TO BE FILLED OUT BY INFORMATION SERVICES

FILE NO: ISR-310-1	ACCEPTED ☑ NOT ACCEPTED ☐		
SIGNATURE: _C. Hampton_	DEPARTMENT: 200	TITLE: Manager, Info. Serv. Div.	TELEPHONE: X2670

REMARKS. This is a project directive. J. Herring is appointed project leader. Advise requestor when

funds are 90% expended.

FORM NO: C-6-1	ADDITIONAL INFORMATION: USE REVERSE SIDE OR EXTRA PAGES

■ Figure 8.6   Context diagram of the logical model for the new A/R system.

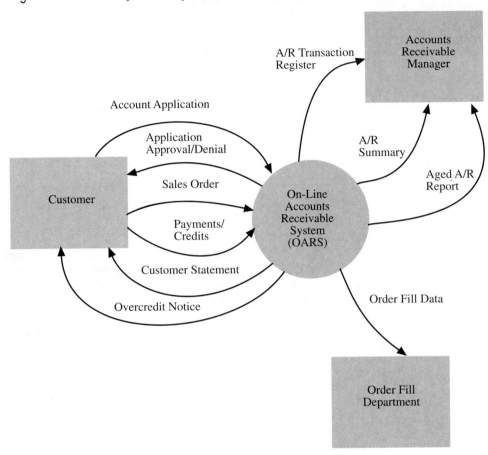

Logical Model of the New System

Figure 8.6 is the context diagram for the new on-line accounts receivable system (OARS) as derived from the project directive. The logical model for the new system at this level, in this case, is the same as the logical model for the old system. If the major problems of the existing system are at a more detailed level or in the physical implementation of the system, it is not uncommon that the old and new system logical models are the same or very similar at the context diagram level. The context diagram identifies the three entities that bound the system: the customer, the A/R department managers, and the order-fill department. The latter is shown because OARS must interface with a perpetual inventory system.

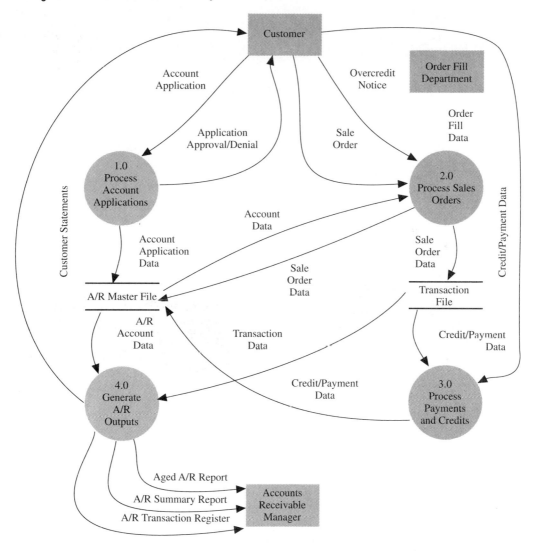

Figure 8.7 is a level-0 data flow diagram that identifies the following four major processes that transform data streams:

1. Process account application
2. Process sales order
3. Process payments/credits
4. Create A/R outputs

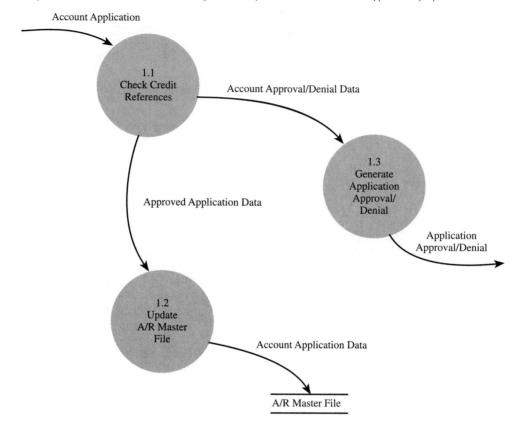

■ Figure 8.8   OARS level-1 data flow diagram. Decomposition of Process Account Applications (1.0).

It also shows an A/R data base, which is in accordance with J. Herring's recommendation to replace the separate customer and A/R master files of the current system.

Figures 8.8, 8.9, 8.10, and 8.11 are the level-1 data flow diagrams for each of the four process bubbles shown on the level-0 DFD. We will not further decompose these level-1 data flow diagrams. However, an actual system would be more complex than our example, and additional levels of decomposition would be required in order to complete the design phase task of preparing a complete structured data processing specification.

This set of data flow diagrams is a useful tool for distinguishing between regions of manual and computer data processing operations. In OARS, for example, credit reference checking is a manual process. Additionally, other background knowledge that the analyst has accumulated in the course of the initial investigation and in-depth

OARS level-1 data flow diagram. Decomposition of Process Sales Orders (2.0).

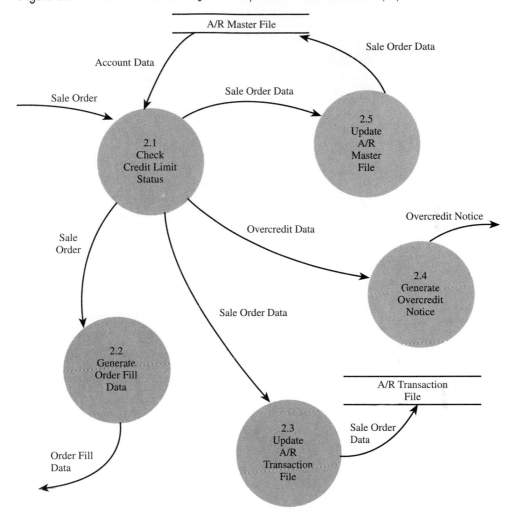

discussions with users also assist in identifying the most suitable presentation techniques and formats for output information. This knowledge is particularly useful in preparing user-oriented output descriptions. This important task is the last of the system performance definition tasks, and it is completed after the general constraints and specific objectives of the computer information system have been fully documented.

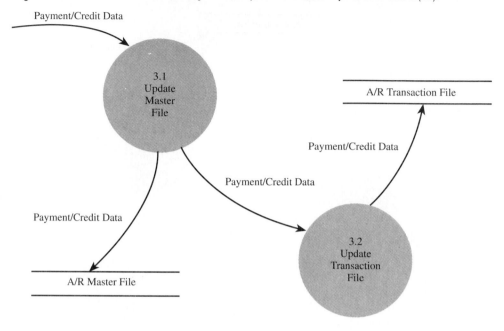

General Constraints

Statement of General Constraints

General **constraints** are those limiting all problem solutions that the systems analyst may consider. Typically, these are constraints that have been imposed from the outset of the project or that have been identified in the course of the initial investigation and discussed with the user-sponsor. There are many possible general constraints. Among the most common are management policy, legal requirements, equipment and facilities (for example, an existing computer center), audit and internal control requirements, fixed organizational responsibilities, cost, and time.

With respect to the cost and time constraints, it is important for the analyst to realize that management often is willing to accept something less than an optimum system provided that it meets basic needs, that its development cost is not excessive, and that it will be available when needed. The analyst who is not able to appreciate the realities of the corporate environment will not enjoy a long and rewarding career. Incidentally, this is one reason why it is often a good strategy, when possible, to segment large systems so that some elements can be installed and can begin to "pay their own way" while the development of other elements continues.

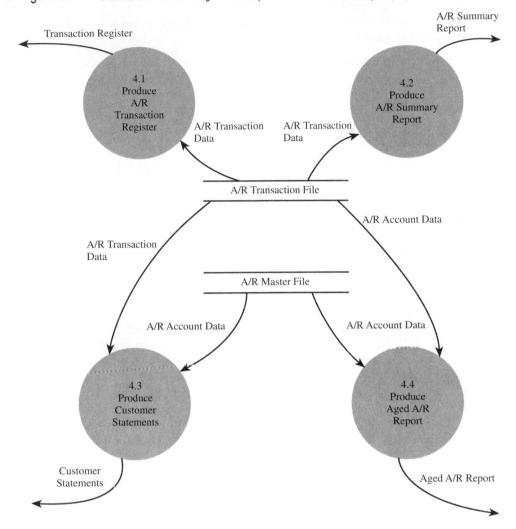

■ Figure 8.11 OARS level-1 data flow diagram. Decomposition of Generate A/R Outputs (4.0).

Example System: General Constraints

For the example system, the ABCO corporation's OARS, some general constraints might be as follows:

1. Development of the on-line accounts receivable system (OARS) is to be completed within fourteen months.
2. OARS is to have a growth potential to handle a minimum of 20,000 customer accounts.
3. OARS is to interface with the existing perpetual inventory system.

4. OARS is to be designed as an on-line system operating in a distributed data processing environment.
5. The design must be compatible with corporate plans to proceed toward a regional profit center concept.

After the system constraints are established, the analyst proceeds to identify specific performance objectives.

Specific Objectives

Identification and Ranking of Specific Objectives

The objective stated in the project directive is the major system objective. However, this objective is usually a general statement of purpose. The systems analyst must derive the specific objectives to which each system output can be related from this general statement. The first step is to analyze the anticipated benefits stated in the project directive. These benefits, in association with the general system objective, help to formulate **specific objectives**, which are measurable performance outcomes. The experienced analyst does not lose sight of the fact that the benefits of a system must be meaningful and measurable in the value system of the principal user.

The anticipated benefits may be tangible or intangible. Figure 8.12 lists six categories of system benefits. They range from the very tangible, for example, cost reduction, to the very intangible, for example, spring cleaning (which means change for the sake of change). Historically, management has tended to emphasize tangible benefits. More recently, many companies have progressed to the use of computer-based systems to achieve competitive advantages and to provide information that aids in policy and planning decisions. These benefits may be visible only in the corporation's profit and loss statement.

Whenever possible, benefits must be translated into specific objectives that can be stated in measurable terms. For example, "To improve customer service," a general objective and statement of purpose, might be supported by the following specific objectives:

1. To increase the percentage of goods shipped on schedule from 40 percent to 80 percent within six months and to 95 percent within a year.
2. To reduce the number of order cancellations from 35 percent to 5 percent within six months.
3. To reduce the number of back orders from 25 percent to 5 percent at a rate of 5 percent per month.

As these examples illustrate, percentage improvements are an effective means of comparing the performance of a new system with that of the existing system. However, the analyst should be careful not to use the present system's performance as the only reference for establishing the new system's objectives. The analyst should focus also on new needs, some of which may not be related to elements of the current system. Frequently, in the course of developing specific objectives—both tangible and intangible—the analyst has to extend fact-finding and analysis to areas or depths not covered in the initial investigation.

■ Figure 8.12   System benefits. Whenever possible, benefits must be translated into specific objectives that can be stated in measurable terms. This, however, does not mean that intangible benefits should not be considered.

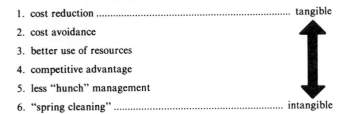

1. cost reduction .... tangible
2. cost avoidance
3. better use of resources
4. competitive advantage
5. less "hunch" management
6. "spring cleaning" .... intangible

Example System: Specific Objectives

We will assume that, after a review of the project directive and the results of the initial investigation, J. Herring prepared the following list of specific objectives for OARS. They are ranked in order of importance.

1. To establish billing cycles for each region.
2. To mail customer statements no later than one day after the close of a billing cycle.
3. To provide the customer with a billing statement two days after the close of a billing cycle.
4. To speed up collections, reducing the float by 50 percent.
5. To examine customer account balances through on-line inquiry at the time of order entry.

Output Description

Output Identification and Description

As the final step in performance definition, the analyst must describe the outputs as they will appear to the user. For example, if the system outputs are to be a display or in a report format, the analyst prepares a layout and a data element description for each output. At this point in the life cycle of a system, it is not necessary to design the output in great detail. The output layout may be a neat sketch that the user can understand and comment upon. However, the sketch should conform to the general rules for good form design. Another option is to develop a prototype of the output using a CASE tool or a data base management system. This approach is described in more detail in chapters 13, "Output Design," and 14, "Input Design." The working prototype may be developed with the user at a terminal. Prototyping often is the best way to develop an output that meets user needs. The output layout can be in any of three forms: a sketch, a prototype, or an example of an existing output.

Reports are the most common computer outputs. These may be actual paper printouts, called "hardcopy" reports, or they may be displays on cathode ray tubes (CRTs), called "softcopy" reports. This discussion of output specifications and data

■ Figure 8.13 Output specification. The output specification form is used by the analyst to describe computer-generated outputs. The layout is a sketch of the proposed output.

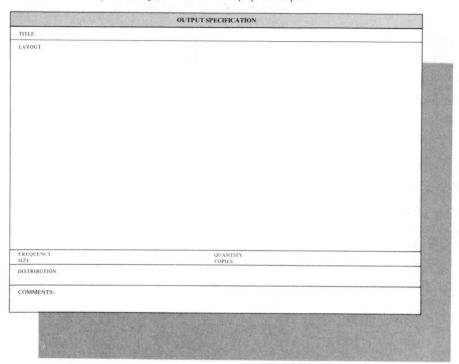

element lists is, in general, applicable to both types of outputs. The specification of output formats and media is necessary not only to complete the system performance definition, but also to trigger the process of selecting the best of alternative systems. This selection process is described in chapter 9, "Candidate System Evaluation." All of the initially chosen outputs and media may not be those selected at the conclusion of the candidate system evaluation. For the remainder of this section and throughout the discussion of OARS, which follows, we will assume that an initial decision was made to present the system outputs in the form of terminal displays whenever feasible, and in the form of printed reports where copies must be sent to customers or filed for future use. Figure 8.13 is an *output specification* form that may be used to describe computer-generated output. It includes:

1. An output title.
2. A layout, that is, a sketch, prototype example, or sample of an existing output.
3. An estimate of the frequency (how often), size (number of pages), quantity (number of unique reports), and number of copies of the output.
4. A distribution list, including the location of feasible distribution points.
5. Special considerations, including identified constraints and controls.

Data element list. Each data element shown in the output layout sketch is described in a data element list. The size, in characters, should be given for each data element. If the format of the data is other than a single string of characters, the format should also be shown on the data element list. This list becomes the basis of data dictionary entries.

DATA ELEMENT LIST		
TITLE:		
DESCRIPTION	FORMAT	SIZE
Billing Cycle: Mo/Day/Yr	*xx/xx/xx*	*8 characters*

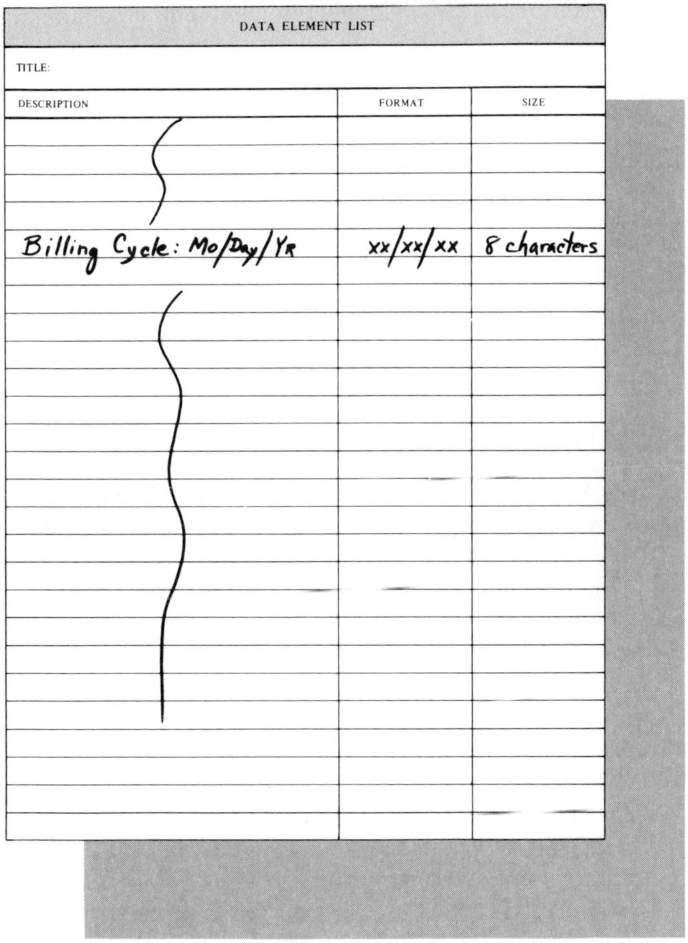

Figure 8.14 is an example of a data element list that should accompany the output specification. The *data element list* contains information describing each data element on the specified report. This information becomes the basis of the data dictionary entries. We will use the typical entry shown in figure 8.4 to illustrate the meaning of the column headings.

1. Description is the name plus any other significant description of the report:

Billing Cycle: Mo/Day/Yr

2. Format is an indication of the appearance of the output on a printed report. The format column should be used whenever any special punctuation or editing is required, for example, $12,456.00 or 02/12/93. Xs are used to represent numbers and characters. Editing symbols are used if they are to be part of the output, for example slashes in dates:

xx/xx/xx

3. Size indicates the number of characters to be printed:

8 characters

By specifying exactly how an output item will appear, the data element list clarifies communication. It leads to an estimate of storage requirements and to meaningful, unambiguous entries in the data dictionary. Of course, as the detailed design process continues or as changes are introduced, data element lists can be retrieved from the data dictionary and output documentation can be kept current. In subsequent phases, the data element list is a basis for file design and for a description of computer program report output.

Example System: Output Description

Sample outputs for the example A/R system are shown in figures 8.15 through 8.22. The first part of each figure is an output specification, the second, a corresponding data element list.

Figure 8.15 illustrates the customer monthly statement along with its data element list. Figure 8.16, the A/R transaction register, contains the same data and is similar to the current system output, but is to be a display as well as a printed report. Figure 8.17, the A/R summary, has been modified from the current output to reflect current balances only. It will be a display showing the data for one customer on each screen. Figure 8.18 is the aged A/R report. It is a monthly report produced at the end of each billing cycle when the customer statements are prepared. Current amounts and 30, 60, 90, and over 90 days past due amounts are shown. Figure 8.19 is the order-fill data transmitted to the Order Fill department. Each sales region will be able to view its customer account list on a terminal on demand. No printed copies will be available. Figure 8.20 is the overcredit notification, which is prepared daily for each account that has exceeded its credit limit and for which the accounts receivable department decides not to grant additional credit. The printed notice is mailed to the customer.

Sample customer monthly statement. The output specification and data element list of the customer monthly statement were developed by the user and the analyst.

OUTPUT SPECIFICATION

TITLE: **Customer Statement**

LAYOUT:

Customer Monthly Statement
ABCO Corporation
Walnut, California

Name and Address

Account No: _____
Billing Date: _____
Due Date: _____
Amount Paid: _____

To insure proper credit, please return this portion with payment.

Account Number	Previous Balance	Finance Charge	Total Purchases	Total Payments & Credits	New Balance

Date	Invoice Number/Description	Purchases	Payments & Credits

FREQUENCY: **Monthly**   QUANTITY **6,000**
SIZE: **1 to 5 pages**   COPIES: **2**

DISTRIBUTION: 1. Customer
2. A/R Department file

COMMENTS: A Delinquent Account message will b
than 30 days over due at the beginning of a billing c

DATA ELEMENT LIST

TITLE: **Customer Monthly Statement**

DESCRIPTION	FORMAT	SIZE
Name		26 characters
Address:		
Street		20 "
City		18 "
State		2 "
Zip Code		5 "
Account No: Region No. - Sequence No.	XX-XXXXXXX	10 "
Billing Cycle Date: Mo/Day/Year	xx/xx/xx	8 "
Due Date: Mo/Day/Year	xx/xx/xx	8 "
Amount Paid	XXX,XXX.XX	10 "
Previous Balance	XXX,XXX.XX	10 "
Finance Charge	X,XXX.XX	8 "
Total Purchases	XXX,XXX.XX	10 "
Total Payments & Credits	XXX,XXX.XX	10 "
New Balance	XXX,XXX.XX	10 "
Date: Date of Purchase, e.g., Jun 15	XXX XX	6 "
Invoice Number/Description		30 "
Purchases	XXX,XXX.XX	10 "
Payments & Credits	XXX,XXX.XX	10 "

■ Figure 8.16   Sample A/R transaction register. The output specification and data element list of the accounts receivable transaction register for this system is to be a display as well as a printed report.

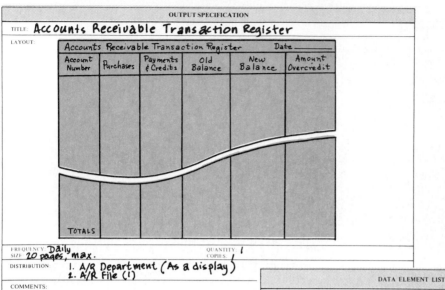

OUTPUT SPECIFICATION

TITLE: **Accounts Receivable Transaction Register**

LAYOUT:

Accounts Receivable Transaction Register	Date_____				
Account Number	Purchases	Payments & Credits	Old Balance	New Balance	Amount Overcredit
TOTALS					

FREQUENCY **Daily**   QUANTITY COPIES: **1**
SIZE **20 pages, max.**

DISTRIBUTION   1. A/R Department (As a display)
                2. A/R File (1)

COMMENTS:

        Account number sequence

DATA ELEMENT LIST

TITLE: **Accounts Receivable Transaction Register**

DESCRIPTION	FORMAT	SIZE
Date: Mo/Day/Year	xx/xx/xx	8 characters
Account No: Region No.-Sequence No.	XX-XXXXXXX	10 "
Purchases	XXX,XXX.XX	10 "
Payments & Credits	XXX,XXX.XX	10 "
Old Balance	XXX,XXX.XX	10 "
New Balance	XXX,XXX.XX	10 "
Amount overcredit	XX,XXX.XX	9 "
Totals	XX,XXX,XXX.XX	13 "

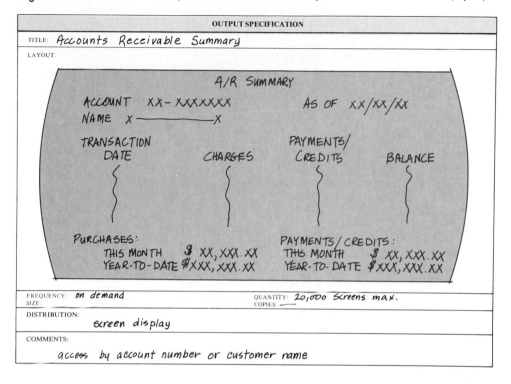

■ Figure 8.17 Sample A/R summary. The accounts receivable summary reflects current balances as a display output.

Figure 8.21 is the application approval form that is mailed to customers who qualify for credit after their account application request has been reviewed and approved. Figure 8.22 is the application disapproval form that is mailed to customers who apply for but do not qualify for credit.

At this point, the analyst has identified the specific objectives of the system and has described the outputs required to meet those objectives. The analyst is now ready to evaluate the alternative physical candidate systems that might produce these outputs.

■ Figure 8.17   continued.

DATA ELEMENT LIST		
TITLE: *Accounts Receivable Summary*		
DESCRIPTION	FORMAT	SIZE
Account Number	XX-XXXXXXX	10 Char.
Current Date (as of)	MM/DD/YY	8 "
Customer Name		26 "
Transaction Date	MM/DD/YY	8 "
Charges	$XX,XXX.XX	10 "
Payments / Credits	$XX,XXX.XX	10 "
Balance	$XXX,XXX.XX	11 "
Purchases:		
This month	$XX,XXX.XX	10 "
Year-to-date	$XXX,XXX.XX	11 "
Payments / Credits:		
This month	$XX,XXX.XX	10 "
Year-to-date	$XXX,XXX.XX	11 "

- Figure 8.18   Sample aged A/R report. The aged accounts receivable report is a printed monthly report produced at the end of each billing cycle.

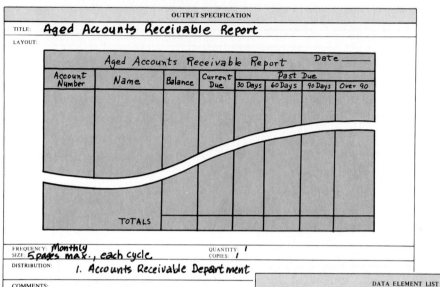

OUTPUT SPECIFICATION

TITLE: **Aged Accounts Receivable Report**

LAYOUT:

Aged Accounts Receivable Report					Date _____		
Account Number	Name	Balance	Current Due	Past Due			
				30 Days	60 Days	90 Days	Over 90
TOTALS							

FREQUENCY: **Monthly**   QUANTITY: **1**
SIZE: **5 pages max., each cycle.**   COPIES: **1**
DISTRIBUTION: **1. Accounts Receivable Department**

COMMENTS:
Run by region on billing cycle date.

DATA ELEMENT LIST

TITLE: **Aged Accounts Receivable Report**

DESCRIPTION	FORMAT	SIZE
Date: Billing Cycle Date: Mo/Day/Yr.	xx/xx/xx	8 characters
Account No.: Region No. - Sequence No.	XX-XXXXXXX	10 "
Name		26 "
Balance	XXX,XXX.XX	10 "
Current Due	XXX,XXX.XX	10 "
Past Due		
30 days	XXX,XXX.XX	10 "
60 days	XXX,XXX.XX	10 "
90 days	XXX,XXX.XX	10 "
Over 90	XXX,XXX.XX	10 "
Totals	XX,XXX,XXX.XX	13 "

■ Figure 8.19 Order-fill data is provided so that a perpetual inventory may be maintained by replacing items when the reorder level is reached.

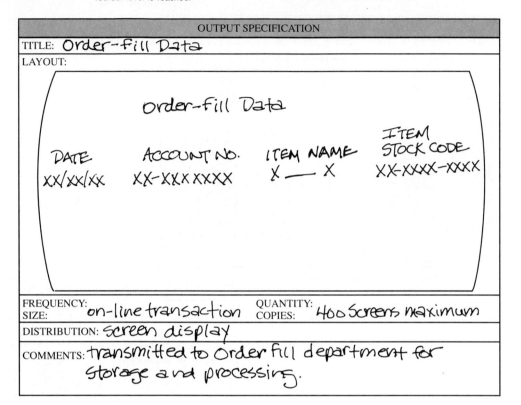

OUTPUT SPECIFICATION
TITLE: Order-fill Data
LAYOUT: Order-fill Data DATE   ACCOUNT NO.   ITEM NAME   ITEM STOCK CODE XX/XX/XX   XX-XXX XXXX   X ___ X   XX-XXXX-XXXX
FREQUENCY: SIZE: on-line transaction   QUANTITY: COPIES: 400 screens maximum
DISTRIBUTION: screen display
COMMENTS: transmitted to order fill department for storage and processing.

■ Figure 8.20   Sample overcredit notification. An overcredit notification will be printed for each account that has exceeded its credit limit and for which the accounts receivable department decides not to grant additional credit to the customer.

OUTPUT SPECIFICATION

TITLE: Overcredit Notice

LAYOUT:

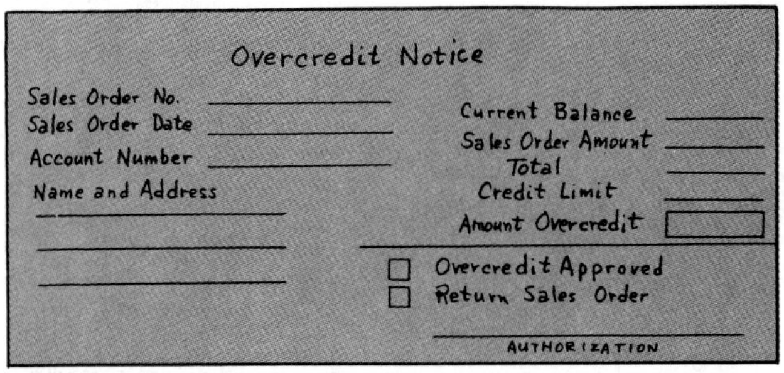

Overcredit Notice

Sales Order No. _____
Sales Order Date _____
Account Number _____
Name and Address
_____
_____
_____

Current Balance _____
Sales Order Amount _____
Total _____
Credit Limit _____
Amount Overcredit [_____]

☐ Overcredit Approved
☐ Return Sales Order

AUTHORIZATION

FREQUENCY: Daily
SIZE: 1 page
QUANTITY: 80 max.
COPIES: 2

DISTRIBUTION: 1. Accts. Receivable Dept.

COMMENTS: ___

DATA ELEMENT LIST

TITLE: Overcredit Notice

DESCRIPTION	FORMAT	SIZE	
Sales Order Number	XXXXXXX	8	characters
Sales Order Date	xx/xx/xx	8	"
Account No: Region No.—Sequence No.	xx-xxxxxxx	10	"
Name		26	"
Address			
Street		20	"
City		18	"
State		2	"
Zip Code		5	"
Current Balance	xxx,xxx.xx	10	"
Sales Order Amount	xxx,xxx.xx	10	"
Total	xxx,xxx.xx	10	"
Credit Limit	xx,xxx.xx	9	"
Amount Overcredit	xx,xxx.xx	9	"

■ Figure 8.21   Application approval form. The application approval form is mailed to customers who qualify for credit after their account application request has been reviewed and found satisfactory.

OUTPUT SPECIFICATION
TITLE: *Application Approval Form*

LAYOUT:

Account Number: _____   Date _____

Name and Address

_____

_____

_____

    We are pleased to inform you that your application for an account has been approved. Your account number is shown above. Your credit limit is _____.

FREQUENCY:	*daily*	QUANTITY: *50/day*
SIZE:		COPIES: *2*

DISTRIBUTION: *1 - Customer*
2 - A/R Department File

SPECIAL CONSIDERATIONS: *Word Processing Application in Credit Check. Account data used to update A/R data base.*

DATA ELEMENT LIST		
TITLE: *Application Approval Form*		
DESCRIPTION	FORMAT	SIZE
Account No.: Region & Seq.	XX-XXXXXXX	8 characters
Date: Current Date	Example: January 27, 1988	
Name		26 characters
Address		
Street		20 "
City		18 "
State		2 "
Zip Code		5 "

■ Figure 8.22   Application disapproval form. The application disapproval form is mailed to customers after their account application request has been reviewed and found unsatisfactory.

OUTPUT SPECIFICATION

TITLE: *Application Denial Form*

LAYOUT:

Name and Address   Date _____

_____

_____

_____

      We regret that we are not able to approve your application for credit at this time. We are returning your account application for the reason below:

    □ Incomplete application
    □ Credit references lacking or unsupported
    □ Other references lacking or unsupported
    □ Other reason:

FREQUENCY: *daily*   QUANTITY: *10/day*
SIZE: COPIES: *2*

DISTRIBUTION: *1. Applicant*
               2. Credit check file

SPECIAL CONSIDERATIONS: *Word Processing Application in credit check.*

DATA ELEMENT LIST		

TITLE *Application Denial Form*

DESCRIPTION	FORMAT	SIZE
Date: Current Date	Example: January 27, 1988	
Name		26 characters
Address		
Street		20 "
City		18 "
State		2 "
Zip Code		5 "

Summary

System performance definition is the transition from a logical performance requirement to a physical one. It includes the statement of general constraints, identification of specific objectives, and description of outputs. The transition is accomplished in four stages:

1. The project directive, prepared at the conclusion of the initial investigation, is used to prepare a context diagram for the new or improved system. This diagram is expanded into a leveled set of data flow diagrams to ensure that all significant data flows are known, the processes that transform them understood, and the appropriate data dictionary entries made. The result is a logical model of a new or modified system.
2. The general constraints, which are the conditions that limit all solutions that the analyst may consider, are stated clearly.
3. The specific objectives that the information system must meet are derived from the objectives stated in the project directive. They are measurable system performance outcomes to which the system outputs can be related.
4. Finally, each system output is described. Output specification sheets are used to show hardcopy and softcopy outputs. These are designed to be user-oriented. They are accompanied by data element lists that explain all of the data elements that appear on the output specification layouts.

Upon completion of the system performance definition activities, the systems analyst is prepared to evaluate the alternative systems that might produce the desired outputs.

For Review

system performance definition   output specification
constraint   data element list
specific objective

For Discussion

1. What is the importance of system performance definition?
2. Identify the major activities that are involved in the transition from a logical model of an information system to a physical one.
3. At what point in the systems development life cycle should the formal description of system outputs occur?
4. What is a general constraint? A specific constraint?
5. How is the project directive used in the system performance definition process?
6. What is the reason for ranking specific objectives in order of importance?
7. What is an output specification sheet? How does it relate to the selection of candidate systems?

8. What is the relationship between a data element list and a data dictionary? A data element list and an output specification sheet?
9. What is a specific objective? How does it relate to the objectives that appear on the project directive? How does it relate to system outputs?
10. What should the relationship between the systems analyst and the principal users of a computer information system be during the system performance definition process?

For Exercise: OARS Hierarchy Chart

Referring to the data flow diagrams shown in figures 8.6 through 8.11, draw a hierarchy chart that shows the levels of functions of this accounts receivable system. The levels shown on the hierarchy chart should reflect the levels of DFDs.

Chapter

9

■ ■ ■

Candidate
System
Evaluation

Preview

The previous chapter described the process of defining the performance required of a computer-based business information system. Next, a candidate system evaluation is performed to choose the system that meets the performance requirements at the least cost. The most essential tasks performed by the candidate system analysis are: (1) the identification and description of candidate systems, (2) the evaluation of candidate systems, and (3) the selection of the best of the candidate systems.

Objectives

1. You will be able to describe the purposes of a candidate system analysis.
2. You will be able to list the steps in performing a candidate system analysis.
3. You will be able to estimate storage requirements by performing an output data source analysis.
4. You will be able to prepare candidate system, candidate evaluation, and weighted candidate evaluation matrices.

Key Terms

candidate system matrix a table that lists functions to be performed and alternative systems for performing them.

candidate evaluation matrix a table that lists evaluation criteria and rates alternative systems in terms of these criteria.

weighted candidate evaluation matrix a table that weights the candidate evaluation matrix entries by their importance and applies a rating number; it is a means of calculating comparative total scores for each candidate.

"best" system the system that meets the performance requirements at the least cost.

Purposes of a Candidate System Evaluation

At this point in the study phase a problem has been identified, an initial investigation has been completed, a project directive has been agreed upon, and system performance definition activities have resulted in:

1. The development of a logical model of the information system, including data flow diagrams, a data dictionary, and process specifications.
2. The initiation of the transition from a logical model to a physical one, subject to constraints, ranked objectives, and output descriptions.

The next step is the candidate system evaluation, which will identify potential physical systems and help us to select the most feasible among these for detailed design and development. Usually, because of the number of computer-related products on the market and because of the large number of possible combinations of input, storage, processing, communications, and output devices, it is possible to develop many candidate systems that appear to meet the physical requirements of the computer information system. Often there is difficulty in keeping the number of candidates to a realistic number so that each can be evaluated within the resources available to the systems team. The process of evaluating the selected candidates is called a candidate system evaluation, and its purpose is twofold:

1. To describe the attributes of each candidate system in detail.
2. To select and recommend the best among them.

In most instances, the best system is the one that satisfies all of the system performance objectives and constraints at the lowest cost.

Steps in a Candidate System Evaluation

The most difficult parts of a candidate system evaluation are the identification of candidate systems and the evaluation of the performance and cost of each. This process is a highly creative one that requires imagination and experience. As with most complex tasks, however, a procedure can be followed. There are seven identifiable steps in performing a candidate system evaluation, as follows:

1. Develop the system candidates.
2. Perform preliminary evaluation of candidates.
3. Prepare detailed descriptions of candidates.
4. Identify meaningful system characteristics.
5. Determine performance and cost for each candidate.
6. Weight the system performance and cost characteristics by importance.
7. Select the "best" candidate.

In the following discussion of the seven steps of the candidate system evaluation, the examples presented to illustrate the process are a continuation of the development of the on-line accounts receivable system (OARS) of the ABCO corporation.

The analyst has been working closely with a team of representatives of the user organization since the beginning of the initial investigation. These user representatives have supplied much needed information about the existing system and the user requirements for the new or modified system.

As we have previously emphasized, the involvement of users and management in planning a system makes the system "their" system. When the people who are going to use the system and/or pay for the system refer to it as "their" system rather than "your" system, the analyst most likely will have cooperation from the users at system reviews and during system conversion.

During the system performance definition, we made a transition from the "what" of the system to the "how" of the system. That is, we went from the logical description to the physical description of the system. The sketches of the various outputs, along with the DFDs, will help us to focus on the system inputs, outputs, and data transformations of the new system.

In preparation for the evaluation of system candidates, the team should review the data flow diagrams to make sure that every member of the team knows the "what" of the new system. This process usually proceeds quickly and without difficulty. The team has sketches and data element lists of all outputs identified during the system performance definition. Additionally, system inputs were identified on the information service request used as the project directive. Returning to the example project, ABCO's OARS, let us assume the following:

> *The system team reviewed and discussed the DFDs and the outputs and inputs identified during the system performance definition activities. Figure 9.1 is the context diagram which along with several levels of DFDs was reviewed by the team. It was approved by Mr. Franklin, manager of the accounting division, during the system performance definition. The team is now ready to proceed with the seven steps of the candidate system evaluation.*

Step 1: Develop the System Candidates

The first step of the candidate system evaluation is to develop candidate physical systems that could produce the outputs identified in the new system data flow diagrams. This step includes a consideration of hardware devices able to accomplish each of the four basic system functions of input, processing, storage, and output.

The system team's task is to brainstorm to create various hardware combinations for each of the four basic functions mentioned earlier. If some team members are not familiar with some of the potentially suitable devices, other members with knowledge of equipment, for example, the data processing representative, can make a presentation to the team.

Figure 9.2 is a table that can be used in the development of system candidates. This table, called a **candidate system matrix,** lists functions to be performed and alternative systems for performing them. It is an effective means of presenting and comparing the basic functions of each candidate. The use of a candidate system matrix is illustrated by continuing with our example system.

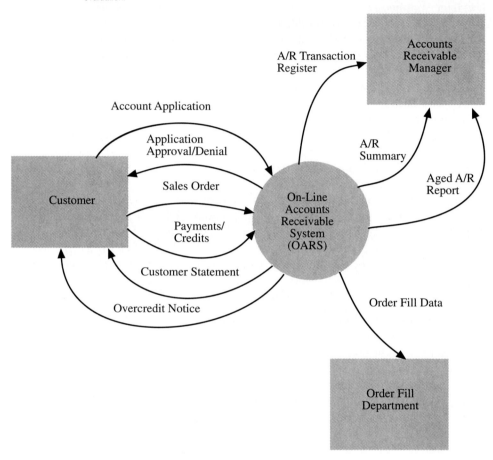

In the ABCO corporation's OARS, the output media initially chosen was computer-printed reports or visual displays, depending upon the nature of the output. These choices were made by the users with the assistance of the analyst, Ms. J. Herring, during the system performance definition activities because they judged them the most likely output media. Those initial assumptions were made so that sketches or prototypes of the outputs could be made with the characteristics of the output device in mind. Those initial assumptions, however, do not now prevent the system team from considering other media.

Possible input media are considered next. Each of the potential media has performance and cost advantages and disadvantages. It is the task of the analyst to help the users understand these advantages and disadvantages so that they, the users, may make the most appropriate choices.

OARS candidate system matrix. This table can be an effective means of presenting and comparing the basic functions of each candidate.

CANDIDATE SYSTEM FUNCTIONS	I	II	III	IV	V	VI
OUTPUT						
INPUT						
STORAGE						
PROCESSING						

The other functions to be considered are processing, storage, and communications. The general processing choices are manual processing and computer processing. In today's world, the processing is accomplished by any of several computerized approaches in most cases, but there are a few applications that are still best served with a manual system. If a potential processing medium is a computer, there are a large number of computers with differing processor capabilities, processor speeds, main storage size ranges, auxiliary storage handling capabilities, and levels of communication support. Computer vendors will be more than happy to provide the system team with information on their equipment and to make recommendations. Representatives of the team, however, should always make it a point to verify data from vendors by making visits or contacts with other users or user groups. Each potential processor has its own advantages and disadvantages. Compromise may be necessary; however, know what you are giving up for what you are getting.

Candidate system matrix. This table contains the descriptions of the three OARS project candidates.

candidate system / functions	I	II	III	
communication	wide area network with mainframe access	wide area network with output download capability	regional local area networks bridged to other regions; distributed data base and processing	
output	all outputs generated at the central site; central printing and local displays	central site generation of all outputs; download for local printing	local generation of displays and printed outputs	
input	local terminals	local micro computers	local micro computers	
storage	data base held and maintained at central site	data base held and maintained at central site	data base distributed among local microcomputers	
processing	all processing at central site; larger mainframe	all processing at central site; larger mainframe	all processing at local sites; existing mainframe	

Step 2: Perform Preliminary Evaluation of System Candidates

Usually the team has far too many candidates to evaluate each one in detail. Hence, the second step in the candidate system evaluation is to make a preliminary evaluation of the system candidates and thus narrow down the number of candidates to a manageable number.

In developing system candidates in step 1, the idea was to brainstorm as many candidates as possible, without attempting any evaluation. In the preliminary evaluation, any system that would not be practical because of its obvious high cost or its overkill for the task at hand is eliminated. Candidate systems that require technical knowledge beyond that available to the company or that do not fit the corporate philosophy should also be dropped from consideration.

The process of elimination should continue until the number of candidates is reduced to a manageable size. The actual number of systems to be considered in detail is, of course, a function of the amount of time and the resources available to the team. The systems to be evaluated in detail are entered into a candidate system matrix.

The system team for the OARS project, headed by Ms. J. Herring, generated a candidate system matrix for OARS. This matrix is shown in part in figure 9.3. All of the candidates are computer-based systems. All of the candidates rely on a central-site computer; however the degree of local processing varies among the candidates.

Step 3: Prepare Detailed Descriptions of Candidates

The third step in the candidate system evaluation is to prepare detailed descriptions of the systems appearing in the candidate system matrix. The detailed descriptions should include data flow diagrams, specific constraints, identified inputs, processing requirements, and storage requirements.

The OARS example illustrates this step with the following assumed situation. In the OARS project, Ms. Herring and the system team have reduced the number of candidates for detailed study to the following three:

1. Candidate I is a computer system utilizing a larger (than the existing) central-site computer with terminals located in each region. All outputs would continue to be produced at the central-site location.
2. Candidate II also requires a larger central-site computer with microcomputers located in each region. All outputs continue to be generated at the central site, but they may be downloaded to the local microcomputers to be displayed or printed locally.
3. Candidate III uses the existing central-site computer as a data repository accessed by microcomputers located in each region. This candidate distributes the accounts receivable data base and processing to each local microcomputer. All outputs, therefore, are generated at the local site.

Both candidates I and II require a central-site computer that is larger than the existing one. Candidate III requires a data base server for distributing the data base over the wide area network, and this candidate is used as the example system for the discussions that follow.

Vendor proposals will be solicited and evaluated early in the design phase, assuming the project gets approval to proceed from the users and management. The data flow diagram of figure 9.1 shows the source of input documents, the path of each document through the transformations, and the generation and distribution of all outputs. Parts a through d of figure 9.4, drawn for candidate III, illustrate details of the description that the team prepared for each candidate. Part a of figure 9.4 is a DFD. It identifies the inputs, outputs, and data transformations of the new accounts receivable system. These descriptions present a comprehensive overview of the candidate system.

Specific constraints are unique to each candidate. They must either be consistent with the general constraints of the project directive or must identify areas where the candidate does not meet the general constraints. If the specific constraints are too restrictive, the candidate will be eliminated or the general constraints of the project directive will have to be modified.

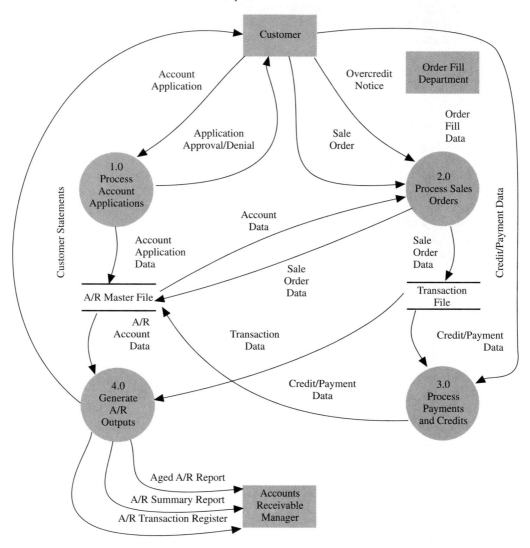

■ Figure 9.4a   OARS project data flow diagram. This DFD emphasizes the inputs, outputs, and data transformations of the new accounts receivable system.

Returning to our example system, part b of figure 9.4 lists the specific constraints for OARS candidate III. Part c identifies the three major OARS inputs and specifies, in general, the equipment to be required by the system. In this case the equipment required is the existing central-site computer and a minicomputer system for each region. Part d presents the estimated number of characters of storage for each master record in the data base, the number of characters for the master file at current customer levels, and the size of the master file at the end of a five-year projection of customer growth. A general constraint affecting the storage estimates is the capacity to process 20,000 customers within five years.

■ Figure 9.4b   OARS specific constraints. Constraints specifically for candidate III.

Candidate III Specific Constraints:

1. This candidate does not require replacement of the central site computer.

2. This candidate requires the installation of a data base server to allow the distribution of the OARS data base among the local microcomputers.

3. The implementation schedule for OARS allows very little time for the acquisition and installation of the required hardware and networks. An evaluation of vendor's products must begin immediately to get an appropriate delivery date for the required hardware and software.

4. A wide area network (WAN) must be provided by bridging regional local area networks.

■ Figure 9.4c   The three major OARS inputs.

OARS System Identified Inputs:

1. Customer Account Applications — maximum of 20 per day

2. Sales Orders — maximum of 1,000 per day

3. Payments/Credit Memos — maximum of 500 per day

■ Figure 9.4d   OARS storage estimates.

OARS System Storage Requirements:

1. Each OARS master record consists of 15 data elements for a total of 167 characters.

2. Assuming a range of 10,000 master records to 20,000 records over the expected 5-year life of the system, from 1,670,000 characters to 3,340,000 characters of data will have to be stored.

3. The data described in 2 above will be distributed among the computers located in the local regions in candidate III.

The gross storage estimates can be developed from a worksheet like the form used in the OARS example, shown in figure 9.5. This worksheet is called an output data element source analysis sheet, and its purpose is to help determine the source of the data elements in the outputs of a system. The data element lists developed to accompany each output sketched during the system performance definition activities are referred to. The completed worksheet identifies the origin of the output data elements as master file, transaction file, or calculated result. In addition, it provides an overview of the output documents and their data element relationships. These worksheets can be used to provide the source data for the data dictionary entries during the design phase activities.

The following are the steps used in performing an output data element source analysis:

1. Complete the heading information.
2. List all output data elements found on the data element lists. Do not list a data element more than one time. Watch for single data elements listed by two or more different data element names. The names used on the data element lists are names that were appropriate and meaningful to that particular output. A slightly different name for the same data element might have been more meaningful on a different output. For example, in figure 9.5 the data element "previous balance" is shown as being used in five of the outputs. The data element lists refer to the same data element as "previous balance" on one output, as "old balance" on two outputs, as "balance" on one output, and as "current balance" on one output. It is obviously the same field in each case, regardless of its name on any one data element list.
3. In the column below each output document, place a check mark opposite each data element appearing on the document. The frequency of check marks opposite the data elements will be valuable information when designing the master record layout.
4. With the frequency-of-use information, decide which data elements should be maintained in a master file or a transaction file, or which ones are to be calculated by the computer program. In the appropriate source of data element column, enter the number of characters for the data element. Data in the master file must originate either in transaction files or as calculated results. Such data is entered in two columns. The number of characters for each data element can be found in the appropriate data element list. Watch for inconsistent data element sizes on the data element list and make adjustments to the lists where required. Note that the numbers of characters entered in the source of data element columns do not include editing symbols, that is, dollar signs, commas, and decimal points, as these would not be stored in the master file or transaction file records.
5. Total each source of data element column. The master file total is a usable estimate of the master record size. It does not take data formats, for example, zoned or packed decimal, into consideration, but it is adequate for study phase planning.

■ Figure 9.5 Output data element source analysis forms for the OARS project.

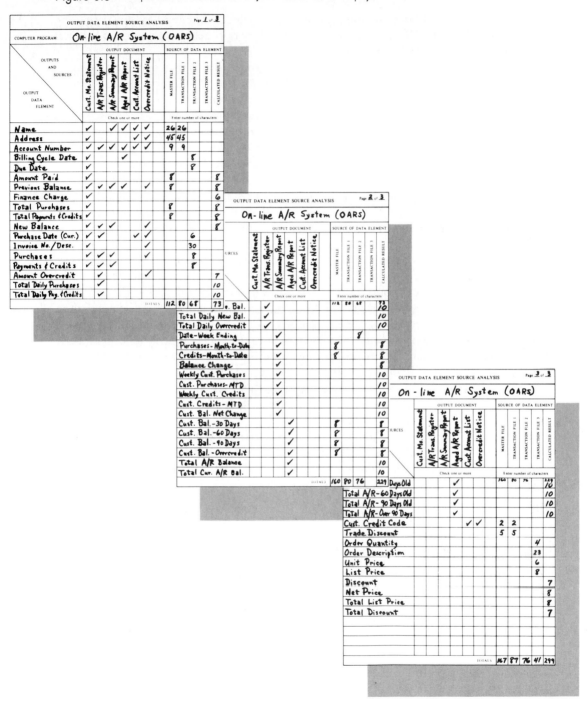

Step 4: Identify Meaningful System Characteristics

Step four of the candidate system evaluation is to select the criteria for evaluating the candidate systems. The candidates are evaluated by two major categories of criteria: performance characteristics and costs.

The performance evaluation criteria relate to the satisfaction of specific objectives identified and ranked in the process of system performance definition. Typical criteria are accuracy, control capability, flexibility, growth potential, response time, storage requirements, and usability. Often these characteristics do not lend themselves to quantitative measurements and must be described qualitatively. In any event, qualitative measurements (that is, best, good, bad, worst) can be used to gauge the relative performance of candidate systems. These measures are based upon the collective judgment of the systems team. System costs include the costs of developing the system and operating it after its implementation. Cost factors that may be particularly important in evaluating a system are those for equipment, facilities, and training. Equipment costs are important when additional equipment, such as computers, must be acquired, or existing equipment must be modified. Existing equipment costs usually need not be considered in the evaluation of a system if these costs would remain the same whether or not the system was adopted. Facility costs reflect the costs of additional buildings or rooms, or the modification of existing facilities. Computer installations requiring additional air conditioning, subflooring to allow for cables, alterations to fire sprinkler systems, or installation of security devices are examples of such costs. Training costs are usually not collected unless they can be easily identified. They can be identified if employees must be sent to equipment vendor schools, or if classes are to be held in-house with overtime being paid to either the employee attending classes or to that person's substitute on the job. However, normal training on the job is usually too difficult to separate from regular job duties to be counted as a system cost.

Figure 9.6 depicts the system evaluation criteria to be used to evaluate the three remaining OARS candidates. This table is called a **candidate evaluation matrix.** When completed, it lists evaluation criteria and rates alternative systems in terms of this criteria.

Step 5: Determine Performance and Cost for Each Candidate

The next step in the candidate system evaluation is to develop the entries for the candidate evaluation matrix. Although the performance ratings are often subjective, the analyst must be fair in making appraisals of system performance and should use consistent units of measure for each candidate.

The "accuracy" of a candidate refers not to the accuracy of the equipment, but of the system. One computer is not likely to be more accurate than another, but a system using one computer can be more accurate than another system using the same computer. Accuracy, therefore, relates to the steps involved in getting source data into the system and the steps that are taken to keep the data as error free as possible. No system will be completely free of bad data. "Control capability" relates to the security of the system; it also provides for auditing of the system. Control capability provides protection from mistakes made by humans and from fraud or illegal data

Candidate evaluation matrix. This table shows the evaluation criteria to be used to evaluate the OARS candidates.

candidate system / evaluation criteria	candidate I	candidate II	
performance			
accuracy			
control			
flexibility			
growth potential			
response time			
storage requirements			
usability			
costs			
system development			
system operations			
payback			

manipulation. "Flexibility" refers to the ease of making adjustments to the system, such as generating modified or new outputs. "Growth potential" is a measure of how much the system can continue to grow without extensive modification to the system or a major component, such as a computer. Such changes are often costly. A system should be expandable for at least two to five years.

The analyst's confidence that the system can produce the desired outputs cycle after cycle is the "reliability" rating. Weak points in the system, or in equipment utilized within the system, that could bring the operation to a halt should be reflected in the reliability rating. A system's "response time" is the total elapsed time between submission of data by a user and its return as a computer output. In a batch processing system, response time includes the system activities of data collection and output distribution, as well as the time required to process the data. In an on-line transaction processing system using a display terminal, the response time is the time from entering the data (or request for data) until seeing the output on the screen.

"Storage requirements" refers to computer-based systems and refers to both main storage size and required auxiliary storage for all files. One of the most important criteria is "usability." Usability, as we have emphasized, is the worth of a system as evaluated by the persons who must use it. It is a measure of the user friendliness (or ease of use) of the system, and it is the final measure of its acceptance. Costs can be

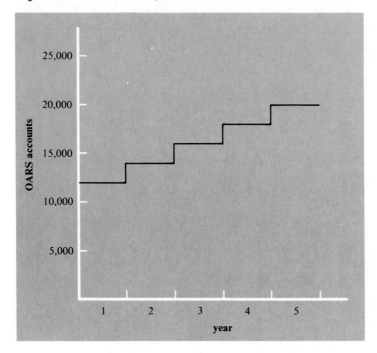

developed most easily when the system benefits are relatively tangible. The most tangible cost comparisons are actual cost savings. The next most tangible comparisons are those related to cost avoidance, usually the case when large growth factors are involved.

For the example OARS, it has been stated that the growth in the number of A/R accounts will double within the next five years. An estimate was made that sales and accounts would increase to 12,000 accounts from the current 10,000 accounts before any new system could be developed and implemented. In addition, it is expected that accounts will increase by approximately 2,000 accounts per year for the next five years. Figure 9.7 depicts this estimated growth. Using this projection, the number of accounts can be estimated for any year over the next five years. Knowing the number of accounts to be processed, the analyst can break the total costs down into "per account" cost for comparison purposes.

The OARS example cost calculations that follow are for OARS candidate III only. Similar calculations were made for the other candidates, and the results are tabulated.

Figure 9.8 illustrates the calculations required to determine the OARS candidate III cost of operation. The figure includes the number of accounts as well as the monthly cost. This information, plus the fact that the number of regions will increase

Candidate III Cost of Operations

year	1	2	3	4	5
number of accounts	12,000	14,000	16,000	18,000	20,000
per region costs:					
communications	$150	$150	$150	$150	$150
*computer	2,000	2,000	2,000	2,000	2,000
system personnel	2,500	2,750	3,000	3,250	3,500
totals	$4,650	$4,900	$5,150	$5,400	$5,650
central-site costs	$6,000	$6,000	$6,000	$6,000	$6,000

*Note: The computer costs are monthly averages which include microcomputers, printers, and maintenance contracts.

to four in year two and to five in year three of the new system, will allow us to calculate the operating costs on a per account basis. Candidate III distributes the processing of the accounts receivable system to each of the regions. Each region, as well as the central site, will therefore incur operating costs. The per region cost includes the cost of communications, the computer, and the system personnel. The central-site cost includes the communications hardware/software and central-site system personnel. Figure 9.9 summarizes the per account costs. As new regions are created and microcomputers are installed, the total cost per account fluctuates from $1.67 up to $2.00 and down to $1.72. Clearly, the personnel cost is the major component of the total cost. The estimated cost to design and develop OARS candidate III is shown in figure 9.10. This cost is the total of the study, design, and development phase costs. Some analysts choose not to include the study phase costs, since they are considered "sunk" costs (or costs already spent). In this example the study phase cost was included in the total cost of all candidates.

Figure 9.11 depicts the rate of spending and the cumulative cost of the study phase, design phase, and development phase over a sixty-week period. For the purpose of comparison, the cost of operating the current A/R system was determined. Figure 9.12 is the same as figure 8.3, except for the added cost due to "float." Float is the cost incurred due to delays in receiving payment from credit customers. The estimated delay in collecting an average two million dollars per month at current interest rates results in an estimated monthly cost of $31,992. This float adds a cost of

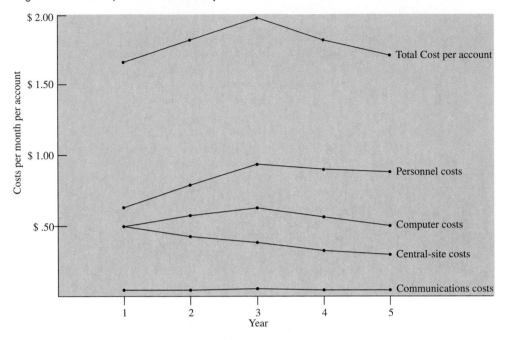

	per week	total	
Study Phase: (10 weeks)			
senior analyst	$1,000	$10,000	
analyst	800	8,000	
			$18,000
Design Phase: (20 weeks)			
senior analyst	$1,000	$20,000	
analyst	800	16,000	
senior programmer	750	15,000	
			$51,000
Development Phase: (30 weeks)			
senior analyst	$1,000	$30,000	
analyst	800	24,000	
senior programmer	750	22,500	
programmers (5)	700	105,000	
computer time	500	15,000	
			$196,500
			$265,500

OARS rate of spending and cumulative cost of the study phase, design phase, and development phase over a sixty week period.

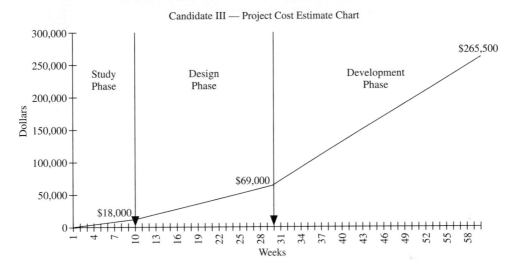

Candidate III — Project Cost Estimate Chart

■ Figure 9.12 OARS cost of operation calculations for the existing system, including float.

Accounts Receivable Operating Cost Summary Including Float (monthly cost per account at 10,000 accounts)		
monthly operating costs:		
computer time	$ 4,400	$ .44/account
personnel cost	12,300	1.23/account
data entry	3,800	.38/account
supplies	4,600	.46/account
operating totals	$25,100	$2.51/account
monthly float cost	$31,992	$3.20/account
total operating costs	$57,092	$5.71/account

■ Figure 9.13 OARS cumulative cost calculations.

year	Ref.-Existing annual	Ref.-Existing cumulative	I annual	I cumulative	II annual	II cumulative	III annual	III cumulative
dev. cost	0	0	215,300	215,300	230,100	230,100	265,500	265,500
1	822,240	822,240	230,000	445,300	239,000	469,100	239,400	504,900
2	959,280	1,781,520	289,000	734,300	290,000	759,100	307,200	812,100
3	1,096,320	2,877,840	340,000	1,074,300	350,000	1,109,100	381,000	1,193,100
4	1,233,360	4,111,200	350,000	1,424,300	360,000	1,469,100	396,000	1,589,100
5	1,370,400	5,481,600	380,000	1,804,300	390,000	1,859,100	411,000	2,000,100

$3.20 per account each month, raising the cost to $5.71. Figure 9.13 depicts the costs for each candidate. Even though the current system is not a viable candidate, its costs have been included to show the relationships between the costs of replacement systems and the cost of maintaining the existing system. The data for figure 9.13 were determined from the following:

1. The number of accounts for each year was taken from the account projection in figure 9.7.
2. The number of regions will increase from three to four in the second year of system operation and to five in the third year.
3. The float cost will increase as the number of accounts increases. This cost was determined to be $31,992; $37,332; $42,660; $48,000; and $53,328 for each of the projected five years.
4. The float cost from number 3 was added to the annual operating costs of candidates I and II.
5. It was estimated that the expanded existing system would remain at $5.71 per account cost each month and that this cost per account would continue over the next five years.
6. The annual operating costs for candidate III were calculated using the data in figure 9.8.

Figure 9.14 illustrates a payback analysis. Its purpose is to show the point in time at which the investment in the new system is recovered—as a result of cost savings or cost avoidance. The payback occurs where the candidate's accumulated cost crosses the accumulated cost of the reference existing system. The performances and

■ Figure 9.14   OARS payback analysis.

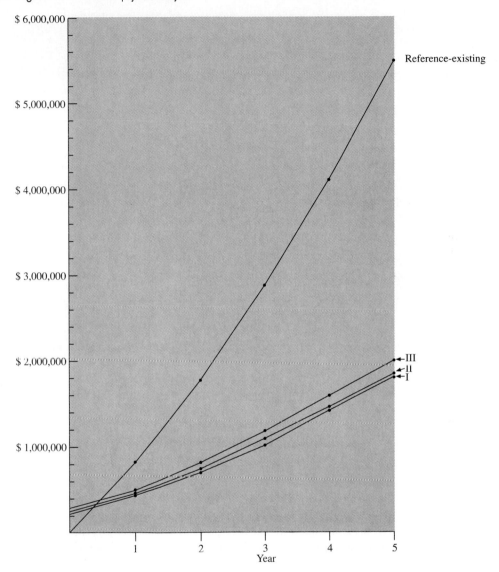

candidate system / evaluation criteria	candidate I	candidate II	candidate III
performance			
accuracy	good	good	very good
control	good	good	very good
flexibility	good	good	very good
growth potential	poor	poor	very poor
response time	good	good	very good
storage requirements	very good	good	very good
usability	fair	good	very good
costs			
system development	$215,300	$230,100	$265,500
system operation	$1.60 to 1.77 to 1.58	$1.66 to 1.82 to 1.63	$1.66 to 1.98 to 1.71
payback	≈ 4 months	≈ 6 months	≈ 8 months

costs of each candidate are summarized in figure 9.15, which is a completed candidate evaluation matrix for candidate III. As the analyst proceeds through the candidate system evaluation, additional system criteria may be identified, and/or criteria identified previously may be discarded. In this figure, all of the criteria identified earlier in figure 9.6 have been retained.

Step 6: Weight the System Performance and Cost Characteristics

In some cases the performance and cost data collected for each candidate will show one candidate as the obvious choice. When this occurs, the task of the candidate system evaluation is completed. Many times, however, the best candidate is still not clearly identified. The eighth step of the candidate system evaluation is to prepare a **weighted candidate evaluation matrix.** This is a matrix that weights the candidate evaluation entries by their importance and then applies a rating number; it is a means of calculating total numeric scores for each candidate.

A weighted candidate evaluation matrix is prepared in five steps, as follows:

1. Divide the evaluation criteria into categories of importance, for example, very important, moderately important, important.
2. Assign a weighting factor to each category. The weighting factors should be in proportion to each criterion's effect on the success of the selected candidate system.
3. Rate each candidate for each criterion relative to the other candidates. This relative rating is often with a scale of 1 to 5, with 5 being the best and 1 the lowest.

candidate system / evaluation criteria	candidate I		candidate II		candidate III	
performance	rating	score	rating	score	rating	score
accuracy (wt 2)	3	6	3	6	5	10
control (wt 4)	3	12	3	12	4	16
flexibility (wt 2)	3	6	3	6	4	8
growth potential (wt 4)	1	4	1	4	5	20
response time (wt 5)	3	15	3	15	5	25
storage requirements (wt 2)	5	10	3	6	5	10
usability (wt 5)	2	10	3	15	5	25
costs						
system development (wt 5)	5	25	4	20	3	15
system operation (wt 2)	5	10	4	8	3	6
payback (wt 2)	5	10	4	8	3	6
total score		108		100		141

4. Calculate the candidate's score for each criterion by multiplying the relative rating by the weight assigned to the category.
5. Add the score column for each candidate to determine its total score.

Figure 9.16 is a weighted candidate evaluation matrix that was developed for OARS by following the previous steps. The relative weights for each criterion were determined cooperatively by the system team, and the ratings of the candidates were developed from data summarized in figure 9.15.

Step 7: Select the "Best" System

The last step is to select the best candidate system. If the analyst has been objective and has judged each of the evaluation criteria for each candidate without prejudice, the weighted candidate evaluation matrix summarizes the facts collected, as well as the subjective impressions about each candidate. The candidate with the highest total score probably is the best system. The analyst must select a candidate to present to the users and to management for their acceptance or rejection. If the total scores of two or more candidates are close, the analyst should reexamine the weights and ratings that differ the most, or in which the team has the least amount of confidence. Finally, the analyst should select the candidate with the highest total score that is consistent with the team's confidence in the data. The analyst usually should not present several candidate choices to management for their selection. They expect a recommendation from the analyst and other team members who have just completed a period of concentrated study of the candidates and are therefore in the best position to recommend a selection.

In the example ABCO corporation OARS, the criterion with the greatest effect on the total scores was the system growth potential. Candidates I and II were not expected to be able to grow as easily as candidate III because of the requirement for a large central-site computer to support them. In addition, the response time and the usability of candidate III are far superior to the other candidates. Candidate III will also allow ABCO to pursue its profit-center concept of organization. Therefore, although its payback period was the longest, candidate III was selected by the team for presentation to management and the users.

The number of candidates that could be considered in the preceding example was necessarily limited. Actual situations usually are more complex, and choices are more difficult. However, there is one important practical guideline that the systems analyst always should keep in mind: The **"best" system** usually is the system that meets the performance requirements at the least cost. This "best" system is not necessarily the system that provides the best performance, or even the best performance-to-cost ratio, if cost is a serious consideration. Overdesign frequently disguised as "the most bang for the buck" is liable to be an expensive luxury in a competitive, cost-conscious business environment. For example, a medium-to-large-scale computer may have a better performance-to-cost ratio than a small computer. However, if a small computer will meet the performance requirement at a lower cost, the additional dollars might be more effectively utilized elsewhere in the corporation. The weighted candidate evaluation matrix example just completed was developed manually, but there are several project management software packages available to automate the procedure. Some of these packages run on mini and mainframe sized computers, but most are designed to run on personal computers. Figure 9.17 is an example from a program running on a personal computer. It shows the same evaluation data as was examined in figure 9.16.

The General System Design

At this point in the system development life cycle, the constraints of the system have been identified, the specific objectives of the new system have been ranked and listed, the system performance requirements have been identified and described, and the "best" candidate system has been selected for presentation. This establishes the general system design that will be presented in the study phase report, presented in chapter 10. If the candidate system that has been selected for presentation to users and management is accepted, this general design will be developed into a detailed design during the design phase.

Computer-generated evaluation matrix. This project management software package generates a separate page for each candidate plus a summary page comparing total scores for all candidates. The darkened portion of each bar graphically shows the actual score of the candidate for that criterion.

Lightyear

SUBJECT:OARS
VERSION:ONE

DETAIL EVALUATION: CRITERIA AND RULES   SCORE WEIGHT

| Candidate III | 26 | 33 |

Criterion	Score	Weight
Response Time	5	5
Usability	5	5
Sys Development	2	5
Control	3	4
Growth	4	4
Accuracy	2	2
Flexibility	2	2
Storage	1	2
Sys Operation	1	2
Payback	1	2

Summary

The purpose of the candidate system evaluation is to identify candidate systems, reduce these systems to a reasonable number, and evaluate the systems on the basis of relative cost and performance. The seven steps in performing a candidate system evaluation are as follows:

1. Develop the system candidates.
2. Perform preliminary evaluation of candidates.
3. Prepare detailed descriptions of candidates.
4. Identify meaningful system characteristics.
5. Determine performance and cost for each candidate.
6. Weight the system performance and cost characteristics by importance.
7. Select the "best" candidate.

Three tables, called matrices, are useful tools in proceeding from step 4 to step 9. These are:

1. A candidate system matrix: A table that lists functions to be performed and an alternative system for performing them.
2. A candidate evaluation matrix: A table that lists evaluation criteria and rates alternative systems in terms of these criteria.
3. A weighted candidate evaluation matrix: A table that weights the candidate evaluation matrix entries by their importance and then applies a rating number.

The weighted candidate evaluation matrix is a means of calculating total scores for each candidate. The candidate with the highest total is identified as the "best" system. The best system usually is the system that meets the performance requirements at the least cost. After completing a period of concentrated study, the analyst should be prepared to discuss all candidates with the principal user and make a recommendation.

The documentation developed in the study phase thus far describes the general system design of the candidate to be presented to users and management for consideration as the accepted system. It provides the heart of the study phase report and is the basis for the design phase activities.

For Review

system team

candidate system matrix

output data element source analysis sheet

system performance

system costs

candidate evaluation matrix

payback analysis

weighted candidate evaluation matrix

"best" system

For Discussion

1. What are the two specific purposes of the candidate system evaluation?
2. What is the purpose of the systems team?
3. What are the five basic functions to be performed by any system candidate? How does considering these functions aid in developing candidates?
4. Why is it necessary to perform a preliminary evaluation of system candidates prior to preparing detailed descriptions?
5. What should be included in a detailed description of a system candidate?
6. What is the purpose of the output data element source analysis worksheet?
7. Is the candidate system evaluation in the study phase the only study of alternatives in the life cycle? Explain.
8. What is the purpose of:
   a. A candidate system matrix?
   b. A candidate evaluation matrix?
   c. A weighted candidate evaluation matrix?
9. What is the relationship among the three matrices cited in question 8?
10. Discuss the statement: "The system that meets all the performance criteria at the least cost is the 'best' system."

For Exercise: Candidate Evaluation Matrix

Set up a candidate evaluation matrix with evaluation criteria to assist in the selection of a new automobile. Include both performance and cost criteria that you believe would be appropriate if you were looking to purchase a car.

Chapter

10

■ ■ ■

Study Phase
Report and
Review

Preview

At the conclusion of the study phase activities the analyst prepares a report and reviews it with users of the computer-based information system. The central element of the study phase report is the performance specification, which is a user-oriented general design specification. The study phase review is attended by the principal user and managers who will be affected by the system, and the outcome of the review is a decision whether or not to proceed with the design of the proposed system.

Objectives

1. You will be able to describe the content of a performance specification.
2. You will be able to prepare a study phase report.
3. You will be able to discuss the purposes of a study phase review.

Key Terms

performance specification a baseline specification that describes what the computer-based system is to do at the general design level.

study phase report a comprehensive report prepared for the user-sponsor of the system and presented at the conclusion of the study phase.

study phase review a review for presenting the results of the study phase activities and determining future action.

Performance Specification

The study phase concludes with a comprehensive review. Prior to the study phase review, the performance specification is completed, and a study phase report is prepared and circulated. The study phase report is based on the **performance specification,** which is the first major baseline document. As such, it is a general design specification that provides visible evidence of systems development life-cycle progress. The performance specification is a primary communication link between the systems analyst and users for whom the system is intended. Figure 10.1 illustrates the general form and content of this specification. It is divided into two parts. The first part describes the relationships between the system and its operating environment. Because it establishes the boundaries of the computer information system, this part of the performance specification is called the *external performance description,* and it includes a *context diagram.* The accompanying documentation describes the major inputs to and outputs from the system to external entities, some of which may be other information systems with which the new or modified system under study must interact. Also resources, such as people, facilities, and equipment, required to support the system should be identified.

The second part of the performance specification is called the *internal performance description* because it describes the environment internal to the system. Generally, it is prepared to include at least the detail characteristic of level-0 and level-1 data flow diagrams. The accompanying documentation describes the data flow diagrams and identifies data storage requirements of the proposed information system at the general design level.

As the central element of the study phase report, the performance specification must be a user-oriented document, written in a language and vocabulary familiar to the user. In subsequent phases of the SDLC, the content of the performance specification is added to and expanded in detail. In particular, the internal performance specification becomes more technical and comprehensive as the system progresses through the design and development phases. Clearly, the graphics and word processing features of a comprehensive CASE tool are of great value in documenting the system specifications as they evolve and in preparing the many reports and presentations that occur throughout the SDLC.

Study Phase Report

Structure and Content

The **study phase report** is a carefully prepared management-oriented document. The report must be free of computer jargon so that it can be understood by senior managers who may not have a computer background. Figure 10.2 is an example of the structure and content of a study phase report.

The discussion of the system scope is based on the project directive and on the performance definition activities by which specific objectives were identified. The problem statement and purpose section is designed to provide a brief discussion of the problem that the system is to solve. It identifies the general objectives of the

■ **Figure 10.1** Performance specification outline. The performance specification is the technical core of the study phase report. It has two major sections: an external performance description and an internal performance description.

> **PERFORMANCE SPECIFICATION**
>
> *A. EXTERNAL PERFORMANCE DESCRIPTION*
> 1. context diagram
> 2. system output descriptions
> 3. system input descriptions
> 4. system resource identification
>
> *B. INTERNAL PERFORMANCE DESCRIPTION*
> 1. data flow diagrams
> 2. data storage description

■ **Figure 10.2** Study phase report outline. The study phase report, completed at the end of the study phase, has five major sections: system scope, conclusions and recommendations, performance specification, plans and cost schedules, and appendices.

> **STUDY PHASE REPORT**
>
> I. SYSTEM SCOPE
>   a. system title
>   b. problem statement and purpose
>   c. constraints
>   d. specific objectives
>   e. method of evaluation
>
> II. CONCLUSIONS AND RECOMMENDATIONS
>   a. conclusions
>   b. recommendations
>
> III. PERFORMANCE SPECIFICATION
>   a. external performance description
>   b. internal performance description
>
> IV. PLANS AND COST SCHEDULES
>   a. detailed nilestones — study phase
>   b. major milestones — all phases
>   c. detailed milestones — design phase
>
> V. APPENDICES — as appropriate

system and the specific benefits that are expected to be realized. In this section the systems analyst may make use of the results of the fact-finding and fact-analysis activities that occurred throughout the initial investigation.

The constraints are of the type referred to in chapter 8 as general constraints. They are ground rules that apply to all the alternative means by which the general objective of the system may be accomplished.

The specific objectives are derived from the general objective and anticipated benefits. They should be complete and quantitative wherever possible. The method of evaluation should describe how the accomplishment of the specific objectives is to be measured during the operation phase of the life cycle.

Major milestones in the design and development phases. The major design and development phase
milestones are included in the study phase report to provide the user-sponsor of the information system
with an overview of the activities and associated costs required to complete the project.

major milestones	
design phase	allocation of functions
	computer program functions
	test requirements
	design specifications
	design phase report
	design phase review
development phase	implementation plan
	equipment acquisition
	computer program development
	system tests
	personnel training
	changeover plan
	system specifications
	development phase report
	development phase review

The conclusions and recommendations are presented next in the report in order
to emphasize them and to accommodate the executive who may not need to read the
entire report. However, the conclusions and recommendations must be substantiated
in the other sections of the study phase report. The conclusions reflect the significant
results of the system performance definition and candidate system evaluation. The
recommendations relate to the user's decision to proceed with a design phase, to redo
portions of the study phase, or to terminate the project.

The performance specification follows the conclusions and recommendations.
Major elements of this baseline document are as outlined in figure 10.1.

The plans and cost schedules prepared at the onset of the study phase are updated
to report actual progress and cost versus schedule for the entire study phase. The
report also includes two additional sets of project plans and cost schedules. A chart
of *major milestones* is prepared for the entire project. The purpose of such a chart
is to make visible to the reviewers the key activities, called milestones, to be completed and the costs to be incurred in order for the proposed system to become operational. Figure 10.3 is a list of key design phase and development phase tasks that
are common to the life cycle of most computer-based business systems. A cost
schedule is prepared to accompany the major milestones project plan.

A *detailed milestone* project plan also is prepared for the design phase. This plan
is required since, after a successful study phase review, the authorization to proceed
applies to the entire design phase. There is another review at the end of the design

■ Figure 10.4   Detailed milestones for the design phase. The detailed milestones for the design phase are included in the study phase report to provide the user-sponser with specific information about the activities and associated costs that are to be authorized for the subsequent phase.

Design Phase — Detailed Milestones

allocation of functions

    manual functions   task definition
                                 reference manual requirements

    equipment functions   function definition
                                 equipment specification

    computer program functions   data base design
                                 computer programs
                                 design (for each program)

  test requirements   systems test requirements
                                 computer program test requirements

  design specifications

  design phase report

  design phase review

phase, when similar detail is given for the development phase. Figure 10.4 lists the milestones that will be described in chapter 11. A cost schedule is prepared to accompany the plan.

Appropriate appendices are included in the study phase report. Typically, they contain the project directive, the significant results of the initial investigation, the feasibility analysis, and pertinent memoranda.

Example Study Phase Report

Exhibit 1 on the following pages shows the study phase report that might be prepared for the example system OARS. It includes all the features outlined in figure 10.2. However, many illustrations that have already been presented in the text are not repeated here but simply referred to. In addition, the content of the appendix is limited to a listing of items typically included.

Study Phase Review

The **study phase review** is held to present the user with the results of the study phase activities and with recommendations for future action. If the recommendation of the analyst is to proceed with the design of the system, the analyst should remember that the user will be making a commitment that transforms the system effort from a study to a formal project.

The analyst should be factual, yet not hesitate to sell a recommendation; after all, it is the analyst who has been working on the study phase for weeks, even months. The analyst *is* knowledgeable about the system and would be less than human in not forming strong convictions. If the analyst is enthusiastic, it should show.

The study phase review should be attended not only by the *principal user,* but also by senior representatives of other affected organizations, including the information services organization. All attendees should be provided with a copy of the study phase report in advance of the review meeting.

If the outcome of the study phase review is a decision to proceed with the design phase, the user-sponsor issues a written approval to proceed. This approval is an example of the renewed, or incremental, commitment that occurs at the end of each life-cycle phase. It extends the project directive by authorizing the expenditure of resources for the design phase.

Summary

At the conclusion of the study phase activities, a study phase report is completed. This report is the basis for a study phase review with the principal user and managers affected by the computer-related business information system. The study phase report has five principal parts:

1. System scope
2. Conclusions and recommendations
3. Performance specification
4. Plans and cost schedules
5. Appendices

The performance specification is the central element of the study phase report. It is written in language that the user can understand, and it describes both the external and the internal performance of the business information system at the general design level. The study phase report includes completed project plan and cost schedules for the study phase, major milestones for all phases to provide visibility for the entire project, and detailed milestones for the design phase, since that is the next major activity. At the study phase review, the systems analyst presents the results of the activities completed and makes recommendations for future effort. If the recommendation of the systems analyst is to proceed, and if that recommendation is approved, the project moves into the design phase.

For Review

performance specification
data flow diagram
system specification
level-0 data flow diagram
internal performance description
study phase report
detailed milestone
principal user

external performance description
design specification
context diagram
level-1 data flow diagram
study phase
major milestone
study phase review

For Discussion

1. What is the purpose of the study phase report?
2. What is the content of the study phase report?
3. Why are the conclusions and recommendations presented early in the study phase report?
4. Discuss the importance of the performance specification.
5. What are the differences between the external performance specification and the internal performance specification?
6. How many sets of project plans and schedules are presented at the study phase review? How do they differ?
7. What is the purpose of the study phase review? Who should attend?

EXHIBIT 1

■ ■ ■

The Study Phase Report— OARS Case Study

The on-line accounts receivable system (OARS), introduced in chapter 7 and continued in chapters 8 and 9, is the basis for this example study phase report.

A principal goal of OARS is to establish geographically separate profit centers. All of the candidate systems that were evaluated were distributed data processing systems with a direct entry capability. These range from "dumb" terminals to workstations with a substantial local data processing capability, and many communications options are available.

OARS Study Phase Report

I. System Scope
   A. System Title
      On-line Accounts Receivable System (OARS)
   B. Problem Statement and Purpose
      The ABCO corporation's present accounts receivable system is at its maximum capacity of 10,000 accounts. The number of accounts is expected to double to 20,000 accounts over a five-year period. The present system cannot meet this projected growth and satisfy the corporate goal of distributing information processing resources to regional profit centers. Serious problems have already been encountered in processing the current volume of accounts. Specific problems that have been identified are as follows:
      1. Saturation of the capacity of the present computer system, causing difficulties in adding new accounts and obtaining information about the status of existing accounts.
      2. Processing delays in preparing customer billing statements because of the batch-oriented design of the current accounts receivable system.

3. Excessive elapsed time between mailing of customer statements and receipt of payments, which creates a high-cost, four-day float.
4. Inadequate control of credit limits.
5. Inability to provide regional centers with timely customer-related information.

Therefore, the purpose of the OARS project is to replace the existing accounts receivable system with one that can eliminate the stated problems and meet ABCO's growth and regional accountability goals.

C. Constraints

The OARS constraints are as follows:

1. Development of the on-line accounts receivable system is to be completed within fourteen months.
2. OARS is to have a growth potential to handle 20,000 customer accounts.
3. OARS is to be designed as an on-line system operating in a distributed data processing environment.
4. The design must be compatible with corporate plans to install regional profit centers.

D. Specific Objectives

The specific objectives of OARS are as follows:

1. To establish billing cycles for each region.
2. To mail customer statements no later than one day after the close of a billing cycle.
3. To provide the customer with a billing statement two days after the close of a billing cycle.
4. To speed up collections, reducing the float by 50 percent.
5. To examine customer account balances through on-line inquiry at the time of order entry.

E. Method of Evaluation

After OARS has been operational from sixty to ninety days:

1. A statistical analysis will be made of customer account processing to verify the elapsed time between the close of the billing cycle and the mailing of customer statements.
2. The float time will be measured, and the cost of the float will be calculated at three-month intervals.
3. Periodically, random samples of customer accounts in each region will be audited for accuracy and to validate the effectiveness of on-line inquiry.
4. The validity of OARS transactions that affect the inventory system will be measured by random sampling and physical count.
5. Personal evaluations of the effectiveness of the system will be obtained from its principal users.

II. Conclusions and Recommendations
  A. Conclusions
      The Candidate System Evaluation of the on-line accounts receivable system (OARS) involved the evaluation of three candidate systems and led to the conclusion that the best system would be one that required minimal modification of the existing central-site computer system and that utilized this system as a host for a network of microcomputers. Candidate III will use the existing central-site computer as a data repository accessed by the networked microcomputers located in each region. This candidate distributes the accounts receivable data base and processing to each local microcomputer. All outputs will be generated at the local site.

      The projected monthly operational cost for the selected system varies from $1.67 per account at a volume of 10,000 accounts in three regions, to $1.72 per account for a volume of 20,000 accounts in five regions. The current system costs $5.71 per account at a volume of 12,000 accounts. It can expand to handle 20,000 accounts at a cost of $5.71 per account; however, it would continue to operate in a batch-oriented mode and would not meet the on-line, distributed data processing goals of the corporation.

      The projected development cost for OARS is $265,500. The savings in the operating cost of the selected system, when compared with the cost of expanding the existing system, will result in recovery of the development costs in eight months of operation.
  B. Recommendations
          It is recommended that the OARS project be approved for the design phase.
III. Design Specification
  A. External Performance Specification
      1. *Context Diagram* Figure E1.1a is the context diagram for OARS. As this diagram shows, the external entities that establish the domain of the system are: the customer, the order-fill department, and the accounts receivable manager. The accompanying narrative appears as figure E1.1b.
      2. *System output descriptions* The eight OARS outputs are as follows:
          a. Customer statement
          b. Accounts receivable transactions
          c. Accounts receivable summary data
          d. Aged accounts receivable data
          e. Order-fill data
          f. Overcredit notice

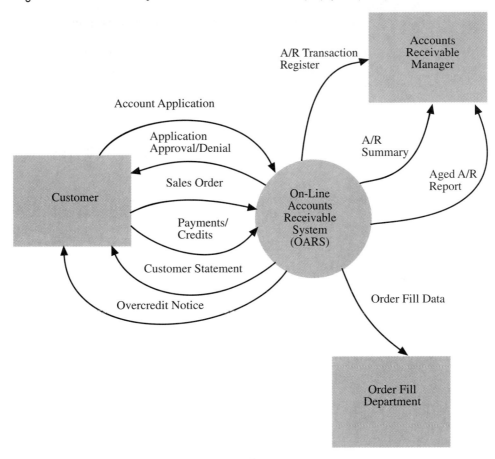

■ Figure E1.1b   Narrative description for an on-line accounts receivable system (OARS) context.

The boundaries of the on-line accounts receivable system (OARS) are set by three external entities: the customer, the A/R manager, and the Order Fill department. These entities provide the inputs to OARS and receive the outputs. There are three inputs and seven outputs. All three inputs are created by the customer, beginning with an account application. The other two inputs are a customer-generated sales order and payments or applied credits. Customer-related outputs are: application approvals, application denials, customer statements, and overcredit notices.

The A/R manager is provided with A/R transaction data, A/R summary information, and aged accounts receivable data, all of which are important in controlling customer accounts and in the management of cash flow. The Order Fill department is provided with order fill data, which is used to pick and ship customer orders and to manage inventory.

g. Application approval notice

h. Application denial notice

An output specification and an accompanying data element list are presented as figure E1.2.

3. *System input descriptions* The three OARS inputs are as follows:

   a. Account applications

   b. Sales orders

   c. Payments/credits

   Figure E1.3 is an example of a system input.

4. *System resource identification* The current central-site computer system will be augmented by regional microcomputers networks. The required microcomputers for each region will have the following general characteristics:

   a. One file server:

      CPU with 32 megabytes of main memory

      One 1 gigabyte magnetic disk drive

      One 24 page/minute laser printer

   b. Eight workstations:

      CPU with 8 megabytes of main memory

      One 500 megabyte magnetic disk drive

B. Internal performance specification

   1. *Data flow diagrams*

      a. Level-0 DFD and narrative description (Figure E1.4a and E1.4b)

      b. Level-1 DFD and narrative description (Figure E1.5a and E1.5b)

   2. *Data storage description*

      a. Each OARS master record consists of 15 data elements for a total of 167 characters.

      b. Assuming a range of 10,000 master records to 20,000 records over the expected 5-year life of the system, from 1,670,000 characters to 3,340,000 characters of data will have to be stored.

      c. The data described in item b above will be distributed among the computers located in the local regions.

IV. Project Plans and Schedules

A. Study Phase

   The study phase was scheduled for a ten-week period, beginning 9/1/xx (this year) and ending 11/10/xx. The funding authorized for the study phase was $18,000. As shown in figure E1.6, the project is on schedule. Only the study phase review remains to be completed.

   As shown in figure E1.7, expenditures are as estimated.

B. Major Milestones—All Phases

   Figure E1.8 is a schedule for the entire project. The design phase is scheduled for twenty weeks, and the development phase is scheduled for thirty weeks. If we proceed as planned, the design phase will be completed 3/30/xy (next year), and the development phase will be completed on 11/17/xy.

■ Figure E1.2   OARS output description: and data element list: overcredit notice.

OUTPUT SPECIFICATION	

TITLE: **Overcredit Notification**

LAYOUT:

```
                    Overcredit Notification
    Sales Order No.  _____
    Sales Order Date _____        Current Balance    _____
                                        Sales Order Amount _____
    Account Number   _____            Total          _____
                                          Credit Limit     _____
    Name and Address _____        Amount Overcredit  [_____]
    _____         ☐ Overcredit Approved
    _____         ☐ Return Sales Order

                                        _____
                                            AUTHORIZATION
```

FREQUENCY: **Daily**
SIZE: **1 page**

QUANTITY: **80 max.**
COPIES: **2**

DISTRIBUTION: **1. Accts. Receivable Dept.**

COMMENTS:

DATA ELEMENT LIST		

TITLE: **Overcredit Notification**

DESCRIPTION	FORMAT	SIZE
Sales Order Number	XXXXXXXX	8 characters
Sales Order Date	xx/xx/xx	8 ''
Account No: Region No.—Sequence No.	XX-XXXXXXX	10 ''
Name		26 ''
Address		
Street		20 ''
City		18 ''
State		2 ''
Zip Code		5 ''
Current Balance	XXX,XXX.XX	10 ''
Sales Order Amount	XXX,XXX.XX	10 ''
Total	XXX,XXX.XX	10 ''
Credit Limit	XX,XXX.XX	9 ''
Amount Overcredit	XX,XXX.XX	9 ''

Exhibit 1   ■   279

CUSTOMER ACCOUNT APPLICATION
ABCO CORPORATION
Walnut, California

FIRM NAME	WHOLESALE ☐ RETAIL ☐	DATE	
STREET ADDRESS		TELEPHONE	
CITY	STATE	ZIP CODE	
BANK REFERENCES:			
NAME	BRANCH	TELEPHONE	
ADDRESS	CITY	STATE	ZIP CODE
NAME	BRANCH	TELEPHONE	
ADDRESS	CITY	STATE	ZIP CODE
OTHER REFERENCES:			
NAME		TELEPHONE	
ADDRESS	CITY	STATE	ZIP CODE
NAME		TELEPHONE	
ADDRESS	CITY	STATE	ZIP CODE
FOR OFFICE USE:	APPROVED ☐		
ACCOUNT NUMBER	DISAPPROVED ☐		
EFFECTIVE DATE	AUTHORIZATION SIGNATURE		
CREDIT CODE			
DISCOUNT CODE			
IF DISAPPROVED, REASON:			

■ Figure E1.4a   Level-0 data flow diagram for OARS.

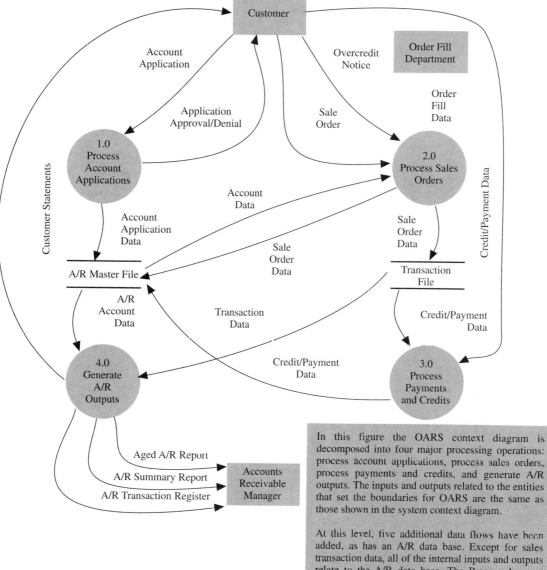

In this figure the OARS context diagram is decomposed into four major processing operations: process account applications, process sales orders, process payments and credits, and generate A/R outputs. The inputs and outputs related to the entities that set the boundaries for OARS are the same as those shown in the system context diagram.

At this level, five additional data flows have been added, as has an A/R data base. Except for sales transaction data, all of the internal inputs and outputs relate to the A/R data base. The Process Account Applications bubble supplies the A/R data base with updated customer account data. The Process Payments and Credits bubble provides the A/R data base with current payment/credit data, and the Process Sales Orders bubble returns sales data to the A/R data base.

The A/R data base has two outputs. The first is the customer account data required to process sales orders, and the second is A/R data used to create the outputs required by the A/R manager. Also, in order to create these outputs, sales transaction data must flow from the Process Sales Orders bubble to the Generate A/R Output bubble.

■ Figure E1.4b   Narrative description for an on-line accounts receivable system (OARS) level-0 data flow diagram.

■ Figure E1.5a   Level-1 data flow diagram for OARS.

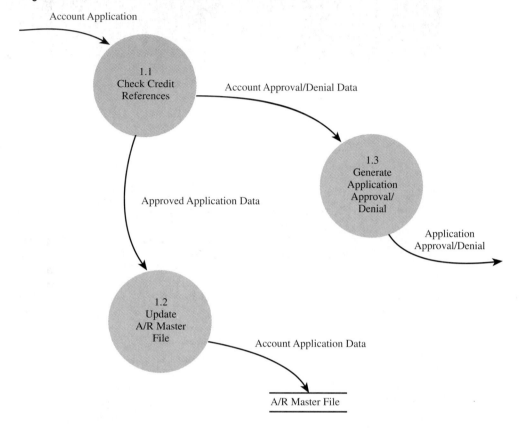

Account Application

1.1
Check Credit
References

Account Approval/Denial Data

1.3
Generate
Application
Approval/
Denial

Approved Application Data

Application
Approval/Denial

1.2
Update
A/R Master
File

Account Application Data

A/R Master File

■ Figure E1.5b   Narrative description for an on-line accounts receivable system (OARS) level-1 data flow diagram.

In this figure the Process Account Application-bubble in the OARS level-0 data flow diagram is decomposed to exhibit three level-1 processing bubbles: Check credit References, Generate Application Approval/Denial, and Update A/R Master File. The Check Credit References bubble has as its input customer account application data and produces as an output either an application approval or denial, which flows to the Assign Credit Limit bubble. This process also generates account data needed to update the A/R data base.

Study Phase 1

Systems analyst work with users of computer information systems to translate their needs into specifications that will produce usable outputs.

Study Phase 2

A user and analyst often evaluate models, or prototypes, of system outputs created during the study phase before proceeding with the detailed design of a computer information system.

Design Phase 1

Many aspects of the detailed design of a computer information system must be reviewed with a user before an information system can proceed to the development phase.

Design Phase 2

The detailed design of a computer information system usually requires the evaluation of many hardware and software alternatives.

Development Phase 1

Computer programs created in the development phase must be tested and debugged.

Development Phase 2

Visual displays for user workstations are generated in the development phase.

Operation Phase 1

Corporate-level data processing and data base management usually are performed by a mainframe computer at a central site.

Operation Phase 2

Knowledge workers are able to retrieve data from and enter data into a remote mini-computer or mainframe computer system.

■ **Figure E1.6** Project plan and status report—study phase.

PROJECT PLAN AND STATUS REPORT																					
PROJECT TITLE OARS — STUDY PHASE	**PROJECT STATUS SYMBOLS** ○ Satisfactory □ Caution △ Critical **PLANNING/PROGRESS SYMBOLS** ▢ Scheduled Progress ∨ Scheduled Completion ■ Actual Progress ▼ Actual Completion											J. Herring PROGRAMMER/ANALYST									
												COMMITTED DATE 11/10/XY	COMPLETED DATE	STATUS DATE 11/3/XY							

ACTIVITY/DOCUMENT	PERCENT COMPLETE	STATUS	PERIOD ENDING (Week)																		
			1	2	3	4	5	6	7	8	9	10									
STUDY PHASE	95	0																		
Initial Investigation	100	0																		
Project Directive	100	0																		
Performance Definition	100	0																		
Candidate System Evaluation	100	0																		
Performance Specification	100	0																		
Study Phase Report	100	0																		
Study Phase Review	0	0																		

■ **Figure E1.7** Project cost report—study phase.

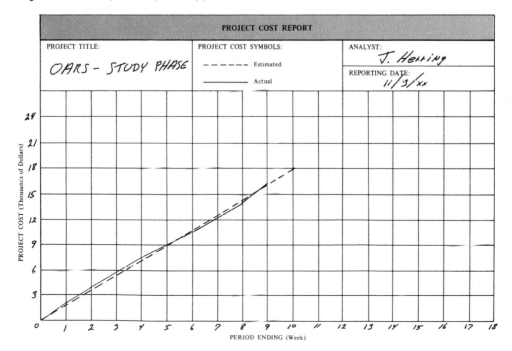

■ **Figure E1.8** Project plan and status report—OARS major milestones.

PROJECT PLAN AND STATUS REPORT																					

PROJECT TITLE: OARS – MAJOR MILESTONES

PROJECT STATUS SYMBOLS
O Satisfactory
□ Caution
△ Critical

J. Herring
PROGRAMMER/ANALYST

PLANNING/PROGRESS SYMBOLS
□ Scheduled Progress   ∨ Scheduled Completion
■ Actual Progress   ▼ Actual Completion

COMMITTED DATE 11/17/XY
COMPLETED DATE
STATUS DATE 11/3/XY

ACTIVITY/DOCUMENT	PERCENT COMPLETE	STATUS	PERIOD ENDING (Week) 2 4 6 8 10 12 14 16 18 20 22 24 26 28 30
STUDY PHASE	95	O	
Initial Investigation	100	O	
Performance Spec.	100	O	
Study Phase Report	100	O	
Study Phase Review	0	O	
DESIGN PHASE			
Allocation of Functions	0	O	
Computer Prog. Functions	0	O	
Test Requirements	0	O	
Design Spec.	0	O	
Design Phase Report	0	O	
Design Phase Review	0	O	

PROJECT PLAN AND STATUS REPORT																					

PROJECT TITLE: OARS – MAJOR MILESTONES

PROJECT STATUS SYMBOLS
O Satisfactory
□ Caution
△ Critical

J. Herring
PROGRAMMER/ANALYST

PLANNING/PROGRESS SYMBOLS
□ Scheduled Progress   ∨ Scheduled Completion
■ Actual Progress   ▼ Actual Completion

COMMITTED DATE 11/17/XY
COMPLETED DATE
STATUS DATE 11/3/XY

ACTIVITY/DOCUMENT	PERCENT COMPLETE	STATUS	PERIOD ENDING (Week) 32 34 36 38 40 42 44 46 48 50 52 54 56 58 60
DEVELOPMENT PHASE	0	O	
Implementation Plan	0	O	
Equipment Acquisition	0	O	
Computer Program Dev.	0	O	
Personnel Training	0	O	
System Tests	0	O	
Changeover Plan	0	O	
System Spec.	0	O	
Dev. Phase Report	0	O	
Dev. Phase Review	0	O	

■ Figure E1.9   Project cost report—total project.

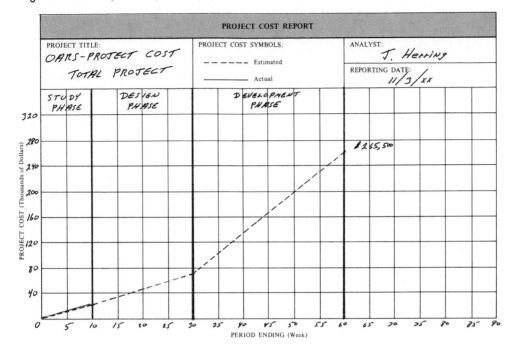

The estimated cumulative cost for the entire project (study, design, and development phases) is graphed in figure E1.9. The total cost is estimated to be $265,500.

C. Detailed Milestones—Design Phase

Since the next phase to be undertaken is the design phase, detailed projections are presented for that phase. Figure E1.10 displays the specific milestones to be achieved in the course of a twenty-week design phase effort.

Figure E1.11 presents the accompanying cumulative cost estimate. The total design phase cost is estimated to be $51,000.

V. Appendices

Note: The appendices include all supporting data for the conclusions of the study. For purposes of this exhibit, such detail is not included.

Exhibit 1   ■   285

PROJECT PLAN AND STATUS REPORT

PROJECT TITLE	PROJECT STATUS SYMBOLS ○ Satisfactory □ Caution △ Critical		J. Herring PROGRAMMER/ANALYST		
OARS — DESIGN PHASE	PLANNING/PROGRESS SYMBOLS ▢ Scheduled Progress ∨ Scheduled Completion ■ Actual Progress ▼ Actual Completion		COMMITTED DATE 3/30/XY	COMPLETED DATE	STATUS DATE 11/3/XY

ACTIVITY/DOCUMENT	PERCENT COMPLETE	STATUS	2	4	6	8	10	12	14	16	18	20							
DESIGN PHASE	0	0																	
Allocation of Functions	0	0																	
Manual Functions	0	0																	
Task Definition	0	0																	
Ref. Manual Def.	0	0																	
Equipment Functions	0	0																	
Function Def.	0	0																	
Equipment Spec.	0	0																	
Computer Prog. Functions	0	0																	
Data Base Design	0	0																	
Data Edit Program	0	0																	
A/R Program	0	0																	
Customer Program	0	0																	
Overcredit Program	0	0																	

PROJECT PLAN AND STATUS REPORT

PROJECT TITLE	PROJECT STATUS SYMBOLS ○ Satisfactory □ Caution △ Critical		J. Herring PROGRAMMER/ANALYST		
OARS — DESIGN PHASE	PLANNING/PROGRESS SYMBOLS ▢ Scheduled Progress ∨ Scheduled Completion ■ Actual Progress ▼ Actual Completion		COMMITTED DATE 3/30/XY	COMPLETED DATE	STATUS DATE 11/3/XY

ACTIVITY/DOCUMENT	PERCENT COMPLETE	STATUS	2	4	6	8	10	12	14	16	18	20							
DESIGN PHASE (cont'd)	0	0																	
Test Requirements	0	0																	
System Test Req.	0	0																	
Computer Prog.Test Req.	0	0																	
Design Spec.	0	0																	
Design Phase Report	0	0																	
Design Phase Review	0	0																	

■ Figure E1.11   Project cost report—design phase (estimate only).

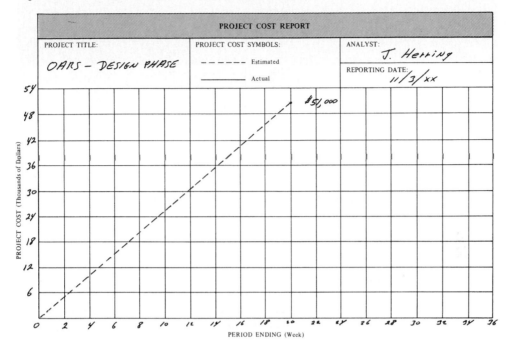

Exhibit 1   ■   287

5

The Design Phase

Design Phase Activities

The **design phase** is the life-cycle phase in which the detailed design of the system selected in the study phase is accomplished. In the course of the design phase, the performance specification developed in the study phase is expanded into the design specification. The design specification becomes a baseline document oriented to the needs of the programmers and other professional personnel who will actually develop the system. A smooth transition from the study phase to the design phase is necessary because the design phase continues the activities begun in the earlier phase. The project becomes enlarged in scope, and personnel are added in this phase.

As the design phase progresses, the user organization assigns additional personnel to participate as members of the project team. These persons are particularly concerned with defining user requirements and developing the resources (for example, training manuals, procedures, and personnel) required by the user organization to ensure successful operation of the system. In addition, the information service organization assigns additional technical personnel, such as analyst/programmers and equipment specialists, to the project. These persons develop the technical requirements for computer programming and operations support. They are particularly concerned with the effective translation of system performance requirements into data base and computer program design requirements. They aid in the selection of the best techniques for utilizing existing computer hardware and software. They also aid in the development of specifications on which to base the selection of new computer systems or components.

The flowchart of figure U5.1 is a pictorial overview of the design phase. The major design phase activities are described and discussed in chapter 11, "Detailed System Design," chapter 12, "Data Modeling," chapter 13, "Output Design," chapter 14, "Input Design," and chapter 15, "Design Phase Report and Review." Each of these activities is described briefly as follows:

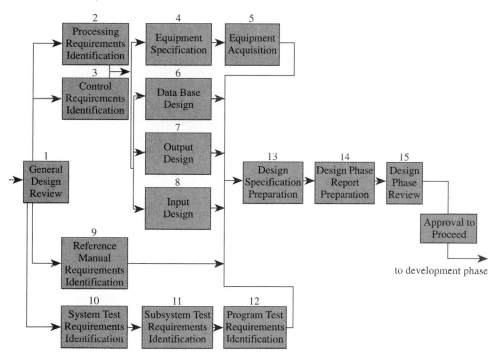

■ **Figure U5.1** Design phase activity flowchart. After the general design review, the major activities are the design of the system processes and the identification of the testing requirements. The design specification and design phase report are prepared prior to the presentation of the system design at the study phase review. If the system design is accepted, the system development process moves to the development phase.

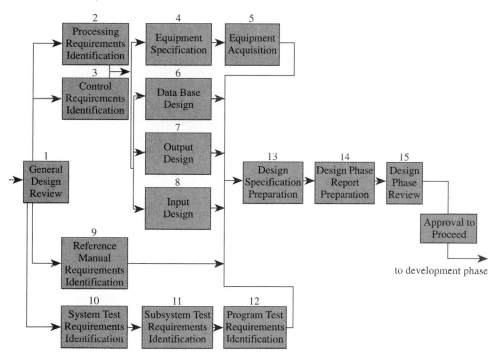

1. *General system review.* The system team, made up of members from both the user and information organizations, reviews the proposed system as described in the performance specification of the study phase. The purpose of this review is to ensure that the system team members understand the required characteristics of the system.
2. *Processing requirements identification.* Manual and automated processing functions are identified. Each has its own output, input, and processing requirements. Special hardware and supporting software requirements also are

identified. As necessary, additional decomposed data flow diagrams are prepared at the computer program and subprogram levels. Narratives, equations, algorithms, and decision tables or trees may be developed as aids in defining the functions of the principle system components.

3. *Control requirements identification.* Many of the computer program components identified in the processing requirements identification activity must include appropriate controls to guard against inaccurate outputs and invalid data within the system data base. Most of these controls will be implemented within the computer program component.

4. *Equipment specification.* The hardware configuration used to convert input data to meaningful output information is described. If existing hardware is not adequate, alternatives, which may range from adding special equipment to procuring an entire computer system, must be considered.

5. *Equipment acquisition.* Since computer hardware may be a long-lead-time item, it may be necessary to initiate procurement of critical equipment during the design phase.

6. *Data base design.* Relationships between data elements, functions to be performed, and file organization choices are studied in detail so that the most efficient data base design can be achieved. The storage requirements for all the data elements on which the computer programs operate are calculated, taking into account the size and volume of the records to be stored. The interfaces between the data base of the system being designed and other data bases are identified by specifying the data that must be shared between them.

7. *Output design.* If the performance specification contains sketches of system outputs, each of these outputs must be designed in detail. These detailed layouts become the specifications for programmers to follow during the development phase. If outputs were prototyped during the study phase, the prototypes should be reviewed for appropriateness.

8. *Input design.* Any inputs that were sketched for the performance specification must now be designed in detail. As in the case of the output design, these detailed layouts become the specification for programmers to follow during the development phase.

9. *Reference manual identification.* All of the manuals that will be required by users, computer operators, and programmers must be identified. The manuals themselves will be developed in the next phase.

10. *System test requirements identification.* Requirements are established for the tests necessary to verify the performance of the entire computer-based system. This is accomplished in parallel with the activities associated with system design.
11. *Subsystem test requirements identification.* Requirements are established for the tests required to verify the performance of major system functions.
12. *Computer program test requirements identification.* Requirements also are determined for the tests necessary to verify the performance of the computer programs. This is done after the definition of the system and subsystem test requirements. (However, these tests are actually performed prior to the subsystem and system tests.)
13. *Design specification preparation.* The design specification represents an expansion of the performance specification into a blueprint for the development of the computer-based business system. This specification is the second major baseline document and is the "build to" specification.
14. *Design phase report preparation.* A design phase report is prepared at the conclusion of the design phase. This report is the outgrowth of the data acquired and added to the project file during the design phase. As an extension of the study phase report, it contains a summary of the results of all significant activities undertaken during the design phase. An important element of the design phase report is a recommendation relative to proceeding with the development phase. If the recommendation is to proceed, a detailed project plan is provided for the remainder of the project. Included as part of the body of this report is the design specification—the second major baseline document.
15. *Design phase review.* The system design is reviewed at the conclusion of the design phase by the management of the user organization and by representatives of the information systems organization. The principal documents upon which the review is based are the study phase report, including the performance specification, and the design phase report, including the design specification. Any changes to the performance specification as a result of the design phase activities are identified and discussed. The detailed progress plan and the cost schedule for the development phase are reviewed, as are the estimates of operational costs. After the conclusion of a successful design phase review, personnel and other resources are committed. Written approval to proceed with the development phase is provided by the user organization.

Chapter

11

■ ■ ■

Detailed System Design

Preview

The design phase is the second of the four systems development life-cycle phases. It is the phase in which the detailed design of the system selected in the study phase is accomplished, and the user-oriented performance specification is converted into a technical design specification. At this point in the system development life cycle, the problem has been identified, alternative solutions have been studied, and a management review has concluded with an authorization to proceed with an approved solution.

The first design phase step, detailed system design, involves the identification of all system functions to be performed. These requirements are usually identified by decomposing the data flow diagrams into a set of leveled DFDs. In addition to the identification of required system functions, it is important to identify the control requirements of the system. This is the appropriate time to identify the reference manuals needed for training and documentation. System and computer program test requirements must also be identified. A very useful technique for detecting and eliminating design and development errors, called a structured walkthrough, is commonly used in this and later phases of the system development life cycle. Computer equipment requirements must be identified; and because of long lead-times, hardware acquisition may begin.

Objectives

1. You will be able to explain how system processing requirements are identified.
2. You will be able to discuss the importance of the early identification of control requirements.
3. You will be able to identify the commonly required reference manuals.
4. You will be able to discuss the importance of identifying test requirements.
5. You will be able to describe the purpose and use of the structured walk-through.
6. You will be able to identify the steps in the hardware acquisition process.

Key Terms

design phase the system development life-cycle phase in which the detailed design of the system selected in the study phase is accomplished.

decomposed data flow diagrams data flow diagrams (DFDs) that have been expanded in their detail until each of the processing functions can be identified. If the DFDs are decomposed to their lowest level, they are known as a leveled set of DFDs.

HIPO charts (Hierarchy plus Input Processing and Output) a series of charts to identify and emphasize the functions of a system.

structured walk-through a technical review to assist the people working on a project; used to discover errors in logic of system components or in computer programs.

Detailed Design Specifications

General System Design

The general system design was presented and approved as a part of the study phase report and study phase review. This general design should now be reviewed to assure the system team members that they understand what was approved and what the new or modified system is to accomplish. This general design is the basis for all of the detailed design which follows.

Identifying Processing Requirements

The first major activity of the design phase is the identification of processing functions. This is accomplished by expanding the general system design into greater levels of detail. The *data flow diagrams* prepared in the study phase are reviewed and decomposed until all functions the system must perform are evident. Because of the importance of identifying what the system does in terms of its functions, the analyst may draw HIPO charts in addition to the data flow diagrams. **HIPO** stands for Hierarchy plus Input Processing and Output. HIPO charts are actually a series of charts. The first chart in the series is the *hierarchy chart.* This chart, sometimes called a *structure chart,* shows the hierarchy or levels of system functions. Its appearance is similar to an organization chart that shows the hierarchy or levels of positions within an organization. The second part of the HIPO series is made up of an *IPO chart*—a three-column chart showing the processes of a system and the inputs and outputs to those processes.

The OARS example illustrates the use of expanded DFDs and HIPO charts. Both of these approaches identify the processing functions of the system.

Figure 11.1 is the context diagram and figure 11.2 is the level-0 DFD that were prepared for OARS during the study phase. Figures 11.3a through 11.3d are level-1 data flow diagrams that were used to identify the processing functions of the system. Together, they graphically show all the major data processing functions that must be performed by the system. Figure 11.4 is an example of a hierarchy chart and an IPO chart used to show the same system processing functions as the DFDs in figures 11.2 and 11.3. A HIPO chart set should include an IPO chart for each block of the hierarchy chart, but in this example only the IPO for the "check credit limit status" function is shown. The major differences between the HIPO charts and DFDs are the chart structure and the emphasis of the HIPO chart on system functions rather than data flows.

Key project personnel, as a team, determine the most effective means of performing each function. This determination is made by studying and evaluating alternatives. The process follows steps similar to those of the candidate system evaluation, but alternatives are studied at a level of greater detail. For example, during the study

Context diagram for the OARS project. This chart was developed during the study phase activities and is presented here as a review of the system overview.

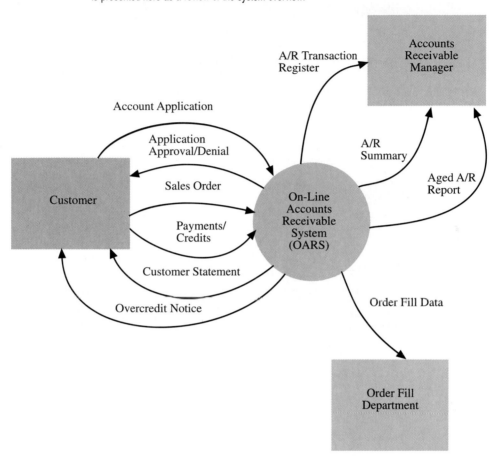

phase it might have been found that a remote terminal was the most cost-effective means of entering data into the system. Now, in the design phase, a particular terminal must be selected from the many models or types available to perform the input function. As another example, it might be decided that certain data could be evaluated more effectively by manual techniques than by a computer. This could be the case if human judgment or particularly rapid handling of an exceptional situation were required.

■ Figure 11.2   Level-0 data flow diagram of the OARS project. This DFD shows the four major processes of process account applications, process sales orders, process payments and credits, and generate accounts receivable outputs.

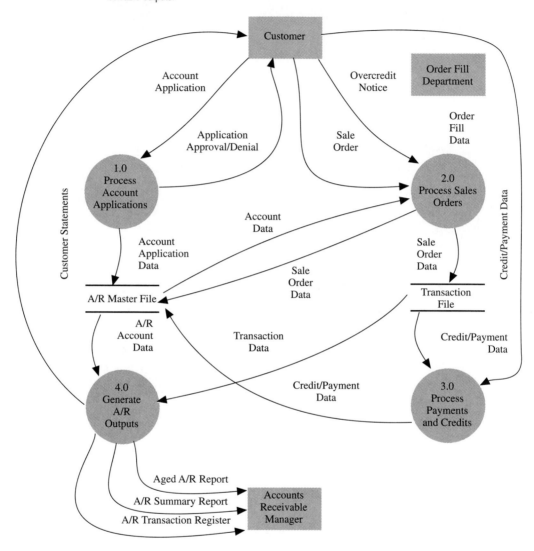

■ Figure 11.3a   Level-1 data flow diagram of the OARS project Process Account Applications subsystem.

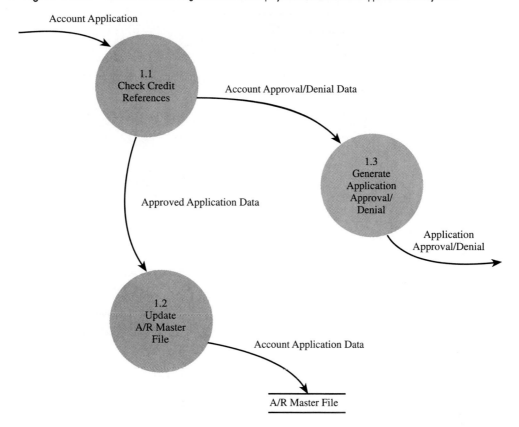

■ Figure 11.3b   Level-1 data flow diagram of the OARS project Process Sales Orders subsystem.

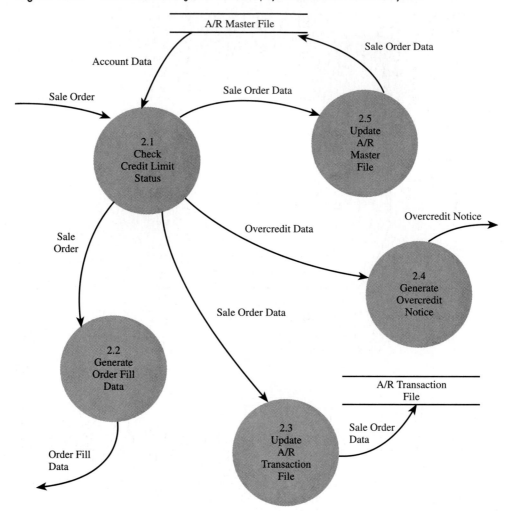

Level-1 data flow diagram of the OARS project Process Payments and Credits subsystem.

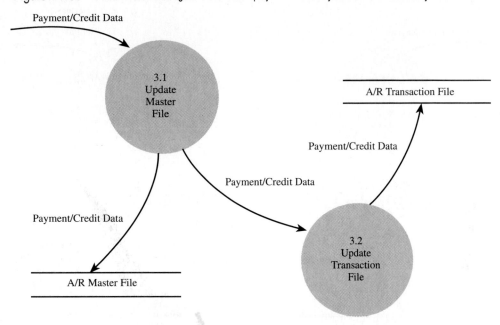

■ Figure 11.3d   Level-1 data flow diagram for the OARS Generate A/R Outputs subsystem.

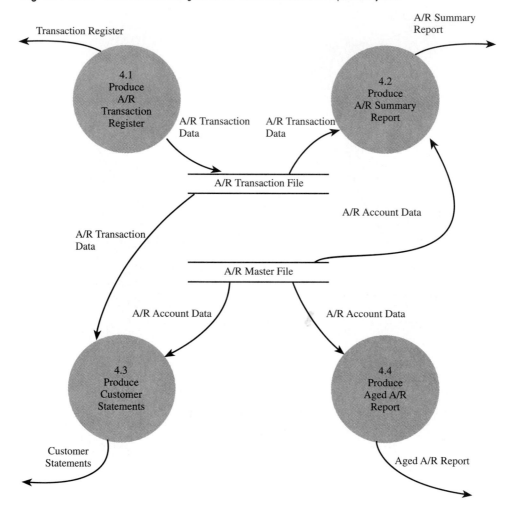

Hierarchy chart and sample IPO chart for the OARS project. The hierarchy chart is also known as a structure chart.

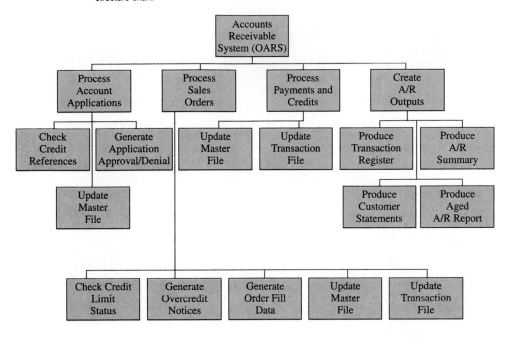

IPO chart: 2.1 Check Credit Limit Status

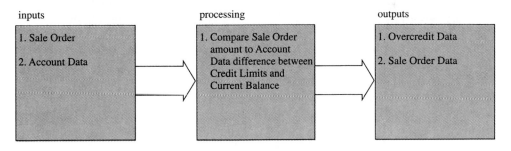

■ Figure 11.5   Example control techniques. Controls are used to minimize incorrect data and should be a part of any information system. Control techniques may be applied to inputting, processing, and/or outputting functions.

Control Techniques:

Input Controls:	1. Define responsibility for input preparation.
	2. Verify data for significant numeric fields.
	3. Utilize self-checking numbers and codes where practical.
	4. Sequence number input data.
	5. Number and take hash totals for batch input.

Processing Controls:	1. Establish a comprehensive program of computer program and system testing.
	2. Centralize the authority for all computer program changes or modifications.
	3. Protect files with backups and limited accessibility.
	4. Provide standards for the development and use of software checks.

Output Controls:	1. Assign responsibility for hard-copy output handling and distribution.
	2. Insist upon an auditable trail from outputs back to inputs.
	3. Inspect all hard-copy output for reasonableness.
	4. Periodically review display output for reasonableness.

Identifying Control Requirements

The purpose of controls is to minimize incorrect data, and so controls are an indispensable part of any information system. To ensure that the appropriate controls are built into the system, the analyst should plan for them early in the design phase. Later in the development phase there will be pressures from programming schedules and test schedules that will tend to distract from the importance of controls.

Although controls may be used to help prevent or detect theft and fraud, the vast majority of problems detected through controls arise from honest mistakes. The principal controls used relate to input, processing, and output. Figure 11.5 identifies some commonly encountered controls with which the systems analyst should be familiar. Some of the controls are simply standards to be established and used; some involve manual operations; others are implemented through the computer program components of the system.

In the OARS example, the A/R system illustrates some of the common system controls. The system includes a process to check for and prevent customers from exceeding their credit limit without specific authorization. Other examples are exercising control of the view and update authority of those users utilizing terminals; and data edit routines in each input function that check for invalid or inappropriate data, for example, invalid inventory codes, nonexistent customer account numbers, and nonnumeric data in numeric fields.

Identifying Reference Manual Requirements

Typically, humans interface with computer-based systems in at least six principal ways, each involving manual tasks:

1. Humans prepare source documents.
2. Humans enter data from source documents for conversion to a machine-readable format.
3. Humans prepare and use control documents.
4. Humans write computer programs.
5. Humans operate the computer.
6. Humans use the computer-produced outputs.

All humans who are involved with a computer-based system must know certain aspects of the system. This information is provided by reference manuals. All the reference manuals to be used by programmers, users, and operators are identified in the design phase. The principal content of each manual is outlined. There may be a large number of these manuals because of the varying needs of many different types of users. The manuals are completed during the development phase, and they are an essential part of personnel training. Training plans and programs, including reference manuals, are discussed in chapter 16, "Preparing for Implementation."

Test Requirements

Identification of Test Requirements

The requirements for tests are established after the identification of processing functions is completed. They are established in the following sequence:

1. System test requirements
2. Subsystem test requirements
3. Program test requirements

The requirements for overall system performance are established first because they will determine the requirements for each subsystem. The requirements for testing the components of each subsystem are defined next. A computer-based business system has manual, equipment, and computer program subsystems. Typically, the most important subsystem is the computer program subsystem. Its components are computer programs. In the design phase, the tests that must be performed are identified in the sequence indicated previously, progressing from the system level to the program level. In the development phase, test plans are prepared to correspond to the test requirements. In this phase, the actual testing also takes place. The tests are performed in a planned sequence, progressing from the program level to the system level. Development phase testing activities are discussed in chapter 16, "Preparing for Implementation."

Structured Walk-throughs

Structured reviews are a technique used in developing efficient and reliable systems. A **structured walk-through** is a technical review to assist the technical people working on a project. It is a "structured" review because it is one of a series of reviews that are a planned part of the system design and development activities. It is referred to as a "walk-through" because the project is reviewed in a step-by-step sequence. Structured walk-throughs can be a valuable tool in the design and development of any system component. They are especially valuable in the design and development of computer programs.

The purpose of a structured walk-through is to discover errors in logic of a computer program or problems with other system components. The underlying philosophy is that others often can see errors that are not obvious to the programmer or analyst. The structured walk-through is a very powerful "test-as-you-go" technique. The review team consists of selected peers of the project developer. For example, if the project is a computer program, the review group consists of other programmers. The project developer "walks" the review group through the logic of the project. If any errors, omissions, or discrepancies are uncovered, they are recorded by one of the group members. The structured walk-through allows problems to be discovered early, when it is easier and less costly to correct them. If the structured walk-through technique is used consistently, fewer errors will be found during system testing, and less debugging time will be required. It should be noted that successful structured walk-throughs must be positive and nonthreatening experiences for the project developer; therefore, management does not attend, and the review must not be a basis for employee evaluation.

The structured walk-through technique is consistent with the entire life-cycle approach to the design and development of systems. The study, design, and development phase reviews are structured reviews. Structured walk-throughs are meaningful supplements to those reviews for the purpose of examining the technical logic of system components. Structured walk-throughs are particularly valuable in the development phase, which usually is much longer and costlier than the study and design phases. Therefore, it is essential that periodic structured management and technical reviews be held as work progresses.

Hardware Acquisition

The identification of processing functions must take into account the computer equipment resources currently available and the additional resources that might be required. The range of possibilities that must be considered include:

1. Acquire a computer system.
2. Replace the current equipment by a new computer system.
3. Greatly modify the current equipment.
4. Add some components to the current equipment.
5. Recognize that the current computer equipment is adequate.

Within each of the first four options, there may be many equipment choices. The process for evaluating specific equipment model choices is similar to that used during the candidate system evaluation activities of the study phase. As an example, consider a situation in which it has been found necessary to replace the current computer system with a system with a larger memory, faster processor speed, and faster input/output in order to handle an anticipated increase in workload. The hardware selection process involves the following steps:

1. Define the functions to be performed by the computer system.
2. Identify the required capabilities of the computer system.
3. Evaluate the candidate computer systems.
4. Select the computer system to be acquired on the basis of its performance and cost.

The definition of the functions to be performed by the system begins with an analysis of the workload that the system is expected to process. This includes the continuing current workload plus the estimated additional future workload. The purpose of analyzing workload is to develop representative samples that can be used to test the performance of various computer configurations. These samples are commonly drawn from actual programs currently in use, a composite made up to represent the *planned workload,* or they are a simulation of the workload and computer. Whichever technique is used, the sample workload should be representative of the tasks the computer must perform. This is called *benchmark testing* because identical series of tasks can be used to compare two or more computer systems. Typical tasks are compilations, updates, sorts, edits, report generation, and input and output handling.

If it is cumbersome to assemble an adequate and representative sample from problems currently being processed, then a composite can be made of tasks currently being performed and expected to be performed. This composite is not an actual production program; it is a series of tasks of the types described previously. It can, however, be used as a benchmark for measuring the relative performance of proposed hardware and software. Another alternative is the use of a simulation program, which makes one computer appear to perform like another computer. The inputs to the simulation program are the input, processing, and output tasks desired, and the frequency of their occurrence. The result of the simulation is data on timing, price, and performance. After the functions to be performed have been converted to a representative workload sample, the additional requirements for the computer equipment can be stated and the candidate systems can be evaluated. Figure 11.6 depicts performance and cost factors that typically are considered in evaluating products of vendors.

Growth is the ability of the equipment to meet not only the current workload but also future workloads. Three common ways of providing for growth are (1) equipment with reserve power, (2) equipment with add-on capability, and (3) equipment that is compatible for upward conversion. Reserve power usually is the least economical way of providing for growth, since it involves paying for capability not being used. Add-on capability is attractive because it offers an increase in capability when needed.

Vendor evaluation matrix. A vendor evaluation matrix is useful to the systems team in comparing the performance and cost factors of equipment to be acquired. Vendor evaluation is another example of a study of alternatives, and it follows the steps discussed in chapter 9 for performing a candidate system evaluation.

VENDOR FACTOR	Vendor A	Vendor B	Vendor C
PERFORMANCE:			
Workload			
Growth			
Hardware			
Software			
Support Services			
COSTS:			
Rental			
Third-Party Lease			
Purchase			

Compatibility for upward conversion provides the potential for replacing the equipment by a more powerful system on which all of the existing programs will run without modification. Since most vendors provide upward-compatible equipment, this often is a feasible route to follow as well. However, possible pitfalls, such as differences between operating systems, should be evaluated carefully.

Hardware performance is measured by factors such as memory size, internal speed of the central processor, and idle time waiting for input or output. Software performance depends on the efficiency of the operating system, the quality and quantity of utility programs, the programming languages provided, and the applications packages that the vendor may supply. Support services include field engineering, for example, maintenance, backup, and response to problems; systems (that is, software) support; and education and training of customer employees.

The three most common ways of acquiring computer equipment are rental, lease, and purchase. If the equipment is to be used for an extended period of time, both purchase and lease plans are less expensive than rental. Many computer manufacturers no longer rent or lease their hardware, but other companies specialize in the leasing of several brands of computers. The lease of equipment from someone other than the vendor is called a third-party lease. There are many leasing companies, and a variety of lease plans are available. Many lease plans provide an option to purchase. Third-party leasing can result in cost savings because the leasing company, anticipating a continuing market, often can spread the cost of the equipment over a longer period of time than can the initial user. If the equipment is to be retained for a long period of time, usually in excess of four years, then outright purchase may be the most economical means of acquisition.

Among the most important factors that affect cost decisions are changes in technology (which still continue to produce more performance for less cost with each new model release), confidence in workload projections, interest rates, flexibility, and lead times for equipment delivery. The equipment acquisition process has not been described in detail. Rather, by identifying the factors that must be considered, we have emphasized the need for evaluation procedures. Systems analysts must realize they cannot rely entirely upon vendors. They must know their own needs, be able to determine their own performance requirements, and be able to evaluate vendor responses to those requirements.

Summary

The design phase is the second of the four system development life-cycle phases. It is the phase in which the system selected in the study phase is designed in detail.

The first step in the design phase is the detailed system design. Detailed system design consists of four major steps, as follows:

1. The review of the general system design approved at the conclusion of the study phase. The system team must always be aware of what the new or modified system is to accomplish.
2. The initiation of a detailed design by identifying all processing requirements. The identification of these requirements is accomplished through the decomposition of the data flow diagrams drawn in the study phase. This decomposition has to reduce the DFDs to a leveled set where the detail of each function can be clearly seen. The system team may elect to use HIPO charts to show the hierarchy or levels of functions of the system and the inputs and outputs of each function.
3. The identification of control requirements. The system controls are an indispensable part of any information system and must be planned for early. If they are not planned for early enough, they either get left out of the system due to the pressures of system development or must be treated as an add-on near the end of the project.
4. The identification of all required reference manuals. Humans interface with systems in several ways and must know how to perform their particular portion of the system tasks. This information is provided through reference manuals.

Another major task to be performed early in the design phase is the identification of the test requirements for the system and each of the system components. These test requirements must be identified as early as possible to ensure that appropriate testing will take place during the development phase. Test requirements are established at the system, subsystem, and component levels.

The structured walk-through is a powerful technique for discovering and eliminating errors as the system is designed and developed.

For Review

design phase	IPO chart
data flow diagram	system controls
decomposed data flow diagram	planned workload
HIPO chart	benchmark testing
hierarchy chart	structured walk-through
structure chart	

For Discussion

1. What is the purpose of reviewing the general system design?
2. How do the decomposed DFDs and HIPO charts aid in the identification of processing functions?
3. What is a "leveled set" of data flow diagrams?
4. Why is it important to plan controls as early as possible in system design?
5. What is the purpose of system controls, and why are they needed?
6. Who determines the most effective means of performing each system function?
7. Name and discuss some ways in which humans interface with computer-based systems.
8. What test requirements must be identified?
9. What studies of alternatives may be required in the hardware acquisition activities?
10. What is a "planned workload"? How is it obtained?
11. What is "benchmark testing," and why is it used?
12. What is a structured walk-through? What is its purpose?

For Exercise: Vendor Evaluation Matrix

You have been given the responsibility to recommend a specific vendor/model for personal computers in your organization. Develop a vendor evaluation matrix, similar to figure 11.6, to compare at least three different vendor/model choices. The performance criteria should include: processor type/clock speed, disk capacity/access speed, monitor type/resolution, upgradeable processor, memory size/maximum, and number of expansion slots. The cost criteria should include initial cost and the annual cost of a maintenance agreement.

Chapter

12

■ ■ ■

Data Modeling

Preview

So far in the design phase the analyst and the system team have developed expanded data flow diagrams to identify each task or function to be accomplished by the system. They have also developed a data dictionary that describes each entity or data structure. They are now ready to continue the system design by designing the data base to be used by the system. In this chapter we focus on the relationships between the system entities using an entity-relationship diagram (ERD).

We will discuss a process called data normalization for decomposing complex data files into simpler forms. It is very common to manage these data files through the use of a data base management system (DBMS). DBMSs allow the analyst to prototype all or part of the system.

Objectives

1. You will be able to draw entity-relationship diagrams (ERDs) to show the relationships between system entities.
2. You will be able to normalize files and be able to describe the advantages of normalizing.
3. You will be able to list the components of a data base management system (DBMS).
4. You will be able to describe the advantages of designing through prototyping.

Key Terms

entity   a person, place, thing, or event for which data exists within a system.

entity-relationship diagram (ERD)   a diagram for graphically showing the logical relationships between entities of a system.

data normalization   the decomposition of complex data files into multiple, simpler files for more effective data retrieval and processing.

first normal form (1NF)   a table (or file) that does not contain repeating groups.

second normal form (2NF)   a table (or file) that is in 1NF and in which every column (field) is dependent on the entire key.

third normal form (3NF)   a table (or file) that is in 2NF and that does not contain columns (or fields) that are determined by any column other than the key.

data base management system (DBMS) software that allows data descriptions to be independent from computer programs. This system provides the capability for describing logical relationships between files to facilitate efficient maintenance and access to the data base.

schema   the DBMS definition of data elements and the relationships between the data elements in a data base.

subschema   the definition of the data elements available to an individual computer program.

row   the equivalent of a record in the relational model of a DBMS.

column   the equivalent of a field in the relational model of a DBMS.

table   the equivalent of a file in the relational model of a DBMS. The table can be visualized as a layout of rows and columns.

data base administrator (DBA)   the authority that regulates the DBMS by controlling the data base schema and subschema.

prototyping   a technique for speeding up the development of a computer-based information system by working with a model of that system that evolves into a final design specification.

Objectives of Data Modeling

In the design of a system's data base, two general types of files must be designed—master files and transaction files. *Master files* contain relatively permanent data, such as customer names, addresses, balances, and year- or month-to-date information. *Transaction files* contain data with a limited useful life, typically one processing cycle. Transaction information concerning sales or payments, for example, is of value only during the current billing cycle. It should be understood that a system can, and typically does, have multiple master and transaction files.

The objectives of file design are to provide for the effective use of data storage media and to contribute to the overall efficiency of the computer program component of the business information system. The data storage media must provide efficient access to the data. The data, in turn, must be organized to minimize duplicated data and the potential for errors.

Understanding the Data and Data Flows

The first step in understanding the data and data flows is to know what data are needed to satisfy the requirements of the users. This was accomplished during the study phase when the outputs and their data elements were identified. Figure 12.1 is the output data element source analysis worksheet prepared during the candidate system evaluation activities. If any modifications to outputs or to their data elements have been made, the output data source analysis worksheets must be updated at this time.

Data Flow Diagrams

The output data element source analysis worksheets together with the output specification forms from the system performance definition activities provide information about the sources and destinations of data, data stores, data transformation steps, and the data that flow between them. This information was used to draw the data flow diagram shown in figure 12.2. Understanding these data flows is critical for the data modeling effort.

The Data Dictionary

Each data structure within the system must be described in detail to show the structure's name, type, and content. An effective tool for providing this description is the data dictionary.

Figure 12.3 is an example of a data dictionary entry for the Sales-Order structure. The entries show that the sales order is a data flow type of structure and name each of the data elements that make up the sales order record. The underlining of the order number data element is to identify the order number as the primary key field for these records. The last four elements are enclosed in braces to show that these elements may repeat within the record. Every data structure of the system should be described in the data dictionary.

Output data element source analysis. The output data element source analysis sheet prepared in the study phase can be used to identify master and transaction file record data elements; they also indicate the number of characters for each data element. The output data element source analysis sheets shown are the same as those in figure 9.5. Of course, the worksheets should be updated to reflect any changes made since the candidate system evaluation.

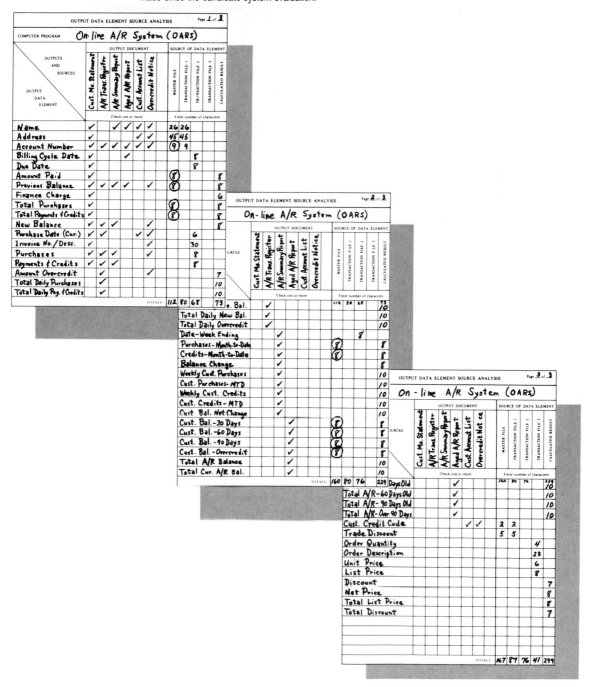

■ Figure 12.2   Data flow diagrams describe the flow of data from entity to process to entity, but not the relationships between entities. Understanding the data flows is the first step in data modeling.

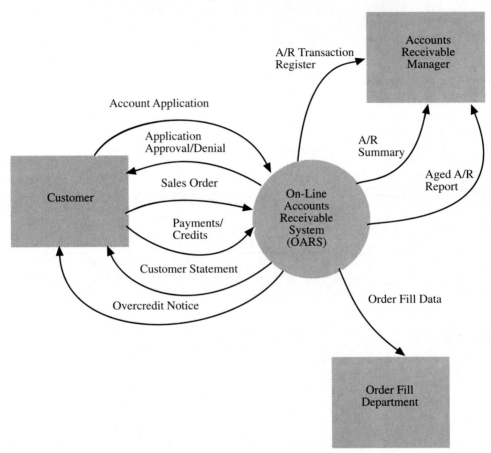

Understanding the Relationships Between Entities

An **entity** was previously defined as any object (i.e. a person, place, thing, or event) for which data exists within the system. Thus the data flows, data stores, and sources/ destinations of data shown in the DFDs are all entities. Note that the data flow diagrams described above show the various entities of the system but do not show how the entities relate to each other. The next data modeling task is to understand the relationships between these entities.

Entity-Relationship Diagrams (ERDs)

The diagram used to graphically describe the logical relationships between entities is called an **entity-relationship diagram (ERD).** ERDs describe how pairs of entities relate to one another and the number of entities involved in the relationship. As

The data dictionary contains the description of the fields that make up the data. This information becomes the foundation for creating the data model.

```
                          Data Dictionary Entry

    Name of Data Structure: Sales-Order

    Type of Data Structure: Data Flow

    Other Names:          none

    Content:
        Sales-Order = Order Number +
                      Order Data +
                      Customer Number +
                      Customer Name +
                      Customer Address +
                      Customer City +
                      Customer State +
                      Customer ZIP Code +
                      Discount Code +
                      Trade Discount +
                    ⎧ Product Code +        ⎫
                    ⎨ Product Description + ⎬
                    ⎪ Quantity Ordered +    ⎪
                    ⎩ Unit Price            ⎭
```

COMMENT: Product Code through Unit Price are repeated for each item ordered.

examples, the ERD will show how two entities relate to one another by describing that relationship with a verb such as receives, places, generates, or lists—a customer (entity) places an order (entity), or an order (entity) generates a customer statement (entity). The number of entities involves describes how many of the first entity relate to how many of the second entity. These relationships are described as one-to-one, one-to-many, or many-to-many.

Drawing Entity-Relationship Diagrams

Figure 12.4 illustrates the general format of the entity-relationship diagram. The rectangle shape is used to show entities and the diamond shape is used to show the relationship.

Of course a single entity may relate to multiple other entities, as illustrated in figure 12.5. The general rule for describing an entity is that the entity should always be stated in the singular. Thus the entities in figure 12.5 are customer, order, and customer statement. That does not mean that the business only has one customer, but that the relationship being expressed in the diagram deals with each entity. The rule for the relation description is that it is always stated as an action verb such as places or generates.

■ Figure 12.4   Entity-relationship diagrams (E-R diagrams) show the relationship between two entities. The entity is a singular person, place, thing, or event which has data associated with it.

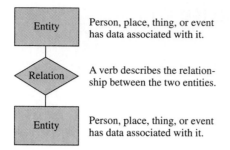

Person, place, thing, or event has data associated with it.

A verb describes the relationship between the two entities.

Person, place, thing, or event has data associated with it.

■ Figure 12.5   The OARS entity-relationship diagram shows the relationships between the customer and an order, and the order and the customer statement. Relationships may be one to one (1:1), one to many (1:M), or many to many (M:N).

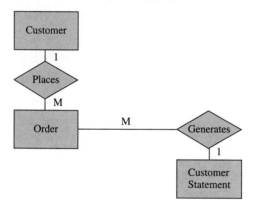

The 1s and Ms refer to the number of entities involved in the relationship. This may be a one-to-one (1:1), one-to-many (1:M), or many-to-many (M:N) relationship. A one-to-one relationship exists when there is only one of the second entity for each of the first entity. A one-to-many relationship exists when many of the second entities relate to only one of the first entity, and the many-to-many relationship exists when many of the second entities relate to each of the first entity and many of the first entities relate to each of the second entity. In figure 12.5 each customer places one or more orders so the relationship is one-to-many (1:M). Many orders generate one customer statement, illustrating the reverse situation, many-to-one (M:1). Although there are multiple orders and multiple customer statements, there are multiple orders reflected in one statement, but there are not multiple statements for one order so it is not a many-to-many relationship.

Normalization of Files

The process of normalizing files involves, in most cases, the breaking up or decomposing of large, complex files into multiple smaller files. Each of the resulting smaller files is easier to use and avoids some errors. It is not uncommon to identify entities not previously known during the normalization process. If additional entities are discovered during normalization, the ERDs will have to be updated.

Purpose of Normalization

The purpose of normalization is to avoid problems, called *update anomalies,* that arise when working with files. These anomalies or problems occur when the system is involved with the processes of updating, making additions, and deleting data.

The updating anomaly may arise if data is repeated or duplicated within the data base. If data are repeated in different places, updating the data base involves making multiple changes. If all occurrences of the data are not updated to the new value, the data base then contains inconsistent data.

An anomaly may occur when one attempts to add data to the data base but the key or identifying field(s) for the record is not yet established for that data. An example of this situation is if customer data were contained within the order record. Data for a new customer could not be added to the data base until that customer placed an order and an order record was created—not a reasonable situation.

Deleting data in files that are not normalized may also cause an anomaly. Consider the case presented above where customer data are a part of the order record, and if the only order for a customer is canceled and deleted we will delete more data than we intend. The customer data will be deleted along with the order data.

All three of these update anomalies can be avoided if we normalize the data.

Normal Forms

Commonly three normal forms are associated with the normalization process. They are referred to as the first normal form (1NF), second normal form (2NF), and the third normal form (3NF). These normal forms are steps that must be completed sequentially; that is, a file is placed into 1NF, then 2NF, and finally 3NF.

The **first normal form (1NF)** requires that all fields be identified by the key field(s) and that each record not contain any repeating fields. As an example, the OARS system uses the data from an order transaction file. This file includes fields of order number, order date, customer data, discount data, product code, product description, quantity ordered, and unit price. If a typical order was for the purchase of multiple items, the product code, product description, quantity ordered, and unit price would be repeated for each item in the order. Figure 12.6 illustrates the layout of the orders file as it was just described. Note that the last four fields are repeated six times to allow for up to six items to be purchased on a single order. This file is not normalized.

The orders file is not normalized because it has repeating fields of product code, product description, quantity ordered, and unit price for each item being ordered.

Orders File:

Order Number
Order Date
Customer Number
Customer Name
Customer Address
Customer City
Customer State
Customer ZIP Code
Discount Code
Trade Discount
Product Code
Product Description
Quantity Ordered
Unit Price
Product Code
Product Description
Quantity Ordered
Unit Price
Product Code
Product Description
Quantity Ordered
Unit Price
Product Code
Product Description
Quantity Ordered
Unit Price
Product Code
Product Description
Quantity Ordered
Unit Price
Product Code
Product Description
Quantity Ordered
Unit Price

The 1NF requires that there be no repeating fields. In this example, each item being ordered must be recorded in a separate record. Since the order number would be the same on each of the multiple records, the order number plus the product code would be required to establish a unique key for the record. Figure 12.7 lists the fields of the orders file without the repeating fields. Note that both the order number and product code are underlined, as they must both be used as a combined key to uniquely identify any given record in the file. This file is now in first normal form (1NF).

The **second normal form (2NF)** requires that the file be in 1NF and that every element within the record be determined by the entire key. If records are identified by a combination of the order number plus the product code, every field must be determined by the entire key and not just the order number or the product code. In our OARS example, several fields do not meet this entire key requirement of 2NF. The quantity ordered can only be identified by knowing the order number and the product code, but that is not the case with any of the other fields in the record. The order

■ Figure 12.7   The orders file is in first normal form (1NF). Each field is determined by the record key, and there are no repeating fields. Note that the key is the order number plus the product code; nothing less will uniquely identify each record in the file.

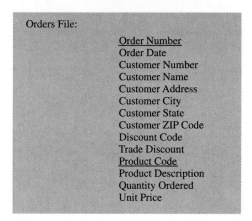

Orders File:

Order Number
Order Date
Customer Number
Customer Name
Customer Address
Customer City
Customer State
Customer ZIP Code
Discount Code
Trade Discount
Product Code
Product Description
Quantity Ordered
Unit Price

■ Figure 12.8   The orders file has now been decomposed into three separate, related files that are in second normal form (2NF). Each field in each file is determined by the whole key.

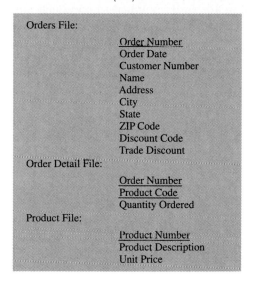

Orders File:

Order Number
Order Date
Customer Number
Name
Address
City
State
ZIP Code
Discount Code
Trade Discount

Order Detail File:

Order Number
Product Code
Quantity Ordered

Product File:

Product Number
Product Description
Unit Price

date and the customer data are determined by the order number, but not by the product code. The product description and the unit price are determined by the product code, but not by the order number. Figure 12.8 shows that the orders file has now been split into three separate files: orders, order detail, and product. The orders file contains only data determined by the order number. The order detail file contains data determined by both the order number and the product code. The product file contains data determined by the product code. These files are now in second normal form (2NF).

The orders file has been further decomposed into five separate, related files. Each field in each file is determined only by the key field or fields and not by any other field in the record. These files are in third normal form (3NF).

Orders File:

    Order Number
    Order Date
    Customer Number

Order Detail File:

    Order Number
    Product Code
    Quantity Ordered

Product File:

    Product Number
    Product Description
    Unit Price

Customer File:

    Customer Number
    Name
    Address
    City
    State
    ZIP Code
    Discount Code

Discount File:

    Discount Code
    Trade Discount

The **third normal form (3NF)** requires that the file be in 2NF and that every field within the record be determined only by the key field(s) and not by any nonkey field within the record. We have two problems with the files as illustrated in figure 12.8. First, the customer data is determined by the order number—a particular customer did place the order, but the customer data is also determined by the customer number field. The second problem is that the trade discount does apply to the order, but it is determined by the discount code field. To be in third normal form, the customer data must be removed from the orders file, and the trade discount should not be left with the discount code. Figure 12.9 depicts the resulting five files required to put the order data into the third normal form (3NF).

Referring to the anomalies discussed earlier, a file that is not normalized can have problems when updating data, adding records, or deleting records. With five separate, but related files as shown in figure 12.9, data can be changed or updated without concern about creating multiple copies of a field; new customers and products can be added to the system without an order record being created; and orders may be deleted without losing product, customer, or trade discount data.

Note that the example OARS order data has been normalized into five separate files and two additional entities have been identified. When compared to the original ERD of figure 12.5, figure 12.10 illustrates the addition of the discount and product entities.

Data Base Management Systems

As the number of computer-based systems within a company increases, larger amounts of data must be stored in support of them. The maintenance and control of a large, complex set of files is a costly and difficult task. Often data elements are duplicated in the files of several different systems. For instance, employee names and

New OARS entity-relationship diagram drawn after normalizing the files. Normalizing a file often points out additional entities and relationships.

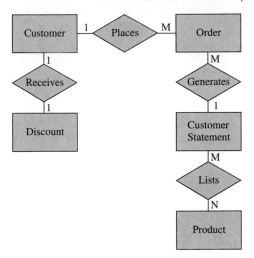

addresses may be recorded in the personnel file, the payroll file, and other employee-related files. These redundant or duplicated data items cause two major problems: (1) they increase the total amount of file storage space needed; and (2) they necessitate multiple updates whenever a change in the data occurs.

A solution for the problem of redundant data is to separate data into multiple, smaller files that can be used in combination where data are recorded only once. These smaller files created through normalization may be used in different combinations by different programs. The *data base* is made up of a series of common, shared files. The creation of common files that are shared by multiple systems introduces two additional problems. First, each program using the files must input and hold all the data in the shared file records, not just the data elements used in the processing by that program, and those multiple files have to be accessed in order to retrieve the required data elements, causing a great increase in the complexity of the programs. Second, data elements that do not apply to a particular system may become available to all system users. This is especially true for on-line inquiry systems, where users might see confidential data they are not authorized to use. Considering the public's right to privacy and the several laws that require privacy of confidential data, this must be a major concern for all organizations. For many companies, the solution to the problems of maintaining and controlling the data base has been the use of a data base management system. A **data base management system (DBMS)** is a software system used to access, maintain, and control multiple, shared files.

Data base management system (DBMS) modules. Data base management systems consist of two major modules. The data manipulation component makes all data retrievals, updates, additions, and deletions to the data base. The data definition component communicates the data requirements of the application program to the data manipulation component.

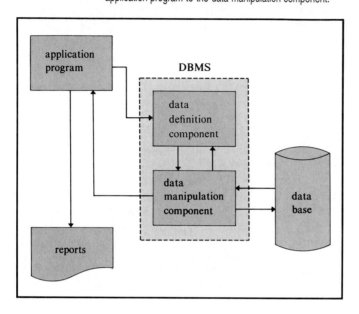

DBMS Components

Five major components are common to most data base management systems. The first two are a data definition component and a data manipulation component. The use of these components is illustrated in figure 12.11. Application programs call for data through the data definition component, which communicates the data requirements to the data manipulation component. All data retrievals, updates, additions, and deletions are accomplished through the data manipulation component. This component then transmits the requested data to the application program, which processes the data and can output the results to the user. These two components are the heart of the DBMS.

A third component is a query language. This is a simplified programming language that allows users to specify the data wanted and the format that will meet user information needs. The query language is easy to use and typically requires only a few key words to create a user output. It is especially valuable in on-line systems where a user can specify the data through the terminal and see the resulting output almost immediately. One popular query language is called Structured Query Language, or SQL. An example of an SQL query is presented in chapter 17, "Computer Program Development."

A report writer is the fourth component. This component allows the user to describe a printer/display layout to generate tabular reports. The report writer permits much more formatting of the requested output than does the query language. It allows the user to specify a title, column headings, and the elements that are to make up the body of the report. The report writer also often provides for the printing of subtotals and totals. An example of a report writer is presented in chapter 13, "Output Design," in the discussion of prototyping printer output. Variations of a report writer can be used to generate display screen inputs and outputs. An example of a screen design is included in the discussion of prototyping VDT screens in chapter 14, "Input Design." Both of these examples use the microcomputer-based dBASE IV system.

The last component is the DBMS utility. It is a series of programs used to create, back up, and restore the data base. These utility programs allow the data processing center to protect itself against possible loss of the data base.

DBMS Functions

Data base management systems have two major functions: (1) to maintain the data base independently from the application programs that use the data; and (2) to provide a measure of data security so that unauthorized users will not have access to the data.

In traditional application programs, all files, records, and data elements used by the program must be defined within the program. If the size of the record or any data element changes, all the application programs using the file must be modified to reflect the change. In a shared file, changes may have been made in only one system, but data definition changes are required in all programs that use the file. Data base management systems avoid this problem by removing the data definitions from the application programs and putting them in the DBMS. This allows the data to be defined once, within the DBMS, instead of within every application program. If any changes are made to the data base, only the DBMS definition must be altered. Application programs are not affected.

The DBMS definition of the data elements and the relationships between the data elements in the data base is called the **schema.** Since the application program no longer contains data definitions, it cannot directly access the data base. When an input or output dealing with the data base is required, the application program will request the data from the DBMS. The DBMS will then access the data base and transfer the data to or from the application program. It should be noted that the application program cannot be written in all languages. Each data base management system is designed to interface with one or more host languages. All data base management systems support COBOL as a host language; many support C, and a few support RPG and other languages.

Although the application program does not contain data definitions, it does use a list of data elements that make up the program's logical record. The definition of the data elements available to the program is called the **subschema.** The data elements of the logical record defined in the subschema may actually come from several different records in several different files. Some DBMSs also refer to the subschema as the *view* of the data. The DBMS manufactures a logical record for the application program to match the subschema. Figure 12.12 shows a portion of a view or subschema. Note that the fields within this view are not all from the same file. If the contents of the subschema are controlled, control can be exercised over the data that the user can see. Data elements that do not apply to the user's program or data that

■ Figure 12.12 Example view or subschema showing fields from multiple files being used as a single logical record. This view was generated using dBASE IV on a microcomputer.

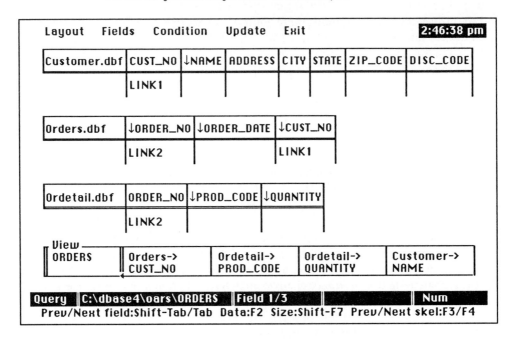

the user is not authorized to see will not be provided to the application program. If different subschema are provided to different users, what the user sees is controlled by their particular subschema.

Users can also be limited in what they do with the data. They may be limited to inquiry only, or they may be allowed to update data elements, add records to the file, delete records from the file, or any combination of these functions. An additional security function in most data base management systems is provided by a system of privacy locks or a password system. Before users can access data through a terminal, for example, they are required to enter personal identification. This identification is in the form of a word called a user ID. In addition, this user ID must be confirmed with a password known only to that user. The user ID communicates to the DBMS the level of authority the user has in dealing with the data.

DBMS Architectures

Data base management systems allow the programmer to view the data base as a set of linked records. The DBMS architecture describes how the records relate to each other. There are three principal architectures: hierarchical, networked, and relational.

A *hierarchical* DBMS links records through a superior-subordinate relationship. As an example, the OARS system has a customer file and a file of orders from those customers. The relationship between the records of these two files could be

Relational model DBMS table. The table is a two-dimensional presentation of the file data. Each row is equivalent to a record, and each column is equivalent to a field.

Record#	PROD_CODE	PROD_DESC	UNIT_PRICE
1	00123	Chrome Gadget	12.95
2	00124	Brass Gadget	17.85
3	00125	Silver Gadget	45.50
4	00125	Gold Gadget	106.25

established with the customer file records being the superior and the orders for that customer the subordinate. Thus if a customer's record is accessed, the DBMS will have links to all orders for that customer. In a hierarchical organization the only way to access subordinate records is through a superior record. A subordinate record may have only one superior record.

The *networked* architecture is similar to the hierarchical, except that each subordinate record can have multiple superior records. This would allow the access of customer records from order records, as well as the reverse. In addition, the order file records could be linked to other superior records, such as in a file of suppliers.

The *relational* architecture is the newest of the DBMS architectures. In the hierarchical and networked architectures, the links between one file and another are established within the DBMS structure. In the relational architecture, the data itself is used to associate it with other files. Thus two files that contain common data elements can easily be associated with each other.

The relational architecture is described as a two-dimensional system with the data elements arranged in rows and columns. Each **row** is a record, and the **columns** represent the data elements that make up the record. The row and column layout of the relational data base file is called a **table.** Figure 12.13 illustrates a relational table. The relational architecture provides a great deal of flexibility in that new files may be added to the data base and be immediately linked to other files without having to modify the structure of the data base. Remember, the files are related to one another through the data in the files, not through the structure of the data base. One disadvantage of the relational architecture has been that performance (or response time) has been slower than with the other architectures. This response time continues to improve with updates of the software, but relational data bases cannot handle as high a number of transactions per second as the other two architectures. The relational data base that has become a standard is called SQL or Structured Query Language. SQL-based systems are now available on the full range of hardware from mainframes to microcomputers.

It should be noted that there are several suppliers of DBMSs. Each of these systems differs from the others in their approach, capabilities, and/or cost. Converting to a DBMS environment from a non-DBMS environment is a complex task that must be planned carefully. Make sure that the best system is selected for your organization and that appropriately trained personnel are available to install it. Once converted to any DBMS it may be very difficult to convert to another DBMS.

Data Base Management Systems and the Personal Computer

Originally DBMSs were strictly for use on mainframe computers. This was due to the fact that DBMSs are composed of large, complex programs that require a relatively large amount of main memory to hold them. The memory requirement for a DBMS has not changed much over the years, but the typical amount of memory found in a computer in all price ranges has changed a great deal. Only a few years ago, a personal computer with 48 KB (kilobytes) or 64 KB of memory was considered to have a lot of memory. Indeed, it hasn't been that long since a mainframe computer with 640 KB or less of memory was typical. Today it is common to find personal computers with at least 4 to 8 megabytes of memory. Several of the newer personal computers have a maximum capability of at least 32 megabytes of main memory.

Today there are personal computer variations of mainframe data base management systems. These personal computer DBMSs use the same codes and commands as do their larger counterparts. This allows a user or programmer to develop applications for the mainframe DBMS on their personal computer and then up load the application to the mainframe and/or use it on microcomputers. It also means that within a distributed data processing (DDP) system a portion of the mainframe data base can be down loaded to a personal computer for specific user manipulation without jeopardizing the main data base. There are also several DBMSs developed specifically for the personal computer. The most popular to date is one called dBASE from Ashton-Tate, a Borland company. Its current version is called dBASE IV. It is a relational DBMS designed for personal computers. The dBASE package includes data definition, data manipulation, query, and report writer components. With these components, the package provides the user with a complete DBMS. In addition, there is a friendly control center mode that provides users with an easy-to-use process for selecting the DBMS functions they require. Thus users can define, collect, and manipulate data without having to possess a programming background. Figure 12.14 shows the control center display of dBASE IV. Several dBASE IV examples are used as illustrations in the next two chapters.

The Data Base Administrator (DBA)

The data base management system separates data descriptions from application programs and provides a measure of data security. The **data base administrator (DBA)** is the authority that regulates the DBMS by controlling the data base schema and subschema. The DBA also authorizes the use of passwords by users. The job of data base administrator may range from a part of a person's responsibilities in smaller companies to a full-time position that includes a staff of several assistants in larger companies. The data base administrator's job is to provide services to both data processing personnel and users; the DBA must be able to work with both groups. The administrator has the ultimate responsibility for the organization and control of the data base.

The dBASE IV control center. The control center is a user-friendly approach to allowing users access to their data without requiring users to become programmers.

```
 Catalog   Tools   Exit                                          2:45:53 pm

                        dBASE IV CONTROL CENTER

                    CATALOG: C:\DBASE4\OARS\OARS.CAT


    Data        Queries      Forms      Reports     Labels    Applications

 <create>     <create>    <create>    <create>    <create>    <create>

 CUSTOMER     ORDERS      ORDERENT
 DISCOUNT
 ORDERS
 ORDETAIL
 PRODUCT



 File:          New file
 Description: Press ENTER on <create> to create a new file
   Help: F1  Use: ┘ Data: F2  Design: Shift-F2  Quick Report: Shift-F9  Menus: F10
```

The Prototyping Engine

As previously noted, **prototyping** is a means of speeding up the SDLC by allowing analysts and users to work together with a model of the actual computer information system throughout the study and design phases. Data base management systems often are able to serve as the prototyping engine that produces a working model of a system before proceeding with full-scale construction of the system. For example, a data-driven prototype can generate examples of screen displays and reports with which a user can identify. It is a method of allowing the user to touch and feel what the real thing will be like when the system is put into operation. Prototyping produces an actual report or screen display that the user can see and use. It is not just a layout document that allows the user to visualize what the final product will be like—it's a working model. A prototype is not necessarily the final version; it is intended to be used and modified until it is exactly the way the user wants it to be. It is an excellent way to create a user-analyst relationship.

Attributes of the Prototyping Engine

There are several CASE tools with which the analyst can develop prototypes, but one approach is to use the tools available with a DBMS. The query language and report writer components of a DBMS can be used to quickly generate screen displays and printed reports. The use of a query language and report writer to develop prototypes is illustrated in the next two chapters.

■ Figure 12.15   This figure shows the steps involved in setting up a model, or prototype, of a system and testing it. The steps in the system prototyping cycle can be repeated until the model is discarded or accepted. In the latter event, the model may become an interim working version to be integrated into other corporate systems or converted into a detailed design specification for a system to be developed.

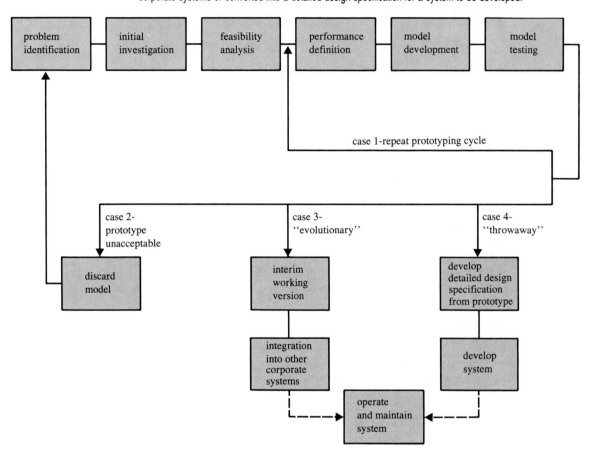

The Prototyping Cycle

The prototyping concept is a simple one: The sooner users can see, become involved in the development of, and experiment with a model of an information system, the more quickly and effectively it can be implemented. However, a prototype is not a quick and dirty approach for solving urgent systems problems. Prototyping, too, is a systematic methodology involving well-defined steps in order to construct a scaled-down, but meaningful, model of a proposed information system. The prototype must exhibit all of the important attributes of the system. The steps involved in developing a prototype of an information system are shown in figure 12.15. These steps are not greatly different from those required by the standard SDLC methodology. It is still necessary to understand and define the problem, analyze the current system, perform a candidate system evaluation, and develop a comprehensive data dictionary in order to ensure the availability of the data required for processing and producing usable outputs. Systems analysis is still of critical importance, and design of the prototype must include realistic data entry screens, report formats, and output screen displays. As contrasted with the standard, more detailed SDLC methodology, the potential advantages of prototyping are as follows:

1. The standard approach is sequential, and change is difficult and expensive, particularly if unforeseen problems are encountered in the design and development phases. Instead of relying upon meeting a set of defined milestones and dates that culminate in acceptance testing by the user, prototyping is a cycle of activities, and many iterations can be made in a relatively short period of time. The cyclical nature of prototyping can effect design and development efficiencies because life-cycle activities that are sequential in the standard approach to the SDLC methodology can be overlapped and worked upon concurrently.
2. With prototyping, the system is not defined, initially, to the same level of detail as in a standard SDLC approach that might require a very detailed analysis and documentation of data flows and user requirements. Instead, using a test data base, the analyst and user can modify the model until the outputs satisfy the user. In effect, the user is involved in acceptance testing of the system from the outset.
3. Prototyping can greatly reduce the cost and time required to test an actual system because successive refinements to the model can easily be made. Also, should the system not prove to be feasible, it can be discarded without excessive loss in time or expense.

Assuming that the prototype is successful, there are two general uses for the completed model. As figure 12.15 also shows, these are:

1. To use it as an interim working version for the new system. This working model could evolve into the new system or be integrated with other corporate systems that share common data bases.
2. To use it as a design specification for a more efficiently programmed system. After the improved version of the system is built and installed, the prototype is thrown away. This is the reason why prototypes often are referred to as throw-away systems.

In sum, prototyping is a powerful systems development tool, capable, in many instances, of reducing the time required to design, develop, and implement computer information systems. It is not a panacea for all systems development projects. However, prototyping does have a broad range of applicability. In particular, it should be strongly considered as a means of designing information systems in which there is a high degree of user-oriented interaction, such as on-line query and decision support systems.

Summary

The two objectives of file design are effective use of storage media and the efficient processing of data. To make this happen, the analyst needs to understand the data and the data flows through a study of the data flow diagrams and data dictionary prepared during the study phase.

While DFDs show the flow of data between sources/destinations and data stores, they do not show how the various entities relate to one another. The tool to describe the relationship between entities is called an entity-relationship diagram (ERD). This diagram graphically illustrates the nature of the relationships that exist between entities within the system. The relationships shown on the ERD may be one-to-one (1:1), one-to-many (1:M), or many-to-many (M:N).

Normalizing files is an approach to avoiding problems called update anomalies that arise from working with files. These anomalies or problems occur when the system is involved with the processes of updating, making additions, and deleting data. The normalization process involves modifying the structure of the files according to the rules of the first normal form (1NF), second normal form (2NF), and third normal form (3NF).

To manage the multiple files created during the normalization process, it may be appropriate to consider a data base management system (DBMS) to maintain these files for the organization. There are five components common to most DBMSs—data definition, data manipulation, a query language, a report writer, and a utility component. The architecture of the DBMS describes how the files in the data base relate to each other. There are three principal architectures: hierarchical, networked, and relational. Today there are personal computer variations of mainframe data base management systems. These personal computer DBMSs use the same codes and commands as do their larger counterparts. This allows a user or programmer to develop applications for the mainframe DBMS on their personal computer and then up load the application to the mainframe and/or use it on microcomputers.

The data base administrator (DBA) is the authority that regulates the DBMS by controlling the data base schema and subschema. The DBA also authorizes the use of passwords by users.

Prototyping is an effective methodology for allowing users to participate in the development of a model of an information system, and to experiment with that model before committing the resources required to develop a full-scale system. All of the steps essential to the standard SDLC process are present; however, prototyping can greatly speed up the systems design and development process because the same level of initial detail is not required, and because the process is cyclical, allowing SDLC activities to overlap as the model is refined.

For Review

master file	data base management system (DBMS)
transaction file	schema
data flow diagram (DFD)	subschema
data dictionary	view
data base	hierarchical DBMS
entity	networked DBMS
entity-relationship diagram (ERD)	relational DBMS
normalization	row
update anomalies	column
first normal form (1NF)	table
second normal form (2NF)	data base administrator (DBA)
third normal form (3NF)	prototyping

For Discussion

1. What are the two main objectives of data modeling?
2. What entities are shown on a data flow diagram?
3. What information is part of a data dictionary entry?
4. What is an entity-relationship diagram?
5. What is the purpose of normalizing files?
6. What are the three normal forms discussed in this chapter?
7. What is a DBMS?
8. What are the major functions of a DBMS?
9. What are the five major components of a data base management system? What is the purpose of each?
10. How might a personal-computer-based DBMS be of value to a user?
11. What are the functions of the data base administrator (DBA)?
12. Define prototyping. What is its purpose?

For Exercise: File Normalization

You have been assigned to a systems team working with the inventory system. Your task is to normalize the inventory system data. The inventory data includes: item description, item location—bin number, item location—code, item location—floor, item quantity-on-hand, item quantity-on-order, stock code (key field), supplier address, supplier city, supplier code, supplier name, supplier state, supplier zip code, and unit price. These fields are listed in alphabetic order, not necessarily in the order of the file(s). Place this data into the third normal form (3NF). For each file, identify the key field(s) by underlining them.

Chapter

13

∎ ∎ ∎

Output Design

Preview

Output design has been an ongoing activity almost from the beginning of the project. In the study phase, outputs were identified and described generally in the project directive. Tentative output media were then selected and sketches made of each output during the system performance definition activities. In the candidate system evaluation, a "best" new system was selected; its description identified the input and output media. The system team must now refine the sketches into detailed descriptions of the outputs. An alternative to describing outputs as sketches is to develop a "live" example or prototype of the output for the user to see and evaluate. To develop a sketch or a prototype, the output must be planned with a specific output medium. The most common output media are computer printers and visual display terminal (VDT) screens. Computer print charts and VDT display layout sheets are used for the detailed description of outputs. Microcomputers are having a dramatic impact upon output design. The availability of graphics software and desktop publishing systems can make the automation of form design a reality for even small organizations.

Objectives

1. You will be able to list the major principles of output design.
2. You will be able to read and draw computer print charts.
3. You will become familiar with the purpose of output prototyping.
4. You will be able to identify the special requirements for preparing VDT display layouts.

Key Terms

print chart   a form used to design computer printer outputs. Each line on the form is divided into printer print positions to allow for the detailed design of titles, column headings, detail lines, and so forth.

display layout sheet   a form used to design VDT screen layouts. The form is divided into 24 lines of 80 characters each to simulate the possible display positions on a screen.

computer output   with few exceptions, output designs describe "lines of characters." The most common output media are the line printer and visual display terminal (VDT). In all cases, the format descriptions are similar. Chapter 14, "Input Design," will also discuss the design considerations of source documents and the design of visual displays.

input/output prototyping   the simulation of system inputs and outputs to help the users to get the "look and feel" of the input or output during its design.

desktop publishing   the production of newsletters, flyers, and similar printed output utilizing the combination of desktop (or personal) computers and laser printers.

General Principles of Output Design

Most outputs have four basic parts: the title, heading, body, and conclusion. The *title* identifies the output. It should be as descriptive and as brief as possible. Examples are "Purchase Order," "Sales Report," and "Sales Order." The title usually is centered at the top of the output. The *heading* contains all the general identification data. For example, it might include the date, form sequence number, and company name and address. The heading data usually is not the principal information the output was designed to show, but that which is necessary for record identification purposes. All data used for reference filing is contained in the heading. The heading may be separated from the remainder of the output by ruled lines or by a box drawn around it. The specific data the output was designed to show is called the *body* of the form. An example is a sales invoice that shows quantities, item descriptions, unit prices, and total prices. The body of the output should read from left to right and from top to bottom. Since the body of many outputs is numeric, it is common to see the body set up in columnar form. It is critical that the body information be at the appropriate level of detail for the involved user. Generally, the higher the user is in the organization, the more general or summary the data of the output body. Users at the operational level in the organization will most likely require very detailed data as compared to what managers require. The last part of a form is the *conclusion.* The conclusion contains summary data such as totals. The basic parts described here are found on most outputs, yet exceptions are common. Output design is a combination of skill and art, however, you should not allow considerations of art or "pretty outputs" to override the principles of good output design.

Printer Output

Designing Effective Printer Layouts

Designing effective printer layouts requires the analyst to keep the needs of the users in mind. Make sure that the data in the body of the report is in a sequence that makes it easy for the user to find and use the information they need. Of course the choice of data sequence must always be that of the user—a major reason for keeping the users involved in the design process.

Since printed outputs may accumulate and be useful for a period of time, it is important that the users be able to determine how old the information is on the report. A simple way to accomplish this is to always provide a date in the heading of the report.

The layout of the printed report can be developed and documented through the use of a printer layout form.

Printer Layout Forms

The detailed description of outputs includes the identification of the print positions to be used for the title, column headings, detail data, and totals. Figure 13.1 depicts a typical form used to make this detailed description. The example **print chart** allows for 144 possible printing positions. Computer printers typically have a maximum of

■ Figure 13.1   Print chart. Print charts are used to prepare detailed descriptions of computer printed outputs. Each of the small squares on the chart represents a possible printing position. The title, column headings, detail, and total lines can be shown exactly as they will appear in the final output.

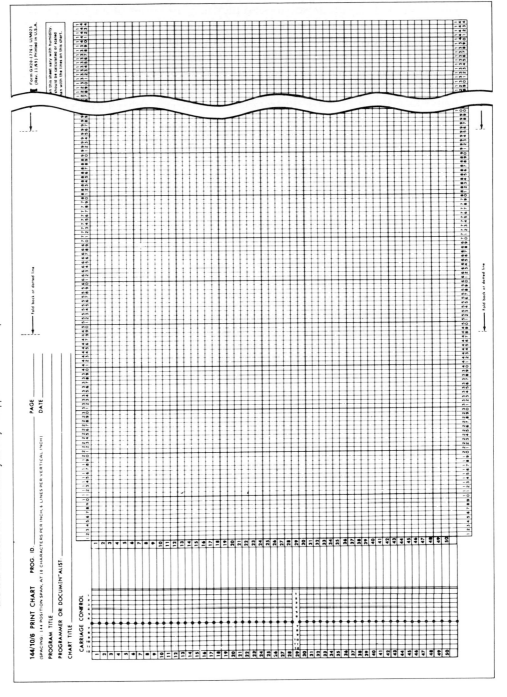

either 120 or 132 print positions, and they may use forms of much narrower width. A vertical line should be drawn on the layout form to indicate the width of the form. Form length also varies with the needs of users. Common form lengths are $3\frac{1}{3}$, $3\frac{1}{2}$, $3\frac{2}{3}$, $5\frac{1}{2}$, 6, 7, $7\frac{1}{2}$, $8\frac{1}{2}$, and 11 inches.

Many years ago, computer printers had a physical device that could read carriage control data from holes punched in a closed loop made of paper or mylar. This closed loop was called a *carriage control tape.* The carriage control data was recorded by punching holes within areas called channels. This carriage control tape is often described on the left side of print charts. Modern printers no longer have a carriage control device that detects holes punched in a loop of paper. Instead, they store the carriage control information within a small memory buffer. The data in the carriage control buffer functions just as the carriage control tape did on the older equipment. Carriage control data are most often used to identify the first and last line of printing on a form. Two standard uses of channels are the *channel 1* signal, which indicates the position of the first line to be printed on a page, and the *channel 12* signal, which indicates the position of the last line of print on a page. Channels 2 through 11 are used at the discretion of the programmer. When printer forms are moved one line at a time, the carriage control unit is used only to detect the channel 12 signal—the bottom of the form. The process of moving the form one, two, or three lines at a time is called *spacing. Skipping* is the process of releasing the form, or moving it rapidly through the printer carriage until a designated channel is detected by the carriage control system. The skipping technique is useful because most printers skip faster than they space when the form is to be moved four lines or more. As examples, let us consider some of the four OARS printer outputs.

The two parts of figure 13.2 depict the sketch and the data element list of the overcredit notification developed in the OARS system performance definition. This information is the basis for preparing the output design of figure 13.3. The field sizes and formats come from the data element list, and the layout comes from the sketch. The width and length of the form are outlined on the print chart. The location of the channel 1 signal in the carriage control system is on the same line as the first line of printing, the title line. A channel 12 indication to locate the last line of printing is not required because each line on this form is different from all others. Thus it is not necessary to determine when the bottom of the form is reached.

Figure 13.4 is an example of an output with several detail lines. When several detail lines of the same format are to be printed, it is not necessary to show all the lines on the print chart. The first two detail lines should be shown to illustrate the spacing of the body. If the report has totals, the last detail line also is required, to show the spacing between detail lines and total lines. The wavy lines between the second and last detail lines indicate that the format is repeated without change.

Edit characters, for example, dollar signs, commas, and decimal points, should be included in field descriptions. For example, if a numeric field could have a value of zero, the number of zeros to be printed should be depicted on the print chart. The placement of a zero in a data field indicates the first significant digit to print. The format XXX,XXO.XX indicates to the programmer that 0.00 should be printed if the field value is zero, 0.99 if the field value is 99 cents.

Sample overcredit notification. Output design is based upon the output specification and data element list developed during the system performance definition activities of the study phase.

■ Figure 13.3 OARS overcredit notification. The OARS overcredit notification print chart was developed from the over-credit notification output specification and data element list developed during the system performance definition activities of the study phase.

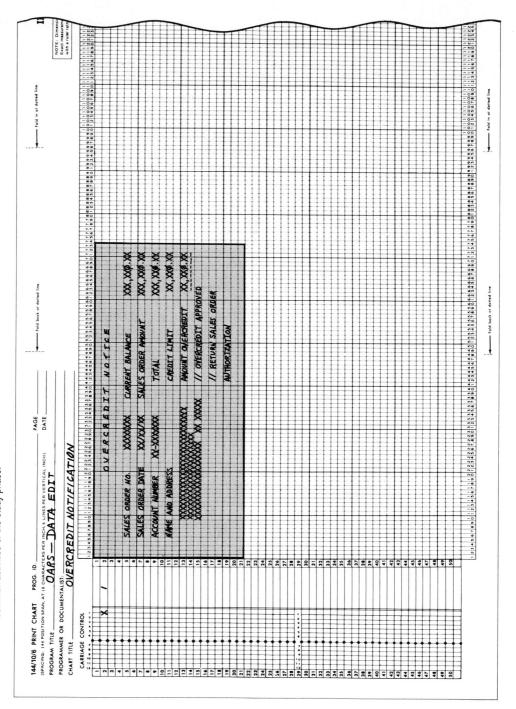

■ Figure 13.4 OARS transaction register. The OARS transaction register print chart was developed from the output specification and data element list developed in the study phase.

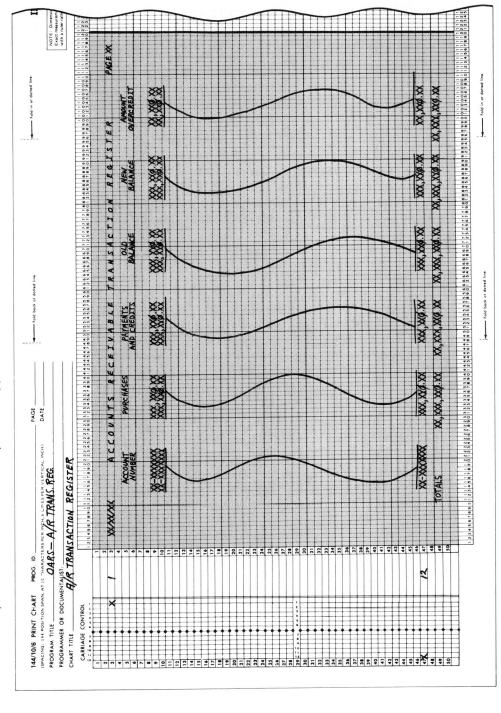

Forms manufacturers can provide a wide variety of specialty forms with pre-printed information on a custom-designed basis. Figure 13.5 depicts the OARS customer monthly statement. There are several advantages of this type of form, as follows:

1. Column headings can be much more flexible with different sizes and styles of type.
2. Numeric fields may be edited by the form itself, for example, dashed vertical lines may be inserted to separate dollars and cents.
3. Fewer lines need to be printed by the computer, saving computer time.

The obvious disadvantages of using specialty forms are higher cost and the need to maintain a larger printer forms inventory. Specialty printer forms include continuous forms with built-in carbon copies (called multipart forms); envelopes; mailing labels; and forms presealed into envelopes, which are printed through the envelope by carbon copy techniques.

Prototyping Printer Outputs

Input/output prototyping is the simulation of system inputs and outputs to help the users to get the "look and feel" of the input or output during its design. Prototyping allows the analyst to show the actual output to the user rather than a sketch or design form. This approach has a reality that users appreciate.

There are many tools available to the systems analyst to develop prototypes of the outputs. The examples shown here were developed using the report generator of the dBASE IV data base management system. Figure 13.3 illustrated a print chart of the Overcredit Notice for the OARS system. Figure 13.6 is the Overcredit Notice layout as seen on the screen of a personal computer while designing the form. The literal values of the title and data labels are typed in and can be changed as the user watches the prototype being developed. If the user does not like what he or she sees on the screen, labels can be easily changed or repositioned.

After the output has been designed, an actual output may be produced with "live" data to show an example of the output to the user. Figure 13.7 is an example of the Overcredit Notice with actual data from the OARS data base on the form. The form may now be modified to better suit the needs of the user or accepted as it is. Prototyping is a very powerful tool for working with users to develop appropriate outputs.

Graphics and Desktop Publishing

Graphics

In the past, all printed output was produced on printers that have fixed character sets. That is, the characters are formed by striking a ribbon with a hammer that has a raised character shape in a certain font. This approach produces a high-quality image of the character, but it limits the characters that may be printed to those fonts on the printer.

■ Figure 13.5 Preprinted form. Some computer-printed output may use forms that contain preprinted information. These specialty forms are obtainable from forms manufacturers on a custom-designed basis. This figure is a layout for a specialty form on which the titles and column headings will be preprinted.

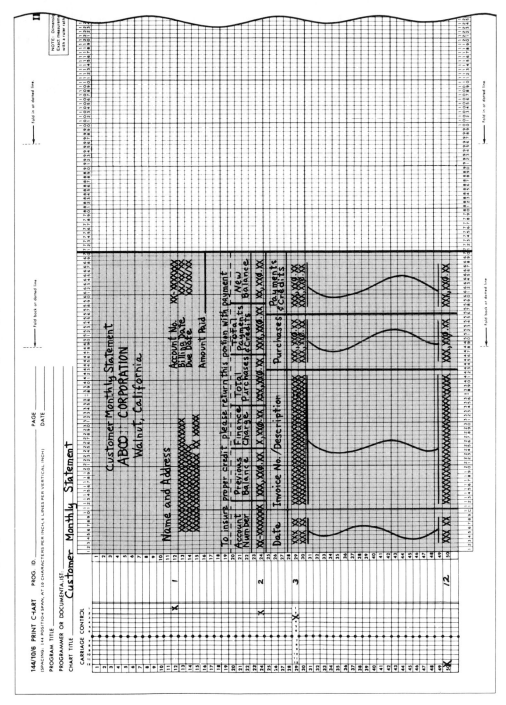

■ Figure 13.6   OARS overcredit notification prototype. The OARS overcredit notification may be designed on-screen and easily modified to suit the requirements of the users. This example is the report generator within the dBASE IV data base management system.

```
 Layout    Fields   Bands   Words   Go To   Print   Exit        4:17:13 pm
 [ . . . . • . ▼ . 1 . . . . • ▼ . . 2 . . ▼ • . . . . 3 . ▼ • • ▼ . 5 . . . . • ▼ . . 6 . . ▼ • . . . 7 . ▼ . • . . .
 Page       Header    Band
                            O V E R C R E D I T   N O T I C E
 Report     Intro     Band
 Detail               Band
       SALES ORDER NO.      XXXXXXXX  CURRENT BALANCE       999,999.99
       SALES ORDER DATE               SALES ORDER AMOUNT    999,999.99
       ACCOUNT NUMBER                 TOTAL                 999,999.99
       NAME AND ADDRESS               CREDIT LIMIT           99,999.99
           XXXXXXXXXXXXXXXXXXXXXXXXX   AMOUNT OVERCREDIT      99,999.99
           XXXXXXXXXXXXXXXXXX         □  OVERCREDIT APPROVED
           XXXXXXXXXXXXXXXXX XX XXXX  □  RETURN SALES ORDER
                                         AUTHORIZATION
 Report  C:\dbase4\oars\OVERCRDT  Line:0 Col:1  View: OVCREDIT   NumCapsIns
            Add field: F5  Select: F6  Move: F7  Copy: F8  Size: Shift-F7
```

■ Figure 13.7   OARS overcredit notification prototype example. The OARS prototype designed with dBASE IV may be used to generate actual outputs for the users to examine. Based upon the user's input, the output design may be modified or accepted as it is.

```
                        O V E R C R E D I T   N O T I C E

 SALES ORDER NO.      00012001      CURRENT BALANCE                0.00

 SALES ORDER DATE     01/14/92      SALES ORDER AMOUNT         2,275.00

 ACCOUNT NUMBER    01-0001022       TOTAL                      2,275.00

 NAME AND ADDRESS                   CREDIT LIMIT               2,000.00

    EDSPEC Incorporated             AMOUNT OVERCREDIT            275.00
    P. O. Box 344                                             =========
    Covina          CA  91723       / / OVERCREDIT APPROVED

                                    / / RETURN SALES ORDER

                                    AUTHORIZATION _____
```

Laser printer sample output. Charts and graphics of all types may be produced with laser printers. As in this example bar chart, shading can be effectively used to produce high-quality black and white charts. Several laser printer manufacturers are now offering printers that produce color prints with excellent resolution for under $10,000.

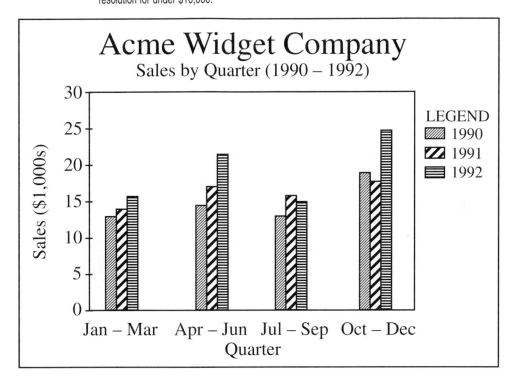

Dot-matrix printers form the printed image by striking the ribbon with a matrix of small rods or pins. Each pin produces a small dot on the paper with the pattern of dots forming the image. The term image is used rather than character because the dot-matrix is not limited to forming characters. The image may be any shape. With this flexibility, dot-matrix printers can print images such as line, bar, and pie charts, data flow diagrams, organization charts, forms, or any other image that can be described. The disadvantage of the dot-matrix printer has been its low quality of print as compared to fixed-character printers. Generally, the quality has not been good enough for business or professional use. The most recent improvement in printers has been the introduction of reasonably priced laser printers. Laser, or page, printers produce an image using hardware similar to that of a copier. The output of the laser printer is produced as a series of dots, as with the dot-matrix printer, but the dots are much smaller and very close together. Figure 13.8 is an example of a bar chart produced with an inexpensive laser printer. The common laser printers print three hundred dots per inch. Laser printers can print any image, including text, pictures, graphs, and so on. Some high-quality (and high-cost) laser printers can produce images with up to twelve hundred dots per inch. This quality is equal to that found in glossy magazines.

Desktop Publishing

Desktop publishing is a term applied to the production of newsletters, flyers, and similar printed output utilizing the combination of desktop (or personal) computers and laser printers. With the flexibility of the laser printer to print any kind of image, text and graphics can be combined on a page. This allows users to produce newsletters, advertising copy, and brochures on their own personal computer. The better desktop publishing software packages also allow direct input into automated typesetting equipment for very high-quality reproduction.

The hardware required for desktop publishing consists of any of several brands of laser printer and a personal computer powerful enough to run the software that can combine text and graphic images. Generally, that means a personal computer such as the Apple Macintosh or an IBM-compatible machine with a fast processor. The desktop publishing software formats the page images in almost any way you desire. The buzzword for desktop publishing is WYSIWYG (pronounced wizzy wig). It means **W**hat **Y**ou **S**ee **I**s **W**hat **Y**ou **G**et: In other words, the layout on the screen is exactly what you will see on the printed page. That includes text rotated and printed up the side, graphics, proportional print, and anything else that you require. Figures 13.9 and 13.10 were both printed with a laser printer. Note that in addition to printing the form itself, data can be merged into the form from a data file as the form is printed.

Visual Display Terminal Screen Output

Designing Effective Screen Layouts

The principles used in designing visual display terminal (VDT) screen output are similar to those of form design and computer printer output design. VDT displays typically include titles, column headings, detail data, and, possibly, totals. These are the same requirements identified with computer print charts. The major differences are: (1) the size of the screen, and (2) the amount of data to be outputted as a record. The typical screen size is 80 characters across and 24 lines down. The VDT display may consist of many detail lines arranged in columns much like a printed output, yet many times only a single record will be displayed. This is especially true with systems that randomly access data.

Screen Layout Forms

Figure 13.11 is an example of the form used for designing VDT displays. This form is called a **display layout sheet**, and it is very similar to the computer print chart in that each display column and line are numbered.

A detailed example of the use of display layout sheets is included in chapter 14, "Input Design."

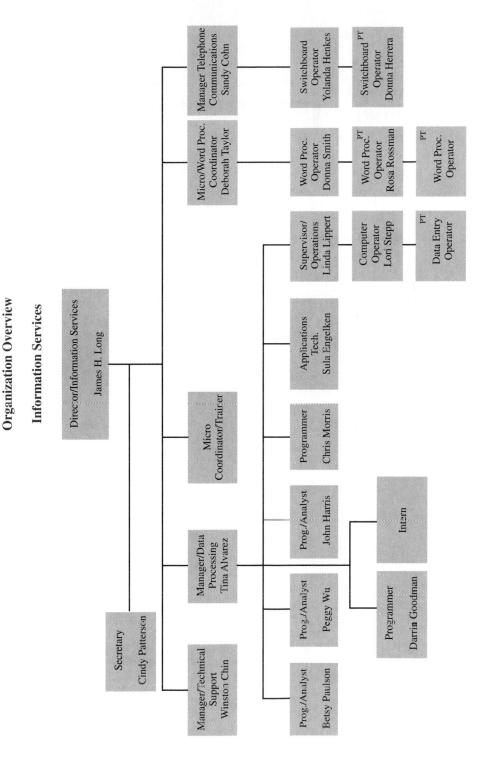

■ Figure 13.9   Organization chart. The time required for the creation or modification of organization charts can be greatly reduced with the use of computer-generated graphics.

Organization Overview

Information Services

Director/Information Services
James H. Long

Secretary
Cindy Patterson

Manager/Technical Support
Winston Chin

Manager/Data Processing
Tina Alvarez

Micro Coordinator/Trainer

Micro/Word Proc. Coordinator
Deborah Taylor

Manager Telephone Communications
Sandy Cohn

Prog./Analyst
Betsy Paulson

Prog./Analyst
Peggy Wu

Prog./Analyst
John Harris

Programmer
Chris Morris

Applications Tech.
Sula Engelken

Supervisor/Operations
Linda Lippert

Word Proc. Operator
Donna Smith

Switchboard Operator
Yolanda Henkes

Programmer
Darrin Goodman

Intern

Computer Operator
Lori Stepp

Word Proc. Operator PT
Rosa Rossman

Switchboard PT Operator
Donna Herrera

Data Entry Operator PT

Word Proc. Operator PT

■ Figure 13.10 Merged data and forms. Complex forms with many different type sizes and styles can be quickly created. Data can be entered into the form from a data file at the same time that the form is printed.

ABCO CORP

Credit Application

Date:

BUSINESS INFORMATION	DESCRIPTION OF BUSINESS		
NAME OF BUSINESS	NO. OF EMPLOYEES	CREDIT REQUESTED	TYPE OF BUSINESS
LEGAL (IF DIFFERENT)	IN BUSINESS SINCE		
ADDRESS	BUSINESS STRUCTURE ☐ CORPORATION ☐ PARTNERSHIP ☐ PROPRIETORSHIP		
CITY	☐ DIVISION/SUBSIDIARY NAME OF PARENT		
STATE	ZIP	PHONE	COMPANY _____ HOW LONG IN BUSINESS _____

COMPANY PRINCIPALS RESPONSIBLE FOR BUSINESS TRANSACTIONS

NAME:	TITLE:	ADDRESS:	PHONE:
NAME:	TITLE:	ADDRESS:	PHONE:
NAME:	TITLE:	ADDRESS:	PHONE:

BANK REFERENCES

NAME OF BANK	NAME OF CONTACT
BRANCH	ADDRESS
CHECKING ACCOUNT NO.	TELEPHONE NUMBER

TRADE REFERENCES

FIRM NAME	CONTACT NAME	TELEPHONE NUMBER	ACCOUNT OPEN SINCE

CONFIRMATION OF INFORMATION ACCURACY AND RELEASE OF AUTHORITY TO VERIFY

I hereby certify that the information in this credit application is correct. The information included in this credit application is for use by XYZ Company in determining the amount and conditions of credit to be extended. I understand that XYZ Company may also utilize the other sources of credit which it considers necessary in making this determination. Further I hereby authorize the bank and trade references listed in this credit application to release the information necessary to assist XYZ Company in establishing a line of credit.

X

SIGNATURE   TITLE   DATE

POLICY STATEMENT: INITIAL ORDER FROM NEW ACCOUNTS WILL NOT BE PROCESSED UNLESS ACCOMPANIED BY THE ABOVE REQUESTED INFORMATION. TERMS: NET 30 DAYS FROM DATE OF INVOICE UNLESS OTHERWISE STATED.

■ Figure 13.11   Display layout sheet. The display layout sheet is very similar to the print chart except that it has 24
rows and 80 columns to match the layout of a VDT screen.

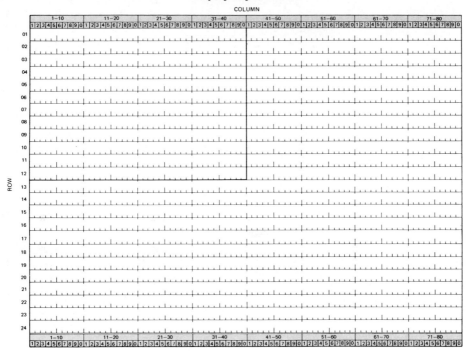

Summary

The output design, an ongoing activity almost from the beginning of the project, follows the principles of form design. Both printed outputs and VDT displays can include a title, column headings, detail data, and totals; they must be described in detail for programmers. Forms called print charts and display layout sheets are used to communicate this design detail. Specialty forms can be designed for printed reports.

Input/output prototyping is an automated approach to the design of forms that allows the systems analyst to develop "live" examples of the outputs of the system. This provides an actual output for the user to see to better evaluate the form.

In the past, all printed output was produced on printers that had fixed character sets. This approach limited the output to text made up of those fixed characters. Dot-matrix printers have more flexibility because the image is made up of dots rather than fixed characters. The problem with dot-matrix printers is their relatively poorer quality of print. The availability of laser printers, along with graphics and desktop publishing software, has given us the high-quality print for text and the flexibility for graphics.

VDT display layout design differs from that of computer print charts because the area is limited by the size of the screen, as is the amount of data that can be displayed in a record.

For Review

print chart	skipping
carriage control	edit characters
channel 1	display layout sheet
channel 12	prototyping
spacing	desktop publishing

For Discussion

1. What are the most common output media?
2. What is the purpose of a print chart?
3. What is the difference between spacing and skipping?
4. What are the usual uses of channels on a carriage control system?
5. Why should at least two detail lines of a report be shown on a print chart?
6. Under what conditions should an analyst consider the use of a preprinted specialty form?
7. What is meant by output prototyping?
8. Why do users usually like to work with prototypes rather than print charts?
9. What is the major advantage of a dot-matrix printer over a fixed-character printer?
10. Relative to dot-matrix and laser printers, what is meant by the term "printed image"?
11. What is the advantage implied by the term WYSIWYG?
12. What are the major differences between the principles for screen design and the design of printed outputs?

For Exercise: Output Display Design

Your task, as the systems analyst, is to do the preliminary design for an inventory system display. The display is to include the following output fields (in alphabetic order): item description, item location code, item quantity-on-hand, item quantity-on-order, stock code (key field), supplier name, and unit price. This display is to be for one inventory item only. Make the display both functional and attractive.

Chapter

14

■　■　■

Input Design

Preview

The most common source of data processing errors is inaccurate input data. Effective input design minimizes errors made during data entry operations. This chapter extends the previous discussions of output design to input form design and important input devices, particularly the visual display terminal (VDT). This chapter provides specific information on designing and documenting the input screen through the use of the screen layout form. In addition, screen design with prototyping software is illustrated. Design considerations for optical mark readers, optical character readers, and bar code readers are also introduced.

Objectives

1. You will be able to list and explain input design principles.
2. You will be able to apply the design techniques for VDT displays.
3. You will be able to describe the uses of a screen design aid.
4. You will be able to identify and distinguish among various input scanners.

Key Terms

automated source document design the use of form design and page layout software to design source documents.

source document control techniques for monitoring the generation and changing of source documents with the use of numerical and functional form control files.

VDT visual display terminal: a terminal with a keyboard for inputting and a display screen for outputs.

display layout sheet a form used to design VDT screen layouts. The form is divided into 24 lines of 80 characters each to simulate the possible display positions on a screen.

Source Document Design

Source document design is the process of converting a user-oriented description of the inputs to a computer-based business system into a programmer-oriented specification.

Source Document Design Responsibility

The task of producing a detailed layout for a source document is the responsibility of a forms specialist. Forms specialists are experts in types and styles of forms, sizes and styles of print, and details of preparing a form layout for reproduction. These specialists are available to the systems analyst from in-house reproduction centers or from the major forms manufacturers.

The only things the forms specialist does not know are (1) what data the user wants to collect with the form, and (2) how the form is going to be used in the system. These things are known only to the user. The analyst must help users develop their form requirements and guide them in the development of cost-effective forms. The coordination of the forms design effort between the user and the forms specialist is the responsibility of the systems analyst. It is the analyst who must verify that proof copy of the form is exactly as required by the user and the system. The forms manufacturers can provide a wide variety of sample forms for ideas, but the analyst must select and check the final form design. The systems analyst is also responsible for the input/output screen design on CRT terminals and printed outputs.

Principles of Source Document Design

Inaccurate input data is the most common cause of data processing errors. If poor input design—particularly where operators must enter data from source documents—permits bad data to enter a computer system, the outputs produced are of little value.

To evaluate the effectiveness of a document, the systems analyst should keep the following four principles in mind:

1. The document must be easy to fill out.
2. The completed document must be easy to use in the system.
3. The document should not collect data that will not be used in the system.
4. The document should not be unnecessarily expensive.

Ease of Data Recording

Business forms should be designed so that they can be filled out quickly and accurately. It is important that the analyst avoid errors induced by the form's design. Design-induced errors can occur whenever the person completing the form is not sure what data is being requested. Whenever a document is used in more than one department or is used infrequently, it is usually wise to include appropriate instructions. The instructions should be placed on the form just before the section to which they apply. It should be noted, however, that including instructions where they are not required hinders clarity and adds to the expense of producing the form.

Data items should be grouped in a logical pattern. Grouping requires fewer instructions and results in fewer errors. Fewer errors will occur if all the logically related data is collected prior to changing the subject. All data entry areas must be clearly labeled. Make sure that the user knows whether the label applies to the line above the label or the line below. If the form will be filled in using a typewriter, the data area label should appear above the data entry area so that the label is visible when the form is in the typewriter. Avoid uncommon abbreviations or uncommon words as labels. Although labels should be brief, they must be complete enough to communicate exactly what data is being requested.

Leave adequate space for the response. Common typewriter horizontal spacing is ten or twelve characters per inch. Make sure that the data area is long enough to allow for reasonable responses. Remember also that handwritten entries require more space than typewritten responses. Vertical spacing also is important to forms design. Forms that are expected to be completed with handwritten responses should allow at least one-half inch of vertical spacing. Forms that may be completed using a typewriter should allow at least one-third of an inch and should be a multiple of one-sixth of an inch. (Most standard typewriters print six lines per vertical inch.) Avoid spacing that requires the typist to realign the typewriter for each line. The minimum of one-third inch would be equivalent to double spacing. If the form is always completed using a typewriter, leave out the horizontal lines to make alignment easier. Aligning the form can take as much of the user's time as actually entering the data.

Ease of Use

Sequence the data on the form in the order in which it is to be used. This is especially true when the data is to be entered into a computer system through a keystroking operation.

The analyst should be aware of the effect of ink and paper color combinations on the legibility and readability of forms. Readability can be improved (or made worse) by the combination of ink color and background color. Figure 14.1 is LeCourier's legibility table, which ranks thirteen ink-background combinations in order of legibility. The common black on white combination ranks sixth, while black on yellow is at the top of the list. Colored paper can be used to distinguish the various copies of a form and to aid in form distribution. However, the use of colored paper should not be allowed to interfere with the legibility of the data. This is particularly problematic for copies at the bottom of a carbon stack. Many businesses input source data into computerized systems with optical scanners. If optical scanning of forms is to be used, the analyst must consider character size and vertical spacing requirements. It is the analyst's responsibility to verify that the form layout is compatible with the scanner hardware.

Required Data

The analyst should verify that all the data items requested on a form are required and actually used in the system. Many times data is collected on a form simply because it was collected on previous versions of the form. Data items not actually required waste the time of the person completing the form and clutter the form for those who use the data. Wasting clerical time adds unnecessary expense to the system.

■ Figure 14.1   Le Courier's legibility table. Le Courier's legibility table shows the effect of ink color and background color combinations on readability. Note that the traditional black on white ranks sixth in this chart.

order of legibility	color of printing	color of background
1	black	yellow
2	green	white
3	red	white
4	blue	white
5	white	blue
6	black	white
7	yellow	black
8	white	red
9	white	green
10	white	black
11	red	yellow
12	green	red
13	red	green

Cost Considerations

The costs of using a form are far greater than the costs of producing it. The area with the greatest potential for cost effectiveness is the efficiency of a form in use, rather than the cost of the form itself. Still, forms should not be unnecessarily expensive. If the company has in-house reproduction capability, there has to be a decision on whether to produce the form in-house or out-of-house. This decision must be based on the required quality and complexity of the form relative to in-house capability. For complex or high-quality forms, in-house production is not always the least expensive.

Design forms in a standard size, such as $8\frac{1}{2}'' \times 11''$ or $8\frac{1}{2}'' \times 5\frac{1}{2}''$. Printers buy their paper stock in standard sizes; if a form of an uncommon size is desired, it may be unnecessarily costly to produce because of the extra cutting or trimming of paper. In general, avoid forms larger than $8\frac{1}{2}'' \times 11''$. Larger forms are often more expensive to store and require larger, and more expensive, file storage. Print forms in reasonable quantities. Bids for printing jobs include a basic setup charge, which stays the same regardless of the quantity of forms produced. It is advantageous, therefore, to buy forms in as large a quantity as is reasonable, considering the rate of use, the likelihood of modification, and the costs of storage. The larger the quantity, the lower the cost per form.

Automated Source Document Design

One of the advantages of the more powerful, larger-capacity personal computers that are popular today, and the sophisticated page layout software that they can run, is the automation of forms design. Page layout programs are designed to work with laser printers to produce near typeset quality output.

With a variety of type styles and type sizes available, forms may be interactively designed on the personal computer display by the analyst and the users. These forms are then printed as high-quality design layouts. In many cases, the print quality of the form produced on the laser printer is good enough to use as a master copy to produce the form. If the print quality of the laser printer is not high enough, page layout systems can output directly to automated typesetting equipment. These capabilities reduce the amount of time required for form design and have the added advantage of allowing the users to see exactly what the final form will look like during the design process. In addition, some form design software can be used not only to create the form but also to fill in the form. This approach is sometimes called working with electronic forms. Figure 14.2 is an example of an electronic order form that can be used to input the data and then be printed as a completed form. This particular example was created using PerForm Pro by Delrina Technology. This software package was designed to be used to design a form and print it as a master copy, or to save the form and print it with the input data.

Source Document Control

A form designed for efficient use is a major step toward controlling the cost of collecting data. However, an equally important consideration is the prevention of a flood of new and modified forms from each department of the company. Departments tend to act independently of other departments when it comes to forms. Departments rarely inquire of each other to find out if a form is already in existence—they simply design a new one. A system of **source document control** is needed.

The solution to the problem is twofold: (1) establish a central forms authority, and (2) establish control files. The central authority should be an individual or a group with complete control over all company forms. The approval of the central authority must be obtained prior to the design or modification of any form. The advantage of this procedure is that this authority will have knowledge (and samples) of all forms currently in use or being designed. Since many forms may meet the needs of more than one department, the coordination of the design or modification of forms can be handled expediently by one authority. The use of one form rather than several similar forms can be a real cost saving in the production, storage, and distribution of forms.

Computer-generated order form. This order form can be filled in using PerForm Pro software and printed as a completed form. PerForm Pro is a product of Delrina Technology.

ABCO
CORP

ORDER FORM

Date _____

SOLD TO:

SHIPPING ADDRESS:

Order Number:

Salesperson:

Telephone:

Ship Via:

Date:

Quantity	Description	Unit Price	Amount

TERMS

☐ Cash
☐ COD
☐ On Account

Subtotal
Delivery Charge
TOTAL
Sales Tax
Balance Due

Two control files are needed to keep track of the forms being used in the company: a numerical file and a functional file. The *numerical file* contains at least one sample of each form being used. The samples are filed by form number, creating a catalog of forms being used. Any form can be accessed by means of its coded form number. The *functional file* contains additional copies of each form. They are filed in order of subject, operation, or function. If a form has multiple uses or functions, it will be found more than once in the file. Whenever a new form is required, the functional file can be checked to determine whether a form already exists for that purpose. When the functional file is originally established, many forms usually can be eliminated or consolidated. The two control files also aid in forms inventory control. Knowledge of which departments use any particular form and their approximate rate of use prevents the buildup of too large an inventory of forms and also is a timely reminder to reorder.

VDT Input Screen Design

Designing Effective Input Screen Layouts

Visual display terminals have become very common as input devices. Effective screen design can not only reduce data entry errors, it can also increase productivity and user satisfaction. Most of the on-line data entry stations are VDTs that provide both a visual verification of input data and a means of prompting the user. As data is entered it is echoed, or displayed, on the screen. The user can modify or delete any data display before sending it to the computer system for storage and processing. The most common size display screen is 24 rows or lines of 80 characters each.

The following are some screen design rules that are important for user satisfaction:

1. Use the same formats with related screens. Users expect to find the same data in the same place.
2. Do not overcrowd the screen. Often two neat, eye-pleasing screens look better and are easier to use than one screen filled with too much data.
3. Provide instructions. Tutorial information that is easily accessible is helpful to users, particularly novices or infrequent users.
4. Use consistent terminology. Changing names of terms (for example, ''erase'' instead of ''delete'') can be confusing.
5. Keep instructions brief and grammatically similar. Nouns and action words are useful. Some examples are: inventory record update, customer record add, and sales amount.
6. Coordinate forms and screen design. This is particularly important for data entry, where data elements are common to the source document and to the screen.

■ **Figure 14.3**   Display layout sheet. The display layout sheet is used to plan the layout of a VDT screen. It allows up to 24 lines of 80 characters each. Each small square on the form is the position of one character. This form is similar to the print chart introduced in chapter 13.

Display Layout Sheet

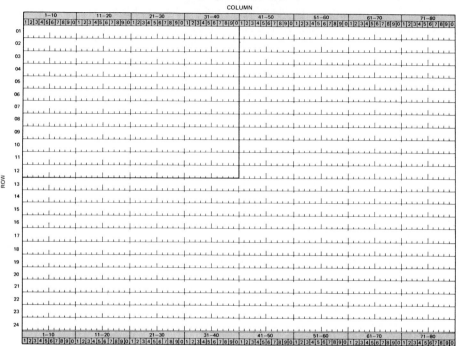

Screen Layout Forms

Figure 14.3 is an example of a design form used to communicate the required layout to programmers. To illustrate the use of a **display layout sheet**, we will use the customer account application data as sample input data. Figure 14.4 depicts the source document for this data. Note that it is not necessary to input all data collected on the form. Only the data blocked off in small squares needs to be inputted. The remaining data are for the use of the personnel department and are not to be entered into the system. Figure 14.5 illustrates the display layout for the customer account application. The screen display is titled, and each data element has a clearly stated prompt.

Customer account application. The customer account application form is a source document for OARS
input data. A display layout must be designed to enter the data shown in the small squares.

Prototyping VDT Screens

Many modern computer systems have software utilities to assist in the design and
development of screen layouts. As an example, IBM has a utility called Screen Design
Aid (SDA). With this utility, it is possible to eliminate filling out the display layout
sheet. The screen layout can be designed at the terminal. The utility allows the designer to add, delete, or move the display components. When the design is completed,
SDA outputs a printed record of the design that looks much like the display layout
sheet. In addition, the utility generates the program code to produce the design display. Figure 14.6 is an example of SDA documentation.

Customer application display layout sheet. This display layout sheet illustrates the completed design of the input screen for the data collected from the customer account application shown in figure 14.4.

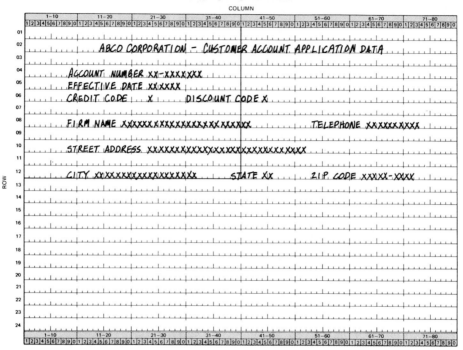

Input Scanners

Optical readers are examples of input devices that can capture data directly. Three important types of optical devices are mark readers, bar code readers, and character readers. *Optical mark readers* are able to accept data in the form of pencil marks on paper. *Optical bar code readers* detect combinations of marks by which data is coded. These systems usually are complex to design; the most widely known bar code is the Universal Product Code (UPC), which appears on most retail packages. Figure 14.7 shows several of the variety of sizes and shapes in which bar codes can be printed. The human-readable characters are printed alongside.

■ Figure 14.6 Screen design aid. Many modern computer systems include utility programs to aid in the design of screens. This example is an IBM utility called screen design aid (SDA). It allows the screen to be designed at a terminal and produces the equivalent of a display layout sheet on a computer printer.

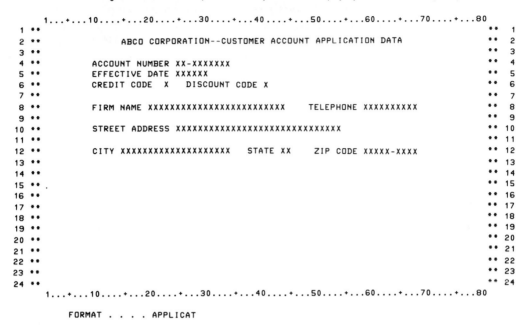

```
         1...+...10....+...20....+...30....+...40....+...50....+...60....+...70....+...80
    1 ••                                                                           ••  1
    2 ••             ABCO CORPORATION--CUSTOMER ACCOUNT APPLICATION DATA            ••  2
    3 ••                                                                           ••  3
    4 ••        ACCOUNT NUMBER XX-XXXXXXX                                          ••  4
    5 ••        EFFECTIVE DATE XXXXX                                              ••  5
    6 ••        CREDIT CODE  X    DISCOUNT CODE X                                 ••  6
    7 ••                                                                           ••  7
    8 ••        FIRM NAME XXXXXXXXXXXXXXXXXXXXXXXXX     TELEPHONE XXXXXXXXXX        ••  8
    9 ••                                                                           ••  9
   10 ••        STREET ADDRESS XXXXXXXXXXXXXXXXXXXXXXXXXXXXXX                      •• 10
   11 ••                                                                           •• 11
   12 ••        CITY XXXXXXXXXXXXXXXXXXX     STATE XX     ZIP CODE XXXXX-XXXX       •• 12
   13 ••                                                                           •• 13
   14 ••                                                                           •• 14
   15 •• .                                                                         •• 15
   16 ••                                                                           •• 16
   17 ••                                                                           •• 17
   18 ••                                                                           •• 18
   19 ••                                                                           •• 19
   20 ••                                                                           •• 20
   21 ••                                                                           •• 21
   22 ••                                                                           •• 22
   23 ••                                                                           •• 23
   24 ••                                                                           •• 24
         1...+...10....+...20....+...30....+...40....+...50....+...60....+...70....+...80

             FORMAT . . . . APPLICAT
```

■ Figure 14.7 Bar codes. Optical bar code readers detect combinations of marks by which data is coded. Bar code systems are commonly found in many types of business systems.

Optical character reader (OCR) devices have been designed for applications that can make use of special, optically readable symbols. A typical design application is embossed credit cards, which produce an imprint that can be read by optical scanners. Documents that use special type fonts are in common use; a typical application is in customer billing. Optical readers are good examples of the expanding trend toward using technology to minimize the role of error-prone humans in creating large volumes of input transaction data. To the extent that human operations can be replaced by machine operations, the integrity of input data, and therefore of system output, can be improved.

Summary

The user is the final authority on the items of data to be collected and the final layout of any form. The forms manufacturer (or in-house reprographics department) is responsible for the final design of the document, according to the requirements specified by the user. It is, however, the responsibility of the systems analyst to coordinate the forms design effort with the user and the forms manufacturer. In many cases this task of coordination is made easier with the use of personal computers and page layout software.

The systems analyst is also responsible for forms control—the coordination of forms design or modification between users and/or departments. This requires the maintenance of two files: a numerical file and a functional file.

The most common source of data processing error is inaccurate input data. The objective of input design is to create an input layout that is easy to follow and does not induce operator errors. The analyst must always be aware of the following principles of form design:

1. The form must be easy to fill out.
2. The completed form must be easy to use.
3. The form should not collect data that will not be used in the system.
4. The form should not be unnecessarily expensive.

One of the most common input devices is the visual display terminal. The screen design must include appropriate labels, or prompts, for the data entry operator. The layout of the screen is designed and documented with the use of a display layout sheet or its equivalent. Many computer systems have software packages that assist in the design and documentation process. This automation of the layout process speeds up the design process and allows the user to see exactly what the final layout will be.

Other input media, such as input scanners, are also used and each has its own particular design considerations. Optical mark readers, bar code readers, and optical character readers (OCR) are the most common types of these input scanners.

For Review

visual display terminal (VDT)
display station
display layout sheet
title
heading
body
conclusion

forms control
numerical file
functional file
optical reader
optical mark reader
optical bar code reader
optical character reader (OCR)

For Discussion

1. What are the forms design responsibilities of the user, the systems analyst, and the forms manufacturer?
2. What is the most common cause of data processing errors?
3. Describe the purposes of the title, heading, and body of a form.
4. What are the screen design rules that are important for user satisfaction?
5. What is automated source document design?
6. What are the advantages of formal forms control?
7. What two types of files are required for effective forms control? Why?
8. What is a screen layout sheet? How is it used?
9. What is input screen prototyping?
10. What are the major advantages of optical readers over keyboard input?

For Exercise: Input Form Design

Assume that you are the systems analyst assigned to design an input form to be used by the receiving department to record inventory items being delivered to us.

The title area is to include "Inventory Received" plus the company name, "Big-deal Incorporated." The heading area is to include the supplier's name, address, city, state, ZIP code, and the date the merchandise was received. The body of the form must allow for a minimum of twelve items being received as part of a single shipment. The data about each of the items, below appropriate column headings, are as follows: item description, item location code, quantity received, stock code (ours), and stock code (theirs). The items should not be in the order listed. Make the form functional and attractive. Use form design software if it is available.

Chapter

15

■ ■ ■

Design Phase
Report and
Review

Preview

At the conclusion of the design phase activities, the analyst prepares a report and reviews it with users of the computer-based information system. The central element of the design phase report is the design specification, which is a detailed "build to" specification. The design phase review is attended by principal users and managers who will be affected by the system; the outcome of the review is a decision whether or not to proceed with the development phase.

Objectives

1. You will be able to describe the content of a design specification.
2. You will be able to prepare a design phase report.
3. You will be able to explain the purposes of a design phase review.

Key Terms

design specification a baseline specification that serves as a "blueprint" for the construction of a computer-based business information system.

design phase report a report prepared at the end of the design phase; it is an extension of the study phase report and summarizes the results of the design phase activities.

design phase review a review for the dual purpose of presenting results of design phase activities and determining future action.

Design Specification

The *design phase* activities are concluded by three major events. These are (1) completion of the design specification, (2) preparation of the design phase report, and (3) conducting of the design phase review.

The **design specification** is the technical core of the design phase report. This second major baseline document is the "blueprint" for constructing the computer-based business system. It is the communication link between the analyst and the programmers who will be assigned to the project. Figure 15.1 displays the content of a typical design specification. The design specification is an extension of the performance specification prepared at the conclusion of the study phase. It also is divided into two parts. The first part is an *external design requirement* that relates to the interaction between the system and its operating environment. The second part of the design specification is an *internal design requirement.* This part establishes design requirements for the overall computer program component of the business information system and for the individual programs that are the building blocks for this component. The requirements for the computer programs result from the design phase activities, which were described in chapters 11, 12, 13, and 14. Note that the performance specification description entries in figure 10.1 expand to become the design phase requirements in figure 15.1. The task of maintaining this type of cumulative documentation is greatly eased through use of the graphics and word processing features of many CASE tools.

Design Phase Report

Structure and Content

The structure and content of the *design phase report* are shown in figure 15.2. As shown in this figure, the design phase report has the same five major parts as the study phase report. Elements of the study phase report, appropriately expanded or modified, are carried forward into the design phase report. For instance, the system scope section is brought forward to refamiliarize reviewers with the project. Of course, the system scope section in the design phase report should identify and explain any changes that occurred during this phase. As mentioned earlier, the design specification is an expansion of the performance specification prepared at the end of the study phase. The life-cycle project plan and the cost schedule, which also were prepared at the conclusion of the study phase, are updated to show progress in reaching the design phase milestones. As with the system scope section, significant departures from or changes in the life-cycle project plan should be noted and explained. A detailed milestone plan and cost schedules are now prepared and presented for the development phase, for which authorization to proceed is being requested. Figure 15.3 lists appropriate development phase milestones. These are explained in Unit Six, which describes the development and operation phases of the SDLC.

■ Figure 15.1 Design specification outline. The design specification is the technical core of the design phase report. It has two major sections: an external design requirement and an internal design requirement.

Design Specification

A. External Design Requirement
1. context diagram
2. system output requirements
3. system input requirements
4. system resource requirements
5. system test requirements
6. training requirements

B. Internal Design Requirement
1. computer program component
   a. top-level data flow diagrams
   b. data base requirement
   c. top-level structure chart

2. computer program design (for each program)
   a. decomposed data flow diagram
   b. data storage requirement
   c. structure chart
   d. transaction file requirements
   e. control requirements
   f. test requirements
   g. special conditions

■ Figure 15.2 Design phase report outline. The design phase report, completed at the end of the design phase, has five major sections equivalent to those in the study phase report: system scope, conclusions and recommendations, design specification, plans and cost schedules, and appendices.

Design Phase Report

I. System Scope
   a. system title
   b. problem statement and purpose
   c. constraints
   d. specific objectives
   e. method of evaluation

II. Conclusions and Recommendations
   a. conclusions
   b. recommendations

III. Design Specification
   a. external design requirement
   b. internal design requirement

IV. Plans and Cost Schedules
   a. detailed milestones — design phase
   b. major milestones — all phases
   c. detailed milestones — development phase

V. Appendices — as appropriate

Development Phase — Detailed Milestones	
Implementation Plan	test plan training plan conversion plan
Equipment Acquisition and Installation	
Computer Program Development	computer program design coding and debugging computer program tests
Reference Manual Preparation	programmer's reference manual operator's reference manual user's reference manual
Personnel Training	
System Tests	
Changeover Plan	
System Specification	
Development Phase Report	
Development Phase Review	

Appendices should be included in the design phase report as needed. It usually is a good idea to place complicated analyses in appendices. These analyses can be referred to, and the significant results can be presented in the body of the report, without diverting the reader from the "mainstream" message. Other materials, such as tables and charts that support the conclusions and recommendations of the design phase report, should be placed in an appendix unless it is appropriate to present them in the body of the report.

Example Design Phase Report

An example of a design phase report based on the ABCO corporation's on-line accounts receivable system (OARS) appears on the following pages as Exhibit 2. As in the case of the example study phase report, only sample illustrations are included from among those that previously appeared in the text.

Design Phase Review

The **design phase review** is a particularly critical review. It is a true test of sponsor confidence. Up to this point, the computer-based business system activities were visible to the user-sponsor. The principal user was able to follow the study phase efforts that resulted in the preparation of the performance specification and the study phase report. This person can comprehend most of the design tasks that are summarized in the design specification. Now the system is on the verge of moving into the development phase. The user must make a decision about future activities that cannot be visualized clearly or followed in detail. The sponsor is being asked to make the most significant cost commitment to date. Usually, this commitment is for a greatly enlarged project scope, involving many complex development activities over an extended time. For example, programmers will be added to the project, and the results of their activities will not be visible to the user until shortly before the system is scheduled to become operational.

The analyst must plan the design phase review with great care. The user should be provided with a well-written design phase report in advance of the review, and given the study phase report as a reference document. At the review, an effective presentation is necessary so that the principal user will retain faith in the analyst's ability to continue with the detailed development of the system.

Summary

When the design phase activities are completed, the systems analyst prepares a report. This report, called the design phase report, is the basis for a comprehensive review with the user-sponsor of the computer-related business information system.

The design phase report contains the design specification, which is the second major baseline document. This document is an expansion of the first major baseline document, the performance specification. There are two parts to the design specification, an external design requirement and an internal design requirement. The greatest difference between the performance specification and the design specification is the expansion of the internal performance definition contained in the study phase report into a completed internal design requirement for computer programs that are the building blocks of the computer program component of the information system.

After the principal user has had an opportunity to study the design phase report, a review is held and a decision is made whether to proceed to the development phase. The design phase review is particularly critical, since the principal user must make decisions about future activities that cannot be followed in detail and about initiating a greatly expanded project scope. The user-sponsor's continued confidence in the ability of the systems analyst to manage the project is an important element of the design phase review.

For Review

design phase
design specification
external design requirement
internal design requirement

performance specification
design phase report
design phase review

For Discussion

1. What is the purpose of the design phase report?
2. What is the content of the design phase report?
3. Discuss the importance of the design specification, including its relationship to the performance specification. How might a CASE tool be used to support this relationship?
4. What project plans and schedules are presented at the design phase review?
5. What is the purpose of the design phase review?

■ ■ ■

The Design Phase Report—OARS Case Study

The in-text case study of an on-line accounts receivable system (OARS) is continued with this example of a design phase report. This exhibit extends the example of the documentation of the SDLC process started in Exhibit 1, *The Study Phase Report—OARS Case Study,* which appeared in chapter 10, "Study Phase Report and Review."

OARS Design Phase Report

I. System Scope
  A. System Title
     On-line Accounts Receivable System (OARS)
  B. Problem Statement and Purpose
     The ABCO corporation's present accounts receivable system is at its maximum capacity of 10,000 accounts. The number of accounts is expected to double to 20,000 accounts over a five-year period. The present system cannot meet this projected growth and satisfy the corporate goal of distributing information processing resources to regional profit centers. Serious problems have already been encountered in processing the current volume of accounts. Specific problems that have been identified are as follows:
     1. Saturation of the capacity of the present computer system, causing difficulties in adding new accounts and obtaining information about the status of existing accounts.
     2. Processing delays in preparing customer billing statements because of the batch-oriented design of the current accounts receivable system.
     3. Excessive elapsed time between mailing of customer statements and receipt of payments, which creates a high-cost, four-day float.
     4. Inadequate control of credit limits.
     5. Inability to provide regional centers with timely customer-related information.

Therefore, the purpose of the OARS project is to replace the existing accounts receivable system with one that can eliminate the stated problems and meet ABCO's growth and regional accountability goals.

C. Constraints

The OARS constraints are as follows:

1. Development of the on-line accounts receivable system is to be completed within fourteen months.
2. OARS is to have a growth potential to handle 20,000 customer accounts.
3. OARS is to be designed as an on-line system operating in a distributed data processing environment.
4. The design must be compatible with corporate plans to install regional profit centers.

D. Specific Objectives

The specific objectives of OARS are as follows:

1. To establish billing cycles for each region.
2. To mail customer statements no later than one day after the close of a billing cycle.
3. To provide the customer with a billing statement two days after the close of a billing cycle.
4. To speed up collections, reducing the float by 50 percent.
5. To examine customer account balances through on-line inquiry at the time of order entry.

E. Method of Evaluation

After OARS has been operational from sixty to ninety days:

1. A statistical analysis will be made of customer account processing to verify the elapsed time between the close of the billing cycle and the mailing of customer statements.
2. The float time will be measured, and the cost of the float will be calculated at three-month intervals.
3. Periodically, random samples of customer accounts in each region will be audited for accuracy and to validate the effectiveness of on-line inquiry.
4. The validity of OARS transactions that affect the inventory system will be measured by random sampling and physical count.
5. Personal evaluations of the effectiveness of the system will be obtained from its principal users.

II. Conclusions and Recommendations

A. Conclusions

The design phase activities substantiate the results of the study phase activities, and no major changes in the OARS project are required. An evaluation of equipment suitable for the regional microcomputers was completed, and the Excalibur Model VI computer system was selected. A letter of intent, subject to confirmation following the design phase review, was placed in order to establish a delivery date that met the development phase schedule. No special problems were encountered during the design phase, and the OARS project is on schedule. The design phase cost was $52,000, which exceeds the estimated cost of $51,000 by $1,000. The extra costs were due to the assignment of an additional person from the accounts receivable department to the project to assist in the microcomputer evaluation and procurement activities.

    B. Recommendations

It is recommended that the OARS project be approved for the development phase. It is also recommended that the letter of intent be converted into a firm order for the Excalibur VI computer system.

III. Design Specification

    A. External Design Requirement

        1. *Context diagram* Figure E2.1a is the context diagram for OARS. The accompanying narrative appears as figure E2.1b.

        2. *System output requirements* The eight OARS outputs are as follows:

           a. Customer statement

           b. Accounts receivable transactions

           c. Accounts receivable summary data

           d. Aged accounts receivable data

           e. Order-fill data

           f. Overcredit notice

           g. Application approval notice

           h. Application denial notice

An output specification and accompanying data element list for the overcredit notice are presented as figure E2.2a. The print chart layout for hardcopy output is shown in figure E2.2b.

        3. *System input requirements* The three OARS inputs are as follows:

           a. Account applications

           b. Customer orders

           c. Payments/credits

Figure E2.3 is an example of a system input, the account application.

        4. *System resource requirements* The current central-site computer system will be augmented by five Local Area Networks, one for each region. Each regional system will have the following configuration:

           a. One file server:

CPU with 32 megabytes of main memory

One 1-gigabyte magnetic disk drive

           b. One 24 page-per-minute laser printer

           c. Eight workstations

CPU with 8 megabytes of main memory

One 500-megabyte magnetic disk drive

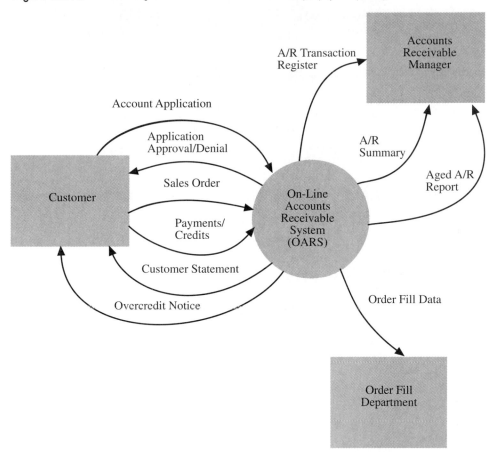

The boundaries of the on-line accounts receivable system (OARS) are set by three external entities: the customer, the A/R manager, and the Order Fill department. These entities provide the inputs to OARS and receive the outputs. There are three inputs and seven outputs. All three inputs are created by the customer, beginning with an account application. The other two inputs are a customer-generated sales order and payments or applied credits. Customer-related outputs are: application approvals, application denials, customer statements, and overcredit notices.

The A/R manager is provided with A/R transaction data, A/R summary information, and aged accounts receivable data, all of which are important in controlling customer accounts and in the management of cash flow. The Order Fill department is provided with order fill data, which is used to pick and ship customer orders and to manage inventory.

OUTPUT SPECIFICATION

TITLE: Overcredit Notification

LAYOUT:

Overcredit Notification

Sales Order No. _____
Sales Order Date _____
Account Number _____
Name and Address _____

_____
_____

Current Balance _____
Sales Order Amount _____
Total _____
Credit Limit _____
Amount Overcredit [_____]

☐ Overcredit Approved
☐ Return Sales Order

AUTHORIZATION

FREQUENCY: Daily
SIZE: 1 page

QUANTITY: 80 max.
COPIES: 2

DISTRIBUTION: 1. Accts. Receivable Dept.

COMMENTS: ___

DATA ELEMENT LIST

TITLE: Overcredit Notification

DESCRIPTION	FORMAT	SIZE
Sales Order Number	XXXXXXXX	8 characters
Sales Order Date	xx/xx/xx	8 "
Account No: Region No. — Sequence No.	XX-XXXXXXX	10 "
Name		26 "
Address		
Street		20 "
City		18 "
State		2 "
Zip Code		5 "
Current Balance	XXX,XXX.XX	10 "
Sales Order Amount	XXX,XXX.XX	10 "
Total	XXX,XXX.XX	10 "
Credit Limit	XX,XXX.XX	9 "
Amount Overcredit	XX,XXX.XX	9 "

■ Figure E2.2b OARS output design requirement: overcredit notice.

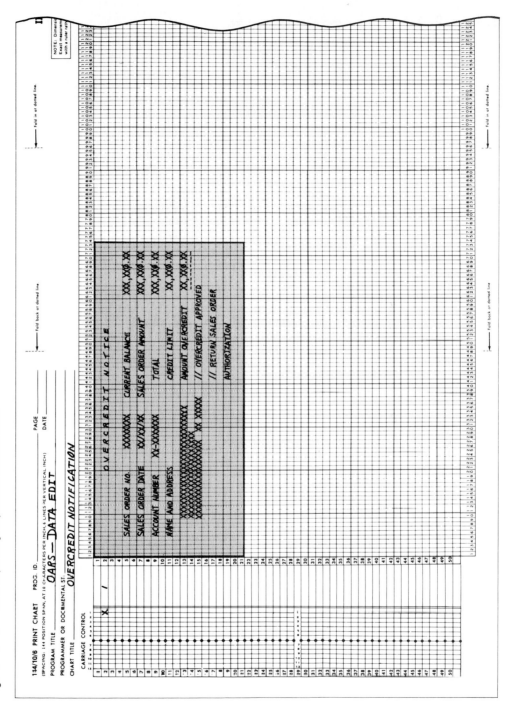

Exhibit 2 ■ 377

■ Figure E2.3   OARS input description: account application.

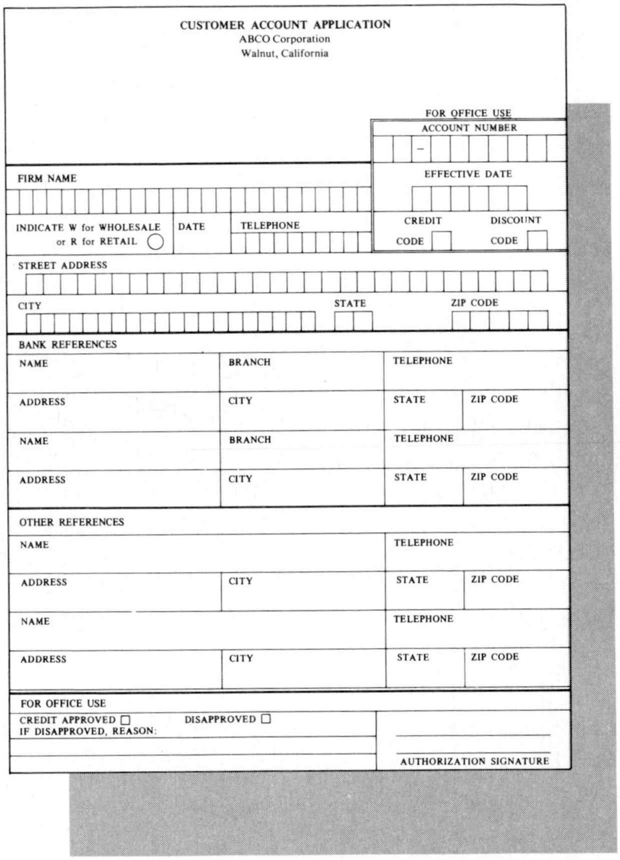

CUSTOMER ACCOUNT APPLICATION
ABCO Corporation
Walnut, California

FOR OFFICE USE
ACCOUNT NUMBER

FIRM NAME

EFFECTIVE DATE

INDICATE W for WHOLESALE   DATE   TELEPHONE
or R for RETAIL

CREDIT   DISCOUNT
CODE   CODE

STREET ADDRESS

CITY   STATE   ZIP CODE

BANK REFERENCES

NAME	BRANCH	TELEPHONE	
ADDRESS	CITY	STATE	ZIP CODE
NAME	BRANCH	TELEPHONE	
ADDRESS	CITY	STATE	ZIP CODE

OTHER REFERENCES

NAME		TELEPHONE	
ADDRESS	CITY	STATE	ZIP CODE
NAME		TELEPHONE	
ADDRESS	CITY	STATE	ZIP CODE

FOR OFFICE USE

CREDIT APPROVED ☐   DISAPPROVED ☐
IF DISAPPROVED, REASON:

AUTHORIZATION SIGNATURE

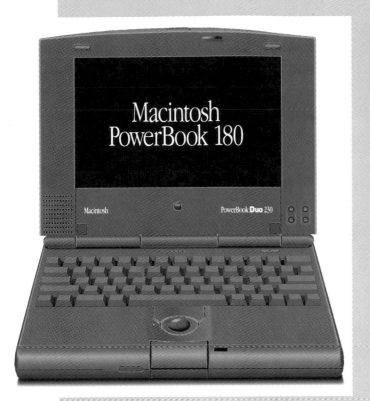

Notebook-size computers, of which the Macintosh PowerBook Duo 230 is an example, serve both as powerful portable computers and as complete desktop systems when connected to peripheral devices such as full-size keyboards, laser printers, large color displays, and file servers. These lightweight personal computers assist systems analysts and users as they work together to perform essential tasks, for example the development of output screens for prototypes of complex information systems.

The productivity of systems analysts can be greatly enhanced by the use of personal computers as workbenches supported by computer-aided software engineering tools designed to automate many complex and time consuming processes throughout all phases of the SDLC.

Knowledge workers of all levels are using microcomputers not only as elements of communications networks, but also as personal computers equipped with productivity improvement software such as electronic spreadsheets, graphics, word processors, and data base managers.

Many knowledge workers, including programmers and systems analysts, will be able to do much of their work at home by using a modem linked to corporate communications network.

Designers of computer information systems are able to take advantage of the rapidly converging multimedia technologies, including graphics, text, voice, image, and animation. Systems such as that pictured enhance user communication and system design and documentation in many ways—ranging from conceptualizing a system to effective presentations to comprehensive reference manuals that aid analysts, programmers, and end-users throughout the life cycle of the system.

5. *System test requirements* The system tests will be conducted in two stages. The first stage of testing will be run as a full prototype of the actual system, using test input and files. The second stage will involve the use of live data and a copy of a live file. Initial tests will be low volume, with the volume gradually increasing as successful tests are completed. All tests will employ user personnel under the supervision of the test team. The computer program component of OARS is to be validated by the test team, top-down, as program modules are developed. Testing will continue until the entire computer program component is tested. Tests will include both valid and invalid data.
6. *Training requirements* One additional programmer will be required prior to the start of the development phase. Staff will be selected from the regional centers for training in the use of OARS.

B. Internal Design Requirement
1. *Computer program component*
   a. Top-level data flow diagrams
      (1) Level-0 DFD and narrative description (figures E2.4a and E2.4b)
      (2) Level-1 DFD and narrative description (figures E2.5a and E2.5b)
   b. Data base requirement (figure E2.6)
   c. Top-level structure chart (figure E2.7) Figure E2.7 is a conceptual-level HIPO chart that shows the major components of OARS. The IPO chart, shown for the credit check limit status module, illustrates how this module must verify that the customer will not exceed their credit limit.
2. *Computer program design (for each program)*
   a. Check Credit Limit Status (figure E2.8)
   b. Data storage requirement
      The OARS data base will be made up of five seperate, related files—Orders, Order Detail, Customer, Product, and Discount. Figure E2.9 shows the data elements of each of these five files.

Exhibit 2　■　379

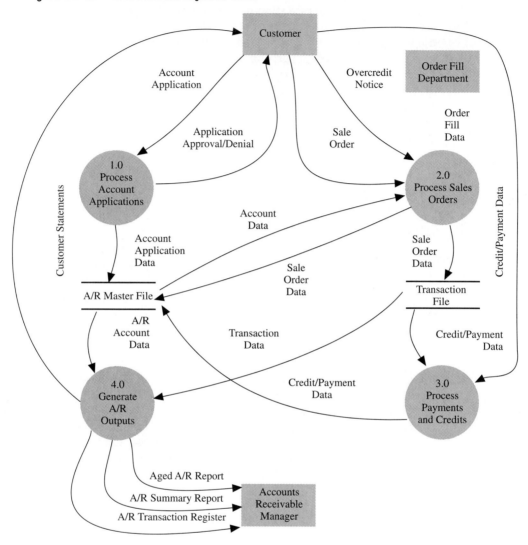

In this figure the OARS context diagram is decomposed into four major processing operations: process account applications, process sales orders, process payments and credits, and generate A/R outputs. The inputs and outputs related to the entities that set the boundaries for OARS are the same as those shown in the system context diagram.

At this level, five additional data flows have been added, as has an A/R data base. Except for sales transaction data, all of the internal inputs and outputs relate to the A/R data base. The Process Account Applications bubble supplies the A/R data base with updated customer account data. The Process Payments and Credits bubble provides the A/R data base with current payment/credit data, and the Process Sales Orders bubble returns sales data to the A/R data base.

The A/R data base has two outputs. The first is the customer account data required to process sales orders, and the second is A/R data used to create the outputs required by the A/R manager. Also, in order to create these outputs, sales transaction data must flow from the Process Sales Orders bubble to the Generate A/R Outputs bubble.

c. Structure chart for data edit module

Figure E2.10 shows the sequence of operations to be performed by the data edit program module. The symbols represent the physical devices that actually will be used. The characteristics of these devices affect the design of the system in two significant ways: the selection and use of programming languages and techniques in the development phase, and the ongoing operation and maintenance of the computer information system.

Exhibit 2   ■   381

■ Figure E2.5a   Level-1 data flow diagram for OARS.

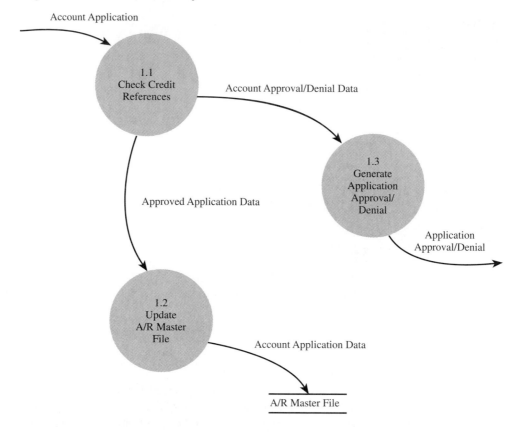

■ Figure E2.5b   Narrative description for an on-line accounts receivable system (OARS)—Level-1 Data Flow Diagram.

In this figure the Process Account Applications bubble in the OARS level-0 data flow diagram is decomposed to exhibit three level-1 processing bubbles: Check Credit References, Generate Application Approval/Denial, and Update A/R Master File. The Check Credit References bubble has as its input customer account application data and produces as an output either an application approval or denial, which flows to the Assign Credit Limit bubble. This process also generates account data needed to update the A/R data base.

■ Figure E2.6   OARS data base requirement.

OARS System Storage Requirements:

1. The OARS database consists of 14 data elements for a total of 167 characters.

2. Assuming a range of 10,000 master records to 20,000 records over the expected 5-year life of the system, from 1,670,000 characters to 3,340,000 characters of data will have to be stored.

3. The data described in 2 above will be distributed among the computers located in the local regions.

■ Figure E2.7   HIPO chart for OARS.

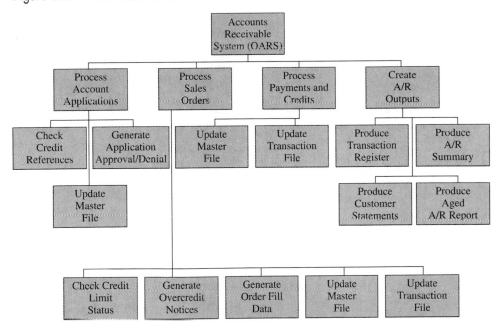

IPO chart: 2.1 Check Credit Limit Status

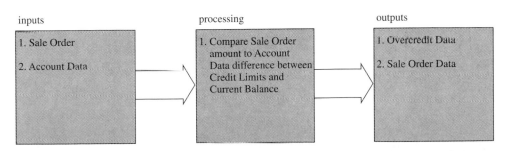

■ Figure E2.8   Decomposed data flow diagram for OARS check credit limit status module.

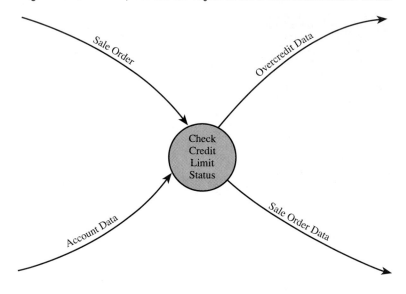

   d. Transaction file requirements

The transaction file requirements for OARS are shown in figure E2.10 and E2.11, which depicts the CRT display for the customer application transaction.

   e. Control requirements

The OARS computer programs will provide the following controls:
1. Edit all input data for validity.
2. Detect overcredit conditions prior to processing invoices.
3. Detect short or out-of-stock conditions prior to processing invoices.

   f. Test requirements

The programmer is responsible for initial testing of a program module in accordance with procedures approved by a programming supervisor. When satisfied that a module is performing according to design specifications, the programmer is to return it, along with all test data and results, to the test team.

■ Figure E2.9   OARS data base files and elements.

Orders File: Customer File:

                Order Number   Customer Number
                Order Date   Name
                Customer Number   Address
                                                          City
Order Detail File: State
                                                          ZIP Code
                Order Number   Discount Code
                Product Code
                Quantity Ordered

Product File: Discount File:

                Product Number   Discount Code
                Product Description   Trade Discount
                Unit Price

Exhibit 2   ■   385

■ Figure E2.10　OARS transaction file requirements: customer application.

Display Layout Sheet

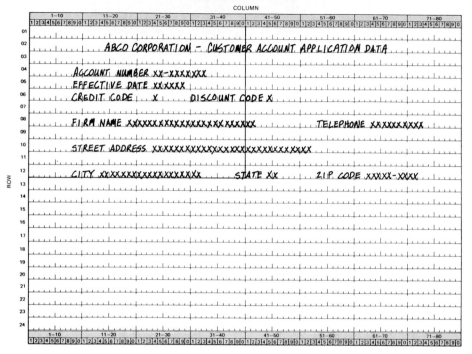

■ Figure E2.11　Screen design for customer account application data.

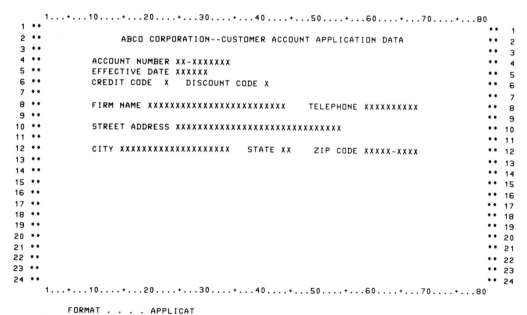

```
     1...+...10....+...20....+...30....+...40....+...50....+...60....+...70....+...80
 1 **                                                                          **  1
 2 **             ABCO CORPORATION--CUSTOMER ACCOUNT APPLICATION DATA          **  2
 3 **                                                                          **  3
 4 **        ACCOUNT NUMBER XX-XXXXXXX                                         **  4
 5 **        EFFECTIVE DATE XXXXXX                                             **  5
 6 **        CREDIT CODE  X    DISCOUNT CODE X                                 **  6
 7 **                                                                          **  7
 8 **        FIRM NAME XXXXXXXXXXXXXXXXXXXXXXXXX     TELEPHONE XXXXXXXXXX       **  8
 9 **                                                                          **  9
10 **        STREET ADDRESS XXXXXXXXXXXXXXXXXXXXXXXXXXXXXX                      ** 10
11 **                                                                          ** 11
12 **        CITY XXXXXXXXXXXXXXXXXXX     STATE XX     ZIP CODE XXXXX-XXXX      ** 12
13 **                                                                          ** 13
14 **                                                                          ** 14
15 **                                                                          ** 15
16 **                                                                          ** 16
17 **                                                                          ** 17
18 **                                                                          ** 18
19 **                                                                          ** 19
20 **                                                                          ** 20
21 **                                                                          ** 21
22 **                                                                          ** 22
23 **                                                                          ** 23
24 **                                                                          ** 24
     1...+...10....+...20....+...30....+...40....+...50....+...60....+...70....+...80

        FORMAT . . . . APPLICAT
```

IV. Plans and Cost Schedules
  A. Detailed Milestones—Design Phase
     Figure E2.12 depicts the detailed schedule for the nearly completed OARS design phase. The design phase is on schedule. The design phase costs are as planned. Figure E2.13 shows the design phase costs.
  B. Major Milestones—All Phases
     Figure E2.14 is a schedule for the entire OARS project. The project is on schedule. The thirty-week development phase is scheduled for completion on 11/11/xx. The estimated cumulative cost for the entire project is graphed in figure E2.15. The total cost is estimated to be $265,500.
  C. Detailed Milestones—Development Phase
     Figure E2.16 presents the detailed projections for the development phase over the thirty-week period. Figure E2.17 is the accompanying cumulative cost estimate for the development phase. The total development phase cost is estimated to be $196,000.

Exhibit 2   ■   387

PROJECT PLAN AND STATUS REPORT																				
PROJECT TITLE	PROJECT STATUS SYMBOLS O Satisfactory □ Caution △ Critical								J. Herring PROGRAMMER/ANALYST											
OARS — DESIGN PHASE	PLANNING/PROGRESS SYMBOLS ☐ Scheduled Progress ∨ Scheduled Completion ■ Actual Progress ▼ Actual Completion								COMMITTED DATE 3/30/XY		COMPLETED DATE		STATUS DATE 3/16/XY							
ACTIVITY/DOCUMENT	PERCENT COMPLETE	STATUS	PERIOD ENDING (Week)																	
			2	4	6	8	10	12	14	16	18	20								
DESIGN PHASE	0	0																		
Allocation of Functions	0	0																		
Manual Functions	0	0																		
Task Definition	0	0																		
Ref. Manual Def.	0	0																		
Equipment Functions	0	0																		
Function Def.	0	0																		
Equipment Spec.	0	0																		
Computer Prog. Functions	0	0																		
Data Base Design	0	0																		
Data Edit Program	0	0																		
A/R Program	0	0																		
Customer Program	0	0																		
Overcredit Program	0	0																		

PROJECT PLAN AND STATUS REPORT																				
PROJECT TITLE	PROJECT STATUS SYMBOLS O Satisfactory □ Caution △ Critical								J. Herring PROGRAMMER/ANALYST											
OARS — DESIGN PHASE	PLANNING/PROGRESS SYMBOLS ☐ Scheduled Progress ∨ Scheduled Completion ■ Actual Progress ▼ Actual Completion								COMMITTED DATE 3/30/XY		COMPLETED DATE		STATUS DATE 3/16/XY							
ACTIVITY/DOCUMENT	PERCENT COMPLETE	STATUS	PERIOD ENDING (Week)																	
			2	4	6	8	10	12	14	16	18	20								
DESIGN PHASE (cont'd)	0	0																		
Test Requirements	0	0																		
System Test Req.	0	0																		
Computer Prog.Test Req.	0	0																		
Design Spec.	0	0																		
Design Phase Report	0	0																		
Design Phase Review	0	0																		

■ Figure E2.13   Project cost report—design phase.

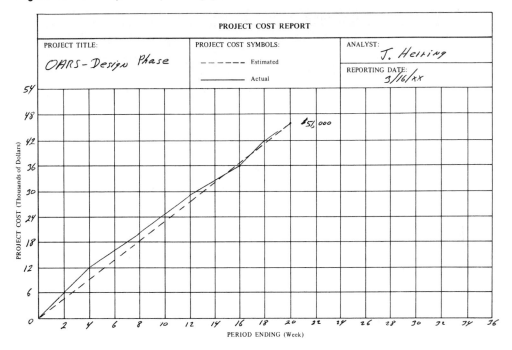

Exhibit 2   ■   389

PROJECT PLAN AND STATUS REPORT

PROJECT TITLE	PROJECT STATUS SYMBOLS		
OARS – MAJOR MILESTONES	O Satisfactory □ Caution △ Critical		J. Herring PROGRAMMER/ANALYST

	PLANNING/PROGRESS SYMBOLS □ Scheduled Progress ∨ Scheduled Completion ■ Actual Progress ▼ Actual Completion	COMMITTED DATE 11/17/XY	COMPLETED DATE	STATUS DATE 3/16/XY

ACTIVITY/DOCUMENT	PERCENT COMPLETE	STATUS	PERIOD ENDING (Week)													
			2	4	6	8	10	12	14	16	18	20	22	24	26	28	30
STUDY PHASE	95	O															
Initial Investigation	100	O															
Performance Spec.	100	O															
Study Phase Report	100	O															
Study Phase Review	0	O															
DESIGN PHASE																	
Allocation of Functions	0	O															
Computer Prog. Functions	0	O															
Test Requirements	0	O															
Design Spec.	0	O															
Design Phase Report	0	O															
Design Phase Review	0	O															

PROJECT PLAN AND STATUS REPORT

PROJECT TITLE	PROJECT STATUS SYMBOLS		
OARS – MAJOR MILESTONES	O Satisfactory □ Caution △ Critical		J. Herring PROGRAMMER/ANALYST

	PLANNING/PROGRESS SYMBOLS □ Scheduled Progress ∨ Scheduled Completion ■ Actual Progress ▼ Actual Completion	COMMITTED DATE 11/17/XY	COMPLETED DATE	STATUS DATE 3/16/XY

ACTIVITY/DOCUMENT	PERCENT COMPLETE	STATUS	PERIOD ENDING (Week)													
			32	34	36	38	40	42	44	46	48	50	52	54	56	58	60
DEVELOPMENT PHASE	0	O															
Implementation Plan	0	O															
Equipment Acquisition	0	O															
Computer Program Dev.	0	O															
Personnel Training	0	O															
System Tests	0	O															
Changeover Plan	0	O															
System Spec.	0	O															
Dev. Phase Report	0	O															
Dev. Phase Review	0	O															

■ Figure E2.15   Project cost report—total project.

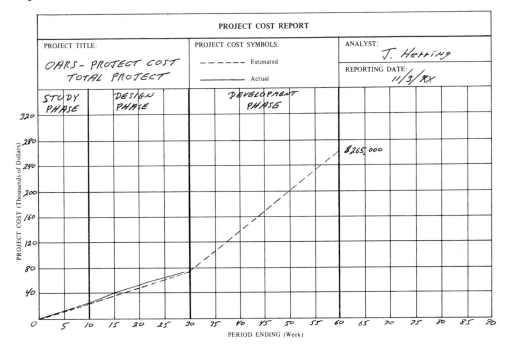

Exhibit 2   ■   391

■ Figure E2.16 Project plan and status report—development phase.

PROJECT PLAN AND STATUS REPORT

PROJECT TITLE	PROJECT STATUS SYMBOLS		J. Herring		
OARS - DEVELOPMENT PHASE	O Satisfactory □ Caution △ Critical		PROGRAMMER/ANALYST		

	PLANNING/PROGRESS SYMBOLS	COMMITTED DATE	COMPLETED DATE	STATUS DATE
	□ Scheduled Progress ∨ Scheduled Completion ■ Actual Progress ▼ Actual Completion	11/17/XY		11/3/XY

ACTIVITY/DOCUMENT	PERCENT COMPLETE	STATUS	PERIOD ENDING (Week)															
			2	4	6	8	10	12	14	16	18	20	22	24	26	28	30	32	34	36
DEVELOPMENT PHASE	0	0																
Implementation Plan	0	0																
Test Plan	0	0																
Training Plan	0	0																
Conversion Plan	0	0																
Equip. Acq. and Instal.	0	0																
Computer Prog. Dev.	0	0																
Computer Prog. Design	0	0																
Coding and Debugging	0	0																
Computer Prog. Tests	0	0																
Reference Manual Prep.	0	0																
Programmer's Man.	0	0																
Operator's Man.	0	0																
User's Man.	0	0																

PROJECT PLAN AND STATUS REPORT

PROJECT TITLE	PROJECT STATUS SYMBOLS		J. Herring		
OARS - DEVELOPMENT PHASE	O Satisfactory □ Caution △ Critical		PROGRAMMER/ANALYST		

	PLANNING/PROGRESS SYMBOLS	COMMITTED DATE	COMPLETED DATE	STATUS DATE
	□ Scheduled Progress ∨ Scheduled Completion ■ Actual Progress ▼ Actual Completion	11/17/XY		11/3/XY

ACTIVITY/DOCUMENT	PERCENT COMPLETE	STATUS	PERIOD ENDING (Week)															
			2	4	6	8	10	12	14	16	18	20	22	24	26	28	30	32	34	36
DEVELOPMENT PHASE (CON'T)	0	0																
Personnel Training	0	0																
System Tests	0	0																
Changeover Plan	0	0																
System Specification	0	0																
Dev. Phase Report	0	0																
Dev. Phase Review	0	0																

■ Figure E2.17   Project cost—development phase.

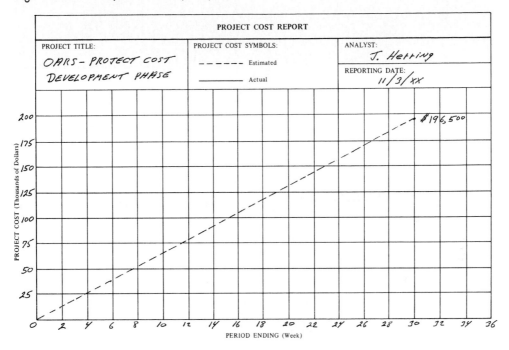

Exhibit 2   ■   393

6

The Development and Operation Phases

Development Phase Activities

The **development phase** is the third of the four life-cycle phases. It is the phase in which the information system is constructed according to the design specification. The principal activities performed during the development phase occur in two major sequences:

1. Activities external to computer program development.
2. Activities internal to computer program development.

The principal development phase activities are depicted and numbered in figure U6.1. They are described and discussed in chapter 16, "Preparing for Implementation," chapter 17, "Computer Program Development," and chapter 18, "Development Phase Report and Review." Following is an overview of each of the activities that comprise the development phase:

1. *Implementation Planning*
   After the initiation of the development phase is approved, implementation planning begins. Essential parts of the *implementation plan* are:
   a. A plan for testing the computer program component, both as the integrated assembly of its individual programs and as an element of the overall business system.

■ Figure U6.1   Development phase activity flowchart. The principal activity sequences of the development phase relate to (1) implementation planning, including conversion to the new system; and (2) computer program design and system testing.

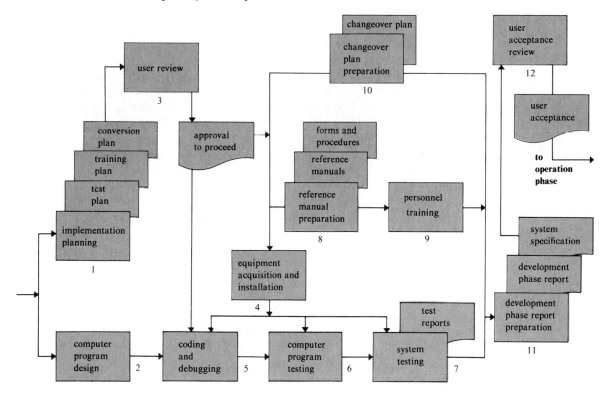

b. A plan for training the personnel who are to be associated with the new system. This includes persons who will provide inputs to, receive outputs from, and operate or maintain the new system.

c. A conversion plan. This plan provides for the conversion of procedures, programs, and files preparatory to actual changeover from the old system to the new one. The *conversion plan* also includes a preliminary plan for actual changeover from the old to the new system.

2. *Computer Program Design*

Computer program design is begun parallel with the implementation planning effort. As necessary, system flowcharts are expanded to show additional detail for the computer program components. The complete data base is developed. Input and output files are identified and computer program logic flowcharts prepared for each computer program component.

3. *User Review*

Reviews are held with the principal user throughout the development phase. The first review block shown in figure U6.1 is indicative of an interim *development phase review.* This type of review normally is not held to reevaluate the decision that initiated the development phase, but rather to keep the user informed of general project progress and to secure cooperation in areas in which the sponsor can be of assistance to the project. As illustrated, a review of test plans, training plans, and conversion plans is essential because user personnel are directly involved in the implementation activities. The user's concurrence with the implementation plan reaffirms support, which is documented by a written approval to proceed. As shown in figure U6.1, the approval to proceed also applies to the ongoing computer program design and development activities.

4. *Equipment Acquisition and Installation*

In the design phase, special hardware required to support the system may have been identified. If not ordered during the design phase, this equipment is ordered at this time, and delivered, installed, and tested. Often all hardware components need not arrive at the same time because needs vary as the computer programs develop from coding through testing. Therefore, an appropriate schedule is established and maintained for the acquisition of hardware items.

5. *Coding and Debugging*

Each of the computer programs that make up the computer program component of the overall system is coded and debugged. This means that each is compiled without error and successfully executes its program logic, using data supplied by the programmer.

6. *Computer Program Testing*

The computer programs are tested in a planned, top-down sequence that includes structured walk-throughs. The testing continues until the programs can be assembled as a component that can be tested as a unit. The analyst supplies data for testing the programs.

7. *System Testing*

    System tests are performed to verify that the computer-based business system has met its design objectives. The system includes the computer program component as one of its major elements. The user is responsible for supplying the input data and for participating in the evaluation of the system test results. System test reports are prepared to validate system performance.

8. *Reference Manual Preparation*

    Appropriate reference manuals for the various individuals who will work with the new computer-based information system must be prepared. These reference documents are based upon the system specification. The three principal manuals are for programmers, operators, and users.

    Forms and procedures are important elements of the reference manuals. Procedures are written, and appropriate forms are designed. The forms are prepared in-house or ordered from a manufacturer of forms.

9. *Personnel Training*

    Operating, programming, and user personnel are trained using the reference manuals, forms, and procedures as training aids. The training schedule is closely coordinated with the schedule for completing the development phase. All essential training must be completed prior to the user acceptance review, which occurs at the end of the development phase.

10. *Changeover Plan Preparation*

    The preliminary changeover plan, which was an element of the conversion plan, is updated. Changeover from the old to the new system takes place at the beginning of the operation phase. The *changeover plan* specifies the method of changeover, giving a detailed schedule of activities to be performed and identifying the responsibilities of all personnel involved in these activities.

11. *Development Phase Report Preparation*

    At the conclusion of the development phase the **development phase report** is prepared, documenting the development of the system in accordance with requirements specified in the design phase report. This report contains a summary of all of the pertinent activities undertaken during the development phase. The development phase report includes a **system specification**—the third major baseline document—which evolves from the performance and the design specifications. The system specification contains the complete technical specification for the computer-related business information system and its components. It contains, for instance, detailed flowcharts, data base specifications, and computer program listings. The system specification contains all of the essential system documentation; it is the baseline reference for the preparation of manuals and training aids.

12. *User Acceptance Review*

At the conclusion of the development phase the computer-based business system is reviewed by the management of the user organization. Representatives of the information service organization and other affected organizations participate in this review. The principal documents upon which the **user acceptance review** is based are the design phase report, the development phase report, test reports, and the changeover plan.

After the conclusion of a successful acceptance review the user organization issues a written memorandum of acceptance and the system enters the operation phase of its life cycle.

Operation Phase Activities

The **operation phase** follows the development phase. Usually it is the longest of the life-cycle phases and is characterized by four distinct stages. Initially, the new system must be introduced into the business activity mainstream. This stage is called change-over. The changeover transition period may take weeks or even months. After it is completed, the system enters the operation and routine maintenance stage. Early in this stage an evaluation should be made based on the comparison of predicted and actual performance measurements to determine whether or not the specific benefits claimed for the system have been achieved. Finally, the new system, like all operational systems, must be able to accommodate change. Change is perhaps the most important characteristic of the final stage in the life of a computer-based business system. Whether or not change can be managed is the final measure of the success or failure of the entire system effort. The major activities of this phase, which are the subject of chapter 19, "System Operation and Change Management," are shown pictorially in the flowchart of figure U6.2. Each of these activities is summarized as follows:

1. *System Changeover*

Normally a period of transition is required to change from an old system to a new one. If all the development phase implementation activities have been performed adequately, the necessary manuals and documentation for the new

■ Figure U6.2   Operation phase activity flowchart. Principal activity sequences of the operation phase relate to change-over from the old system to the new; routine operation; and system change, which usually results from system interaction with the business environment.

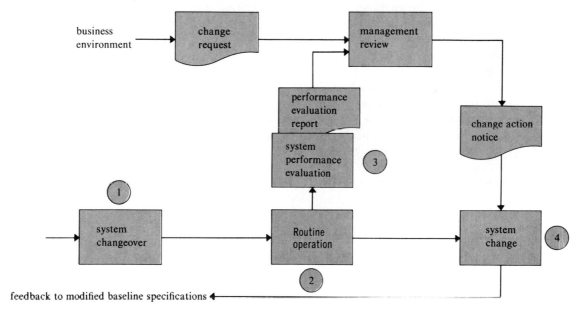

system are available. There is a nucleus of trained personnel (user, programming, and operations) to assume responsibility for the new system. However, it is critically important for the project team to remain heavily involved and in control during changeover. Changeover usually is a one way process; it must result in a system that is operationally acceptable. No matter how completely changeover activities are planned, numerous unforeseen incidents and problems will arise. **System changeover** is the most critical period in the entire life cycle of the computer-based system. Positive support by all user organizations is essential.

2. *Routine Operation*

   At the conclusion of the changeover process the system is considered to be operational. The user organization and other operating personnel assume their respective responsibilities, and procedures are established for change control. Except for routine surveillance and participation in subsequent change activities, the systems analysts' responsibilities for the project are reduced. They and other members of the project team become available to assume other assignments.

3. *System Performance Evaluation*

   After the computer-based business system has been operational for a reasonable period, its performance is formally evaluated. The results of the evaluation are documented in an evaluation report, which should be presented to a management review board, typically called a performance review board. Although the information service organization should be represented, the performance review board should be mainly user-oriented. The board should be headed by the principal user of the system.

4. *System Change*

   The modern business system environment is dynamic, subject to many internal and external influences. As shown in figure U6.2, the business environment may trigger a change request, which is then reviewed by management. This process may range from a brief analysis of the requested change to an extensive investigation. This investigation may cause a return to an early point in the life cycle. How far back in the life cycle the investigation might reach would depend upon the original baseline specification affected by the change. The investigation could cause a return to the study phase, in which case the resulting new design and development activities might yield a greatly modified system.

At the conclusion of the review and analysis of the requested change, the responsible management organization issues a change action notice. The actual change action is then taken. The potential impact of the change action is shown in figure U6.2 by the arrow that indicates feedback to the modified baseline specifications.

Chapter

16

■ ■ ■

Preparing for Implementation

Preview

In the development phase the computer information system is constructed from the specification prepared during the design phase. A principal activity of the development phase, conducted in parallel with the development of the computer programs, is preparation for implementation. This is an activity that continues throughout the development phase. It culminates in bringing a developed system into operational use. An implementation plan is needed in order to schedule and manage all of the tasks related to activating a new system. The implementation plan provides for test plans, training plans, equipment installation, and a plan for converting from the old to the new system.

Objectives

1. You will be able to describe the major development phase implementation activities.
2. You will be able to relate the importance of plans for testing, training, and installing equipment to converting to the new system.
3. You will be able to explain how CASE contributes to top-down testing.
4. You will be able to distinguish among the three changeover methods.

Key Terms

development phase the systems development life-cycle phase in which the system is constructed according to the design phase specification.

implementation plan a plan for implementing a system that includes test plans, training plans, an equipment acquisition plan, and a conversion plan.

top-down computer program development a structured technique that starts with a general description of the system and expands into successively greater levels of detail.

development phase report a report prepared at the end of the development phase; it is an extension of the design phase report and summarizes the results of the development phase activities.

system specification a baseline specification that contains all of the essential system documentation; it is a complete technical specification.

user acceptance review a review held with the user organization at the conclusion of the development phase to determine whether or not to enter the operation phase.

implementation the process of bringing a developed system into operational use and turning it over to the user.

conversion the process of performing all the operations that directly result in the turnover of the new system to the user.

changeover the process of changing over from the old to the new system; the transition from the development phase to the operation phase.

Implementation Planning

The Implementation Process

Implementation is the process of bringing a developed system into operational use and turning it over to the user. Implementation activities extend from planning through conversion from the old system to the new. At the beginning of the development phase a preliminary implementation plan is created to schedule and manage the many different activities that must be integrated into the plan. The implementation plan is updated throughout the development phase, culminating in a changeover plan for the operation phase.

The Implementation Plan

A common implementation management technique is to assign the responsibility for each element of the implementation plan to a team. The head of each team is selected from the organization best qualified to perform the specific implementation task. For example, a user-manager would head the conversion team, and the data processing manager would head the equipment installation team.

The major elements of the **implementation plan** are test plans, training plans, an equipment installation plan, and a conversion plan. We will discuss each of these elements in later sections of this chapter.

Test Plans

The implementation of a computer-based system requires that test data be prepared and that the system and its elements be tested in a planned, structured manner. The computer program component is a major subsystem of the computer-based information system, and particular attention should be given to the testing of this system element as it is developed. As we have previously stated, the structured, top-down approach to systems analysis and design can greatly reduce the effort and cost of developing computer information systems. This is accomplished by validating most of the performance of the system at the analysis and design levels, where changes are more easily accommodated and less costly than in the development phase. This is illustrated in figure 16.1, which shows that the distribution of effort among the analysis, design, and development phases of the SDLC is dramatically altered when CASE tools and prototyping techniques are employed. This redistribution of effort is called *front-end loading* and tends to reduce the introduction of errors that, if unchecked, most likely would proliferate throughout later stages of the SDLC, where it becomes very difficult and expensive to correct them.

Within the development phase, additional economies can be achieved by adhering to a structured approach to computer program development and testing. This approach, called the "top-down method," is a departure from the historical "bottom-up" method, and it has greatly reduced the severity of problems associated with the older method.

■ Figure 16.1   In the early, traditional approach to the SDLC, most of the effort was concentrated in the costly devel-
opment phase. The structured techniques shifted this effort toward the analysis and design phases.
Current CASE techniques, including rapid prototyping, further extend the shift toward front-end loading.
As a result, costly errors can be avoided and the time for the entire SDLC process reduced.

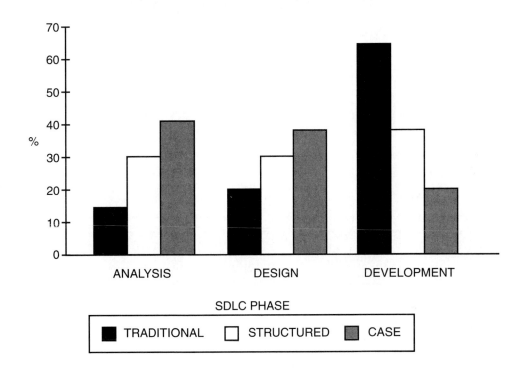

Bottom-up Computer Program Development

The older method for scheduling and managing the tests of computer programs is to
develop a hierarchical structure within which the lowest-level programs are tested
individually and then combined into higher-level modules, which are tested next. This
process, which sometimes is called "string testing," is illustrated in figure 16.2, as an
example of *bottom-up computer program development.*

A typical development and testing sequence (from 1 to 11) is shown in this figure.
Modules that have been coded from the bottom up and those that are not yet coded
are shown. Eventually, all the modules will be strung together at successively higher
levels to form the complete computer program.

There have been many difficulties with this traditional method of developing
computer programs. Often special programs, called "driver" programs, have to be
written to test the higher-level modules as they are created. For example, in figure
16.2, modules 3, 4, and 8, which are the highest-level coded modules at the stage of

■ Figure 16.2   Bottom-up computer program development. The bottom-up method for developing computer programs
is based upon proceeding from lower-level modules to higher-level, more complex ones. Failure of all
of the modules to mesh at the highest level often produced cost overruns and inabilities to meet
schedules.

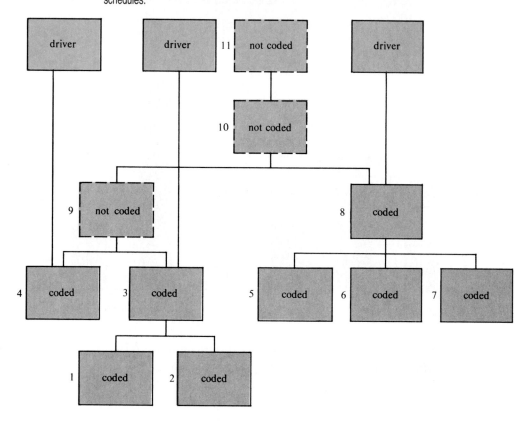

development depicted, must be tested with driver programs that supply calling and
control instructions not yet available from other modules in the computer program
development hierarchy.

In addition, interfaces between modules must be developed, and the modules
must be integrated successfully to create a complete and functional computer program. Failure of some components to mesh at the end of the project has caused serious errors. Changes made at this time, high in the level of the system hierarchy,
could cause much of the lower-level development and testing to be redone, causing
overruns in cost and failures to meet schedules. Because of these problems, the historical method is seldom practiced exclusively, and the top-down method for developing computer programs has become an accepted part of the life-cycle method.

An exception is the object-oriented methodology described in chapter 6. This
approach to system design and development is based upon reusable program modules
developed by means of an object-oriented programming language. These modules are
bottom-up building blocks.

Top-down computer program development. The top-down method for computer program development is based upon proceeding from less-detailed, higher-level modules to more-detailed, lower-level ones. This approach reduces system testing and problems related to final system integration.

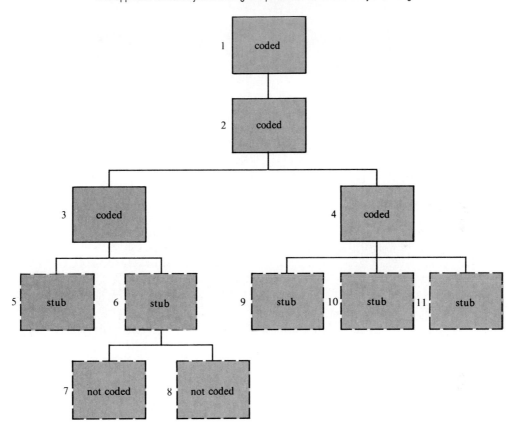

Top-down Computer Program Development

The **top-down computer program development** and testing approach is a structured technique that starts with a general description of the system and expands into successively greater levels of detail.

The top-down approach to computer program development and testing is shown in figure 16.3. This structured technique for computer program development is a logical extension of the top-down, hierarchical approach to system design characteristic of structure charts such as *HIPO charts*.

As the typical development sequence (from 1 to 11) in figure 16.3 shows, modules are developed downward from the nucleus at the top of the computer program hierarchy. Driver programs are not necessary. Instead, modules that display a message acknowledging receipt of higher-level program control are used. These modules are called *stubs;* their use is also illustrated in figure 16.3.

■ Figure 16.4 Comparative machine usage for top-down and bottom-up computer program development. With the top-down method for computer program development the initial investment in machine usage is higher. The total machine usage, however, is less.

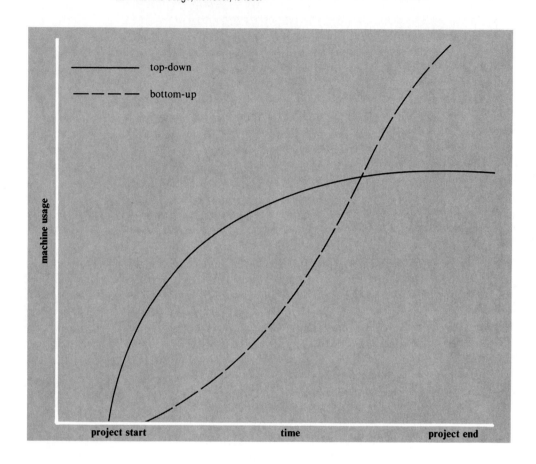

A major advantage of top-down structured testing and development is that the computer program continues to operate as stubs are removed and modules added. Managers thus have continuous control over the computer program development process, and the problems that can arise from an overall integration effort are minimized. An important aspect of this advantage is illustrated in figure 16.4. A major end-of-project integration effort is eliminated, and total machine usage for testing is reduced, which, again, illustrates the cost savings that can be achieved in computer program development through front-end loading. Thus top-down testing of computer programs is generally the approach of choice. There are circumstances, though, when bottom-up testing is appropriate. An example is a minor change to a small system with which the analyst and user are thoroughly familiar. Another is the existence of critical low-level functions that might make the redesign of higher-level functions necessary.

Annotated test plan format. A plan is necessary for testing the programs that make up the computer program component of computer-based information. The scope of the plan, the data to be collected and identified, and special procedures are included.

(subsystem/system) test plan

scope

1. *name*	A name or number that identifies the test
2. *purpose*	**Why:** the specific objectives of the test, including identification of the computer program components involved in the test
3. *location*	**Where** the test is to be performed
4. *schedule*	**When** the test is to be performed
5. *responsibilities*	**Who:** the individuals involved in the test and their specific duties
6. *general procedures*	**What:** a general overview of the test inputs, events, and anticipated results

data collection and evaluation

1. *data to be used*	**What:** a detailed description of live or simulated input data to be used in the test
2. *data to be collected*	**What:** a detailed description of the data to be obtained as test results
3. *method of data recording*	**How** the data is to be recorded, for example, listings, magnetic disk, and so forth
4. *method of data evaluation*	**How** the test results are to be analyzed

special procedures

What procedures are unique to this test, for example, equipment operating procedures, operator intervention procedures, abnormal condition procedures.

In practice, the preferred testing method is a predominantly top-down approach which can accommodate, when necessary, an early need to deal with critical or complex low-level functions.

Formal Test Planning

Plans must be made for the formal evaluation of the computer program as it is developed, as well as for internal technical reviews, such as *structured walk-throughs*. The results of these tests should become part of the cumulative development phase documentation.

A standardized test plan document is useful. A general format for a test plan is shown and annotated in figure 16.5. The comments relate to the questions of "why, where, when, who, what, and how" that a test plan should answer. The format illustrated is suitable for both computer subsystem and overall system tests. An entry identifying the type of test is inserted at the top of the test plan document.

At the conclusion of each test a written report is prepared to record the results; a standardized test report document relating to the test document can be used. Figure 16.6 outlines a general test report format and describes the entries to be made on the document.

Annotated test report format. A written record of test results is required. This report defines the tests performed and describes the results of the tests.

(subsystem/system) test report	
scope	
1. *name*	the name shown on the corresponding test plan
2. *purpose*	the purpose stated on the corresponding test plan
3. *references*	identification of the corresponding test plan and other pertinent documents, such as previous test results
description of results	
1. *test methods*	how the test was performed
2. *objectives met*	identification of specific test accomplishments
3. *problem areas*	discussion of problems encountered
4. *recommendations*	specific actions to be taken, for example, accept test results, perform additional tests, revise coding

Final system tests are performed after the subsystem tests have been completed. Their purpose is to exercise the entire system, including the computer program subsystem, under "live" environmental conditions. The main objective of system tests is to subject the computer-based business system to all foreseeable operating conditions. The user should specify and conduct these tests; system test responsibility should not be delegated to programmers or even to systems analysts.

Systems tests become progressively more complex. Initial tests may involve selected samples of input data and a small test file; later, pilot tests (called "history processing") can be performed using complete files and a large number of past data transactions.

The persons who will be involved in the "live" operation of the system should prepare the system test data for computer processing. If the user is involved appropriately in the system-level tests, progress can be made toward two supplementary goals: user training and user acceptance. User training is vital to the successful conversion to the new system. User participation in earlier top-down tests of the computer program subsystem and in structured walk-throughs is a powerful training technique. The final system tests, if sufficiently thorough, can serve as acceptance tests, which can assure the user that the system is ready for operation.

Training

Training: An Overview

Training plans are an important element of the implementation plan. Their purpose is to ensure that all the personnel who are to be associated with the computer-based business system possess the necessary knowledge and skills. Operating, programming, and user personnel are trained using *reference manuals* as training aids. The training schedule is coordinated with the schedule for completing the development phase, for all essential training must be completed prior to the user acceptance review at the end of this phase. However, training should not be completed too far in advance of need, or the personnel are liable to lose interest or forget their training.

Training programs begin with the selection of appropriate participants and the preparation of different types of training programs for programmers, operators, and user personnel. User personnel are those persons who will prepare inputs, follow procedures, and use outputs. Additional training programs must be conducted for management-level personnel, not only to familiarize managers with the new system, but also to obtain their active support and cooperation during implementation.

Before training programs can be initiated, materials must be prepared. The basic training resources are reference manuals appropriate to the needs and interests of each type of trainee—programmer, operator, or user. These reference manuals are based largely upon the *system specification*. This baseline document usually is not in a final format before the end of the development phase, at which time it is included in the development phase report. However, because the design specification is added to continuously throughout the development phase, an interim system specification exists. Since this specification usually is maintained by word-processing software, drafts of the reference manuals can be prepared for the initial training programs from the interim specification. The reference manuals are prepared in their final formats at the end of the development phase, and they are available for training purposes throughout the life of the system.

In the next section we will describe the training programs established to meet the needs of programmers, operators, and users, outlining the general content of the training manuals.

Programmer Training

Programmers are assigned to the computer-based business system project at the beginning of the development phase. The programmers assigned to develop the computer program modules are indoctrinated by the analysts and programmer/analysts who prepared the design specification. They help to create the programmer's reference manual, which is used to train other programmers assigned to the system throughout its operational life.

Programmer's reference manual. The programmer's reference manual is a comprehensive guidebook, containing both internal (to the computer program component), and external (to the computer program component) system specifications.

guide to programmer's reference manual

1. *title*   name of computer-based system

2. *purpose*   general description of system and its major objectives

3. *external specification*   a. data flow diagram

                               b. output, input, and interface descriptions

                               c. system-level test input-output samples

                               d. equipment specification

4. *internal specification*   a. computer program component:

                                        1) process-oriented flowcharts

                                        2) expanded system flowcharts

                                        3) data base specification

                                        4) control specifications

                                        5) test input-output samples

                               b. computer programs:

                                          1) detailed system flowcharts

                                        2) logic flowcharts

                                        3) transaction file specifications

                                        4) control specifications

                                        5) interface specifications

                                        6) listings

                                        7) test input-output samples

The programmer's reference manual is the most comprehensive of the reference manuals. It informs an experienced programmer, unfamiliar with the system, about all of the aspects of the computer program. The manual should enable this person to (1) understand existing program components; (2) modify existing program components; and (3) write new program components. Figure 16.7 is a guide to typical contents of such a manual. The external specification relates to elements of the system external to the computer program subsystem; the internal specification relates to elements internal to the computer program subsystem.

Operator Training

If new equipment is to be installed, operator training is completed in conjunction with its installation and checkout. If new equipment is not required for the computer-based system, operators still must become familiar with the operational requirements of the new system. Different kinds of operational personnel may be involved in the operation of the system, such as computer operators, console operators, and data entry operators. Therefore, more than one type of manual may be required. Each manual should acquaint the operators with the system and its purpose and provide a

Operator's reference manual. An operator's reference manual contains all the information an operator needs to perform specific tasks. It includes input, processing, and output descriptions and instructions for handling errors and exceptions.

guide to operator's reference manual

1. *title*   name of computer-based system
2. *purpose*   general description of system
3. *operating procedures*   as appropriate to specific operational duties:

    a. operator inputs: a complete description of all inputs, including:
       1) purpose and use
       2) title of input
       3) input and media
       4) limitations
       5) format and content
    b. operator outputs: a complete description of all outputs, including:
       1) purpose and use
       2) title of output
       3) output media
       4) format and content
    c. file summary: a complete description of all files, including:
       1) file identification
       2) medium
       3) type: master, transaction, and so forth
    d. error and exception handling: procedures for handling hardware and software error conditions

ready reference to specific duties and step-by-step operating instructions. These instructions should cover both normal and abnormal situations. They should be written in a style that is easily understood by the intended users of the manual; detailed discussions of complex and lengthy system descriptions should not be included. A guide to the typical contents of a reference manual is shown in figure 16.8.

Training programs for operators are scheduled to coincide with the needs of the computer-based business system as it is developed, tested, and approaches operational status. Users, analysts, and programmers may participate in the training of operators

User Training

For the system to begin operation, a sufficient number of users must be trained before the end of the development phase. Thereafter, additional personnel are trained, and training continues throughout the operational life of the system. As with operator's reference manuals, usually more than one type of user's reference manual is required. Each one should be self-contained and should explain the system in terms of the user's specific needs. The text should be factual, concise, specific, and clearly worded and

User's reference manual. A user's reference manual contains all the information needed to train a user of the computer-based information system in input, output, and operating procedures.

guide to user's reference manual	
1. *title*	name of computer-based system
2. *purpose*	general description of system and its major objectives, including an information-oriented flowchart and/or data flow diagram
3. *user procedures*	as appropriate to each user:

a. instructions for input preparation:
  1) title
  2) description
  3) purpose and use
  4) media
  5) limitations
  6) format and content
  7) relation to outputs
b. instructions for output use:
  1) title
  2) description
  3) purpose and use
  4) media
  5) limitations
  6) format and content
  7) relation to inputs
c. operating instructions: procedures for operating equipment with which the user must be familiar

illustrated. Sentences should be simple and direct; discussions of theory and detailed technical matters should be avoided. The manual should provide users with a general overview of the system. However, primary emphasis is on the specific steps to be followed, the results to be expected, and the corrective actions to be taken when such results are not obtained. Figure 16.9 lists the typical contents of a user's reference manual.

Training sessions for user personnel usually involve larger numbers of people than do operator or programmer training programs. These sessions should be planned to meet the needs of each type of user. Normally, several sessions should be scheduled for all trainees so that they fully understand the new system and have an opportunity to familiarize themselves with the handling of documents and equipment.

The training team should be certain that sufficient user personnel are thoroughly trained and prepared to support the new system at the time of its implementation. Individuals who are not willing to cooperate or who cannot follow procedures can cause great difficulties at the time of changeover from the old system to the new.

Management Orientation

The life-cycle process for the development of computer-based business systems automatically includes numerous reviews to keep user management informed of and committed to the support of the project. However, before changeover to a new system, it is important to augment the scheduled reviews with a series of management presentations. The purpose of these presentations is to inform all managers affected by the new system and to solicit their support during its implementation. These presentations, which should be made by the senior personnel involved in the development of the system, should include these subjects:

1. Review of system objectives, costs, and benefits.
2. Organizational and procedural changes associated with the new system.
3. Responsibilities of the organizations that report to the management attendees.

It is important that the implementation team's responsibilities be understood and that each organization involved in the implementation be assigned a constructive role during the critical changeover period.

Equipment Installation

Earlier in the life cycle of a computer-based system, fundamental equipment decisions were made. During the study phase, for example, alternative configurations were evaluated and decisions made about using available in-house equipment and obtaining new computer components or systems. Early in the design phase, when functions were allocated between manual, hardware, and software tasks, a final process of equipment evaluation and vendor selection took place. If new equipment was needed, it was placed on order. The development phase implementation plan must include all activities related to the installation and check-out of equipment scheduled to be delivered at various times throughout the development phase.

The principal equipment-related activities that must be implemented are (1) site preparation, (2) equipment installation, and (3) hardware and software check-out.

Equipment vendors can provide the specifications for equipment installation. They usually work with the project's equipment installation team in planning for adequate space, power, and light, and a suitable environment (for example, temperature, humidity, dust control, and safety measures). After a suitable site has been completed, the computer equipment can be installed. Although equipment normally is installed by the manufacturer, the implementation team should advise and assist. Participation enables the team to aid in the installation and, more importantly, to become familiar with the equipment.

Usually manufacturers will check out the hardware and the software they supply. The implementation team also should perform its own check-out tests, using application-oriented test programs.

Conversion

Conversion: An Overview

Conversion is the process of performing all of the operations that result directly in the turnover of the new system to the user. Conversion has two parts:

1. The creation of a conversion plan at the start of the development phase and the implementation of this plan throughout the development phase.
2. The creation of a system changeover plan at the end of the development phase and the implementation of the plan at the beginning of the operation phase.

Conversion Activities (Development Phase)

A conversion plan is prepared at the start of the development phase. Its principal elements concern procedures, program, and file conversion.

Procedures Conversion

Often a new system will incorporate many of the old system's forms and procedures, but some of these may require modification to fit into the new system. Also, the new system may interface with a network of other systems; this, too, may cause some modification of procedures. The procedures that require change must be identified, and the changes explained during training of personnel.

Program Conversion

The new computer-based system may include some computer programs that are part of an existing system. A conversion problem may arise if new equipment is installed, if the inputs and outputs of existing programs change, or if the existing programs are not efficient in their new environment. Even if new equipment is not involved, all the existing programs must be reevaluated. Reprogramming should be considered when programs are poorly documented, heavily patched, or not efficient enough. For instance, many small programs might be replaced by a single program that performs a repetitive function more effectively.

System interfaces with other computer programs also must be examined. Programming modifications may be required to enable the new system to supply or receive data through these interfaces.

File Conversion

File conversion can be the most time-consuming and expensive step in the entire project. The magnitude of this task often is underestimated. For example, if many thousands of customer account records are to be stored on a magnetic disk instead of kept in filing cabinets—possibly located in different parts of the company—the conversion effort could be extensive. Existing files must be converted into a format acceptable to the computer program and equipment. Duplicate files must be consolidated and errors corrected before changeover to the new system starts. Otherwise a series of data errors may plague users of the new system for a considerable time after its implementation.

File conversion activities include many basic systems analysis activities, such as fact finding and analysis, forms design, procedure writing, and computer program design. We can divide file conversion into a sequence of three major activities. These are (1) collection of file conversion data, (2) conversion of files, and (3) testing of converted files.

In many circumstances file conversion data must be collected from a variety of sources. Some data may already be in machine-readable form; however, it often is necessary to create new data to supplement that which is already filed in some form. Forms may have to be designed and procedures written to transfer data from an existing file to a new file.

Verifying data going into the new files is an important and often laborious task. All too often a high percentage of "current" data is incomplete or in error. Discrepancies are common, for instance, between data stored in two redundant files that are to be consolidated into a shared data base. Before consolidation can take place, it must be determined which (if either) file is correct. Verification usually requires the extensive assistance of user personnel. The analyst must remember that the new file manager is to be a computer, which will not be as flexible as the human file manager it may replace. Humans often can detect and ignore "garbage." The computer usually cannot.

Computer programs are required to perform the actual file conversion. These programs must be written and checked out before they are needed. They must sort data, validate data, and create the file in the new format. After the files have been converted, the conversion team must check their accuracy. Even if the original files have been "purified" before the data stored on them is entered into the new system, errors may be introduced during conversion. All file data should be printed out and verified. This, again, requires the assistance of user personnel. Special file correction forms may have to be designed, and several conversion runs may be required if a large data base is being assembled. Involving the user in file conversion activities is healthy because it tends to build user confidence in the new data base and in the computer-based system.

Changeover Plan (Operation Phase)

The activities described in the preceding sections were the elements of a conversion plan that is implemented throughout the development phase. By the time of the acceptance review at the end of the development phase, forms and procedures have been prepared and used, computer programs have been written and tested, and old files have been converted to new files. The next step in the conversion process is the actual changeover from the old system to the new, which takes place at the beginning of the operation phase.

A changeover plan that identifies and schedules all changeover activities should be available at the acceptance review. It should specify the method of changeover and identify the roles and responsibilities of all personnel. The three general methods of **changeover** from the old system to the new system are parallel operation, immediate replacement, or phased changeover.

In *parallel operation,* data is processed by both the old and new systems. In theory, this method offers many advantages. Users have maximum flexibility because they do not have to begin using the new system until they are certain it is producing acceptable outputs. They know they can always revert to the old system in the event of disaster. In practice, unfortunately, there are several reasons why a "pure" parallel operation method of changeover seldom is possible:

1. The new system is different from the old system. It probably has been designed to perform functions and produce outputs that were not available with the old system.
2. Parallel processing may be too time-consuming or expensive, particularly if personnel are not available to operate both systems. This is particularly true if the volume of work is large.
3. Determining which system is in error can be difficult. People tend to be biased toward the familiar; in this case, toward the old system.
4. Parallel processing tends to delay adoption of the new system. People tend to cling to a "security blanket," thus prolonging the problems the new system was designed to solve.

Immediate replacement—requiring immediate use of the new system—is a risky alternative. The outputs of the new system may be compared with the last outputs of the old system to identify errors. Correcting errors usually creates crisis situations during the early stages of immediate replacement. The circumstances under which immediate replacement usually occurs are those in which:

1. A high percentage of outputs are new.
2. The system is not so critical that failure is a disaster.
3. No type of parallel processing is possible.
4. The user exerts "pressure" for use of the system outputs.
5. An alternate, or fallback, system is available.

Phased changeover is a compromise between parallel operation and immediate replacement; it is recommended over the other two methods. In this method users process some percentage, perhaps 10 percent of their normal volume of transactions, through the new system, with the remainder processed through the old system. Thus users can become familiar with the operation of the new system, and the task of correcting errors is manageable with existing resources. After the users are assured that normal transactions are being processed correctly, more complex transactions can be introduced. The volume of data handled by the new system can then be increased until the old system is phased out. The success of phase changeover is enhanced if the changeover plan is properly scheduled for sequence and timing, for introducing elements of the new system, and for terminating corresponding parts of the old system.

Whatever changeover method is selected, problems will arise. We will discuss the actual changeover in chapter 19, "The Operation Phase."

An initial operating schedule should also be prepared. Its purpose is to demonstrate how the new computer program can perform its functions in a timely fashion in the "real world." The schedule should identify groups of computer program components that must be run without interruption on a regular basis. These groups are called run modules. Such a schedule is prepared in conjunction with the operations staff of the data processing department.

Implementation Management

We have discussed the four major elements of the implementation plan: test plans, training plans, an equipment installation plan, and a conversion plan. Each of these elements may be complex, involving the combined efforts of a large number of people, many of whom are unfamiliar with the new system. At the beginning of this chapter we suggested that one technique for managing the entire implementation task was to establish implementation teams, each one to be responsible for a major element of the implementation plan. However, for the team approach to be effective, there must be a central reporting point. Often the implementation teams will report to a coordination committee. The membership of such a committee should include the heads of the implementation teams, the primary users of the system, and representatives from the information service organization. The senior systems analyst is responsible for forming this committee and for selecting its members. In doing so, the analyst should consult with the principal user of the new system.

The responsibility for heading the *implementation committee* belongs to the principal user, not the systems analyst. This user already has a major commitment to the success of the system. With the principal user as head of the implementation committee, his or her emotional commitment and readiness to accept the system as it approaches operational status will increase. There are also other advantages:

1. User leadership will demonstrate that the system is "real" and not just an "exercise."
2. The user, as a "line" manager, can bring additional authority to the project. The user can take direct action to resolve and to prevent problems.
3. Because of involvement in implementation management, the user will be prepared to conduct a knowledgeable acceptance review at the end of the development phase. The user will be predisposed to accept a system that he or she feels is ready for operational status.
4. The user's involvement in and commitment to the success of the system will carry over into the operation phase. This will help the analyst during the critical changeover period.

Although the systems analyst does not head the implementation committee, the analyst is an important member. Often the systems analyst functions as the committee secretary, providing the planning and scheduling skills needed to manage the many implementation tasks. Because these tasks can be defined and are similar for almost all computer-based systems, it is appropriate to consider using critical path networks, such as PERT, which was described in Chapter 4, Project Management.

Summary

The development phase is the third of the four life-cycle phases. This is the phase in which the computer-related business information system is developed to conform to the requirements prepared in the design phase. The information system project is expanded to include additional personnel, such as programmers. The principal activities performed during the development phase relate to implementation planning, including preparation of a changeover plan; equipment acquisition; computer program design, debugging, and testing; personnel training; and system tests.

Implementation is the process of bringing a developed system into operational use and turning it over to the user. Often it is effective to form implementation teams. An implementation plan is necessary; its major elements include test plans, training plans, an equipment installation plan, and a conversion plan. The test plan provides for the preparation of test data and for testing the system in a planned, structured manner. Top-down computer program development, as contrasted with bottom-up computer program development, is a contemporary technique for testing computer program modules as they are developed. Test reports document the performance of the system and its subsystems.

Training plans are necessary to ensure that all persons who are associated with the computer-related information system have the necessary knowledge and skills. Reference manuals are prepared to assist in the training of programmers, operators, and user personnel. An important activity related to training is management orientation.

Equipment implementation is an activity that is completed during the development phase. The principal equipment-related activities are: site preparation, equipment installation, and hardware and software check-out.

Conversion is the process of initiating and performing all of the physical operations that result directly in the turnover of the new system to the user. There are two parts to conversion: (1) a conversion plan, which is implemented throughout the development phase, and (2) a changeover plan for moving the system from the development phase into the operation phase. The conversion plan includes procedures conversion, program conversion, and file conversion. The changeover plan also specifies the method of changeover from the old to the new system. Choices of changeover methods include parallel operation, immediate replacement, or phased changeover. The latter usually is the recommended method.

An implementation management team, which includes the head of each implementation team, primary users of the system, and members of the information service organization, oversees the implementation preparation activities. Implementation activities are complex. PERT is a management planning analysis tool that is often used in such situations.

For Review

development phase
implementation plan
conversion plan
development phase review
changeover plan
development phase report
system specification
user acceptance review
implementation
bottom-up computer program
   development
top-down computer program
   development

HIPO chart
stub
structured walk-through
reference manual
system specification
conversion
changeover
parallel operation
immediate replacement
phased changeover
implementation committee
front-end loading

For Discussion

1. Distinguish between implementation, conversion, and changeover.
2. Define and discuss the advantages and disadvantages of bottom-up and top-down testing of computer programs.
3. What is the preferred method of computer program testing?
4. What is front-end loading?
5. In what way does this chapter illustrate how CASE tools can reduce the time and cost associated with the SDLC?
6. Discuss the importance of testing prior to changeover.
7. What are the principal reference manuals? Describe the content of each.
8. What is the value of including management orientation sessions in a training program?
9. Describe and compare the three general changeover methods.
10. What is an implementation team? An implementation committee?
11. Describe the roles of the systems analyst and the principal user throughout the system implementation process.
12. What is the purpose of the development phase report? The acceptance review?
13. What is the system specification? How does it relate to cumulative documentation?
14. How might PERT be used to assist in the management of the development phase activities?

For Exercise: Development Phase PERT Network

The development phase is one in which many important activities occur, often in parallel. PERT is a useful tool for planning complex, interrelated activities. Referring to the Unit Six Overview and to this chapter, prepare a PERT chart that you, as project manager, might use to manage the development phase activities.

Chapter

17

■ ■ ■

Computer
Program
Development

Preview

It is the responsibility of programmers to write the computer programs that make up the computer program component of the overall business information system, but it is the systems analyst who provides the programmers with the program requirements. These requirements include a written statement of the problem; a copy of the detailed data flow diagrams; and copies of the input, output, and file design specifications. The analyst provides these written requirements along with the documentation produced in the design phase.

Objectives

1. You will be able to list the steps that are used by programmers to develop computer programs and to ensure that the programs function properly.
2. You will be able to describe how programmers use design specifications to develop the computer programs using procedural programming languages.
3. You will be able to identify nonprocedural programming languages.

Key Terms

algorithm   a set of rules or instructions used to accomplish a task.

coding   the process of writing instructions in a programming language, such as C, COBOL, dBASE, or RPG.

debugging   the process of testing a computer program for errors and correcting any errors found.

structured walk-through   a review technique that is used to uncover flaws in program definition, planning, or coding. It is a team effort by two or more programmers to review or "walk through" the definition, plan, or code with the programmer assigned to the program.

procedural programming languages those languages that are oriented toward the step-by-step procedures or instructions that the computer must follow to produce the desired output.

nonprocedural programming languages those languages that emphasize the data rather than the procedural steps required to access the data.

Creating a Computer Program

The steps in the development of each of the computer programs that make up the computer program component of a system are as follows:

1. Define the function of the program.
2. Plan the logic of the program.
3. Code the program.
4. Test and debug the program.
5. Complete the documentation.

Defining the Problem

Although the programmer is responsible for writing the computer program, the systems analyst must communicate the computer program requirements to the programmer. The function of each program was defined for the programmer when functions were allocated during system design. Detailed data flow diagrams are prepared for each program from the decomposed DFDs created during the design phase. These DFDs define the function of each program.

Planning the Problem Solution

In program planning, the logic to be used to solve the problem is developed. Algorithms, computer program logic flowcharts or pseudocode, and structure charts are useful tools for program planning. **Algorithms** are sets of rules or instructions used to accomplish tasks. They are stated as formulas, decision tables, or narratives. The program logic flowchart, pseudocode, structure chart, and algorithms that result from program planning are retained and become part of the project documentation.

Writing the Program

The next step, writing, or **coding,** a program, is the actual writing of computer instructions. These instructions will be translated to machine code and followed by the computer; they should follow the steps of the program logic plan. Several *programming languages,* particularly C, COBOL, dBASE, and RPG, are commonly used to solve business problems. An example of one of these procedural programming languages is given later in this chapter. In addition to these traditional languages, organizations using data base management systems may choose to generate programs using the query language of the DBMS. These query languages are a part of a package of programming tools known as fourth-generation languages. An example of a non-procedural language is presented later in this chapter. Each language has its advantages and disadvantages. Most computer installations have a standard language used by their progammers. Programmers usually are not given a choice of languages unless special circumstances exist.

Testing the Program

Testing and debugging a program involve (1) translating the coded program into machine language, a process called *compilation;* and (2) testing the translated program with sample data and checking the result. If the results of testing are not correct, the program is said to have "bugs." **Debugging** is the process of correcting computer programs to obtain correct results. As emphasized in chapter 16, testing must be planned and structured to reduce the change that errors will be overlooked.

Completing the Program Documentation

The last step is to complete the documentation for the program. The documentation must include a statement of the purpose of the program (from step 1), a description of the solution logic (step 2), a listing of the program instructions (step 3), and sample outputs from the completed programs (step 4). Information provided to the programmer by the analyst, such as descriptions of program inputs, outputs, and files, should be included. Instructions to operators explaining how the program is to be used must be written before the program documentation is complete.

Procedural Programming Languages

Procedural programming languages are those that are oriented toward the step-by-step procedures or instructions that the computer must follow to produce the desired output. C, COBOL, and dBASE are all common examples of procedural languages. The emphasis of these languages is on the processing steps. The vast majority of all business programs are written in one of these procedural programming languages.

These traditional business programming languages are all referred to as third-generation programming languages. These languages, also called high-level programming languages, represented a tremendous improvement in programmer productivity over the assembler-level (low-level) languages commonly used during the 1960s and 1970s.

The productivity improvement resulting from the use of high-level languages came from two characteristics: (1) the instructions are made up of English words rather than mnemonic codes, and (2) each written instruction accomplishes more than most individual instructions written in assembler. In addition, high-level languages are not machine dependent. That is, the programs can be moved to different computer systems with little or no modification. Programs written in a low-level language generally cannot be run on any computer system other than the one for which they were written.

Structured Programming Concepts

Structured programming is a top-down approach to the creation of a program that is comparable to the approach defined by the system development life-cycle concept. It is more than a technique used in coding a program; it describes the development of the program from program function definition to documentation.

Structured programs are made up of a series of program modules, each of which performs a single function. The first (top) module of the program logic has the most general function. All following modules develop the logic to more detailed levels, with the last modules each performing one specific, detailed function. The program functions must be carefully defined, and each of the modules that will carry out these functions must be planned in detail. If the planning is properly completed, the actual coding of the program is not a difficult task. Structured programs are made up of combinations of only four logical structures, as follows:

1. Sequence—the structure where instructions are executed in the sequence they are coded.
2. If-Then-Else—the decision structure that states a condition and "then" what should be done if the condition is true, "else" what to do if the condition is false.
3. Iteration (looping)—the structure that causes a module to be repeated.
4. Case—a selection structure that allows for the execution of one of several modules, depending upon a data element value.

Any program can be written using only these four logical structures. The major advantages of structured programs are as follows:

1. The initial development time and cost of the program are less because even complex structured programs are easier to code, test, and debug than are nonstructured programs.
2. The time and costs associated with modifying a structured program are less because the program logic is easier to understand and update.

Program Coding and Debugging Example

The data edit program of OARS provides an example of computer program development. The problem definition is provided for the programmer in the form of a data flow diagram of the data edit function. Figure 17.1 illustrates the required detail. This data flow diagram was developed during the design phase activities.

Before the programmer can code the computer program, additional details of the input, storage, and output must be provided. Input layouts were developed during input design (chapter 14), print charts and screen layouts during output design (chapter 13), and file descriptions during the data modeling activities (chapter 12). Figure 17.2 is a print chart developed during the output design.

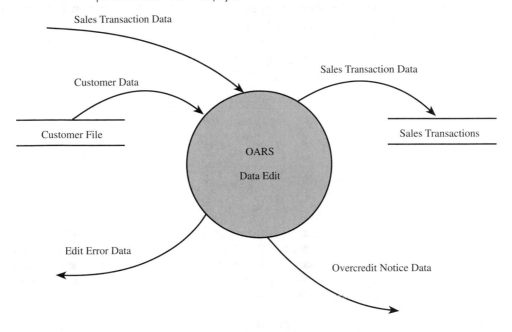

To aid the programmer, algorithms to express the rules or logic of solving the problem in the form of *decision tables, structured English,* or *decision trees,* may be provided. The programmer then develops a computer program logic flowchart and/ or a logic description in *pseudocode.* Figure 17.3 is a decision table that depicts the logic used to determine the requirement for an overcredit notice. Figure 17.4 shows one page of a computer program logic flowchart. Figure 17.5 shows the equivalent logic plan using pseudocode.

After completing the logic plan, the programmer can code the program logic. Figure 17.6 depicts the coding of the segment in figure 17.4 or 17.5. It uses the procedural programming language called COBOL (**CO**mmon **B**usiness **O**riented **L**anguage).

Each program must be tested by the programmer until all errors are found and corrected. Each output must match the planned output in the print charts and display layouts. Figure 17.7 illustrates the overcredit notice produced by the data edit program. Note that the output corresponds to the print chart of figure 17.2.

After testing and debugging each program, the programmer turns over all documentation to the analyst so that the program can replace its "stub" in the overall top-down procedure for the design, development, and testing of the computer program component of the computer-based business information system.

■ Figure 17.2 Overcredit notification print chart. Output descriptions created during the design phase are used to communicate system output requirements to the programmers.

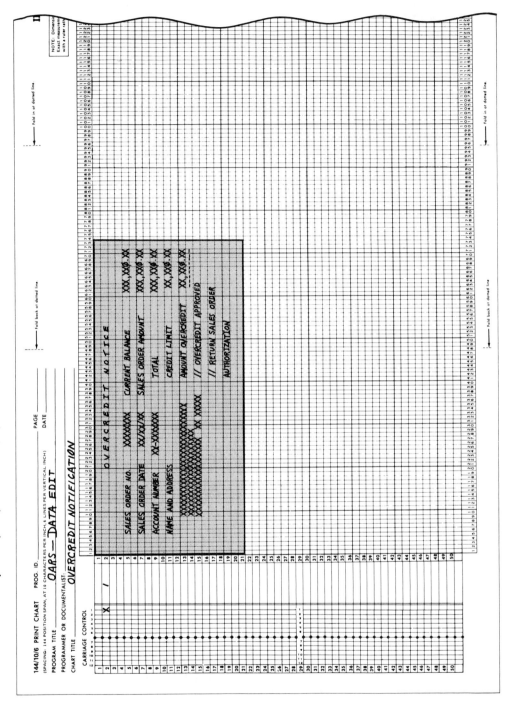

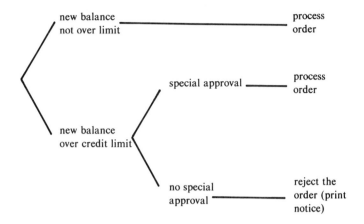

Structured Walk-Throughs

Structured walk-throughs are a review technique used to uncover flaws in program definition, planning, or coding. It is a team effort by two or more programmers to review or "walk through" the definition, plan, or code with the programmer assigned to the program. As the programmer in charge of the program verbally describes and explains what he or she has accomplished to date, weaknesses in the definition, plan, or code are brought out. This is due to the fact that when you hear yourself explain something to other programmers, it sounds different than when the ideas are just thoughts within you. In addition, the other programmers will often recognize procedures that are not well defined or that will not work as the programmer hoped they would. On the positive side, the other programmers in the team will suggest improvements to the approaches, or even better approaches to the solution of the problem. The motivating factor that encourages other programmers to participate in the structured walk-through and make an effort to contribute to developing the program is that they too will be conducting structured walk-throughs on their projects and will want the same quality of assistance.

Nonprocedural Programming Languages

Nonprocedural progamming languages are those languages that emphasize the data rather than the procedural steps required to access the data. RPG is an example of an early programming language that uses the description of the inputs, calculations, and outputs rather than coding the procedure steps to access the input data and to create the required outputs. Other than to organize the sequence of calculation steps,

■ Figure 17.4   OARs computer program flowchart segment. The programmers will use flowcharts or other planning techniques to design the computer program logic. This example includes the logic of the decision tree shown in figure 17.3.

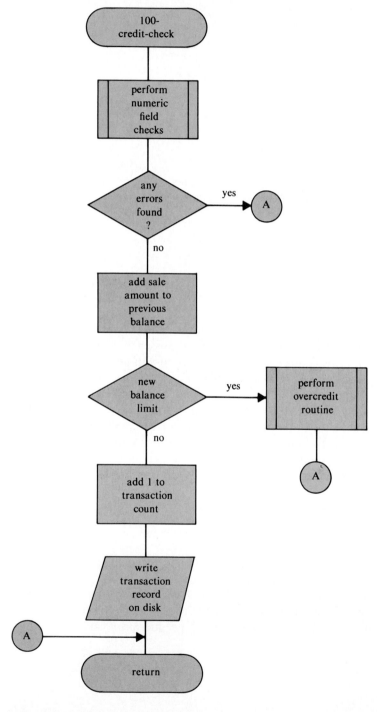

OARS pseudocode segment. Pseudocode is a common alternative to flowcharting for planning program logic. This pseudocode example conveys logic that is equivalent to the flowchart of figure 17.4.

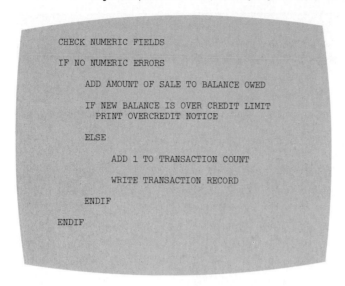

```
CHECK NUMERIC FIELDS

IF NO NUMERIC ERRORS

        ADD AMOUNT OF SALE TO BALANCE OWED

        IF NEW BALANCE IS OVER CREDIT LIMIT
           PRINT OVERCREDIT NOTICE

        ELSE

                ADD 1 TO TRANSACTION COUNT

                WRITE TRANSACTION RECORD

        ENDIF

ENDIF
```

■ Figure 17.6   OARS data edit coding sample. This coding sample, using COBOL, was written following the logic plan depicted in figures 17.4 and 17.5.

```
080010******************************************************
080120*                                                    *
080030*        THIS ROUTINE IS PERFORMED FOR CREDIT LIMIT   *
080040*        CHECKS.  IT ALSO CHECKS ALL NUMERIC FIELDS   *
080050*        TO VERIFY THAT THEY CONTAIN VALID NUMERIC DATA. *
080060*                                                    *
080070******************************************************
080080
080090 100-CREDIT-LIMIT-ROUTINE.
080100     PERFORM 1001-NUMERIC-FIELD-CHECK.
080110     IF NUMERIC-ERRORS IS EQUAL TO 'NO'
080120         ADD SALE-AMOUNT TO ACCOUNT-BALANCE
080130         IF ACCOUNT-BALANCE IS GREATER THAN CREDIT-LIMIT
080140             PERFORM 1002-OVERCREDIT-ROUTINE
080150         ELSE
080160             ADD 1 TO TRANSACTION-COUNT
080170             WRITE TRANSACTION-RECORD.
```

OARS data edit sample output. This overcredit notification is an example of an actual output produced by the OARS system. It matches the output design for overcredit notification shown in figure 17.2.

OVERCREDIT NOTIFICATION

Sales Order No. 00069721	Current Balance	2,320.50
Sales Order Date 10/15/93	Sales Order Amount	1,516.02
Account Number 02-0000367	Total	3,836.52
Name and Address	Credit Limit	3,500.00
ABC Corporation	Amount Overcredit	336.52
2234 Washington Blvd.		
Big City CA 91789	/ / Overcredit Approved	
	/ / Return Sales Order	
	Authorization	

there is nothing for the programmer to flowchart. RPG is still very commonly used in the programming of business systems with the midrange-sized computers such as the IBM AS/400. Even though the RPG language has been used for many years, it continues to be updated and improved to keep pace with today's requirements.

Most of the nonprocedural progamming languages are referred to as *fourth-generation languages* (4GLs) and are a component of data base management systems (DBMSs). There are several different types of data base management systems, as described in chapter 12, "Data Modeling." Each brand name of DBMS has its own variation of a fourth-generation language, called a query language. Nonprocedural programming languages fall into the categories of structured query language (SQL), natural languages, or object-oriented programming systems (OOPS).

Structured Query Language (SQL)

In the mid-seventies, a query language standard was developed called *Structured Query Language (SQL)*. Today, many DBMSs support the SQL standard, sometimes in addition to their own query language. The productivity improvement of fourth-generation languages, such as SQL, over earlier languages is significant. The productivity was enhanced in essentially two ways: (1) the commands are briefer with a less rigid syntax; and (2) each command accomplishes as much as several commands in third-generation languages. Fourth-generation languages are available not only on

■ Figure 17.8   OARS Customer table creation This SQL command creates the table called Customer for the OARS project. Each field is named and described by the type of data and the length of the field.

```
 Layout Words  Go To  Print   Exit
[···◆···▼1···◆·▼··2····▼····3·◆·▼····4▼···◆···▼5····◆·▼··6····▼····?··▼·◆····]
 CREATE TABLE CUSTOMER
     (CUST_NO        CHAR(10),
      NAME           CHAR(26),
      ADDRESS        CHAR(20),
      CITY           CHAR(18),
      STATE          CHAR(02),
      ZIP_CODE       CHAR(05),
      DISC_CODE      CHAR(02),
      CUR_BAL        NUMERIC(10,2),
      BAL_30         NUMERIC(10,2),
      BAL_60         NUMERIC(10,2),
      BAL_90         NUMERIC(10,2),
      BAL_OV_90      NUMERIC(10,2),
      CR_LIMIT       NUMERIC(08,2));




 SQL        C:\dbase4\oars\oarssql\    Line: 15 Col:1     DB: OARSSQL       Num   Ins
```

mainframes, but also on midrange computers and microcomputers. In most cases, the query commands are exactly the same on mainframes, midrange computers, and microcomputers. This allows for developing the program on one size machine, and then uploading it to a larger machine or downloading it to a smaller machine.

Figure 17.8 is an example of the command required to create a table (or file) in SQL. The statement consists of a list of the fields (or columns) and their description for each record (or row). Remember that files in the relational model of a DBMS are called tables which are made up of rows and columns. This SQL example was done using the SQL support within dBASE IV. One approach to adding data to the SQL table is with the insert command, as shown in figure 17.9. The values must be in the same sequence as the fields in the table.

When the data is to be retrieved from a table, a select command is used. Figure 17.10 illustrates a simple select command that will retrieve all fields from the table called Product. The asterisk means "all fields." If only some of the fields were required, the field names would be listed instead of the asterisk. Figure 17.11 depicts the output result of the select command shown in figure 17.10.

It should be noted that SQL commands may not only be used to make on-line queries, but may be imbedded within the code of a procedural programming language. It is very common to imbed SQL within a COBOL program so that the data access is handled by SQL and the calculations and output formatting are handled through COBOL.

■ Figure 17.9   Inserting data into the OARS Product table. This SQL command inserts a record into the table called
Product. The data to be inserted must be in the same sequence as the fields appear in the table.

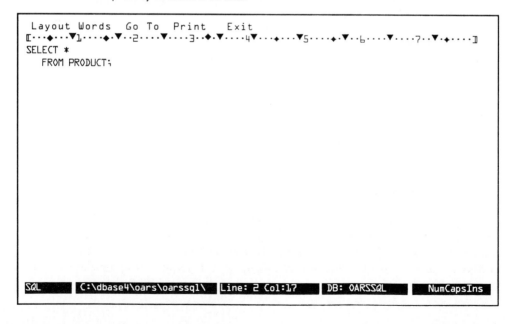

```
 Layout  Words   Go  To   Print    Exit
[[···◆···▼]]····◆·▼··2····▼····3··◆·▼····4▼···+····▼5····+·▼··b····▼····7··▼·+····]]
INSERT INTO PRODUCT
   VALUES ("00123", "Chrome Gadget", 12.95);




SQL        C:\dbase4\oars\oarssql\    Line:  2 Col:45    DB: OARSSQL        Num Caps Ins
```

■ Figure 17.10   Accessing data in the Product table. This SQL select command retrieves all the data in the table called
Product. The asterisk means "all fields." If only some of the data were required, the asterisk would be
replaced by the names of the fields.

```
 Layout  Words   Go  To   Print    Exit
[[··◆····▼]]····◆·▼··2····▼····3··◆·▼····4▼···+····▼5····+·▼··b····▼····7··▼·+····]]
SELECT *
   FROM PRODUCT;




SQL        C:\dbase4\oars\oarssql\    Line: 2 Col:17    DB: OARSSQL        NumCapsIns
```

OARS Product table data. This is the output of the SQL select command illustrated in figure 17.10. In a relational table, each row is a record and each column is a field.

```
PROD-CODE  PROD-DESC       UNIT-PRICE
00123      Chrome Gadget        12.95
00124      Brass Gadget         17.85
00125      Silver Gadget        45.50
00126      Gold Gadget         106.25




SQL        C:\dbase4\oars\oarssql\            DB: OARSSQL      NumCaps
```

Natural Languages

While the SQL commands are relatively brief, they still require a specific syntax for the computer to understand them. That means that anyone using interactive SQL, including users, must also memorize the SQL commands and the syntax. Natural languages are an attempt to avoid having to learn specific commands or command syntax.

A *natural language* allows users to ask for the data they require using English statements. An example of a natural language statement might be "List all names of customers with a balance greater than 3,000." The system searches through the statement looking for words that it recognizes as action terms (list all); field names, file names, and constants (names of customers and balance); and relationships (greater than 3000). With this information, the system forms the appropriate computer command to retrieve the requested data.

Natural language systems do a lot for the user and, therefore, require powerful computers or workstations in order to have acceptable response times.

Object-Oriented Languages

One of the newest of the nonprocedural progamming language approaches is the object-oriented programming system. *Object-oriented programming systems (OOPS)* are those that are oriented toward objects such as invoices, sales orders, and the like.

They are a natural extension of the data orientation of the nonprocedural programming languages, the difference being that the data orientation is at the object level rather than at the level of the individual data elements that make up an object.

Code Generators

Code generators are software packages that generate the program code from descriptions of the data and processing. Often code generators are included in CASE tool packages and DBMSs as well as being available as stand-alone packages.

Code generators as a part of an integrated CASE tool are a natural extension of developing a system using computerized tools. The current CASE packages that include integrated code generators are the "high-end" packages and are quite expensive.

Even DBMSs for microcomputers, such as dBASE IV, include a code generator. Complete dBASE IV programs can be generated without knowing anything about being a programmer. This gives users and programmers a very powerful tool for developing systems.

The user of a code generator has to supply a description about the data, required menus, decision logic, and all inputs and outputs. While code generators can do much of the programming task, they do not do the systems analysis and design. You must know what you want from the system before you can use a code generator.

Summary

It is the responsibility of programmers to write the programs required for the computer program component of a business information system. These programs, however, must be written according to the specifications provided by the analyst. The specifications provided usually include the design of the inputs, outputs, and files, along with a copy of the appropriate data flow diagrams.

Five steps in the development of a computer program are: (1) define the problem to be solved, (2) plan the logic for a solution to the problem, (3) write the program following the logic plan, (4) test and debug the program, and (5) complete the documentation for the program. When these steps are completed, the program and its documentation are ready to be included in the system tests. The modern approach to writing programs is called structured programming. This approach dictates that the program be written in single-function modules that are written from the most general to the most detailed functions. This is a top-down approach that is consistent with the system development life-cycle concept.

An aid to the development of error-free programs is a review technique called a structured walk-through. In this review, the programmer describes and explains his or her problem definition, logic plan, or code to a team of two or more other programmers. The team has the responsibility of pointing out flaws in the logic and suggesting alternative approaches to the programmer.

Improved programming languages called nonprocedural languages or fourth-generation languages (4GLs) are used with data base management systems. These languages are query languages with very powerful commands. They vary from powerful query languages such as SQL to natural languages written in a near-English syntax. As compared to procedural languages, nonprocedural languages concentrate on the data rather than the processing steps. The most advanced of these data-oriented language approaches is one called object-oriented programming systems (OOPS).

For Review

program	decision tree
structure chart	structured English
algorithm	pseudocode
coding	structured walk-throughs
programming languages	nonprocedural programming languages
compilation	fourth-generation languages (4GLs)
debugging	structured query language (SQL)
procedural programming languages	natural languages
structured programming	code generators
decision table	

For Discussion

1. What are the five steps in computer program development?
2. What is program planning?
3. What is an algorithm? Give an example.
4. Who is responsible for testing a computer program? For subsystem testing?
5. What is pseudocode? What is its relationship to structured English?
6. What are the responsibilities of the systems analyst for computer program development?
7. What is meant by the top-down approach in structured programming?
8. What are the five programming structures used in structured programming?
9. What is a structured walk-through? Who is involved?
10. What makes the structured walk-through so successful in finding potential errors as compared to an individual programmer approach?
11. What is the difference between procedural and nonprocedural programming languages?
12. What is a natural language? What is its advantage over other language systems?

For Exercise: Computer Program Development Report

Visit a local business that has computer-based information systems and determine what computer hardware and programming languages they use. Write a brief report on your findings. Some questions to ask are:

Do they have a mainframe computer?

What programming languages are used on this computer?

Are most programs for the mainframe purchased, contracted, or developed in-house?

Do they have midrange-sized computers?

What programming languages are used on these computers?

Are most programs for the midrange computers purchased, contracted, or developed in-house?

Do they have microcomputers?

What programming languages are used on the microcomputers?

Are most of the microcomputer programs purchased, contracted, or developed in-house?

Chapter

18

■ ■ ■

Development Phase Report and Review

Preview

At the conclusion of the development phase, the analyst prepares a report and reviews it with the principal user of the computer-based business information system. The central element of the development phase report is the system specification, which is an "as built" specification. The development phase review is attended by all of the users and managers who will be affected by the system. This is a particularly critical review, since a successful outcome initiates the changeover from a project to an operational system.

Objectives

1. You will be able to describe the content of a system specification.
2. You will be able to prepare a development phase report.
3. You will be able to explain the purposes of a development phase review.

Key Terms

development phase report a report prepared at the end of the development phase; it is an extension of the design phase report and summarizes the results of the development phase activities.

system specification a baseline specification that contains all of the essential system documentation; it is a complete technical specification.

development phase review a review held with the user organization at the conclusion of the development phase to determine whether or not to enter the operation phase.

System Specification

The development phase is concluded by the completion of three major milestone activities. These are:

1. Preparation of the system specification
2. Preparation of the development phase report
3. Conducting of the development phase review

The **development phase report** is built around the system specification—the third and final major *baseline document.* The system specification evolves from the design specification, just as that baseline specification evolved from the performance specification. Whereas the *design specification* is a "build to" specification, the **system specification** is an "as built" specification. It is the major reference document for all personnel who will use, maintain, or operate the computer-based business system. Figure 18.1 illustrates the content of a typical system specification. Like the performance and design specifications, the system specification is divided into two parts. The first part is an external specification relating to the interaction of the information system with its environment; the second part is an *internal system specification* that completely documents the computer program component of the system. The system specification is the result of documenting the development phase activities previously described in chapters 16 and 17.

Development Phase Report

Structure and Content

Figure 18.2 displays the structure and content of the development phase report, which is similar to the study phase and design phase reports. It has the same five major divisions and is an extension of the cumulative documentation performed in the predecessor phases. When completed, the development phase report completely documents the information system design.

Unless changes to the performance definition, the design specification, or both, occur during the development phase, the system scope section is not altered. If there have been any changes in scope, these should be discussed fully. The conclusions and recommendations relate to the next life-cycle phase, the operation phase, and focus on the next major decision. This is the decision to change over from the existing system to the new system. Important inputs to the changeover decision are (1) the completed system specification, (2) satisfactory system test reports, (3) the availability of trained personnel, and (4) a changeover plan.

In preparing conclusions and recommendations, the analyst must take into consideration the environment in which the computer-based business information system will be maintained and operated after conversion from the old to the new system is completed. Preliminary operational schedules, prepared as part of the *changeover plan,* should be used to demonstrate that the new system will mesh with the schedules for ongoing data processing jobs.

System specification outline. The system specification is the technical core of the development phase report. It has two major sections: an external system requirement and an internal system requirement.

SYSTEM SPECIFICATION

A. EXTERNAL SYSTEM SPECIFICATION
   1. context diagram
   2. system output specifications
   3. system input specifications
   4. system resource specifications
   5. system test specifications
   6. training specifications

B. INTERNAL SYSTEM SPECIFICATION
   1. computer program component
      a. top-level data flow diagrams
      b. data base specification
      c. top-level structure chart
      d. system test specifications
         (1) test data
         (2) test results — samples

   2. computer program design (for each program)
      a. decomposed data flow diagram
      b. data storage specification
      c. structure chart
      d. transaction file specifications
      e. control specifications
      f. program listings
      g. test specifications
         (1) test data
         (2) test results — samples
      h. special conditions

The system specification, plans and cost schedules, and appropriate appendices follow the position of conclusions and recommendations in the development phase report. The system specification is used to prepare the programmer's, operator's, and user's reference manuals. Also, it is the basis for developing materials needed to inform and train all personnel who will use or be affected by the information system. The documentation and graphics display capabilities of a CASE tool can greatly assist in creating and maintaining the baseline specifications and in the preparation of manuals and training aids.

The systems analyst updates the major milestones project plan and the cost schedules to display the completion of the development phase. The analyst identifies and describes significant changes that have occurred since the design phase review and also prepares cost estimates for operating and maintaining the new system elements. The appendices that appeared in the design phase report are reviewed, modified, and updated as necessary.

■ Figure 18.2   Development phase report outline. The development phase report, completed at the end of the development phase, has five major sections equivalent to those in the study phase and design phase reports: system scope, conclusions and recommendations, design specification, plans and cost schedules, and appendices. The content is expanded to include the results of the design phase activities.

DEVELOPMENT PHASE REPORT

I. SYSTEM SCOPE
   a. system title
   b. problem statement and purpose
   c. constraints
   d. specific objectives
   e. method of evaluation

II. CONCLUSIONS AND RECOMMENDATIONS
   a. conclusions
   b. recommendations

III. SYSTEM SPECIFICATION
   a. external system specification
   b. internal system specification

IV. PLANS AND COST SCHEDULES
   a. detailed milestones–development phase
   b. major milestones–all phases
   c. changeover plan
   d. operational plan

V. APPENDICES–as appropriate

Example Development Phase Report

An example of a development phase report appears on the following pages as *Exhibit 3—OARS Development Phase Report.*

Development Phase Review

A successful **development phase review** marks the beginning of the transition from a project to an operational system. The immediate consequence of an approval to proceed is the initiation of the changeover activity. Therefore, it is critically important that all the factors that will ensure an effective transition from the old system to the new system be considered. All organizations involved in or significantly affected by the pending conversion should be alerted and be invited to participate in the review. The development phase report should be distributed to them beforehand; the study phase and design phase reports, prepared at the conclusion of earlier phases, are provided as reference documents. In addition, the review group should have had an opportunity to read the changeover plan and the test reports. A commitment to the changeover activities should be obtained from each major participant before a decision is made to embark on the operation phase.

Summary

Upon completion of the development phase activities, the systems analyst prepares a development phase report. This report contains the system specification, which is the complete technical specification for the computer-based business information system. The system specification is the expansion of the design specification into the final baseline specification. The system specification contains two parts: an external system specification and an internal system specification. The external specification relates to the interaction of the information system with its environment. For example, it contains the training procedures and user manuals. The internal specification provides the complete documentation for the computer program component of the information system.

After the principal user has had an opportunity to study the development phase report, a review is held and a decision is made whether or not to enter the operation phase. A decision to proceed marks the transition from a project to an operational system. Therefore, the changeover plan is an important element of the development phase review, and a commitment to the changeover activities must be obtained from all major users of the system prior to initiation of the operation phase.

For Review

development phase report	internal system specification
baseline document	changeover plan
design specification	external system specification
system specification	development phase review

For Discussion

1. What is the purpose of the development phase report?
2. What is the content of the development phase report?
3. Discuss the importance of the system specification, including its relationship to the performance and design specifications.
4. What project plans and schedules are presented at the development phase review?
5. What is the purpose of the development phase review?

E X H I B I T **3**

■ ■ ■

The Development Phase Report— OARS Case Study

The in-text case study of an on-line accounts receivable system (OARS) introduced in chapter 7, "Initial Investigation," is continued with this example of a development phase report. This exhibit completes the SDLC documentation process started in chapter 10 as Exhibit 1, *The Study Phase Report—OARS Case Study,* and continued in chapter 15 as Exhibit 2, *The Design Phase Report—OARS Case Study.*

OARS Development Phase Report

I. System Scope
   A. System Title
      On-line Accounts Receivable System (OARS)
   B. Problem Statement and Purpose

The ABCO corporation's present accounts receivable system is at its maximum capacity of 10,000 accounts. The number of accounts is expected to double to 20,000 accounts over a five-year period. The present system cannot meet this projected growth and satisfy the corporate goal of distributing information processing resources to regional profit centers. Serious problems have already been encountered in processing the current volume of accounts. Specific problems that have been identified are as follows:

   1. Saturation of the capacity of the present computer system, causing difficulties in adding new accounts and obtaining information about the status of existing accounts.
   2. Processing delays in preparing customer billing statements because of the batch-oriented design of the current accounts receivable system.
   3. Excessive elapsed time between mailing of customer statements and receipt of payments, which creates a high-cost, four-day float.
   4. Inadequate control of credit limits.
   5. Inability to provide regional centers with timely customer-related information.

Therefore, the purpose of the OARS project is to replace the existing accounts receivable system with one that can eliminate the stated problems enumerated above and meet ABCO's growth and regional accountability goals.

C. Constraints

The OARS constraints are as follows:

1. Development of the on-line accounts receivable system is to be completed within fourteen months.
2. OARS is to have a growth potential to handle 20,000 customer accounts.
3. OARS is to be designed as an on-line system operating in a distributed data processing environment.
4. The design must be compatible with corporate plans to install regional profit centers.

D. Specific Objectives

The specific objectives of OARS are as follows:

1. To establish billing cycles for each region.
2. To mail customer statements no later than one day after the close of a billing cycle.
3. To provide the customer with a billing statement two days after the close of a billing cycle.
4. To speed up collections, reducing the float by 50 percent.
5. To examine customer account balances through on-line inquiry at the time of order entry.

E. Method of Evaluation

After OARS has been operational from sixty to ninety days:

1. A statistical analysis will be made of customer account processing to verify the elapsed time between the close of the billing cycle and the mailing of customer statements.
2. The float time will be measured, and the cost of the float will be calculated at three-month intervals.
3. Periodically, random samples of customer accounts in each region will be audited for accuracy and to validate the effectiveness of on-line inquiry.
4. The validity of OARS transactions that affect the inventory system will be measured by random sampling and physical count.
5. Personal evaluations of the effectiveness of the system will be obtained from its principal users.

II. Conclusions and Recommendations

A. Conclusions

The on-line accounts receivable system (OARS) is ready for operation. The system tests have been successfully completed; all required personnel have completed training; and the changeover plan has been reviewed and approved. All phases were completed on schedule and within budget.

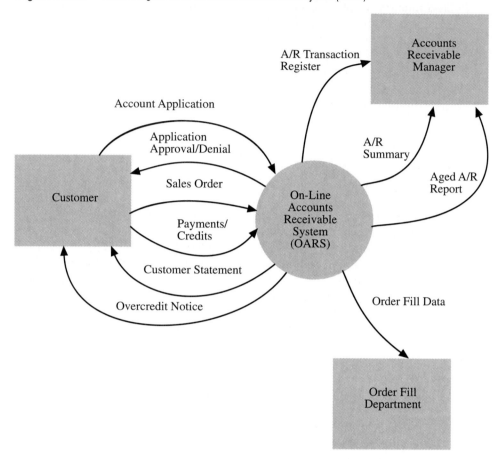

B. Recommendations

It is recommended that the OARS project be accepted for changeover from the old to the new system.

III. System Specification

A. External System Specification

1. *Context diagram* figure E3.1a is the context diagram for OARS. Figure E3.1b is the accompanying narrative.

2. *System output specification* The eight OARS outputs are as follows:

a. Customer monthly statement

b. Accounts receivable transactions

c. Accounts receivable summary data

d. Aged accounts receivable data

Narrative description for an on-line accounts receivable system (OARS) context diagram.

> The boundaries of the on-line accounts receivable system (OARS) are set by three external entities: the customer, the A/R manager, and the Order Fill department. These entities provide the inputs to OARS and receive the outputs. There are three inputs and seven outputs. All three inputs are created by the customer, beginning with an account application. The other two inputs are a customer-generated sales order and payments or applied credits. Customer-related outputs are: application approvals, application denials, customer statements, and overcredit notices.
>
> The A/R manager is provided with A/R transaction data, A/R summary information, and aged accounts receivable data, all of which are important in controlling customer accounts and in the management of cash flow. The Order Fill department is provided with order fill data, which is used to pick and ship customer orders and to manage inventory.

e. Order-fill data

f. Overcredit notification

g. Application approval notice

h. Application denial notice

An output specification and accompanying data element list for the overcredit notification are presented as figure E3.2a. The print chart layout for the overcredit notice is shown in figure E3.2b.

3. *System input specification* The three OARS inputs are as follows:

a. Account applications

b. Customer orders

c. Payments/credits

Figure E3.3 is an example of a system input, the account application.

4. *System resource specification* One Excalibur VI microcomputer system was acquired from the vendor during the development phase. An additional four systems will be required, providing one system for each of the five sales regions. Each system has the following configuration:

a. One file server:

CPU with 32 megabytes of main memory

One 1-gigabyte magnetic disk drive

b. One 24 page-per-minute laser printer

c. Eight workstations:

CPU with 8 megabytes of main memory

One 500-megabyte magnetic disk drive

Exhibit 3   ■   449

OUTPUT SPECIFICATION

TITLE: Overcredit Notification

LAYOUT:

Overcredit Notification

Sales Order No. _____
Sales Order Date _____
Account Number _____
Name and Address
_____
_____
_____

Current Balance _____
Sales Order Amount _____
Total _____
Credit Limit _____
Amount Overcredit [_____]

☐ Overcredit Approved
☐ Return Sales Order

_____
AUTHORIZATION

FREQUENCY: Daily
SIZE: 1 page

QUANTITY COPIES: 2   80 max.

DISTRIBUTION: 1. Accts. Receivable Dept.

COMMENTS:

DATA ELEMENT LIST

TITLE: Overcredit Notification

DESCRIPTION	FORMAT	SIZE
Sales Order Number	XXXXXXXX	8 characters
Sales Order Date	xx/xx/xx	8 "
Account No: Region No.—Sequence No.	XX-XXXXXXX	10 "
Name		26 "
Address		
Street		20 "
City		18 "
State		2 "
Zip Code		5 "
Current Balance	XXX,XXX.XX	10 "
Sales Order Amount	XXX,XXX.XX	10 "
Total	XXX,XXX.XX	10 "
Credit Limit	XX,XXX.XX	9 "
Amount Overcredit	XX,XXX.XX	9 "

■ Figure E3.2b OARS output design requirement: overcredit notice.

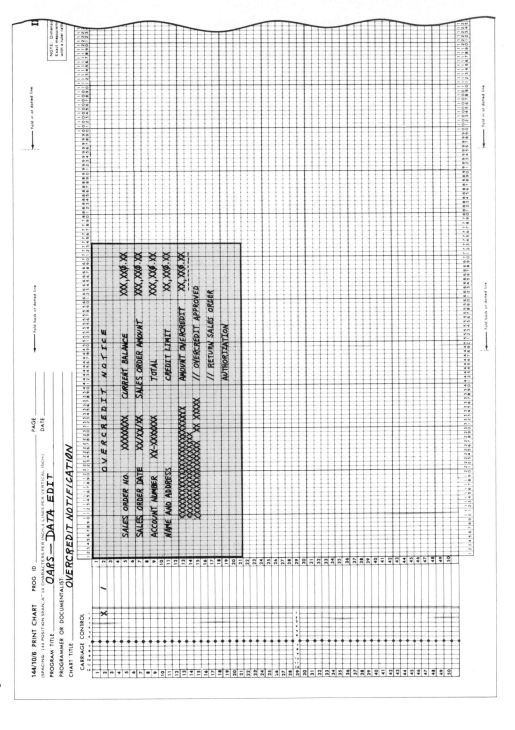

Exhibit 3 ■ 451

CUSTOMER ACCOUNT APPLICATION
ABCO Corporation
Walnut, California

FOR OFFICE USE
ACCOUNT NUMBER

FIRM NAME

EFFECTIVE DATE

INDICATE W for WHOLESALE
or R for RETAIL   DATE   TELEPHONE

CREDIT   DISCOUNT
CODE   CODE

STREET ADDRESS

CITY   STATE   ZIP CODE

BANK REFERENCES

NAME	BRANCH	TELEPHONE	
ADDRESS	CITY	STATE	ZIP CODE
NAME	BRANCH	TELEPHONE	
ADDRESS	CITY	STATE	ZIP CODE

OTHER REFERENCES

NAME		TELEPHONE	
ADDRESS	CITY	STATE	ZIP CODE
NAME		TELEPHONE	
ADDRESS	CITY	STATE	ZIP CODE

FOR OFFICE USE

CREDIT APPROVED ☐   DISAPPROVED ☐
IF DISAPPROVED, REASON:

AUTHORIZATION SIGNATURE

5. *System test specification* System tests were performed according to the OARS test plan. Prototype testing was completed and extended to include live data and a copy of a live file. Initial tests were for a low volume of transactions. Volume was increased, and full-system tests were performed successfully, with user personnel monitored by the test team. Test specifications and recorded results are documented in the appendix section.

6. *Training specifications* The user's reference manual, programmer's reference manual, operator's reference manual, and a reference listing of instructional materials appear as an appendix to this section.

B. Internal System Specification
   1. *Computer program component*
      a. Top-level data flow diagrams
         (1) Level-0 DFD and narrative description (figures E3.4a and E3.4b)
         (2) Level-1 DFD and narrative description (figures E3.5a and E3.5b)
      b. Data base specification (figure E3.6)
      c. Top-level structure chart (figure E3.7)

      Figure E3.7 is a HIPO chart that displays the major components of OARS. The IPO chart, shown for the credit check limit status module, illustrates how this module must verify that the customer will not exceed their credit limit.
   2. *Computer program design (for each program)*
      a. Decomposed data flow diagram for credit check limit states program (figure E3.8)
      b. Data storage specification

         The OARS data base will be made up of five separate, related files— Orders, Order Detail, Customer, Product, and discount. Figure E3.9 shows the data elements of each of these five files.
      c. Transaction file specification

         Figures E3.10 and E3.11 show the display for a customer application transaction, an illustration of a transaction file.
      d. Control specifications

         The OARS computer programs will provide the following controls:
         1. Edit all input data for validity.
         2. Detect overcredit conditions prior to processing invoices.
         3. Detect short or out-of-stock conditions prior to processing invoices.
      e. Program listings

         An indexed reference to the complete set of program listings is included as an appendix to this report
      f. Test specifications

         All tests were performed in accordance with the test plan. A description of the OARS test plan, summaries of test results, and references to documents containing test data and test results are included in an appendix.

Exhibit 3   ■   453

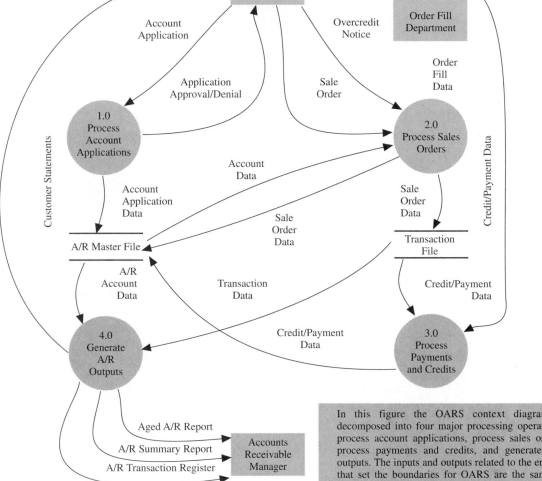

■ Figure E3.4b   Narrative description for an on-line
accounts receivable system (OARS)
level-0 data flow diagram.

In this figure the OARS context diagram is
decomposed into four major processing operations:
process account applications, process sales orders,
process payments and credits, and generate A/R
outputs. The inputs and outputs related to the entities
that set the boundaries for OARS are the same as
those shown in the system context diagram.

At this level, five additional data flows have been
added, as has an A/R data base. Except for sales
transaction data, all of the internal inputs and outputs
relate to the A/R data base. The Process Account
Applications bubble supplies the A/R data base with
updated customer account data. The Process
Payments and Credits bubble provides the A/R data
base with current payment/credit data, and the
Process Sales Orders bubble returns sales data to the
A/R data base.

The A/R data base has two outputs. The first is the
customer account data required to process sales
orders, and the second is A/R data used to create the
outputs required by the A/R manager. Also, in order
to create these outputs, sales transaction data must
flow from the Process Sales Orders bubble to the
Generate A/R Outputs bubble.

■ Figure E3.5a   Level-1 data flow diagram for OARS.

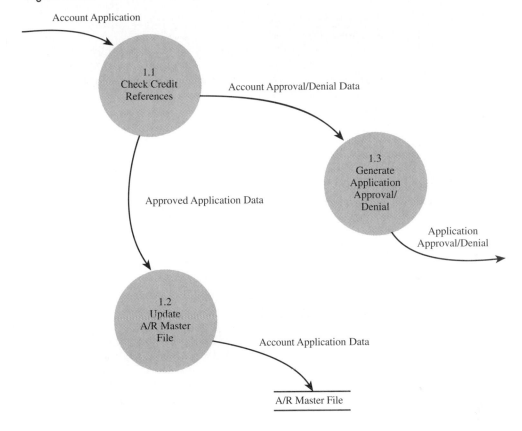

■ Figure E3.5b   Narrative description for an on-line accounts receivable system (OARS) level-1 data flow diagram.

In this figure the Process Account Applications bubble in the OARS level-0 data flow diagram is decomposed to exhibit three level-1 processing bubbles: Check Credit References, Generate Application Approval/Denial, and Update A/R Master File. The Check Credit References bubble has as its input customer account application data and produces as an output either an application approval or denial, which flows to the Assign Credit Limit bubble. This process also generates account data needed to update the A/R data base.

Exhibit 3   ■   455

■ Figure E3.6   OARS data base requirement.

OARS System Storage Requirements:

1. The OARS database consists of 14 data
   elements for a total of 167 characters.

2. Assuming a range of 10,000 master records to
   20,000 records over the expected 5-year life of
   the system, from 1,670,000 characters to
   3,340,000 characters of data will have to be
   stored.

3. The data described in 2 above will be distributed
   among the computers located in the local regions.

■ Figure E3.7   HIPO chart for OARS.

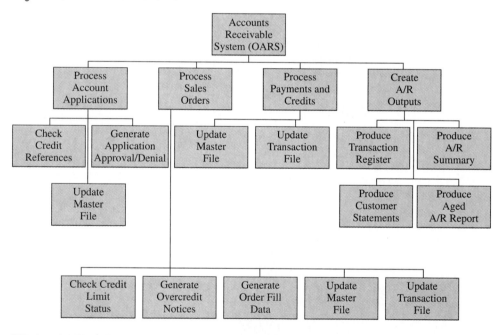

IPO chart: 2.1 Check Credit Limit Status

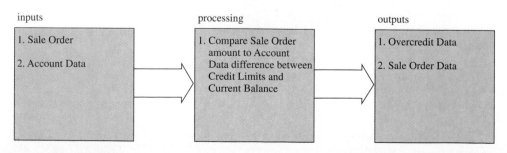

■ Figure E3.8   Decomposed data flow diagram for OARS credit check limit status module.

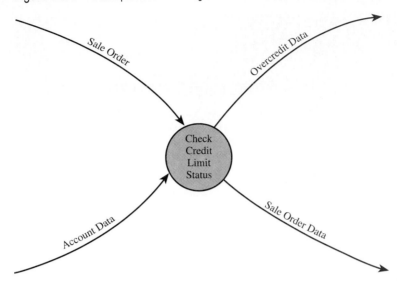

Exhibit 3   ■   457

■ Figure E3.9   OARS data base files and elements.

Orders File:

    Order Number
    Order Date
    Customer Number

Order Detail File:

    Order Number
    Product Code
    Quantity Ordered

Product File:

    Product Number
    Product Description
    Unit Price

Customer File:

    Customer Number
    Name
    Address
    City
    State
    ZIP Code
    Discount Code

Discount File:

    Discount Code
    Trade Discount

■ **Figure E3.10**   OARS transaction file requirements: customer application.

Display Layout Sheet

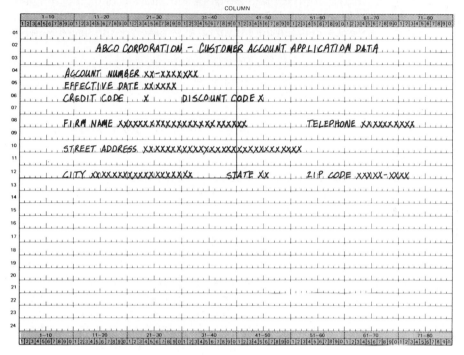

■ **Figure E3.11**   Screen design for customer account application data.

Exhibit 3   ■   459

IV. Plans and Cost Schedules
   A. Detailed Milestones—Development Phase
      The project progress for the OARS development phase is depicted in figure
      E3.12. The development phase was completed on schedule with the
      acceptance review scheduled for 11/10/xx. The costs for the development
      phase are shown in figure E3.13.
   B. Major Milestones—All Phases
      The progress plan and status report for the OARS project is included as
      figure E3.14. Figure E3.15 depicts the total OARS project costs.
   C. Changeover Plan
      The approved changeover plan appears in the appendix section of the
      report.
   D. Operational Plan
      The OARS program operates continuously and produces reports both
      periodically and on demand. The calculated recurring costs per account for
      OARS are as shown in figure E3.16.

PROJECT PLAN AND STATUS REPORT

PROJECT TITLE	PROJECT STATUS SYMBOLS		
OARS - DEVELOPMENT PHASE	O Satisfactory / ☐ Caution / △ Critical		J. Herring
			PROGRAMMER/ANALYST

PLANNING/PROGRESS SYMBOLS	COMMITTED DATE	COMPLETED DATE	STATUS DATE
☐ Scheduled Progress V Scheduled Completion / ■ Actual Progress ▼ Actual Completion	11/17/XY		11/3/XY

ACTIVITY/DOCUMENT	PERCENT COMPLETE	STATUS	PERIOD ENDING (Week) 2–36
DEVELOPMENT PHASE	0	0	
Implementation Plan	0	0	
Test Plan	0	0	
Training Plan	0	0	
Conversion Plan	0	0	
Equip. Acq. and Instal.	0	0	
Computer Prog. Dev.	0	0	
Computer Prog. Design	0	0	
Coding and Debugging	0	0	
Computer Prog. Tests	0	0	
Reference Manual Prep.	0	0	
Programmer's Man.	0	0	
Operator's Man.	0	0	
User's Man.	0	0	

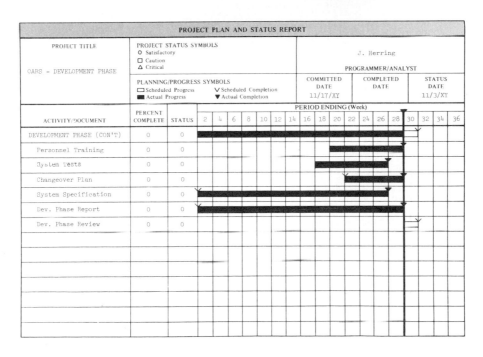

PROJECT PLAN AND STATUS REPORT

PROJECT TITLE	PROJECT STATUS SYMBOLS		
OARS - DEVELOPMENT PHASE	O Satisfactory / ☐ Caution / △ Critical		J. Herring
			PROGRAMMER/ANALYST

PLANNING/PROGRESS SYMBOLS	COMMITTED DATE	COMPLETED DATE	STATUS DATE
☐ Scheduled Progress V Scheduled Completion / ■ Actual Progress ▼ Actual Completion	11/17/XY		11/3/XY

ACTIVITY/DOCUMENT	PERCENT COMPLETE	STATUS	PERIOD ENDING (Week) 2–36
DEVELOPMENT PHASE (CON'T)	0	0	
Personnel Training	0	0	
System Tests	0	0	
Changeover Plan	0	0	
System Specification	0	0	
Dev. Phase Report	0	0	
Dev. Phase Review	0	0	

Exhibit 3   ■   461

■ Figure E3.13   Project cost—development phase.

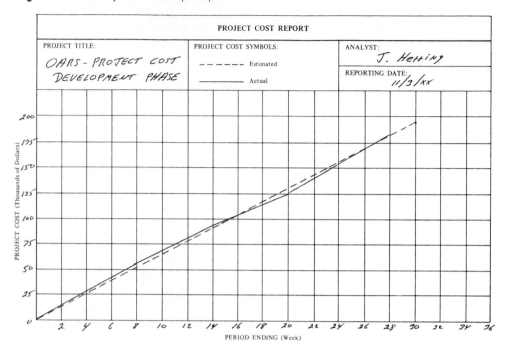

PROJECT COST REPORT

PROJECT TITLE:
OARS - PROJECT COST
DEVELOPMENT PHASE

PROJECT COST SYMBOLS:
– – – – – Estimated
——————— Actual

ANALYST:
J. Herring

REPORTING DATE:
11/3/xx

PROJECT COST (Thousands of Dollars)

200
175
150
125
100
75
50
25
0

2 4 6 8 10 12 14 16 18 20 22 24 26 28 30 32 34 36

PERIOD ENDING (Week)

■ Figure E3.14   Project plan and status report—OARS major milestones.

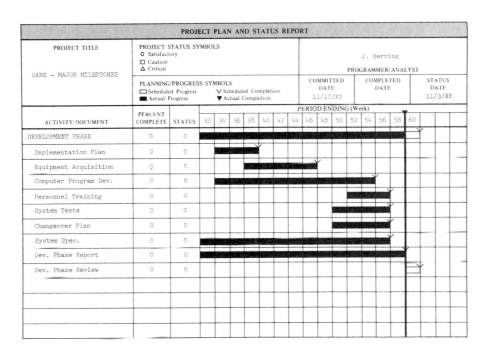

Exhibit 3   ■   463

■ Figure E3.15   Project cost report—total project.

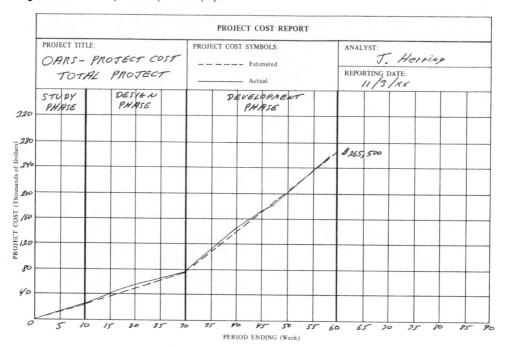

■ Figure E3.16   Weekly operating costs per account.

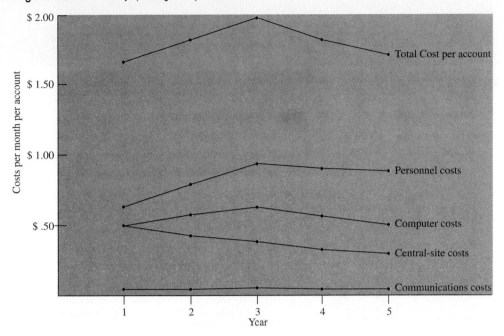

Exhibit 3   ■   465

Chapter

19

■ ■ ■

System Operation and Change Management

Preview

The operation phase is the fourth, and last, of the systems development life-cycle phases. It also is the longest in duration of the life-cycle phases. The system that was designed and developed in the preceding phases is operated by its users and maintained as an ongoing system. During the operation phase, computer information systems are characterized by four distinct stages: system changeover, routine operation, system performance review and evaluation, and system change. Changeover from an old system to a new computer information system is a difficult period in the systems development life cycle because of the probable occurrence of a multitude of unforeseen problems. Even after the new system has settled down, routine operation usually is not really "routine" because of the dynamic nature of the business environment in which the information system must operate. Therefore, the success of the system will depend upon its usability and the relationships the organization providing computer services maintains with its user-customers.

Periodic reviews of the actual performance of a computer-related business information system are needed in order to ensure that the system is continuing to do the job for which it was designed and developed. One structured method for performing these reviews is by means of a performance review board (PRB). This board should have strong user representation. The PRB can also play an important role in the management of change by determining when, and to what degree, a computer information system must be modified. The value of the life-cycle methodology and the assistance available from CASE tools are reemphasized whenever change becomes necessary.

Objectives

1. You will be able to define and to distinguish between the four major stages of the operation phase.
2. You will be able to illustrate by example the difficulties of changeover and the challenges of routine operation.
3. You will be able to describe and discuss the functions performed by an information services organization.
4. You will be able to explain the importance of periodic performance evaluation throughout the operation phase.
5. You will be able to describe a technique, based upon the establishment of a performance review board, for managing change.
6. You will be able to define redevelopment engineering and to distinguish between reverse engineering and reengineering.

Key Terms

operation phase the phase involving changeover from the old to the new system, where the system is operated, evaluated, and changed as necessary.

system changeover the period of transition from the old system to the new system.

standards the rules under which personnel in an information services organization work.

usability the value of an information system as perceived by its users.

performance review board a user-oriented board responsible both for the periodic evaluation of the performance of a computer-based business information system and for maintaining its integrity.

change a system modification that requires performance review board action.

maintenance a system modification that does not require performance review board action.

change control the means by which major modifications to computer-based business information systems are managed.

redevelopment engineering automated software techniques for modifying existing computer information systems, based on the SDLC concept and CASE technology.

Changeover

The Changeover Crisis

The acceptance review, held at the conclusion of the development phase, assured the principal user that the new computer-based business system was ready for operation. At that review the user was presented with evidence that system-level tests had verified the performance of the system; with assurances that personnel had been trained; and with a detailed plan for system changeover. The principal user then decided to proceed to the first stage of the operation phase, changeover from the old system to the new one. It might seem, then, that there are no further obstacles to prevent successful implementation and that the project team can be released for new assignments. Nothing could be farther from the truth. Changeover, which is the period of transition from the old system to the new system, is often the most critical and problem-beset period in the life of computer information systems. The reasons for *changeover crisis* are as follows:

1. Implementation planning, however complete, cannot possibly take into account all the real-life situations that can occur.
2. The more complete the implementation planning, the fewer the unforeseen problems. However, no matter how complete rehearsals have been, it is unrealistic to expect perfect harmony during the initial system performance. For this to occur, all the computer programs must function without error; people must not make mistakes; equipment must not malfunction; files must not contain residual elements of contaminated data; and, above all, everyone should be pulling for the success of the system. It is unlikely that the orchestration will be this perfect when the system goes "on stage" for the first time.
3. All changeover methods contain risks. In chapter 16, "Preparing for Implementation," we discussed three changeover methods: parallel operation, immediate replacement, and phased changeover. All introduce new tasks into an actual operational environment. Therefore, mistakes and problems are to be expected.
4. Changeover is an emotional activity. Change suddenly becomes a reality. Things will be different. This realization is sufficient to create tensions that cause and amplify mistakes.

If we were to prepare a graph to illustrate the frequency of the occurrence of crises during a typical changeover, it might look like figure 19.1. Initially, everything appears to go wrong at once. Then, after a period of time, the crisis environment begins to improve. The frequency and the magnitude of the crises tend to become less. Finally, a relatively tranquil state is reached.

Changeover crisis frequency. Changeover from an old to a new system is a critical period beset by frequent crises. With effective implementation planning and strong user support, crises tend to abate with time.

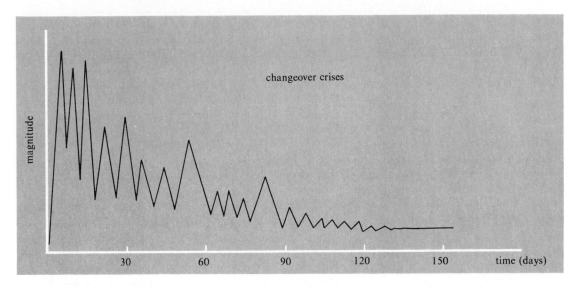

Changeover Activities

Contemporary systems analysis and design methods that include CASE tools and prototyping techniques serve to greatly mitigate the changeover crisis. This is particularly true if the joint applications development team of systems and user personnel is kept intact and available. Here are some practical guidelines for the team's activities during turnover:

1. Compare new outputs with old outputs as much as possible. If outputs differ only in format, it usually is possible to verify content.
2. Check inputs and outputs to be certain that they conform to specifications.
3. Follow up immediately on all errors. Correct the manual or machine processes causing the errors.
4. Keep a log. Use a *changeover action log* to record actions, responsibilities, assignments, and completion dates. Figure 19.2 is an example.
5. Attend to all problems promptly. Seek the cooperation of the user groups in resolving problems and in deciding on immediate corrective measures.
6. Defer any refinements or changes in the system until changeover has been completed.
7. Never expect problems that have not been solved before changeover begins to be solved during changeover. Unsolved problems only tend to become larger and to multiply.

Changeover action log. An action log is a useful management tool during changeover. This log lists in numbered sequence the actions needed, responsibilities for actions, and dates of action assignment and completion.

ACTION NUMBER	ACTION DESCRIPTION	RESPONSIBILITY	DATE ASSIGNED	DATE COMPLETED

CHANGEOVER ACTION LOG

Changeover is the time at which the project leader must make every effort to keep team spirits high. The project must maintain its momentum. The situation is similar to a football team that has the ball on the two-yard line: the entire team must be psyched up to carry the ball over the goal. At this time the earned support and confidence of user groups will pay off. Even a flawed system can be made to work with user support. Without it, a good system will fail. Systems are never more vulnerable to attack than during changeover. If allowed to stay on the sidelines, some users (who are perhaps a bit fearful of the system anyway) will derive satisfaction from the "failures of the computer." It appears to be human nature to mock the failure of a machine, even if the machine is only performing as instructed. To keep them involved, the team should assign specific responsibilities to all users. They should be made responsible for the prompt solution of systems problems that arise in their areas of operation. The project leader should strive to sell success: The leader must keep the team success-oriented by emphasizing the obstacles overcome, rather than those yet to be encountered. Success will breed more success. The crisis environment will begin to abate, and the system will approach a level of performance that justifies its turnover to its users.

User Turnover

When crises have been reduced to manageable proportions, the project leader can consider turning over the system to its users. At this time, all the error conditions noted during changeover will have been corrected, and the system will have gone through several cycles of successful operation. It then becomes the responsibility of the users to operate the system. The project team can be disbanded and its members can return to their own organizations. Although the information services organization will retain some responsibilities for the system, these will be of a maintenance nature until such time as a need for a major change arises. An analyst will be assigned as a liaison with the user, to participate in resolving system problems.

User turnover initiates a new stage in the operation phase. This stage is called routine operation, and the data processing department assumes full responsibility for data processing activities.

Routine Operation

Organizing for Data Processing

We concluded our discussion of changeover by stating that after the system had been turned over to the user, its routine operation became the responsibility of the data processing department. In a large data processing department, routine day-to-day processing is anything but "routine." The operations environment itself is crisis-laden. The typical environment is one in which a large number of jobs, some scheduled and some unscheduled, must be processed amid changing priorities and daily emergencies.

Figure 19.3 illustrates a typical contemporary organization structure. The director of corporate systems and the director of data processing report to the vice-president of information services. The corporate systems activity includes both systems analysis and programming. The organization structure is mixed. Systems projects are set up for each new application and, as such, are carried through to turnover to the user. Thereafter, the operational systems become the responsibility of a systems maintenance group. In the event of significant changes, a particular application can revert from maintenance status to project status.

System support activities are considered to be functional because they are not oriented toward specific applications. In addition to conventional systems functions such as forms design, records management, and work measurement and quality assurance, the support activities may include the development of tools and techniques such as CASE tool kits, critical path methods, prototyping, and data base management. Support is provided for a distributed data processing environment, including communications networks and automated office applications. As also shown in figure 19.3, the data processing organization usually is more oriented toward functions than projects. An exception would be the dedication of a computer system to a single large project, of which large aerospace and airline reservation systems are examples. Other important functional operations are data entry, computer operations, and operations control. Figure 19.4 is a brief summary of typical jobs and duties associated with the organization chart shown in figure 19.3.

■ Figure 19.3   Contemporary information services organization. In a typical contemporary information services organization two principle functions—both reporting to a vice-president of information services—are systems
and data processing. The former includes all systems and applications programming activities. The latter
includes data processing operations and also communications and reprographics.

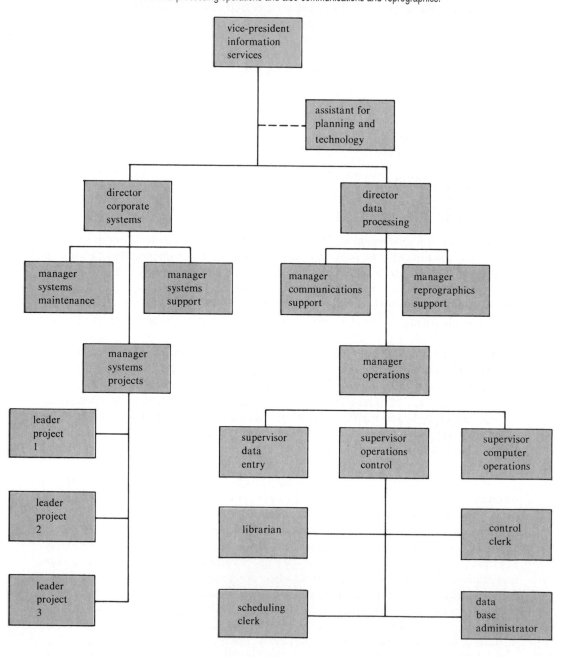

Typical data processing job descriptions. There are many career opportunities in data processing. Several of those associated with operations are listed and described here.

JOB TITLE	DESCRIPTION
Supervisor of Data Entry	Supervises staff responsible for entry of data for computer processing. Schedules workloads and distributes work assignments.
Supervisor of Operations Control	Supervises library activities, preparation of schedules, production control procedures, and data base maintenance.
Librarian	Stores and issues program documentation and data files kept on disk or tape.
Scheduling Clerk	Prepares and maintains daily, weekly, and monthly schedules for all appointed jobs.
Control Clerk	Checks receipt and acceptability of input data. Establishes controls. Checks output. Maintains error records. Dispatches acceptable output to users.
Data Base Administrator	Maintains the integrity of a data base. Organizes, reorganizes, and controls data base definitions and changes. Controls access to the data base.
Supervisor of Computer Operations	Supervises the operation of all computing equipment. Maintains records of equipment performance. Develops techniques to improve performance.

A data processing operation is evaluated by the service it provides to its users, or clients. Two important jobs that affect service to users are data base administrator and manager of communications. The job of data base administrator has come into existence because of the increasing number and complexity of the data bases being created to support integrated and distributed data processing systems. The data base administrator is responsible for the integrity of the data base, or repository. This person monitors the data base, controls changes to it, maintains its structure, and reorganizes it as required. A data base administrator is essential to the successful implementation and maintenance of the data base management systems (DBMSs) and to the successful application of CASE tools and prototyping techniques..

In a client/server environment, portions of a centralized data base may be *down loaded*, that is, made available by electronic means, to remote users. Hence the position of manager of communications support is becoming increasingly important as increasingly more complex electronic networks are developed and as corporations continue to downsize their mainframes in order to distribute more capability and resources to distant users.

Data Processing Standards

The Standards Manual

The foregoing discussion is an example of the need for a sets of rules under which analysts, programmers, operators, and other personnel in an information service organization must work. The rules are called **standards**, and they are the reference against which the performance of the information services organization can be measured. Standards vary from organization to organization. While it is not essential that standards be the same in all organizations, it is essential that complete and current written standards exist and be understood. Some general reasons for the importance of standards are these:

1. The work of analysts and programmers must be understood by other analysts and programmers. This provides backup.
2. The field of systems analysis, particularly where computers are involved, is changing rapidly. Techniques can be kept current.
3. Communications within a department and between departments are improved.
4. New employees can be trained and can become effective sooner if they learn standard procedures.
5. Changes can be implemented more easily when existing standards can be used as references.

Because they affect all members and functions of the information system organization, standards should be established at an appropriate management level. For example, in the information system organization shown in figure 19.3, the establishment and maintenance of standards could be a responsibility of a group that reports to the assistant to the vice-president of information systems. An information systems organization that lacks standards is not organized and therefore is poorly equipped to provide lasting user satisfaction. A *standards manual* is an essential tool. Figure 19.5 lists major topics typically found in standards manuals. The standards policy is a statement to the effect that all work performed in an organization will be in accordance with the content of the manual. Administrative standards relate to organization charts, job descriptions, training of personnel, and administrative information. Systems analysis standards govern the analysts' activities throughout the life cycle of a business system. For example, standards for using CASE tools, performing prototyping, establishing and managing projects, and participating as members of applications development teams would appear in a manual for information system development.

■ **Figure 19.5**   Contents of a standards manual. Standards manuals contain the rules under which personnel in an information services organization work. Thus a standards manual for developing information systems must, in addition to a policy statement, contain detailed administrative, systems analysis, programming, and operating standards.

standards manual for the development of information systems

table of contents

    i. standards policy

   ii. administrative standards

  iii. systems analysis standards

  iv. programming standards

   v. operating standards

Programming standards are rules for activities such as computer program flow-charting, language selection, programming techniques, and program documentation. Operating standards relate to computer and peripheral equipment operations. The need to comply with standards sometimes appears to conflict with a need for timely user support. Actually, standards contribute to accuracy and so lead to faster service and better customer relations because there are fewer errors and complaints about the usability of the system.

Customer Relations

Good customer relations are important because there will be times when the good will and patience of users are essential to the success of routine operations. Fast response, coupled with standards to ensure a quality product, is not always possible. Most computer installations are not sized to handle peak loads, such as might occur at month end and year end. Priority tasks will arise without warning. At these times performance may slip. Also, there always will be unplanned unproductive periods that will cause schedules to slip. Typical causes are machine malfunction and human error. Without customer understanding and constructive support, these periods can be demoralizing and can impair the effectiveness of the entire information services organization.

Security

Management concern about the security of computers is often inflamed by highly publicized incidents of computer-related fraud. The data processing center is expected to provide not only adequate input, processing, and output controls, but also protection against fraud and disaster. This protection should be a shared responsibility. It is the responsibility not only of the data processing manager, but also of top management, insurance companies, security specialists, and users of data processing services. To provide protection against disasters, certain steps should be taken, as follows:

1. *Physical Location*
   Select a computer site away from natural hazards. Take steps to reduce known risks. For example, water risk can be reduced by storing data in high locations and by providing drains, pumps, and plastic covers for equipment.
2. *Physical Access Control*
   Use badges and controlled entry points. However, the key factor is an alert computer staff who will challenge all strangers.
3. *Fire Protection*
   Locate the computer center away from fire hazards. Construct the computer area of flame retardant materials. Minimize combustible materials in the computer area. Provide early warning devices, fire detectors, portable extinguishers, and emergency procedures.
4. *Media Protection*
   Store vital files in a separate room or vault.
5. *Backup and "Fall Back" Capabilities*
   If possible, make arrangements with similarly equipped data processing centers to take over processing in the event of an emergency.
6. *Risk Insurance*
   Evaluate insurance policies to cover data processing losses.

In spite of publicity to the contrary, natural disasters are more frequent causes of catastrophe than is fraud. Nonetheless, there are valid reasons for increased concern about security because of the growth in distributed data processing, which has led to a proliferation of microcomputer workstations, growth in department-level, multiuser networks, and continuing increases in the amount of sensitive information stored in large data bases. In such environments it is difficult to enforce security measures because individuals often are not particularly careful about keeping their passwords, or user IDs, confidential. Also, passwords and other access control methods can be overcome by technically skilled invaders, called "hackers." It is a well-known fact that insiders are responsible for far more unauthorized accesses than are outsiders. For this reason, many corporations have installed very sophisticated security systems. Security has become an industry within an industry, and there are many sources of hardware and software for securing data processing systems. These range from various forms of access control to full-scale data encrypting. Access control usually is accomplished by restricting individuals to a level of data base access on the basis of a need to know. IDs may be changed frequently, and access may be limited to certain time intervals. Usually data encrypting involves protecting the communications networks through which sensitive information is transmitted. Protection is accomplished by hardware and software techniques that scramble data prior to transmission and unscramble them afterwards.

Real security, however, cannot be based only upon hardware and software. It involves recognition that security is more of a people problem than a technical one and requires a management commitment to an ongoing program to educate and remind all employees about security hazards and their personal responsibility to protect sensitive information. Management actions that can be taken to minimize insider security risks include:

1. Division of duties in data processing.
2. Built-in system controls.
3. File and program change controls.
4. Use of a security specialist.
5. Frequent audits by external auditors.
6. Thorough personnel investigations before hiring.
7. Bonding of staff.
8. Prompt removal of discharged personnel.
9. Protection against voluntary termination by good documentation and cross-training of personnel.

Performance Review and Evaluation

Performance Review Board

A system cannot be forgotten after it has been accepted for routine operation. The dynamic nature of business information systems is an essential aspect of the systems development life-cycle concept. Internal and external factors will cause changes to the operating environment of the system. Typical internal factors that can affect system performance are changes in equipment, work load, programming languages, and personnel. Among the external factors that affect performance are new or revised reporting needs, increases in required output, and changes in schedules. In fact, changes to systems are caused by all of the information generators that affect the business system environment.

Thus the life-cycle management process continues throughout the operational life of the system. Computer-based business information systems tend to fall apart rapidly if formal management control is removed, principally because the validity of system documentation is destroyed. One way in which this occurs is the introduction of many small and inadequately documented changes by programmers who deal informally with members of user groups. Although an informal relationship can be healthy, it should not be permitted to destroy the integrity of the system. If laxity in documentation is tolerated, sooner or later a disaster will occur, and the good relationship with the user will disappear. Another type of change, which often is poorly documented, is the system patch. A *patch* is a "quick fix" programming change that is made under the pressure of an immediate operational need. Most often the patch changes one or more of the computer program modules. At the time the change is made, the intent is to remove the patch and to rewrite the affected routines in the future—but this particular future never arrives, unless the intent is supported by a standard procedure. In an environment in which managed actions continually are secondary to crisis responses, the original system quickly becomes completely hidden by patches.

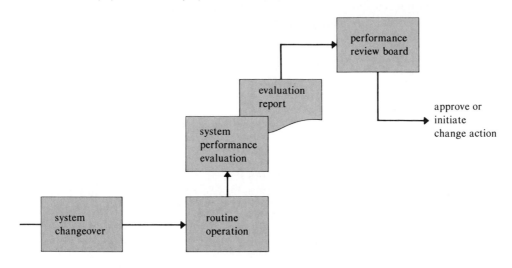

■ Figure 19.6   Performance evaluation. After systems changeover is completed and after the computer-related information system enters routine operation, formal performance evaluation occurs. An evaluation report is prepared for review by a performance review board.

One technique for ensuring system integrity is the establishment of a **performance review board (PRB).** Both the user and information systems are represented on the PRB. It is, however, a user-oriented board, which should be headed by the principal user. The PRB is continuously aware of the computer-based system through user organization involvement in the routine operation of the system and through a designated member of the systems maintenance staff. The PRB should not be involved continuously in operational problems but should respond only to exceptional conditions of a nonroutine nature. In addition, periodic reviews (perhaps quarterly) should be scheduled. The first of these scheduled reviews should take place two to three months after the new system has been installed, to compare actual results with planned results. This review is called the *post-installation review.* Other PRB actions are triggered by requests for changes to the system. The functions of the PRB related to post-installation and periodic reviews are illustrated in figure 19.6.

Post-Installation Review

System performance evaluation begins with the *post-installation review,* which is intended to determine how well actual performance compares with promised performance. The promises were documented as the specific performance objectives, which were in turn derived from the general objectives and anticipated benefits originally stated in the project directive.

The post-installation review should not be scheduled until the changeover crisis is over. The review should be performed by persons who are not directly responsible for system implementation and operation. They can be selected from the user and system staffs, or they can be outside auditors or consultants. The first review activity

System performance evaluation report. The systems performance evaluation report is prepared as part of the post-installation performance review; it compares actual performance with the specific objective of the computer information system.

```
SYSTEM PERFORMANCE EVALUATION REPORT

1.  Name of system:

2.  Specific performance objectives:

3.  Method of evaluation:

4.  Results of evaluation:

5.  Recommendations:
```

is to gather information related to current system operation. Information gathering techniques, such as those discussed in chapter 7, "Initial Investigation," can be employed. For example, as a member of the review team, you should:

1. Examine the actual system outputs. Compare them with the outputs in the system specification.
2. Use the distribution list to send correspondence inquiring about the operating status of the system and its effectiveness. Ask about any problems that have been encountered or that still exist. Solicit suggestions for improvements.
3. Follow up correspondence by interviews with appropriate users of the system outputs, with operating personnel, and with user management.
4. Prepare data flow diagrams to compare the planned and actual data streams and data transformation processes.

After completing its information gathering, the team should compare observed current performance with the specific performance objectives. Some specific objectives with which actual performance can be compared are:

1. elimination of duplicated files
2. reduction or reassignment of personnel
3. cost savings achieved
4. cost avoidance accomplished
5. comparison of past and present error rates

The team then prepares a system performance evaluation report for submission to the PRB. A typical format is shown in figure 19.7. The main elements of the performance evaluation report are as follows:

1. *Name of System*
   Identifies the computer-based business system being evaluated.
2. *Specific Performance Objectives*
   States the specific performance objectives of the computer-based system.
3. *Method of Evaluation*
   Describes how the system performance was reviewed and evaluated.

```
specific objectives of on-line
accounts receivable system (OARS)


1.  establish billing cycles for each region

2.  mail customer statements no later than one day after
    the close of the billing cycle

3.  provide customers with a billing statement no later
    than three days after the close of the billing cycles

4.  speed up collection, reducing float from an average of four
    days to two days

5.  establish regional profit centers

6.  examine customer account balances through on-line
    inquiry during order entry
```

4. *Results of Evaluation*
   a. Compares measured performance with the specific performance objectives.
   b. Summarizes other factors, such as user and operator satisfaction, intangible benefits, and pertinent observations of the review team.
5. *Recommendations*
   Recommends actions to the PRB. The range of possible recommendations includes (a) accept the system "as is"; (b) recommend minor modification; (c) recommend major revision; and (d) reject and start over.

As examples of some specific performance objectives that might be evaluated after implementation, let us again consider the ABCO corporation's on-line accounts receivable system (OARS).

Figure 19.8 lists the objectives presented in chapter 8, "System Performance Definition." Each of these objectives is measurable. Each can be evaluated by examining system outputs over several billing cycles and by interviewing users of the system. Thus actual performance measurement, coupled with an assessment of users' satisfaction and suggestions, results in a meaningful performance evaluation report. This example, by contrast, clearly illustrates the dilemma that management all too often faces in evaluating systems for which specific performance objectives have not been established.

Periodic Review

The post-installation review is followed by *periodic reviews,* which are intended both to ensure that the integrity of the system is maintained and to identify special areas requiring management attention. Two major requirements for system integrity are correct, current documentation and valid outputs. Management can help to keep documentation valid by supporting performance standards that do not accept undocumented changes. Systems and programming staffs often are under pressure to "perform" and not "record," but continual pressure of this kind usually is due to management's lack of understanding of the true cost of poor documentation. The PRB can rectify this situation, in most cases, by allocating the resources necessary to keep the system intact. Problems of this type are reduced when there is a corporate commitment to a CASE environment that includes an understanding of the resources needed to record changes and to maintain the integrity of the system data bases and documentation.

Management also can help to maintain the validity of system outputs. Errors may remain undetected long after changeover has been completed, or they may creep in as a result of changes made to the system. The PRB should request a periodic audit of the accuracy of system outputs. Audits may be performed "around" or "through" the system. Those performed around the system are external, not an integral part of the system data processing operations. Audits performed through the system are designed into the system; they are computer programs that operate upon system data as it is being processed. This type of audit is becoming more common. Statistical sampling techniques also are coming into use as auditing tools. The results of periodic audits should be reported to the performance review board.

Special areas for management attention may come to light only after the system has operated for an extended period. An example is the performance of the system under unplanned circumstances, such as an overload due to unanticipated volumes of data to be processed. Some manifestations of problems are subtle. For example, an increase in circumvention of procedures may be the result of system deficiencies that need to be corrected. As another example, absenteeism can disclose much about the effectiveness of the system. If personnel are misplaced or are subjected to continuing high levels of stress, they will take time off in order to get relief. Reassigning people and rescheduling some of the processing from peak to slack periods may correct this problem. Throughout all of its reviews, the PRB should be particularly sensitive to users' evaluations of the system. In the final analysis, a system is effective only as long as it has usability, meaning that it must continue to be accepted by its users.

Change Management

Guidelines for System Modification

Computer-based business systems are dynamic. They must be able to accommodate changes in information needs resulting from changes in the business environment. These changes occur not only during the study, design, and development phases of the life cycle of the system but also throughout its operational life. Provision must be made for *modification* of an operational system, for if it cannot be modified without destroying the integrity of its data base and its outputs, it is a failure. Change can be managed by continuing the life-cycle management process by which the system was created. The performance review board has an important role to play in the management of change, because, in addition to conducting post-installation and periodic reviews, the PRB also should evaluate requests for modification of the operational system. Some requests will be planned; others will be unplanned. Some will be extremely significant; others much less so. Obviously, the PRB should not be involved on a continuing daily basis, but only when requirements for system modification rise

Modification categories for computer-based business information systems. System modifications may require ordinary maintenance or action by the performance review board. The latter constitutes a system change and generally relates to the type of activity that occurs early in the systems development life cycle.

modification category	baseline specification affected
change (PRB action)	performance specification
	design specification
maintenance (no PRB action)	system specification

above a certain threshold of importance. We can identify this threshold by dividing system modifications into two categories and relating each one to the type of baseline specification it affects, as has been done in figure 19.9. The modification categories shown in this figure are change and maintenance. **Change** is defined as a system modification that requires performance review board action. **Maintenance** is defined as a system modification that does not require performance review board action.

The need for PRB action depends upon the impact of a proposed modification, a concept that can be illustrated by again referring to figure 19.9. Let us first consider the two extremes. We recall that a user-oriented performance specification was created at the end of the study phase. In figure 19.9, the first entry in the "baseline specification affected" column refers to the user-oriented performance specification (as this baseline specification was carried forward into the final system specification). This type of modification always involves the users of the system. Therefore, the PRB always should be involved. For example, a change in company credit policy could change the method of billing customers. As another example, a new tax law requiring state withholding tax payroll deductions could affect all of the employees of a company.

At the other extreme, it is not likely that the PRB would be concerned with modifications to the content of the system specification that are not derived from the original performance specification or the original design specification. Examples are the development of a more efficient computer program component and minor changes in hardware and software. We can define this type of modification as technical maintenance rather than as change.

However, we must be careful not to include major programming, hardware, and operating system changes in this definition of technical maintenance. These are changes that should be brought to the attention of the performance review boards for all operational computer-based business systems. The reason is that data processing changes of large magnitude probably cannot be made without errors or without affecting the users of the computer information system. As a result strange and sometimes catastrophic things tend to happen to user outputs. Therefore, it is imperative to have the concurrence and support of all principal users throughout the process of planning and implementing major changes to the computer-based business system environment. To make sure that the potential impact of technical maintenance modifications is not underestimated because of errors of judgment by programmers or the data processing operations staff, the analyst assigned to maintain the system should approve *all* modifications made to an operational system. Together with the supervisor of programming, the analyst should make certain that specification and documentation standards are observed regardless of the pressure of work load. Following standards is as necessary for a change in a single instruction as it is for the rewriting of large and complicated parts of the overall computer program component.

In between the extremes shown in figure 19.9 are modifications to the system specification, which are derived from the design specification written at the conclusion of the design phase. The maintenance analyst must judge whether or not the PRB should be involved. Typical situations are those resulting from modifications to the internal system design. Examples are changes in file structure, changes in internal data flow, and minor output revisions. For example, if a report were to be modified slightly by changing the relative position of two output items and by adding a subtotal, the maintenance analyst probably could handle this situation as routine maintenance and deal directly with the users of the report (who probably requested the modification in the first place). However, for any proposed design changes that could have a significant impact on persons supplying input to the system, maintaining the data base, or using the outputs, the maintenance analyst should request the concurrence of the PRB.

We can summarize the discussion of change and maintenance type modifications with the following guidelines for the analyst responsible for systems maintenance:

1. Evaluate *all* system modifications.
2. Decide whether the modification is maintenance or change.
3. If it is change, bring the modification to the PRB for a decision.
4. Maintain a log and present a written summary of all maintenance modifications at the next periodic meeting of the PRB.

The importance of establishing guidelines and standards for system modification is underscored when we consider the size of the company investment that the maintenance analyst must safeguard. It is estimated that 25 to 50 percent of all systems and programming effort is spent on maintenance. The continuing annual cost to support a newly operational system is approximately 15 percent of the cost to develop it. Because companies have such large stakes in maintaining computer-based systems, a major value of the life-cycle management process is to provide a framework within which modifications can be accomplished, documented, and approved by management. We call this framework change control.

■ Figure 19.10   Change management process. Changes can be complex and may involve life-cycle activities similar to those that created the computer-based information system. Therefore, a formal change control process is necessary.

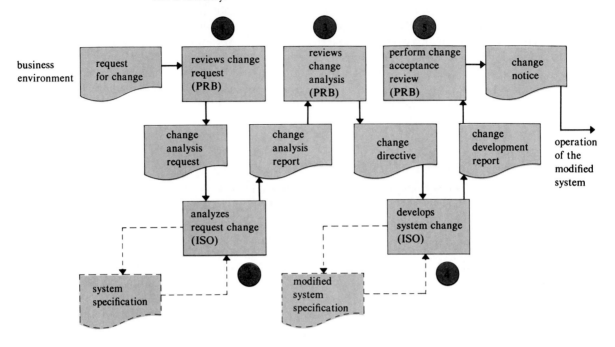

Change Control

Change control is the means by which major modifications (changes) to a computer-based business information system are managed. By extension, change control also includes the activities and documentation required to preserve the integrity of a system throughout minor modifications (maintenance). Change control is a management process centered on the PRB, which acts as the change control agency. It also relies upon the completeness of the documentation of the computer-based business system. Figure 19.10 is a flowchart that illustrates this process. The process symbols identified by (PRB) refer to action of the performance review board; those identified by (ISO) refer to actions by the information service organization. With reference to figure 19.10:

1. The PRB receives all change requests. These may be internal or external in origin. The major internal sources of requests for change are the systems analyst who is responsible for maintaining the system and the operational users of the system. They usually are the persons who can best decide whether a modification is minor and can be handled as maintenance, or whether it is

Analysis request format. A change analysis request is the formal means of introducing a request to change a computer information system. The change request is submitted to the performance review board for consideration.

```
CHANGE ANALYSIS REQUEST

1.  Name of computer-based system:

2.  Description of change:

3.  Reason for change:

4.  Date of need:

5.  Special considerations:
```

major and must be handled as a change. There are many possible external sources of change, for example, a change in the tax laws. Usually external changes must be implemented, but the process is similar to that for implementing internally generated changes.

The PRB reviews all requests for change. Those the board does not reject are transmitted to the information services organization by means of a *change analysis request.* Figure 19.11 outlines its general content. This request initiates a new systems analysis activity. If appropriate, the change analysis request should be accompanied by an information service request (ISR) of the type discussed in chapter 7, "Initial Investigation."

2. Upon receipt of the change analysis request, the information services organization assigns a responsible systems analyst, who will determine the effect of the change on the operational system. The effect depends on the nature of the change and on its impact on the system specification. As a result of an investigation, the analyst determines how far back in its life cycle the system is affected by the change. The process of analyzing the system specification to determine the effect of the change is shown by the first dashed-line feedback loop of figure 19.10.

After completing the analysis of the proposed change, the responsible analyst prepares a *change analysis report,* for which figure 19.11 outlines a general format. If the change is feasible, the analyst drafts an information service request (ISR) to accompany the change analysis report.

3. The PRB receives the change analysis report and reviews it with the systems analyst and with other persons who know the system well. If the board decides to implement the change, an ISR is sent to the information systems organization. The ISR is labeled a change directive.

4. Upon receipt of the change directive, the information service organization transfers the computer-based system from maintenance to project status. A project leader is assigned and a joint applications development team is

Change analysis report. The change analysis report, prepared by the information services organization, is the basis for a decision whether or not to implement a request for a change to a computer information system.

```
CHANGE ANALYSIS REPORT

1.  Name of computer-based system:

2.  Description of change:

3.  Reason for change:

4.  System modifications:
    a.  external specification:
    b.  internal specification:

5.  Date of availability:

6.  Special considerations:
```

appointed to begin the revision of the system. The steps followed are identical to the life-cycle process for developing a new system, with the point of reentry into the life cycle dependant on which baseline specification is modified. On some occasions it is necessary to start at the beginning and to develop new performance, design, and system specifications. The effort to change the ongoing system sometimes is greater than the effort to develop it in the first place. The requirement for reentering the life-cycle process to modify the system is shown by the second dashed-line feedback loop in figure 19.10 as leading to a modified system specification.

The change activities correspond to those previously derived from the life-cycle process presented in the first chapter of this text in figures 1.6 and 1.7, and they include the preparation of a change study report and a change design report, if required. As shown in figure 19.12, the final documented result of the change activities is a *change development report,* which is analogous to the development phase report prepared when the original system was developed. This report is presented to the PRB for a change acceptance review, which is similar to the acceptance review for the original system.

After a successful acceptance review, the PRB issues a *change notice.* This notice informs all personnel of the changes to the system and their effective date. The change notice also acts as a cover sheet to which the replacement pages for all affected specifications and other system documentation are attached. Figure 19.13 shows a typical format for a change notice which ensures that the changes are included as a part of current system documentation.

■ Figure 19.13   System change notice format. After the performance review board has accepted a system change, a
system change notice is issued. This notice informs users and all other affected personnel about the
change and provides the information needed to effect the change.

```
SYSTEM CHANGE NOTICE

1.  Name of computer-based system:

2.  Summary of change:

3.  Effective date of change:

4.  Log of specification/documentation changes:

    specification/documentation        change pages
```

Redevelopment Engineering

It is a fact of life that most enterprises have a significant number of computer information systems that were developed in the past, perhaps five or ten or more years ago, without full implementation of the systems development life-cycle methodology, and certainly without the use of tools and techniques such as CASE packages and prototyping. Generally the most critical of the corporate information systems are found among them, and these have been patched and modified and patched so often that their operation is uncertain and their maintenance is a complex and expensive burden. **Redevelopment engineering,** sometimes referred to as *design recovery,* is a general term for automated software tools designed to modify existing computer information systems in a manner that is compatible with the SDLC and CASE technologies. These tools make possible the recovery of data and logic design information from an existing system and the entry of this information into a CASE repository. Redevelopment engineering includes the development of data structures and structure charts from existing computer code and the "cleanup" of that code. Redevelopment engineering, in effect, approaches the SDLC in a backwards direction, from the operation and development phases toward the design and study phases.

Reverse engineering and reengineering are two major types of redevelopment engineering, and, increasingly, they are compatible with or designed into integrated CASE products. With reference to figure 19.9, reverse engineering relates to maintenance and reengineering to change.

Documentation structure for computer-based business information systems. Structured relationships among documents essential to management of the life-cycle process for creating computer-based business information systems are summarized here.

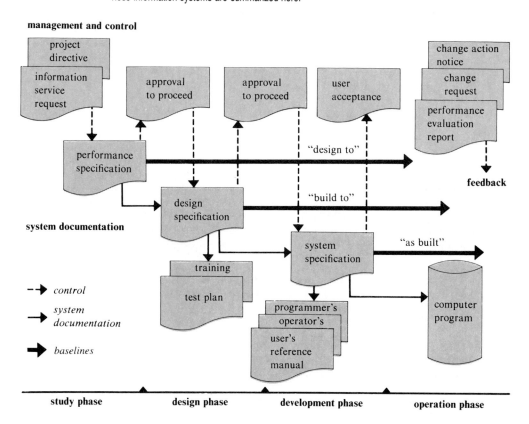

Reverse Engineering

Reverse engineering is a form of redevelopment engineering that applies automated software engineering tools and techniques to systems maintenance. It focuses on reducing the complexity and cost of maintaining existing systems by working backwards from the programming code through the system design, analysis, and definition of requirements. Within the context of figure 19.14, which displays the documentation that must be generated and maintained in a repository throughout the SDLC, reverse engineering is a means of extending the useful life of a system by recovering, or recreating, the specifications and other documentation that define the functions the system is to perform and the design for performing those functions. For example, reverse engineering tools can be used to derive structure charts, data flow diagrams, and data base structures from an existing COBOL program. Reverse engineering enables users and analysts to improve their understanding of what a system does and how it does it, and it assists them in assessing the risks and cost involved in effecting continued maintenance versus making a major change or a "new system" decision.

Reengineering

Reengineering is a form of redevelopment engineering that applies automated software engineering tools to change the functions performed by an existing computer information system or to modify that system by introducing major changes in hardware or software technology. Whereas reverse engineering might include minor technological changes, such as upgrading the data processing or networking environment, reengineering deals with modifications that have a broad impact on users and that require performance review board action. Reengineering uses reverse engineering techniques to provide an improved understanding of the information system; however, it goes beyond reverse engineering because its purpose is to implement change. The general procedure for reverse engineering is identical to that outlined in figure 19.11 and previously described in this chapter.

Reengineering is not a panacea. It is not always possible to satisfactorily recover the design of a critical and complex system that has a history of many poorly documented quick fixes; nonetheless, reengineering techniques often can extend the life of existing systems and provide insights that help to make "change" versus "new system" decisions.

Clearly, reengineering and other emerging structured, CASE-related tools have not yet begun to achieve their full potential or universal acceptance. However, it is equally clear that in the 1990s the rate of change in computer technology, the growing volume and complexity of user requirements, and the need to replace systems developed in the 1970s and 1980s will combine to place an increasing strain on existing tools and techniques, including those that we have studied in this text, for the design and development of computer information systems. This will provide a continuing impetus toward the development and use of advanced CASE products, powerful prototyping software, expert systems, and other tools that will bring increasing rigor and discipline to the SDLC process.

As a current example, the IBM corporation has committed major resources to the development of CASE/repository technology in its Applications Development Cycle (AD/Cycle) and Repository Manager products. And, IBM is joined in this commitment to improve the quality of information systems by other major computer hardware and software vendors. Figure 19.15 illustrates the use of CASE technology to modify an existing major software application. In this case, the application is IBM's manufacturing, accounting, production, and inventory control system (MAPICS), which is a key element of its computer integrated manufacturing (CIM) architecture.

In the years ahead we will see the structured methodologies evolve into an integrated set of computer-aided disciplines called information engineering, which hold great promise for increasing productivity by automating the tedious tasks associated with the systems development life cycle.

■ Figure 19.15   CASE technology and change management. IBM's Application Development/Cycle (AD/Cycle) is an example of commitment to the use of CASE technology to develop and to maintain complex computer information systems. In this instance AD/Cycle is used to redevelop portions of MAPICS, a major software application.

[LARKSPUR, CALIF.]

Synon Chosen for MAPICS Rewrite

IBM development group will use CASE tool for two MAPICS modules

By Grant Evans

In yet another official endorsement of its CASE technology, Synon recently announced that it has been selected by IBM to provide the AS/400 CASE tool for the rewrite of two modules of IBM's manufacturing application package, MAPICS/DB.

According to Jim Smith, Synon director of business development, the Synon/2E product will be employed by IBM's MAPICS Development Group to re-engineer the Inventory Management and Order Entry and Invoicing modules of MAPICS/DB. Smith notes that in addition to being a welcome development for Larkspur, Calif.-based Synon, the announcement underscores IBM's commitment to AD/Cycle and AD/Cycle products.

"By using a designated AD/Cycle product for internal product development and enhancement, IBM is saying 'We're serious enough about AD/Cycle that we're implementing it within the company and using it on a flagship product like MAPICS,' "notes Smith. Synon became IBM's fourth AD/Cycle Business Partner in April 1990.

According to Smith, MAPICS users will benefit greatly from the increased ability to customize MAPICS and more easily add supplemental applications using Synon's technology. Synon Consulting, the professional services subsidiary of Synon, currently is working with the IBM MAPICS development group to provide on-site education and services for the project.

Synon/2E is an interactive application development environment for the AS/400. It helps developers design, code, document and maintain applications. It generates native AS/400 source code in RPG or COBOL.

Summary

The operation phase is the fourth and longest of the systems development life-cycle phases. The operation phase has four distinct stages: system changeover, routine operation, system performance evaluation, and system change.

At the conclusion of a successful acceptance review, the computer-based business information system enters the operation phase. The first stage of the operation phase, called changeover, is a period of transition from the old system to the new system. Changeover is characterized by a series of crises, which usually subside after a period of time. During the changeover period problems must be handled promptly, and it is useful to maintain a changeover action log.

After changeover is completed the system is turned over to its principal user(s) and enters a stage called routine operation. Routine operation seldom is routine, since the day-to-day operating environment is subject to unscheduled priorities and emergencies. Routine operation can best be managed if the information services organization reports to an appropriate level. Typically, this reporting level is that of a vice-president of information services. The key to success in managing routine operations is to maintain the usability of the system by providing timely and accurate information to its users. Maintaining good customer relations and data security contribute to the usability of computer-related information systems.

Computer-related business information systems must be reviewed after they are installed and changeover is completed to be certain that they perform as planned. They also must be reviewed periodically thereafter both to ensure that the integrity of the system and its documentation are maintained and to respond to changes due to the dynamics of the business environment. One method for performing these reviews and for managing change is to establish a user-oriented performance review board (PRB). All system modifications are not significant enough to require prior approval by the PRB. We distinguish between maintenance tasks, which do not require PRB approval, and changes, which do require approval. All modifications do affect baseline specifications; however, changes usually relate more to fundamental decisions made in preparing the performance specification and design specification than do maintenance tasks.

Change control is the means by which major modifications (changes) to a computer-based business information system are managed. The change control process involves the PRB, which reviews all change requests. The PRB may request further analysis from the information service organization prior to rejecting, modifying, or implementing the change request. When a decision is made to change the system, the PRB issues a change directive to the information service organization, and the life cycle is reentered at a point that depends upon the extent of the modification. Sometimes the effort required to change a system is greater than that required to develop it initially.

Redevelopment engineering is a general term for automated software tools designed to modify existing computer information systems in a manner that improves user and analyst understanding and is compatible with the SDLC and CASE technologies. These tools make possible the recovery of data and logic design information from an existing system and the entry of this information into a CASE repository. Redevelopment engineering approaches the SDLC in a backwards direction, from the operation and development phases toward the design and study phases. Reverse engineering and reengineering are two major types of redevelopment engineering. Reverse engineering relates to system maintenance. Reengineering builds upon reverse engineering and relates to change and its management. As these and other computer-related disciplines evolve, the emerging field called information engineering will progress toward maturity.

For Review

operation phase

system changeover

system performance evaluation

system change

changeover crisis

changeover action log

user turnover

routine operation

down load

standards

standards manual

usability

patch

performance review board (PRB)

post-installation review

periodic review

modification

change

maintenance

change control

change analysis request

change analysis report

change directive

change notice

redevelopment engineering

design recovery

reverse engineering

reengineering

For Discussion

1. Define operation phase.
2. What are the four stages of the operation phase?
3. Why is the operation phase usually the longest of the four life-cycle phases?
4. Give some examples of events that could cause extensive changes in an operational business information system. How far back in the life cycle would each extend?
5. What is the "changeover crisis"?
6. Describe actions that can be taken to manage changeover.
7. What occurs at user turnover time?
8. Why are so-called routine data processing operations not routine?
9. What standards are contained in a data processing standards manual? Distinguish among them.
10. Discuss steps that may be taken to protect the computer center against natural disasters and against fraud.
11. Discuss security actions that may be taken to protect the computer center.
12. What is the purpose of the performance review board? Who should be on this board?
13. Under what circumstances are undocumented changes acceptable?
14. What is the purpose of the post-installation review? When should it be scheduled?
15. Why are periodic reviews necessary?
16. Distinguish among modification, change, and maintenance.

17. Describe the change management process.
18. Relate the concept of usability to post-changeover evaluation of a computer information system.
19. Why is change usually more complex than the original computer information system development process?
20. What is redevelopment engineering? Using examples, distinguish between reverse engineering and reengineering.

For Exercise: Coping with Change in the "Real World"

Visit your campus computing center, or a similar industrial activity, and interview the manager of that operation. In your interview, ask how they cope with change, specifically changeover, performance review and evaluation, change management, and redevelopment engineering. Prepare and submit a report that summarizes your discussion. Comment on the relationship between the content of this chapter and your "real world" findings.

Glossary

Acceptance review The final user review of the completed system in the development phase; also called the development phase review.

Achievement Index (AI) The ratio of actual achievement to planned achievement.

ACM Association for Computing Machinery, a professional organization.

AD/Cycle A full-function CASE product developed by IBM.

Activity The application of time and resources to achieve an objective.

Agile enterprise An enterprise that is able to anticipate and react quickly to an external, customer-driven environment. One that combines CIE and TQM. *See* **Computer-Integrated Enterprise (CIE), Total Quality Management (TQM).**

AI *See* **Artificial Intelligence** and **Achievement Index.**

Algorithm A set of rules or instructions used to accomplish a task.

Alphabetic derivation code A code where characters are taken or derived from the name or description of the coded item according to a set of rules; an alphanumeric code.

Alphanumeric code A code that describes items by the use of letter and number combinations. *See* **Mnemonic code** and **Alphabetic derivation code.**

American National Standards Institute (ANSI) A national organization that provides the forum for the establishment of standards within the United States.

Analysis The process of breaking something into its parts so that the whole may be understood.

Anomalies Problems that arise when updating, deleting data from, or adding data to a file.

Applications generator A nonprocedural command language used in conjunction with a data base management system to generate computer instructions.

Attribute Any property that describes an entity.

Automated source document design The use of form design and page layout software to design source documents.

Back-end CASE system *See* **Lower CASE workbench.**

Background analysis An analysis by the systems analyst to become familiar with an organization's environment and the physical processes related to the new or revised system.

Bar chart A chart using horizontal or vertical bars to depict relationships among elements.

Baseline specification One of three essential life-cycle reference documents: performance specification, design specification, or system specification.

Benchmark testing Using an identical set of tasks to evaluate two or more computer systems.

"Best" system The system that meets the performance requirements at the least cost.

Block sequence code A sequence code consisting of a series of consecutive numbers and/or letters divided into blocks, each block reserved for identifying a group of items with a common characteristic.

Body The part of a form or display that contains the specific data to be shown.

Bottom-up computer program development A hierarchical method of developing computer programs in which lower-level modules are tested and combined into higher-level modules.

Boxed style A form style where each data element has a specific amount of space allocated to it, clearly identified by name or by a brief description.

Bugs Programmer term for errors within a program; may be logical in nature or syntax errors.

Business A system of systems, each of which uses resources in order to accomplish its purpose.

Business information system A system that uses resources to convert data into information needed to accomplish the purposes of the business.

Candidate evaluation matrix A table that lists evaluation criteria and rates alternative systems in terms of these criteria.

Candidate system An alternative physical system.

Candidate system evaluation A procedure for identifying system candidates and selecting the most feasible.

Candidate system matrix A table that lists functions to be performed and alternative systems for performing them.

Carriage control tape Formerly used to control position of first and last lines to be printed on a page. *See* **Channel 1, Channel 12.**

CASE *See* **Computer-Assisted Systems Engineering.**

Cathode Ray Tube (CRT) A visual display terminal utilizing a TV picture tube approach for the display.

CD-ROM Compact Disk Read Only Memory.

Central repository The core of all CASE tools, it stores all of the information related to the computer information system, including the data base, process specifications, and tools needed for project management.

Change A system modification that requires performance review board action.

Change control The means by which major modification to computer-based business information systems are managed.

Changeover The process of changing over from the old to the new system. The transition from the development phase to the operation phase.

Changeover action log A log to record actions, responsibilities, assignments, and completion dates during the changeover activities.

Changeover crisis A problem-filled period in the SDLC that occurs whenever a new system first becomes operational.

Changeover plan A plan that identifies and schedules all changeover activities.

Channel 1 A signal that indicates the first line to be printed on a page.

Channel 12 A signal that indicates the last line to be printed on a page.

Chart A graphical or pictorial expression of relationships or movement (trends).

Class A group of objects that have the same structure and behave in the same way.

Classical life-cycle methodology Use of flowchart symbols to emphasize the physical attributes of a system.

CI *See* **Cost Index.**

Code dictionary A listing of codes and their corresponding data descriptions.

Code generator Software that generates program code from the descriptions of data and processing requirements.

Code plan The identification of particular characteristics that need to be contained within a code.

Coding The writing of program instructions in a programming language.

Column The equivalent of a field in the relational model of a DBMS.

Communication The process of transferring information from one point to another.

Compilation The translation of a high-level programming language into machine language.

Computer Information System (CIS) In this text, a computer-based business information system.

Computer program code generator A back-end CASE tool that can convert a detailed design specification directly into applications software.

Computer program test requirements definition The requirements established for the tests necessary to verify the performance of the major computer programs (design phase).

Computer-Assisted Systems Engineering (CASE) An engineering approach toward automating all phases of the systems development life-cycle methodology.

Computer information system (CIS) A computer-related business information system. *See* **Business information system.**

Computer-Integrated Enterprise (CIE) An enterprise that employs flexible, fast-response corporatewide computer information systems and in which all elements, from business plan to delivery of a product or service, are linked by an organized and shared collection of information.

Computer system In this text, refers to the entire computer information system.

Connectivity The ability to link networks of computers and computer systems.

Conclusion The part of a form or display that contains summary data.

Constraint A condition, such as time or money, that limits the solutions that an analyst may consider.

Context diagram A diagram that identifies the domain of a system; it identifies the net input and output data flows between the system and the external entities with which it interacts.

Control The actions taken to bring the difference between an actual output and a desired output within an acceptable range.

Conversion The process of performing all the operations that directly result in the turnover of the new system to the user.

Conversion plan A plan, created at the start of the development phase, for performing all of the conversion activities (procedures, computer programs, and files) that lead to turning a new system over to its users.

Cost Index (CI) The ratio of actual costs to planned costs.

Cost report A line chart showing both planned and actual expenditures; used for project control.

CPM Critical Path Method. *See* **Critical path.**

Critical path The longest path from start to finish in a critical path network; it identifies the required time for the project.

Critical path network A management tool that uses a graphical format to depict the relationships between tasks and schedules.

CRT *See* **Cathode Ray Tube.**

Cumulative documentation The concept that describes the collection and transformation of the documentation as the design specification grows from the system performance specification and the system specification grows from the design specification.

Data Raw, recorded facts.

Data base The collection of data available for processing. A series of common, shared files.

Data Base Administrator (DBA) The authority that regulates the data base management system by controlling the data base schema and subschema; also authorizes the use of passwords by users.

Data Base Management System (DBMS) Software that allows data descriptions to be independent from computer programs. This system provides the capability for describing logical relationships between files to facilitate efficient maintenance and access to the data base.

Data carrier Any entity, e.g. a document, that contains data. *See* **Data flow.**

Data definition component That portion of a data base management system that holds the definition of the data within the data base.

Data dictionary A central repository that contains the definitions and descriptions of all of the system data structures.

Data-oriented model A structured design methodology that focuses upon the optimization of data bases, with processing requirements derived from data structures.

Data element The smallest unit of data that is meaningful to a system; a field.

Data element analysis The analysis of data elements and data structures by system analysts to assure that they understand the meanings of the data names and codes that appear in the manuals, procedures, charts, and other forms of documentation they have collected.

Data element list Information describing the name, format, and size of each data element in a specified output.

Data flow Directed lines that identify input and output data flows for each transformation process.

Data Flow Diagram (DFD) A network that describes the flow of data throughout a system, data stores, and the processes that change or transform data flows.

Data manipulation component That portion of a data base management system that accomplishes all data retrievals, updates, additions, and deletions.

Data normalization The decomposition of complex data files into multiple, simpler files for more effective data retrieval and processing.

Data storage In a data flow diagram, a repository, or store, for data that are related. *See* **File.**

Data structure Refers to a structured relationship between data elements; composed of data elements and other data structures.

DB 2 An IBM relational data base management system utilizing SQL as the query language (larger systems).

DBA *See* **Data Base Administrator.**

DBMS *See* **Data Base Management System.**

DBMS utility A series of programs used to create, back up, and restore the data base.

Debugging The correcting of errors in a computer program or system.

Decision Support System (DSS) An information system designed to assist an executive in decision making through an exploration of consequences.

Decision table A table used to describe logical rules.

Decision tree A network-type chart that is the logical equivalent of a decision table.

Decomposed data flow diagram A data flow diagram that has been expanded in its detail until each of the processing functions can be identified.

Decomposition Subdivision of a high-level data flow diagram into a hierarchy of lower-level data flow diagrams.

Design phase The systems development life-cycle phase in which the detailed design of the system selected in the study phase is accomplished.

Design phase report A report prepared at the end of the design phase. An extension of the study phase report that summarizes the results of the design phase activities.

Design phase review A review held with the user organization at the conclusion of the design phase to determine whether or not to proceed with the development phase.

Design recovery *See* **Redevelopment engineering.**

Design specification A baseline specification that serves as a blueprint for the construction of a computer-based business information system.

Desktop publishing A combination of microcomputers, laser printers, and software that combine text and graphics into a single image.

Destination In a data flow diagram, an external entity that is a termination for a data flow.

Development phase The systems development life-cycle phase where the system is constructed according to the design phase specifications.

Development phase report A report prepared at the end of the development phase. An extension of the design phase report that summarizes the results of the development phase activities.

Development phase review A review held with the user organization at the conclusion of the development phase to determine whether or not to enter the operation phase; also called the acceptance review.

DFD *See* **Data Flow Diagram.**

Display layout sheet A form used to design VDT screen layouts; it is divided into 24 lines of 80 characters to simulate the possible display position on a screen.

Display station *See* **Visual display terminal.**

Distributed data processing Computer information systems that place data processing power wherever it is needed whenever it is needed.

Domain The boundaries of the system being studied.

DPMA Data Processing Management Association, a professional association.

DSS *See* **Decision Support System.**

Edit characters Special characters, e.g. dollar signs, used to describe a data element, or field.

Entity Any object, physical or abstract, about which we store data.

Entity-relationship diagram A diagram that uses predefined symbols to identify entities and to display the relationships among them. *See* **Entity.**

Equipment specification The description of the hardware configuration used to convert input data into meaningful output information.

Error checking tool A CASE tool that enables systems analysts to detect (and correct) errors and other design flaws as they occur throughout the SDLC.

Event A point in time when an activity begins or ends.

Event-driven system *See* **real-time system.**

Expert systems Systems that can diagnose problems and propose solutions.

External entity In a data flow diagram, an entity that is a source or destination of a data flow; it is represented by a rectangle.

External performance specification The part of the performance specification that establishes the relationship between the computer information system and its operating environment.

Fact analysis The analysis of facts collected during the initial investigation to provide the analyst with insight into the interaction among organizational elements, personnel, and information flow.

Fact-finding The initial investigation activity when the analyst collects data from written documents and personnel who are knowledgeable about or involved in the operation of the system under study.

Feedback The comparing of actual output or results to the desired output or results to determine if the exercise of control is necessary.

Field *See* **Data element.**

First normal form (1NF) A table (or file) that does not contain repeating groups.

File The collection of logically related records .

Forms control The coordination of form needs of multiple departments or users to control form costs.

Fourth-Generation Language (4GL) An automated software development package that includes a data base management system, a query language, and a report writer.

Front-end CASE workbench. *See* **Upper CASE workbench.**

Front-end loading Resource commitment to validate system performance at the analysis and design phases, reducing the duration and cost of the system development phase.

Full-function CASE workbench An integrated assembly of tools that apply to all phases of the SDLC.

Functional file A file used in form control that contains copies of forms filed by subject, operation, or function of the form.

Functional prototyping Prototyping based on interviews with persons who are expert in specific functions characteristic of an enterprise.

Gantt-type chart A horizontal bar chart used to show a project schedule and report progress on that schedule.

Goal A broadly stated purpose of a business.

Graphics Images other than text; charts, data flow diagrams, and forms.

Grid chart *See* **Table.**

Group classification code A code that designates major, intermediate, and minor data classification by successively lower orders of digits.

Hardware The physical components of a computer system.

Heading Contains all of the general information about a form or display.

Hierarchical DBMS A data base management system that links files through a superior-subordinate relationship; one superior to one or more subordinate.

Hierarchy chart A structure chart that shows the levels of functions of a system or of a computer program; appearance is that of an organization chart.

HIPO Hierarchy plus Input Processing Output; a package consisting of both a hierarchy chart and IPO charts.

Hygiene factor Factors that add to the pleasantness of a job; they do not contribute as much to job satisfaction as do motivating factors. *See* **Motivating factor.**

Identification code A means of uniquely and concisely describing the characteristics of an object.

Immediate replacement A system changeover approach where the old system is replaced by the new system in one step.

Implementation The process of bringing a developed system into operational use and turning it over to the user.

Implementation Committee A coordinating committee responsible for ensuring that all of the tasks identified in the implementation plan are completed. *See* **Implementation plan.**

Implementation plan A plan for implementing a system that includes test plans, training plans, an equipment acquisition plan, and a conversion plan.

Incremental commitment The concept within the SDLC that allows users and management to commit to a project one phase at a time.

Information The interpreted data outputted from a system.

Information engineering A computer-aided, systems engineering approach to the design and development of complex information systems.

Information flow The network of administrative and operational documentation.

Information generator A business information need, either external or internal in origin.

Information resource center A center staffed by information system professionals who assist users, most often to select microcomputers or workstations.

Information resource management Refers to a centralized responsibility for selecting, distributing, and managing the data processing, automated office, and communications resources of an enterprise.

Information Service Request (ISR) A written request from a user for information services support.

Information system levels Different levels in an organization call for different levels of detail from an information system; these information system levels are operational, lower management, middle management, and top management.

Inheritance Pertains to a hierarchy of classes that share attributes and operations. *See* **Class.**

Initial investigation An investigation performed to clarify the business information system problem and develop a project directive.

Input-output analysis A general term for all analysis techniques based upon the perception of a system as a process that converts inputs into outputs.

Integrated CASE system *See* **Full-function CASE workbench.**

Intelligent memory The tasks related to the management of peripheral devices are shifted from the CPU to the devices themselves.

Internal performance specification The part of the performance specification that describes the environment internal to the computer information system.

Interview A one-on-one, two-way oral communication for the purpose of collecting information.

IPO charts   Part of the HIPO package; consists of detail-level charts listing the inputs, processing steps, and outputs of each functional module of the hierarchy chart.

ISR   *See* **Information Service Request.**

Joint Applications Design (JAD)   A series of intensive meetings with users for the analysis and design of a computer information system.

Knowledge-based system   A system that diagnoses problems and proposes solutions.

LAN   *See* **Local Area Network.**

Laser printer   A page printer using a photocopy approach with excellent printing resolution.

Le Courier's legibility table   A table showing the effect of ink color and background color combinations on form readability.

Level-1 data flow diagram   The data flow diagram derived from a decomposed level-0 data flow diagram.

Level-0 data flow diagram   The data flow diagram level derived from a decomposed context diagram.

Leveled DFDs   The set of data flow diagrams that have been decomposed until a bottom set is arrived at for each major transformation process.

Life cycle   The period of the creation and existence of a business information system. *See* **Systems Development Life Cycle.**

Life-cycle manager   The systems analyst.

Life-cycle methodology   Alternate name for the systems development life cycle (SDLC).

Life-cycle phases   *See* **Systems Development Life Cycle.**

Line chart   A chart constructed by connecting a set of plotted points; also called a graph.

Line position   A position within an organization that has a direct authority relationship with other positions.

Link pins   An organizational position characteristic of a superior-subordinate relationship. A position between an upper and a lower element of the organization.

Local Area Network (LAN)   A network of computers within a restricted geographic area that is wholly owned and controlled by the organization.

Logical model   A data flow diagram or other chart that depicts the logical functions of a system without committing to a physical implementation.

Lower CASE workbench   An integrated assembly of tools that apply to development and operation phases of the SDLC.

Maintenance   A minor system modification that does not require performance review board action.

Manuals   Printed and assembled pages of instructional material (i.e., employee manuals, policy, and procedure manuals).

Master file   A file that contains relatively permanent data, i.e., data good for more than one processing cycle.

Microcomputer   Desktop-sized computers based upon a microprocessor; also called personal computers.

Microelectronics The electronics technology that made it possible to reduce the size of transistors and integrate large numbers of circuit elements into very small chips of silicon.

Mnemonic code A coding system where letter and number combinations are obtained from descriptions of the coded item; often a strict abbreviation of the item description.

Modification Refers to the maintenance or change of a computer information system. *See* **Maintenance, Change.**

Modified information service request The information service request as modified by the systems analyst after completing the initial investigation.

Motivating factor Primary cause of job satisfaction; relates to job content.

MPU MicroProcessor Unit; a central processing unit (CPU) on a single integrated circuit chip.

Multitasking The ability to run multiple applications concurrently.

Narrative A written communication that tells a story; the most informal type of technical writing.

Natural languages Systems that are able to translate human speech into commands that computers can be programmed to understand.

Networked DBMS A DBMS architecture that links files through a superior-subordinate relationship (as does the hierarchical DBMS), but each subordinate file may have more that one superior.

Nonprocedural programming languages Programming languages that emphasize the data rather than the procedural steps required to access the data.

Numerical file A file used in forms control; it contains an example of each form filed by its code.

Normalization *See* Data normalization.

Object A reusable software module that encapsulates both attributes, represented by data structures, and the operations performed on data that cause a certain behavior.

Object-oriented model A system design methodology based on the development of a library of reusable software modules from which systems analysts can make selections when there is a need to create a new system. *See* **Object.**

Objective A concrete, specific accomplishment necessary to the achievement of a goal.

OCR *See* **Optical Character Reader.**

OMR *See* **Optical Mark Reader.**

Operation phase The life-cycle phase in which the system is installed, operated, maintained, and changed as necessary.

Optical bar-code reader Input device that scans data coded as bars; most common bar code is the Universal Product Code (UPC).

Optical Character Reader (OCR) Optical input device for reading characters of data from a form; the characters may be typed or handwritten.

Optical Mark Reader (OMR) An input device that can detect pencil marks on a paper form; best use is for marking a choice from a printed list of options.

Optical reader Reader that uses a light source to directly input from documents without the use of a keyboard.

Oracle An Oracle Corporation relational data base management system based upon the SQL query language; available on many different machines from mainframes to microcomputers.

Organization chart A flowchart that identifies organizational elements of a business and displays areas of responsibility and lines of authority.

Organization function list A document that describes the major activities performed by each organization shown on an organization chart.

Output data element source analysis sheet A worksheet used to determine the source of the data elements in the outputs of a system; may also be used in the preparation of the data dictionary.

Output specification A form used to describe computer-generated output.

Parallel operation A changeover approach where the old system is left in place when the new system is implemented; data is processed by both the old and new systems for a period of time.

Parent-child relationship In a data flow diagram, a process that is common to (i.e., serves as a link-pin to) a process and a next lower or higher level of detail.

Partition *See* **Decomposition.**

Patch A "quick fix" programming change that is made under the pressure of an immediate operational need.

Payback analysis An analysis to determine the point in time at which the investment in the new system is recovered—the result of cost savings or cost avoidance.

Performance indices An index approach to summarizing past project performance and to predicting future performance. *See* **Achievement Index, Cost Index,** and **Status Index.**

Performance review board A user-oriented board responsible both for the periodic evaluation of the performance of a computer-based business information system and for maintaining its integrity.

Performance specification A baseline specification that describes what the computer-based system is to do.

Periodic review A series of post-installation reviews to ensure that the integrity of the system is maintained and to identify special areas requiring management attention.

PERT *See* **Program Evaluation Review Technique.**

Phased changeover A changeover approach in which the new system is phased in and the old system is phased out in several steps.

Picosecond One trillionth of a second; 1/000,000,000,000 second.

Pie chart A chart for presenting relationships as percentages of the whole.

Planned workload A composite of sample programs used to simulate an actual workload for the purpose of evaluating systems and hardware.

Policies Broad written guidelines for conduct or action; often presented with procedures.

Post-installation review A review to determine how well actual performance of the system compares with promised performance.

Presentation Oral communication of plans or results made in order to influence people and to obtain decisions.

Presentation graphics High-quality charts and graphs used as illustrations within printed documentation and as visual supplements to oral presentations.

Primitive Each transformation process in a leveled data flow diagram; a transformation that cannot be further decomposed.

Principal user The person who, in practice, will accept or reject the computer-based business information system.

Print chart A form used to design computer printer outputs. Each line on the form is divided into printer positions to allow for the detailed design of titles, column headings, detail lines, and total lines.

Procedural programming languages Programming languages based on step-by-step procedures or instructions that the computer must follow to produce the desired output.

Procedures Written, specific statements that tell how policies are to be carried out; often presented with policies.

Process specification The rules by which a process transforms input data flows into output data flows.

Process-oriented model A structured design methodology that focuses upon the processes that transform data flows, with data structures derived from input, output, and processing requirements.

Product flow The flow of raw materials into finished goods.

Production enterprises Businesses that produce tangible end products such as manufacturing, farming, construction, and agriculture.

Program The logical steps to be followed by a computer.

Program Evaluation Review Technique (PERT) A graphical format to depict the relationships between tasks and schedules; a critical path network.

Programming language One of many languages available for writing a computer program in the form of instructions that a computer can follow. *See* **Coding.**

Program stubs *See* **Stubs.**

Progress plan A schedule of milestones over the duration of a project.

Progress plan and status report A Gantt-type chart for showing planned and achieved progress for a project.

Project cost report A line chart comparing the estimated costs (the plan) and the actual costs as they are incurred.

Project directive The final version of an information service request. The written contract between the user and the information systems organization; establishes the scope of the information system project.

Project file The file in which pertinent project documents and working papers are stored.

Project reviews A series of reviews or meetings with users and management to apprise them of the progress of the project.

Protocol A software-defined standard for data communications between two computer systems.

Prototyping A technique for speeding up the development of a computer information system by working with a model of that system that evolves into a final design specification.

Pseudocode A structured English approach to design and/or describe the logic of a computer program.

Query language A simplified programming language that allows users to specify the data wanted and the format that will meet user information needs; a component of a data base management system.

RAM *See* **Random Access Memory.**

Random Access Memory (RAM) Semi-conductor-based main memory of a computer.

Rapid Applications Development (RAD) The prototyping version of the SDLC, which focuses on the rapid cycling through study and design phase alternatives until an acceptable design specification is created.

Rapid prototyping *See* Rapid Applications Development.

Read Only Memory (ROM) Special memory that has software built into it. The stored software can be used, but not changed.

Real-time Processing transactions as they occur rather than batching them for later processing; also called transaction processing.

Real-time system A system that responds to external inputs in a time-sensitive manner.

Real-time system CASE workbench A workbench used to design systems that must respond to inputs in a time-sensitive manner.

Recurring data analysis An analysis technique to detect data duplication within the system.

Reengineering A form of redevelopment engineering that applies automated software engineering tools to significantly modify the system hardware and/or software.

Redevelopment engineering Refers to automated software tools designed to restructure existing systems for compatibility with CASE technologies. The process moves from the back to the front of the SDLC. *See* **Redevelopment-engineering CASE workbench.**

Redevelopment-engineering CASE workbench A workbench used to analyze an existing, operational system in order to redevelop its specifications in structured form.

Reference manual identification The identification of the reference manuals required by user personnel, programmers, and equipment operators during the design phase.

Relational DBMS An architecture in which the links are established by the data rather than within the DBMS. Relational DBMS files are called tables and are made up of rows and columns.

Report A written formal communication of results and conclusions due to a particular set of actions; it summarizes work that has been performed.

Report use analysis An analysis technique performed during the initial investigation to identify data elements, and possibly entire outputs, not required by many of the individuals or groups on the current distribution list for a system output.

Report generator A nonprocedural language used to access a database in order to generate a report formatted to user specifications.

Resources The personnel, facilities, materials, and equipment used by a business information system.

Response time The elapsed time between the release of input data by a user and the receipt of computer output.

Reverse engineering A form of redevelopment engineering that applies automated software engineering tools to systems maintenance.

ROM *See* **Read Only Memory.**

Routine operation The stage in the operation phase that follows system changeover.

Row The equivalent of a record in the relational model of a DBMS.

SDLC *See* **Systems Development Life Cycle.**

Schema The DBMS definition of data elements and the relationships between them in a data base.

Second normal form (2NF) A table (or file) that is in the first normal form (1NF) and in which every column (or field) is dependent on the entire key.

Service enterprises Businesses whose main product is a service, such as transportation, communications, medicine, and education.

SI *See* **Status Index.**

Significant digit code A numeric code in which the numbers describe a measurable physical characteristic of the item.

Simple sequence code A code system in which a series of consecutive numbers and/or letters are assigned to a group of items that have been organized into a meaningful sequence.

Skipping The process of moving a form more rapidly than spacing. *See* **Spacing.**

Software The collection of programs that facilitates the use of a computer.

Source In a data flow diagram, an external entity that is an origin for data flow.

Spacing The process of moving a form one, two, or three lines at a time.

Specialty forms Forms that are complex enough in their construction to require special equipment for their manufacture or use; most are designed by a forms manufacturer.

Specific objective A measurable performance outcome.

Specifications Written reference documents that contain basic detailed data.

SQL *See* **Structured Query Language.**

SQL/DS A relational data base management system product from IBM that utilizes SQL as its query language (smaller systems).

Staff position An organizational position that has a service relationship to other positions in the organization rather than a direct or line authority.

Standards The rules under which personnel in an information services organization work.

Standards manual A document that contains the standards that govern the operation of an information services organization; it includes administrative, systems analysis, programming, and operations standards.

Status Index (SI) The ratio of the achievement index to the cost index; an indication of the overall status of a project.

Step chart A basic chart used in place of a line chart to convey patterns of motion when relatively few points are plotted and when individual levels are to be emphasized; has a staircase appearance.

Structure charts Design tools for describing a system according to its functions. *See* **HIPO charts.**

Structured diagramming tool A CASE tool that enables systems analysts to create, verify, and modify design diagrams, e.g., data flow diagrams, in an interactive mode.

Structured English A method for displaying a logical process in an outline format using English statements.

Structured life-cycle methodology A methodology that uses flowchart symbols that identify data flows to develop a logical model of a system.

Structured methods SDLC methodologies that use special flowcharting symbols to identify data flows within a system in order to create and work with a logical model of the system. *See* **Data flow diagram.**

Structured programming A top-down approach to the creation of a program that is comparable to the approach defined by the systems development life-cycle concept; the general modules are developed first, and then the more detailed or specific modules are developed.

Structured Query Language (SQL) The standardized query language used with relational data base management systems.

Structured walk-through A technical review to assist the people working on a project; used to discover errors in logic of a computer program or in other system components.

Stubs Temporary modules placed in a computer program until the real module has been written.

Study phase The life-cycle phase in which a problem is identified and analyzed, alternate solutions evaluated, and a system solution recommended at the general design level.

Study phase report A comprehensive report prepared for the user-sponsor of the system and presented at the conclusion of the study phase.

Study phase review A review for presenting the results of the study phase activities and determining future action.

Subschema The definitions of the data elements available to an individual computer program.

Subsystem A system that is part of a larger system.

Superior-subordinate relationships A relationship in which one position has direct authority over another.

Synchronous data transmission An approach that involves the continuous high-speed transmission of data in a well-defined sequence.

Synthesis The process of putting parts together to form a new whole.

System A combination of resources working together to convert inputs into outputs.

System changeover The period of transition from the old system to the new system.

System controls Approaches designed to minimize the occurrence of incorrect data in a system.

System of systems The acknowledgment that almost all systems are actually subsystems of a larger system; a business.

System performance definition The transition from a logical performance requirement to a physical one; includes the statement of general constraints, the identification of specific objectives, and the description of outputs.

System performance review board A user-oriented board responsible for the post-installation review of a computer information system. *See* **Post-installation review.**

System specification A baseline specification that contains all of the essential system documentation. A complete technical specification of the system.

System team A group of people from user areas, management, and information services that works with the systems analyst throughout the SDLC.

System test requirements definition Requirements for the tests necessary to verify the performance of the entire computer-based system (design phase).

Systems analysis In this text, a structured process for designing and developing effective computer information systems. Includes both analysis and synthesis. *See* **Analysis, Synthesis.**

Systems analyst An individual who performs systems analysis during any, or all, of the life-cycle phases of a business information system.

Systems Development Life Cycle (SDLC) A sequence of related activities through which all business information systems must pass. The four life-cycle phases are: study, design, development, and operation.

Table A chart made up of intersecting horizontal and vertical lines to form rows and columns, called a grid chart. Also, the equivalent of a file in a relational model of a DBMS, where the table can be viewed as a layout of rows and columns.

Task-oriented tools Computer programs designed to automate specific SDLC tasks.

Technical writing A document written for the purpose of communicating facts.

Third normal form (3NF) A table (or file) that is in the second normal form (2NF) and does not contain columns (or fields) that are determined by any other column than the key.

Title Identifies the purpose of a form or display.

Tool kit A collection of tools used by a CASE product. *See* **Lower CASE, Upper CASE,** and **Full-function CASE workbenches.**

Top-down A structured technique that starts with a general description of the system or program and expands that description into successively greater levels of detail.

Top-down computer program development A structured technique that starts with a general description of the program and expands into successively greater levels of detailed modules.

Total Quality Management (TQM) A set of quality management principles that focuses on customer satisfaction and continuous improvement.

Transaction file A file that contains data with a limited useful life, typically one processing cycle.

Transformation process In a data flow diagram, a process, represented by a ''bubble,'' that transforms data streams.

Type *See* **Form type.**

Upper CASE workbench An integrated assembly of tools that apply to analysis and design phases of the SDLC.

Usability The worth of a computer system as perceived in the value system of its principal users; the total quality management concept of user satisfaction.

Usability engineering A field of engineering that has as its goal improving the comfort of users when they interact with computers.

User acceptance review A review held with the user organization at the conclusion of the development phase to determine whether or not to enter the operation phase; also called the development phase review.

User turnover The stage in the operation phase when the data processing department assumes full responsibility for the system. The beginning of routine operation.

View *See* **Subschema.**

Visual Display Terminal (VDT) A terminal that utilizes a screen for output display; may be a cathode ray tube (CRT) or a flat panel type of screen.

Weighted candidate evaluation matrix A table that weights the candidate evaluation matrix entries by their importance and applies a rating number; it is a means of calculating comparative total scores for each candidate.

Word processing The entering, editing, and formatting of text using a computer terminal or personal computer.

Word publishing Word processing software with graphics capabilities.

Workbench An integrated assembly of CASE tools.

WYSIWYG What You See Is What You Get; refers to seeing an accurate image on a terminal screen of what will be printed.

Credits

Color Plates

1: Courtesy of International Business Machines Corporation; 2, 3, 4: © Comstock, Inc.; 5: © Holt Confer/The Image Works, Inc.; 6: © Bob Coyle; 7, 8: © Comstock, Inc.; 9: Apple Computer, Inc.; 10, 11: © Comstock, Inc.; 12: © Bob Coyle; 13: Courtesy of International Business Machines Corporation

Index

a

ABCO Corporation. *See* OARS
    (on-line accounts
    receivable system)
    example
Acceptance reviews. *See* User
    acceptance reviews
Accounts receivable. *See* OARS
    (on-line accounts
    receivable system)
    example
Accuracy of candidate systems,
    252
Achievement index (AI), 98, *99*
Action stubs and entries, 143
Activity, critical path, 102, 104
AD/Cycle CASE product,
    164-65, 489-*90*
Administrative standards, 474
Agile enterprise concept, 58,
    161
Algorithms, **423**, **424**, 427
Alphabetic derivation codes,
    142-43
Alphanumeric codes, 140-43
Analysis, 14
    background, 184
    change, 485, *486*
    data element, 173, 190-91
    fact, 173-74, 189-98
    feasibility, 174-75, 200 (*see
        also* Candidate system
        evaluation)
    input-output, 173, 191-*94*,
        212, 213
    output data element source,
        250-*51*, 312, *313*
    payback, 258-*59*
    recurring data, 174, 195,
        196
    report use, 174, 195, *197*
    structured, *21-22*, 118
    systems (*see* Systems
        analysis)

b

Appendices
    design phase report, 368
    study phase report, 271
Applications. *See* Computer
    programs; Software
Applications generators, 158
Artificial intelligence, 167
Association for Computing
    Machinery, 17
Association for Systems
    Management, 17, 189
Attributes, **117**, **135**
Automated office, 6, *9*
Automated source document
    design, **351**, 355, *356*

b

Back-end systems, CASE, 164
Background analysis, 184
Backup capabilities, 323, 476
Baldridge Award, 54, *56*
Bar charts, 78, *79*
Bar codes, 360-*61*
Baseline specifications, **5**,
    13-14, 72. *See also*
    Design specifications;
    Performance
    specifications; System
    specifications
Benchmark testing, 305
"Best" system, **241**, 261-**62**
Billing systems, 36
Block sequence code, 138-39
Body (output), 334
Bottom-up computer program
    development, 405-6
Businesses
    agile enterprise concept, 58
    characteristics of, 34-37
    feedback and control in,
        51-53
    goals and objectives of, 34

    information generators in,
        48
    information structure of,
        44-48
    information system levels
        in, 48-51
    management uses of
        information in, 48-53
        (*see also* Management)
    organization charts of,
        38-44
    organization function lists
        of, 44
    personnel (*see* Computer
        operators; Computer
        programmers; Systems
        analysts; Users)
    product flow and
        information flow in,
        33-48
    as systems of systems,
        34-37
    total quality management
        (TQM) principles for,
        53-58
Business information systems,
    5, **10**-*11*. *See also*
    Information systems

c

Candidate evaluation matrix,
    241, 252-60
    weighted, 260-61
Candidate system evaluation,
    174-75, **177**
    "best" system selection,
        261-62, *263*
    candidate descriptions,
        247-51
    candidate development,
        243-46
    general system design as
        result of, 262

*Italicized numbers refer to figures

identification of meaningful system characteristics, 252

performance and cost determination, 252-60

performance and cost weighting, 260-61

preliminary evaluation, 246-47

purposes of, 242

steps in, 242-62

Candidate system matrix, **241**, *243-46*

Candidate systems, 174

Careers in systems analysis, 14-17

Carriage control tape, 336

Central repositories, CASE, 166

Change, 401, **467**, **482**

analysis reports, 485, *486*

analysis requests, 485

control, 467, 484-87

development reports, 486

forces of, and SDLC, 24-27

management (*see* Change management)

notices, 486, *487*

Change control, **467**, **484**-87

Change management, 481-*90*

change control, 484-87

guidelines for system modification, 481-83

redevelopment engineering, 487-*90*

Changeover, 398-99, **403**, **417**

action logs, 469, *470*

activities, 469-70

crisis, 468-69

plans, 397, 417-19, 442

system, 398-99, 467

user turnover and, 471

Channel 1, 336

Channel 12, 336

Character readers, optical, 362

Charts. *See also* Reports

HIPO, 294, *301*, 407

milestones, 270-71

organizational, 33, 38-44, 210, 213

performance, 97-100

presentation graphics, 77-81

project cost, 96-97

project planning (Gantt), 93-96, *101*

Check-out tests, 415

Chen, Peter, methodology of, 161

Class concept, 161-62

COBOL language, 323, 427, *431*

Code generators, 166, 436

Code plans, 136-37

Codes. *See* Identification codes

Coding, 396, **423**, **424**. *See also* Computer programs

OARS example, 426-35

Collection systems, 36

College majors for systems analysts, 16

Columns, **311**, **325**

Communication, **65**, **66**

documentation (*see* Documentation)

documents (*see* Documents)

effective, 66-69

elements of, 66-69

interviewing techniques, 69-70

presentations, 73-76

process, 66, *67*

technical writing, 70-72

Communications, manager of, 473

Compilation, 425

Computer-assisted systems engineering (CASE), **5**, **26**, **153**, **154**

automating SDLC with, 26-27

front-end loading with, 404-5

hardware and software developments and, 154-57

nonprocedural languages and, 158-59

prototyping and, 327-29 (*see also* Prototyping)

reengineering with, 489-*90*

structured methodologies and, 159-62

tools and workbenches, 162-*68*

user involvement in SDLC and, 157-58

Computer information systems (CISs), **5**, **6**

business information systems, 10-11

as college major, 16

information system concepts, 6-10 (*see also* Information systems)

projects (*see* Projects)

Computer-integrated enterprises (CIEs), **5**, **6**

Computer-integrated manufacturing (CIM), 6-*8*

Computer operators

reference manuals for, 72, 413

training of, 412-13

Computer output, **333**

Computer programmers. *See also* Systems analysts

reference manuals for, 72, 411-12

training, 411-12

Computer programs. *See also* Software

applications generators, 158

bottom-up development of, 405-6

code generators, 166, 436

coding, 424

conversion of, 416

creating, 424-25

debugging, 396, 423, 425

defining problems for, 424

designing, 396

documenting, 425 (*see also* Documentation)

natural languages, 435

nonprocedural programming languages, 429-36

OARS example, 426-35

object-oriented languages, 435-36

planning problem solutions for, 424

procedural programming languages, 425-29

standards, 475

structured programming, 426

structured query language (SQL), 325, 432-35

structured walk-throughs
of, 429
testing, 396, 425
test requirements for, 291,
303
top-down development of,
407–9
Computer systems, defined, 10.
See also Hardware;
Software
Conclusions (output), 334
Condition stubs and entries,
143
Constraints, 34, *35*, **207**, **222**
candidate system, 247–49
OARS example, 222–24
Context diagrams, **117**, **122**–25
external performance
descriptions and, 268
OARS example, *211*, 213,
218
processing requirements
identification and, 294,
295
Contracts. *See* Project
directives
Control, **33**, **51**. *See also*
Security
capability of candidate
systems, 252
feedback and, for
management, 51–53
identifying requirements
for, 290, 302
Conversion, **403**, **416**
Conversion plans, 395
development phase
conversion, 416–17
operation phase
changeover, 417–19
Correspondence, 185–*86*, 479
Costs. *See also* Project cost
reports
of candidate systems, 174,
252–61
constraints, 222
of hardware, 304–7
OARS example, *211*, 213
planning, 96–97, *102*
of source documents, 354
Costs index (CI), 98, *99*
Critical path, defined, 102, 105
Critical path method (CPM),
102–3

Critical path networks, **89**, **100**
critical path method (CPM),
102–3
program evaluation and
review technique
(PERT), 104–10
Cumulative documentation
concept, 76
Customer payment notices,
478
Customer relations, 54, 475

d

Data, 6
analysis of recurring, 174,
195, *196*
carriers, 21, 190. (*see also*
Documents)
codes (*see* Identification
codes)
collection, 173, 184–89
data flows and, 312–*14* (*see
also* Data flows)
elements (*see* Data
elements)
encrypting, 476
files (*see* Files)
modeling (*see* Data
modeling)
structures (*see* Data
structures)
Data base administrators
(DBAs), **311**, **326**, 473
Data base management systems
(DBMSs), **311**, **321**
architectures of, 324–25
components of, 322–23
data base administrators
(DBAs) and, 311, 326,
473
functions of, 323–24
personal computers and,
326, *327*
purposes of, 320–21
Data bases, 321
design of, 290
down loaded, 474
Data definition components of
DBMS, 322
Data dictionaries, **117**, **131**
data elements and data
structures, 127–31
data modeling and, 312,
315

definition and entries of,
131–35
entities and attributes of,
135
entity-relationship diagrams
for, 135–36
functions of, 118
identification codes,
136–43
symbols, 131
Data elements, **117**, **130**, 135
analysis of, 173, 190–91
data structures and, 127–31
example data dictionary
entry for, *134*
lists of, 227–28
Data flow diagrams (DFDs),
117, **119**
computer program coding
and, 426, *427*
data dictionaries (*see* Data
dictionaries)
data modeling and, 312,
314
as fact-analysis tools, 174,
193–*94*
functions of, 118
guidelines for drawing, 127,
128–30
internal performance
specifications and, 268
OARS example, *219*–23
processing requirements
identification and,
294–*300*
process specifications,
143–46
symbols of, 119–*20*
transformations and
decomposition of,
120–27, 294
Data flows, 21, 119, 130
data and, 312–*14*
entities and, 135 (*see also*
Entities)
example data dictionary
entry for, *132*
product flow and, 44–48
Data manipulation component
of DBMS, 322
Data modeling. *See also* Data
dictionaries; Data flow
diagrams (DFDs)
data and data flows, 312–*14*

data base management
systems, 320–27
normalization of files,
317–20
objectives of, 312
prototyping engines and,
327–29 (*see also*
Prototyping)
relationships between
entities, 314–16
Data normalization, **311**
Data-oriented model, 160–61
Data processing, distributed,
17–19, *20. See also*
Processing; Routine
operation
Data Processing Management
Association, 17, 189
Data stores. *See* Files
Data structures, **117**, **130**
data elements and, 127–31
example data dictionary
entry for, *133*
dBase IV software, 326, *327,*
340, *342,* 433–35, 436
Debugging, 396, **423**, **425**
Decisions, management, 51–53
Decision support systems
(DSSs), 53
Decision tables, **117**, **143**–45,
427, *429*
Decision trees, **117**, **145**, 427
Decomposed data flow
diagrams, **293**
Decomposition of data flow
diagrams, **117**, **122**–27,
294
Deming Award, 54–55
Design
general system, 294
object-oriented, 162
recovery (*see*
Redevelopment
engineering)
structured, 21–22, 118
system (*see* Detailed system
design; Design phase)
Design phase, 12, **288**–91,
293. *See also* Data
modeling; Design phase
reports; Design phase
reviews; Detailed
system design; Input
design; Output design

Design phase reports, **365**
design specifications and,
366
OARS example, 372–93
preparation of, 291
structure and content of,
366–68
Design phase reviews, 291,
365, **368**–69
Design specifications, 13, 291,
365, **366**, *367*
detailed, 294–303
OARS example, 276–78,
374–*86*
Desktop publishing, **65**, **84**,
333, **344**
maintaining organization
charts, 41–43
printer output design, 344
text/graphics formatting,
84–86
word publishing, 84
Detailed milestones project
plan, 270–71
OARS example, *286, 368,*
388, 461
Detailed system design
detailed design
specifications, 294–303
general system design, 294
hardware acquisition,
304–7
identifying control
requirements, 302
identifying processing
requirements, 294–*301*
identifying reference
manual requirements,
303
structured walk-throughs,
304
test requirements, 303–4
Development phase, 12, **394**,
403
activities, 394–98
computer program
development (*see*
Computer programs)
conversion plans, 416–19
equipment installation, 415
implementation
management, 419
implementation planning,
404

management orientation,
415
reports (*see* Development
phase reports)
reviews, 441, 444
system specifications, 442,
443
test plans, 404–10
training plans, 411–15
Development phase reports,
397–98, **403**, **441**, **442**
OARS example, 446–65
structure and content of,
442–44
system specifications and,
442
Development phase reviews,
396, **441**, **444**
Diagrams. *See* Context
diagrams; Data flow
diagrams (DFDs); Entity-
relationship diagrams
(ERDs)
Disaster protection, 476
Display layout sheets, **333**,
344, 347, **351**, **358**–*60*
Displays. *See* Visual display
terminals (VDTs)
Distributed data processing,
17–19, *20,* 326
Distribution systems, 36
Documentation
analysis of, 190–98
computer program, 425
cumulative, 76
desktop publishing for,
84–86
generating, 76–86
life-cycle, 12–14
periodic reviews of, 480–81
presentation graphics for,
77–84
structured analysis and
design, 118
word processing for, 77
Documents. *See also* Input
design; Output design
baseline specifications,
13–14, 72 (*see also*
Design specifications;
Performance
specifications; System
specifications)

changeover action logs, 469, *470*
as data carriers, 190
data collection and, 185
information flow paths and, 46–48
questionnaires, 185–86
reports (*see* Reports)
source (*see* Source document control; Source document design)
Domains of systems, 122
Dot-matrix printers, 343
Down loaded data bases, 474
Driver programs, 405

e

Edit characters, 336
Employee manuals, 72
Encryption, data, 476
Encyclopedias, CASE, 166
Enterprise models, 6, *7*, 164–65
Entities, **117**, **135**, **311**, **314**
attributes and, 135
external, 119
relationships between, 314–16
Entity-relationship diagrams (ERDs), **117**, **135**–36, **311**, **314**-16
after normalization, *321*
Equipment. *See* Hardware
Error-checking tools, CASE, 165
Event, critical path, 102, 104
Event-driven systems, 164
Exception reporting, 52, 108
Expert systems, 166
External design requirements, 366
External entities, 119, 135
External information needs, 48
External performance descriptions, 268
External system specifications, 442

f

Facility costs, 252
Fact-analysis techniques, 173–74, 189–98
Fact-finding techniques, 173, 184–89

Fall Back capabilities, 476
Feasibility analysis, 174–75, 200. *See also* Candidate system evaluation
Feedback, **33**, **51**
communication and, 66, 68
control and, for management, 51-53
loops in study phase, 175
Files. *See also* Data base management systems (DBMSs); Data bases; Data modeling
conversion of, 416–17
as data stores, 119, 130, 135
example data dictionary entry for, *133*
master and transaction, 312
normalization of, 317–20
project, 181
of source documents, 355, 357
Fire protection, 476
First normal form (1NF), **311**, **317**-18
Flexibility of candidate systems, 253
Float costs, 255, 258
Flowcharts, 19–22
Forms, specialty, 340, *341*, 352. *See also* Input design; Output design; Source document design
Fourth-generation languages (4GLs), 159, 432
Fraud, computer-related, 475–76
Front-end loading, 404–5
Front-end systems, CASE, 163
Full-function CASE workbenches, **153**, **164**, *165*
Functional files, 357
Functional prototypes, 166

g

Gane-Sarson methodology, 160
Gantt charts, **89**, **93**-96, *101*
Goals, **33**, **34**
Graphics
desktop publishing, 84–86
presentation, 77–80
printer output, 340–44

Graphics service companies, 84
Graphs, 78, *79*
Group classification code, 139–40
Growth potential of candidate systems, 253, 305

h

Hackers, 476
Hardcopy reports, *47*, *48*, 225
Hardware, 10
acquisition, 290, 304–7, 396
CASE and developments in, 154–57
costs, 252
input scanners, 360–62
installation of, 415
machine usage for testing, 408
microcomputers, 154–55
micro-to-mainframe links, 155–57
personal computers and DBMS, 326
printers, 340, 343–44
testing, 305, 415
visual display terminals (*see* Visual display terminals (VDTs))
Headings (output), 334
Herzberg, Frederick, 188
Hierarchical DBMS, 324–25
Hierarchy charts, 294, *301*, 407
High-level languages, *425*
HIPO (Hierarchy plus Input Processing and Output) charts, **293**, **294**, *301*, 407
Histograms, 80
History processing, 410
Horizontal integration, 50
Hygiene factors, 188

i

Identification codes, **117**, **137**
code plans, 136–37
types of, 137–43
Immediate replacement changeover, 418
Implementation, 394–95, **403**, **404**

Implementation committee, 419

Implementation plans, 394–95, **403, 404**
  conversion plans, 416–19
  equipment installation plans, 415
  test plans, 404–10
  training plans, 411–15

Incremental commitment concept, 76

Indices, performance, 97–100

Information, defined, 6

Information carriers, *47*

Information flow, **33, 44**–48

Information generators, **33, 48**

Information memorandum, 181, *183*

Information resource centers, 17

Information resource management, 17, *18*

Information service requests (ISRs), **172, 177,** 178–81
  limited, 180, *182*
  modified, 180–81, 198–200
  project directive as, 174, 181 (*see also* Project directives)

Information services organizations, 41–*43,* 471–74

Information systems
  business, 10–11
  concepts, 6–10
  engineering (*see* Information systems engineering)
  forces for change in, 24–25, *26, 27*
  levels of, and management, 48–51
  market growth for, *26*
  projects (*see* Projects)
  user spending for, *27*

Information systems engineering
  classical life-cycle methodology, 19–*21* (*see also* Systems development life cycle (SDLC))

computer-assisted systems engineering (CASE), 26–27 (*see also* Computer-assisted systems engineering (CASE))
  evolution of, 19–*24*
  prototyping, 22–*24* (*see also* Prototyping)
  structured analysis and design methods, 21–22, 118 (*see also* Structured methodologies)
  task-oriented tools, 25

Inheritance concept, 161–62

Initial investigation, **172**–74, **177**
  background analysis, 184
  fact-analysis techniques, 173, 189–98
  fact-finding techniques, 173–74, 184–89
  OARS example, 210–13
  problem identification, 178–81
  project initiation, 181–84
  user review, 198–201

Input controls, *302*

Input design, 290
  input scanners, 360–62
  source document design, 352–57
  visual display terminal screen design, 357–60

Input media, candidate system, 244

Input-output analysis, 173, 191–*94*
  OARS example, *212,* 213

Input scanners, 360–62

Installation of equipment, 415

Insurance, risk, 476

Integrated CASE (ICASE) systems, 164

Integration, horizontal and vertical, 50

Interim reviews, 75

Internal design requirements, 366

Internal information needs, 48

Internal performance descriptions, 268

Internal system specifications, 442

Interviews, **65, 69**
  for fact finding, 186–88
  techniques for, 69–70

Inventory systems, 36

IPO charts, 294, *301*

j

Jackson, Michael, methodology of, 161

Jobs
  data processing, 473
  for systems analysts, 15, *16*

Joint application design (JAD), **89, 92**

k

Knowledge-based systems, 166

l

Languages, programming
  coding computer programs, 424 (*see also* Computer programs)
  natural, 435
  nonprocedural, 429–36
  object-oriented, 435–36
  procedural, 425–29
  pseudocode, 146

Languages, query
  as DBMS components, 322
  report generators and, 158–59
  structured query language (SQL), 325, 432–35

Laser printers, 343–44

Lease of equipment, 306–7

LeCourier's legibility table, 353, *354*

Life cycle, **5, 11**. *See also* Systems development life cycle (SDLC)

Limited information service requests, 180, *182*

Line charts, 78, *79*

Line positions, 41

Link pins, 38, 122

Local area networks (LANs), 19, *20*, 155–57

Logical models, 208
    OARS example, 218–*22*,
        223
Lower CASE workbenches,
    153, *163*, **164**
Lower management
    information systems, 49

m

Mainframe computer links to
    microcomputers,
    155–57
Maintenance, **467**, **482**. *See
    also* Change
Major milestones charts, 270
Malcom Baldridge National
    Quality Improvement
    Act, 54
Management
    of change, 481–*90*
    data processing operations,
        473
    feedback and control for,
        51–53
    of implementation, 419
    information system levels
        and, 48–51
    interest and commitment
        patterns of, 74–76
    life-cycle, 12–14 (*see also*
        Systems development
        life cycle (SDLC))
    by objectives, 94–96
    orientation, 415
    total quality management
        (TQM) principles,
        53–58
    uses of information by,
        48–53
Management information
    systems (MIS) majors,
    16
Manager of communications,
    473
Manuals
    reference (*see* Reference
        manuals)
    standards, 474–75
    technical writing and,
        70–71, 72
Many-to-many relationships,
    136, 316
MAPICS application, 489–*90*
Mark readers, optical, 360

Martin, James, methodology of,
    161
Maslow, Abraham, 187
Master files, 312
Media protection, 476
Methodologies. *See* Structured
    methodologies
Microcomputers, 154–55
    distributed data processing
        and, 17
    mainframe links to, 155–57
    personal, and DBMSs, 326
Middle management
    information systems, 49
Milestones, 93, 270–71
    OARS example, *284, 286,
        390, 461, 463*
Mneumonic codes, 141
Modeling. *See* Data modeling
Models
    design, 160–62
    logical and physical, 208,
        218–*22, 223*
Modifications, 481–83. *See also*
    Change; Maintenance
Modified information service
    requests, 180–81,
    198–200
Motivating factors, 188
Motivation and Personality
    (Maslow), 187
Multitasking, 155

n

Narratives, 71–72
Natural languages, 435
Need identification, 172, 178
Needs of individuals, 187
Networked DBMS, 325
Networks
    critical path (*see* Critical
        path networks)
    distributed data processing,
        17–*20*
    local area, 19, *20*, 155–57
Nonprocedural programming
    languages, **423**, **429**–36
    applications generators, 158
    code generators, 436
    fourth-generation languages
        (4GLs), 159
    natural languages, 435
    object-oriented languages,
        435–36

query languages and report
    generators, 158–59,
    432–35
Normalization, 317–20
    normal forms, 317–20
    purpose of, 317
Numerical files, 357

o

OARS (on-line accounts
    receivable system)
    example
    ABCO company history,
        208–9
    candidate system
        evaluation, 243–*63*
    design phase report,
        372–93
    detailed design
        specifications, 294–*301*
    development phase report,
        446–65
    entity-relationship diagrams,
        315–*16, 321*
    general constraints, 222–24
    initial investigation, 210–13
    logical model of new
        system, 218–*22, 223*
    output description, 225–37
    printer output design,
        337–39, *341–42*
    project directive, 213–*17*
    specific objectives, 224–25
    study phase report, 274–87
Objectives, **33**, **34**
    specific, 207, 224–25
Object-oriented design (OOD),
    162
Object-oriented model, 160,
    161–62
Object-oriented programming
    (OOP) languages, 162,
    435–36
Objects, defined, 161
Observation, 188
Office, automated, 6, *9*
One-to-many relationships, 136,
    316
One-to-one relationships, 136,
    316
Operation, routine. *See* Routine
    operation
Operational information
    systems, 48–49

Operation phase, 12, **398**-401, **467**. *See also* Change management; Changeover; Performance review and evaluation; Routine operation

Operators. *See* Computer operators

Optical readers, 360-62

Oral communication
    interviews, 69-70
    presentations, 73-76

Organization charts, **33**, **38**-44
    OARS example, 210, 213

Organization function lists, **33**, **44**, *45*

Output
    controls, *302*
    data element source analysis, 250-*51*, 312, *313*
    identification and description, 225-*37*
    input/output analysis, 173, 191-*94*, *212*, 213
    media, candidate system, 244
    periodic reviews of, 481
    specifications, 226

Output design, 290
    general principles of, 334
    printer output, 334-344
    visual display terminal screen output, 344-47

P

Parallel operation, 418

Parent-child relationships, 122, *124*

Partitioned data flow diagrams, 117, 122-27, 293-94

Passwords, 324

Patch, defined, 477

Payback analysis, 258-*59*

Paying systems, 36

Payoffs, information system, 52

Performance definition. *See* System performance definition

Performance indices, **89**, 97-100

Performance review and evaluation, 400, 477-81
    performance review boards (PRBs), 477-78
    periodic reviews, 480-81
    post-installation reviews, 478-80
    system performance evaluation, 400

Performance review boards (PRBs), **467**, 477-**78**

Performance specifications, 13, 118, 173, **267**, **268**

PerForm Pro software, 355, *356*

Periodic reviews, 480-81

Personal computers. *See* Microcomputers

Personal interviews. *See* Interviews

Personnel. *See* Computer operators; Computer programmers; Management; Systems analysts; Users

Personnel training, 397

PERT (program evaluation and review technique), 104-10

PERT-COST programs, 103

Phased changeover, 418-19

Physical access control, 476

Physical location security, 476

Physical model, 208

Pie charts, 78, *80*

Pilot tests, 410

Planned workloads, 305

Playscript format, 70, *71*

Policies and policy manuals, 70-71, 72

Post-installation reviews, 478-80

Presentation graphics, **65**, **77**
    bar charts, 78, *79*
    effective charts, 81
    line charts, 78, *79*
    pie charts, 78, *80*
    software, 81-84
    step charts, 79-80
    types of charts, 77-80

Presentations, **65**
    outcomes of, 74-76
    preparing, 73
    scheduling, 73-74

Primitives, data flow diagram, 125

Principal user, **89**, **91**
    implementation committees and, 419
    performance review board and, 400
    study phase review and, 272
    user review and, 198

Print charts, **333**, **334**-40, *428*

Printer output, 334-44
    design, 334
    desktop publishing, 344
    graphics, 340-44
    layout forms, 334-40
    prototyping, 340

Printers, 340, 343-44

Problem identification, 178-81, 424

Procedural programming languages, **423**, **425**-29
    OARS example, 426-29
    structured programming concepts, 426
    structured walk-throughs, 429

Procedures and procedure manuals, 70-71, 72

Procedures conversion, 416

Process-driven model, 160

Processing
    candidate systems and, 245
    controls, *302*
    identifying requirements for, 289-90, 294-*301*

Process specifications, **117**, **143**
    decision tables and, 143-45
    decision trees and, 145
    structured English and, 146

Process versus progress, 57

Product flow, **33**, **44**-48

Production enterprises, 34

Production systems, 36

Program evaluation and review technique (PERT), 104-10

Programmers. *See* Computer programmers

Programming languages. *See* Languages, programming

Programs. *See* Computer
 programs
Progress plans, **89**, **93**-96
 OARS example, *283-84,*
 388, 390, 392
Progress versus process, 57
Project cost reports, **89,**
 96-97, *102*
 OARS example, *283, 285,*
 389, 391, 393, 462,
 464
Project directives, **174**, **177,**
 181, 200-*201*
 OARS example, 213-*17*
Project management
 cost planning and status
 reporting, 96-97
 critical path networks,
 100-110
 OARS example, 278-87
 performance indices and
 charts, 97-100
 progress planning and
 status reporting, 93-96
 project planning and
 reporting, 93-100
 project reviews, 89, 110-11
 software, 100, *101, 102,*
 262, *263*
 systems teams, 90-92
Project reviews, **89**, **110**-11
Projects
 contracts (*see* Project
 directives)
 cost reports, 89, 96-97,
 102
 elements of communication
 in, 66-69
 generating documentation
 for, 76-86
 initiation of, 181-84 (*see*
 also Initial
 investigation)
 interviewing techniques,
 69-70
 management (*see* Project
 management)
 milestones, 270-71
 presentations, 73-76
 reviews, 89, 110-11
 summary status reports,
 97-100
 technical writing for, 70-72

Prototyping, **5**, **22**, **311**, **327,**
 333, **340**
 CASE tools for, 166 (*see*
 also Computer-assisted
 system engineering
 (CASE))
 cycle, 328-29
 engines, 327-29
 front-end loading with,
 404-5
 output, 225
 printer output, 340, *342*
 screen input, 359, *361*
 version of SDLC, 22-*24*
Pseudocode, 146, 427, *431*
Purchasing systems, 36

q

Quality management, 53-58
Query languages. *See*
 Languages, query
Questionnaires, 185-*86*

r

Rapid applications
 development (RAD), 23
Rapid prototyping, 23, 166
Real-time system CASE
 workbenches, 164
Receiving systems, 36
Recurring data analysis, 174,
 195, *196*
Redevelopment engineering,
 164, **467**, **487**-*90*
 reengineering, 489-*90*
 reverse engineering,
 488-89
Redevelopment-engineering
 CASE workbenches, 164
Reengineering, 489-*90*
Reference manuals
 identifying requirements
 for, 290
 preparation of, 397
 technical writing and, 72
 as training aids, 411-14
Relational DBMS, 325
Reliability of candidate
 systems, 253
Rental of equipment, 306-7
Report generators, 158-59
 as DBMS components,
 322-23

Reports. *See also* Charts;
 Design phase reports;
 Development phase
 reports; Documents;
 Study phase reports
 change analysis and
 development, 485-87
 cost planning and status,
 96-97
 exception, 52, 108
 hardcopy and softcopy, *47,*
 48, 225
 progress planning and
 status, 93-96
 project performance,
 97-100
 technical writing and, 72
 test, 409-10
 use analysis of, 174, 195,
 197
Research, 189
Response time of candidate
 systems, 253
Reverse engineering, 488-89
Reviews
 design phase, 291, 365,
 368-69
 development phase, 441,
 444
 general system, 289
 management orientation,
 415
 operation phase (*see*
 Performance review and
 evaluation)
 as presentations, 75-76
 project, 89, 110-11
 structured walk-throughs,
 293, 304, 409, 423, 429
 study phase, 175, 267,
 271-72
 user (*see* User reviews)
Risk insurance, 476
Routine operation, 400
 costs, 254-57, *465*
 customer relations, 475
 data processing standards,
 474-77
 organizing for data
 processing, 471-74
 security, 475-77
 standards manuals, 474-75
Rows, **311**, **325**

S

Salaries for systems analysts, 15, *16*
Sales systems, 36
Scales of charts, 81
Scheduling methods. *See* Critical path networks
Scheduling of presentations, 73-74
Schemas, **311**, **323**
Screen Design Aid (SDA), 359, *361*
Screens. *See* Visual display terminals (VDTs)
Second normal form (2NF), **311**, **318**-19
Security, 323-24, 475-77. *See also* Control
Sequence codes, 137-39
Service enterprises, 34
Sets of leveled DFDs, 125
Significant digit codes, 140, *141*
Simple sequence codes, 137-38
Simulation programs, 305
Site preparation, 415
Skipping, defined, 336
Slack time, defined, 105
Softcopy reports, *47*, *48*, 225
Software, 10. *See also* Computer programs
  automated forms design, 355, *356*
  CASE (*see* Computer-assisted Software Engineering (CASE))
  critical path network programs, 103
  data dictionary, 135
  desktop publishing (*see* Desktop publishing)
  languages (*see* Languages, programming; Languages, query)
  presentation graphics, 81-84
  project management, 100, *101*, *102*, 262, *263*
  screen design, 359, *361*
  word processing, 77, 84
Source document control, **351**, **355**-57

Source document design, 352-57
  automated, 355, *356*
  control files, 355-57
  principles of, 352-54
  responsibility for, 352
Spacing, defined, 336
Specialty manuals, 72. *See also* Reference manuals
Specifications
  baseline, 13-14, 72 (*see also* Design specifications; Peformance specifications; System specifications)
  output, 226
  process (*see* Process specifications)
Specific objectives, **207**, **224**, 479
  OARS example, 224-25, *480*
Staff positions, 41
Staircase charts, 79-*80*
Standards, **467**, **474**
Standards manuals, 474-75
Status index (SI), 98, *99*
Status reports
  cost planning and, 96-97
  OARS example, *283-84*
  progress planning and, 93-96
Step charts, 79-*80*
Storage
  data, 119
  requirements of candidate systems, 253
String testing, 405, *406*
Structure charts, 294, *301*
Structured analysis and design methods, 21-22, 118
Structured diagramming tools, CASE, 165
Structured English, **117**, **146**, 427
Structured methodologies
  for analysis and design, 21-22, 118
  CASE diagramming tools, 165
  classification of, 160-62
  for computer programming, 159, 426

distribution of effort in SDLC with, 404-*5*
  evolution of, 159-60
Structured programming, 159, 426
Structured Query Language (SQL), 325, 432-35
Structured walk-throughs, **293**, **304**, 409, **423**, **429**
Stubs
  condition and action, 143
  module, 407, 427
Study phase, 11, 172-75, 177. *See also* Candidate system evaluation; Initial investigation; Study phase reports; Study phase reviews; System performance definition
Study phase reports, **175**, **177**, **267**, **268**
  OARS example, 271, 274-87
  performance specifications and, 269
  structure and content of, 268-71
Study phase reviews, 175, **267**, **271**-72
Style sheets, 84-86
Subschemas, **311**, **323**-*24*
Subsystems, 10-*11*, 36-*37*
  test requirements for, 291, 303
Superior-subordinate relationships, 38-*39*
Symbols
  classical method flowchart, 19, *21*
  data dictionary, 131-*34*
  data flow diagram, 119-*20*
  entity-relationship diagram, 135-36, 315-16
  organizational chart, 40-41
  structured method flowchart, 21-*22*
Synthesis, defined, 14
System(s), **5**, **6**, *9*, 10-*11*
  "best" candidate, 261-62
  business as system of, 34-37
  candidate, 174 (*see also* Candidate system evaluation)

change (*see* Change)

changeover (*see* Changeover)

control (*see* Control)

costs and performance, 252-61

design (*see* Design phase)

domains, 122

information (*see* Information systems)

performance definition (*see* System performance definition)

performance evaluation, 400 (*see also* Performance review and evaluation)

standards, 474

testing, 397

test requirements, 291, 303

System changeover, 398-99, **467**. *See also* Changeover

System performance definition, **174**, **177**, **207**, **208**

general constraints, 222-24

logical model of new system, 218-22

OARS example, 208-17

output description, 225-37

specific objectives, 224-25

transition from logical to physical model, 208

Systems analysis, **5**, **6**, **14**. *See also* Businesses; Systems development life cycle (SDLC)

information systems, 6-11

information systems engineering (*see* Information systems engineering)

methodologies (*see* Structured methodologies)

projects (*see* Projects)

structured analysis and design, 21-22, 118

systems analysts and, 14-19

usability concept, 19

Systems analysts, **5**, **14**

careers of, 14-17

functions performed by, 14-15

management of projects (*see* Project management; Projects)

opportunities and compensation for, 15, *16*

personal qualifications for, 15-17

professional societies for, 17, 189

systems teams and (*see* Systems teams)

Systems development life cycle (SDLC), **5**, **11**. *See also* Systems analysis; Systems analysts

activities, 12, *13*

automating, 24-27

CASE and, 26-27, 167-68 (*see also* Computer-assisted systems engineering (CASE))

classical, 19-*21*

distribution of effort with traditional, structured, and CASE, 404-5

flowchart, 12-14

forces of change and, 24-25, *26*, *27*

management and documentation, 12-14

market growth in information processing, *26*

phases, 11-12 (*see also* Design phase; Development phase; Operation phase; Study phase)

prototyping version of, 22-24, 328-29 (*see also* Prototyping)

structured methodologies (*see* Structured methodologies)

systems analyst salaries and, *16*

task-oriented tools, 25

users and, 17-19, *20*

user spending for information processing, *27*

System specifications, 14, **397**-98, **403**, **441**, **442**

OARS example, 448-*59*

reference manuals and, 411

Systems teams, **89**, **90**

candidate system evaluation and, 243

changeover and, 470

joint application design (JAD) approach and, 92

members, 90-91

principal user and, 91 (*see also* Principal user)

roles and responsibilities, 91-92

usability engineering, 92

t

Tables, **311**, **325**

Task-oriented tools, 25

Teams. *See* Systems teams

Technical writing, **65**, **70**-72

Testing

computer programs, 396, 425

converted files, 417

hardware, 305, 415

identifying requirements for, 291, 303

plans for, 404-10

structured walk-throughs as, 293, 304, 409, 423, 429

systems, 397

Test plans, 404-10

bottom-up computer program development and, 405-6

formal, 409-10

top-down computer program development and, 407-9

Third-generation languages, 425

Third normal form (3NF), **311**, **320**

Third-party leasing, 307

Time constraints, 222

Titles (output), 334

Tool kits, CASE, 162

Tools

CASE, 162-*68*

task-oriented, 25

trap, 180

Top-down computer program
development, **403**,
407-9
Top-down design, 14
Top management information
systems, 50
Total quality management
(TQM), **33**, **53**-58
Training
costs, 252
management orientation,
415
operator, 412-13
overview, 397, 411
plans, 395, 397
programmer, 411-12
user, 413-14
Transactions files, 312
Transformations, data flow
diagram, 119, 120-27

U

Universal Product Code (UPC),
360-*61*
Update anomalies, 317
Upper CASE workbenches,
153, **163**
Usability, **5**, **19**, **467**
of candidate systems, 253
Usability engineering, 92
User acceptance reviews, **398**,
403, 468
User IDs, 324

User reviews, 174, 198-201,
396
acceptance reviews, 398,
403, 468
modified information
service requests,
198-200
project directives, 200-*201*
Users
communicating with (*see*
Communication)
distributed data processing
and, 17-19, *20*
information resource
management and, 17,
18
interviewing, 65, 65-70,
186-88
involvement of, in SDLC,
157-*58*
need for information
systems, 172, 178
principal (*see* Principal
user)
prototyping and, 23 (*see
also* Prototyping)
reference manuals for, 72,
413-14
reviews (*see* User reviews)
SDLC and, 17-19, *20*
training of, 397, 413-14
turnover, 471
usability concept, 19

V

VDT. *See* Visual display
terminals (VDTs)
Vendor evaluation matrix, 305,
306
Vertical integration, 50
Views (subschemas), 323-*24*
Visual display terminals
(VDTs), **351**
input screen layouts,
357-*60*, *361*
output screen layouts, 344,
347
prototyping screens, 359,
361

W

Weighted candidate evaluation
matrix, **241**, **260**-61
Word processing, **65**, **77**, 84
Word publishing, 84
Workbenches, CASE, **153**,
162-*68*
Workloads, planned, 305
Workstations. *See*
Microcomputers
Writing, technical, 65, 70-72
WYSIWYG (What You See Is
What You Get), 344

Y

Yourdon-Constantine-DeMarco
methodology, 160